Trial of Strength

Music advisor to Northeastern University Press
GUNTHER SCHULLER

Trial of Strength

WILHELM FURTWÄNGLER
IN THE THIRD REICH

Fred K. Prieberg

Translated by Christopher Dolan

Northeastern University Press
BOSTON

Originally published in German as
Kraftprobe: Wilhelm Furtwängler im Dritten Reich
Copyright 1986 by F. A. Brockhaus GmbH, Wiesbaden
First English publication in Great Britain by Quartet Books Ltd.,
London, in 1991
Translation copyright 1991 by Quartet Books Ltd.
First U.S. publication in 1994 by Northeastern University Press,
by agreement with Quartet Books Ltd.

Library of Congress Cataloging-in-Publication Data

Prieberg, Fred K.
[Kraftprobe. English]
Trial of strength : Wilhelm Furtwängler in the Third Reich : Fred
K. Prieberg : translated by Christopher Dolan.
p. cm.
Translation of Kraftprobe : Wilhelm Furtwängler im Dritten Reich.
Originally published : London : Quartet Books, 1991.
Includes bibliographical references and index.
ISBN 1-55553-196-2
1. Furtwängler, Wilhelm, 1886–1954. 2. Conductors (Music)—
Germany—Biography. 3. National socialism and music. I. Title.
ML422.F92P7513 1994
784.2'092—dc20
[B]   94-6520

Printed and bound by Thomson-Shore, Inc., Dexter, Michigan.
The paper is Glatfelter Supple Opaque Recycled, an acid-free sheet
MANUFACTURED IN THE UNITED STATES OF AMERICA
99 98 97 96 95 94   5 4 3 2 1

CONTENTS

INTRODUCTION: A BOOK ABOUT WILHELM FURTWÄNGLER

Any book about Wilhelm Furtwängler could only be a further addition to this noteworthy musician's already lengthy bibliography, which, including articles in journals and a few of the major daily newspapers but excluding several new centennial biographies, numbers some two hundred items. Because of this, it seemed important not to restate what had already been said elsewhere, a practical and undemanding method of selling the reader short which unfortunately is widespread in the musical literature. Only a few authors and publishers remain who are not satisfied with presenting information gleaned at second, third or even fourth hand. Most, however, are content to exploit their subject matter, seeing centennial celebrations of famous artists as an opportunity to promote themselves. An occasion such as the 'European Year of Music' in 1985, for example, appeared to legitimate such an approach, especially as music has long been accorded an almost mystical veneration here in Germany.

Furtwängler accepted both the admiration and slander which were directed at him; he became the victim of almost hysterical love and of mindless hatred. Is this simply the artist's lot? In his case love and hatred were aroused not so much by his brilliant musicianship as by his contemporaries' political barbarity. That is why this additional book about him had to be quite different to the previous ones; not another music history but the story of a musician under the Nazi regime. The personal conduct of a well-known personality under a dictatorship – if it does not happen to be a 'left-wing' dictatorship – still makes unpopular reading, because it automatically raises questions of collective responsibility. When the German Interior Minister proposes an amendment to the archive laws which would make it common practice to delete people's names from files and documents, the purpose behind such proposals is clear; the blame and implication, action and inaction, grief and misery, in other words the complicated interactions of acting and suffering individuals, are to be obliterated from history, which will then become a highly stylised mythology of 'the people's destiny', to be accepted without question.

Nevertheless, the constitution, at least as it now stands, protects the right to talk of well-known personalities within their historical context. This encouraged me to delve back into file collections which largely survived the war and as yet have not been tampered with. As well as previously unknown documents originating from the Reichsmusikkammer, the Reichsradio, the Gestapo offices and some ministries, I was able to use all the conductor's previously unpublished diaries, notes and correspondence – including that of his secretary, Berta Geissmar – and other literary remains and press reports. As there were gaps in this material I had to use eyewitness accounts to fill in the picture, although – knowing how susceptible memories are to both time and personal interpretation – only very sparingly and where they could be corroborated by documentary evidence. This methodology should not be taken as a sign of general mistrust of Furtwängler's contemporaries' testimonies – but the publication of a musical biography is not the same as a trial in which a witness is obliged to tell the truth and nothing but the truth. This book aims, however, to present evidence like that admissible in a court of law: demonstrably true facts about the course of events and the motives behind them in particular situations, in this case the twelve years of Wilhelm Furtwängler's life which he spent under extreme political conditions.

It is a theme to which many authors and publishers have devoted themselves in recent years, but just how little importance biographers and music historians attach to the fundamental prerequisite of such work, namely the presentation of historically relevant facts, is clear from the way in which, until now, quotations have been taken from the few previously published documents, while most of the rich archival resources have not been touched at all. As a result the Furtwängler literature continues to perpetuate the dispute between supporters and opponents; the same drab facts and correspondingly colourful opinions are trotted out again and again, and the political dispute over the conductor has yet to be settled. It is after all easier to make a strong case if the documentary evidence on all sides is ignored.

I hope – in all modesty – that this book will help to counter tendencies both to hero-worship and to demonisation, and that by doing so it will demonstrate the importance of verifying the facts and their inter-connections, without which opinions can be nothing more than unfounded expressions of emotion.

Fred K. Prieberg

1

THE SCAPEGOAT

In considering what has so far been written on the German conductor
Furtwängler, one is immediately struck by one thing in particular,
namely the state of mind of those who have judged him so harshly, and
without taking the facts into account. These people's motive in expressing their hostility was to enhance their own reputations. They were
blind, and they raised their blindness to a virtue, although it was that
which had allowed them to hate in the first place. It is a fact that the
emigration from the Reich had many consequences for those who were
part of it, of which their hatred of those who remained was by far the
greatest. An emigrant who could hate improved his chances of survival;
one has to bear in mind that the majority of those who left Germany
did not do so openly or willingly. There were some who left voluntarily,
as a public statement against the Nazi regime, but they were in a
minority and often were able to escape with comparative ease, either
because they already had property, a job or friends abroad, or because
they were cosmopolitan enough to be able to set themselves up quite
quickly. This group established itself abroad without undergoing great
hardship. The majority of emigrants however were refugees and out-
casts. They had no choice. They were not making a statement, they
were forced to flee, and those in power who pursued Jews, communists,
socialists and other 'enemies of the state' across the border were not
concerned with what befell these undesirables in whichever country they
ended up.[1]

Those who were forced to emigrate, robbed of possessions and the
means to earn a living, were forced to come to terms with their loss,
and it was a multiple, often total loss which sometimes left them with
nothing but the clothes on their backs – their environment, home,

language, profession, social standing and citizenship were all suddenly removed. When it became clear that the Reich's democratic neighbours did not even intend to challenge Hitler's regime but were cultivating diplomatic relations with the National Socialists, signing treaties and turning a blind eye to atrocities, it became terribly clear that to return home was out of the question, and that they had to find some way of adjusting. As immigrants they had no social standing; they tried to integrate as quickly as possible to avoid ending up in ghettos, the lot of the long-term homeless. Thus they had every reason to reject the old country and identify with a new one. In such a situation it was not their memories and the old ties to Germany which were of immediate use, but rather their ability to use every opportunity to adapt to their new surroundings. Anyone who could bring himself to give up his mother tongue and his father's name, anyone who could merge completely into the host society, thereby won himself a new identity. That person was no longer an emigrant.

Hatred eased this complicated process of integration. Through it, the emigrants distanced themselves from their native land and symbolically destroyed it. They dismissed those who had rejected them, their former countrymen, as a bunch of criminals and barbarians. The emigrant from Hitler's Germany came to feel that he no longer had anything to do with Germany or the Germans. Hatred consoled him, eased the pain of loss, and enabled a process of identification with the people, culture and politics of the host country. The process of adaptation was not simple and suffered numerous setbacks: in their new countries the emigrants were by and large considered a nuisance which had to be tolerated, but which could generally be marginalised through compulsory bureaucratic measures. In such circumstances, to declare publicly one's hatred of the Nazis could gain one political credibility – if the authorities of the host country were not curbing such 'propaganda' in the interests of their own diplomatic relations with Hitler's ever-stronger Reich. For what was understood by the word 'German' in countries neighbouring on the Reich was changing rapidly. 'German' no longer just described one's origins, it also described those qualities with which the Führer was trying to impress the world: 'German' meant inconsiderate, inhuman, arrogant, violent, and had become synonymous with murder and shame. To avoid thus being wrongly categorised, emigrants cultivated their hatred; but ultimately this proved no protection. When in 1939 Hitler unleashed his armies, emigrants were suddenly seen as a security risk, and were put under guard, or, as 'hostile foreigners', were interned, often alongside party members from German embassies and consulates,

2

tourists and people whose passports had expired, in camps which differed little from the German concentration camps.[2]

This raised levels of hatred still further. However, if one recognises that such a violent uprooting had consequences which prevented any critical assessment, calm reflection or even differentiation one can hardly respond with reproaches. Even among these people the qualities of self-control and adherence to custom and good manners, which had formerly defined the modern civilised citizen, just withered away. Blind, vengeful old-testament-style hatred remained a reality long after the war was over. Among those who prior to emigration had been involved in cultural activities, a further psychological factor came into play which makes their feelings of hatred still more understandable.

It is common enough for artists to come to believe that they are irreplaceable, and musicians are in a category of their own. This may be accounted for by the nature of the musical world. A musician who has won position, followers and a good press after a long struggle against keen competition is quite inclined to believe that this hard-won position is his by right, as it were, and that no one else could possibly fill it successfully. Therefore he believes that his departure will leave a gap which cannot be filled. The musicians who emigrated or were thrown out of Germany from 1933 onwards indeed felt they were irreplaceable and in consequence believed firmly that Hitler's Germany would, following their departure, become a dreary and empty cultural wasteland. This would inevitably cause the rapid collapse of the regime. Behind these notions lies the rather romantic idea that high culture provides some sort of elixir of life for the community, and that a state whose greatness does not find symbolic representation in the arts cannot survive. They indulged in a kind of wishful thinking with which it is not difficult to sympathise. What a disillusionment to discover that it was fed by a misplaced hope – namely that the artist was the possessor of spiritual and moral strengths, and of a share in some emancipatory power to change the human soul and topple thrones.

The reality of musical life in the Nazi state differed even from the way it was portrayed in anti-Semitic propaganda. The ratio of Jews to non-Jews in the musical world – from musical directors down to private music teachers – was actually about ten times greater than in the population as a whole. One reason for this was unquestionably their highly developed musical talent. However, this six per cent neither defined German musical culture nor stole jobs from Aryans. For all that, when, as a result of persecution and changes in the law, Jews were prevented from being practising artists – a process which took place over a number of years – vacancies did arise and many non-Jewish musicians were

3

promoted. This caused occasional difficulties in filling positions, and some loss of quality, but these were only temporary. Furthermore, those Jewish musicians who were expelled were by no means all of top quality; they represented a broad spectrum of ability, an undeniable fact which post-war musical historiography has tended to conceal in the interests of making us believe that it was only geniuses who fell victim to the 'purges'.

Despite these events, and to the discomfort of the emigrants, musical activity in the Reich continued as intensely as ever. The fact that their absence did not produce the hoped-for consequences shattered any illusions they had about their own indispensability. This fuelled their hatred still further and gave it a new sense of direction. After all, it was the musicians who had stayed in the Reich who had both forgotten about their former Jewish colleagues and rendered them superfluous. Sufficiently prominent 'traitors' could not be attacked on the grounds of poor musicianship; denouncing them as Hitler's lackeys made do instead. The favourite target of such hate campaigns was Wilhelm Furt-wängler. One could attack him easily because he did not counterattack, and repeatedly let it be known how deeply it hurt him.

The extreme virulence of the attack on him was due to his position. He was a symbol. For the public at large and even in the headlines of the world press he was, in a way no other German musician could claim to be, the embodiment of German music. Even prior to 1933, at the time of the republic, his position was such that, in the eyes of the public, person and occupation were inseparable; under the Reich Furtwängler continued to represent brilliant artistry and moreover came to symbolise the driving force behind the Reich's music. What a provocation for emigrants! An incomparable artist living in Germany under Nazi rule, who refused to acknowledge what was happening to them, or even at least to share their enforced exile by turning his back on the barbarity which was taking place! He remained there in Germany, despite everything that happened, and for reasons which were not self-evident; these seemed to be of a personal nature and in no way political.

There is certainly no other German musician who faced such a storm of moral indignation as Furtwängler. He made a welcome victim. The attacks began when, soon after taking power, Hitler's first anti-Semitic transgressions made the headlines of the international press. Attention-seekers took up and added their voices to the emigrants' initial bewildered accusations; anti-fascist speeches and articles became quite the fashion. Pointing an accusing finger is one way of saying 'I'm not like that'. It seems to demonstrate one's own worthiness and sense of

4

values . . . and how necessary they were in those post–1933 years. Did not the so-called democracies sign treaties, negotiate and deal with Hitler? Even the Vatican accepted him as a suitable partner for a concordat. Did not the democracies maintain diplomatic relations with the Nazi state, treat the Führer as an equal, as in no way a criminal? Did not Stalin allow the signing of the non-aggression pact with him, and tolerate the presence of a branch of the Nazi Party in Moscow? Of course there were political motives for this, which only serves to emphasise that politics and morals do not mix. Rigorous morals do not allow pacts. It was left to politicians to absorb the Nazi dictatorship into the international scene. They did of course express criticism, but if a journalist in London, Paris or Zürich wrote anything too explicit it was immediately declared 'an affront to a foreign head of state', and suppressed.

Furtwängler was not protected by any particular law. From 1933 to 1945 he was subjected to attacks accusing him of complicity with the Nazis even if they did not go as far as holding him primarily responsible for their deeds. These attacks continued after the war and even, as if by some sort of compulsion, posthumously. That he had been a Nazi was the least of the accusations, and an absurd one given that roughly twenty million Germans were on the membership rolls of the Nazi Party and affiliated groups: Wilhelm Furtwängler's name is not among them. This did not bother his enemies in the least. They worked with suppositions rather than facts. They were concerned with destroying a symbol, and used numerous means to do so. Certain American newspapers and the licensed press in the American post-war occupied zone were noteworthy examples, whose style was then copied by Swiss journalists. Klaus Mann accused Furtwängler of having 'produced the most effective cultural propaganda for an imperialist regime over a period of thirteen years, all the while failing to recognise the real nature of his function'.[3] Erika Mann chipped in and baptised him 'Hitler's favourite maestro and musical propagandist abroad',[4] in her report for Berlin's American newspaper on Fürtwängler's first post-war concert with the Berlin Philarmonic, at the end of which the conductor was given a fifteen-minute ovation.

Bruno Walter made the accusation

> that for many years your talent was used as an extremely effective propaganda weapon by the satanic regime, and that you, thanks to your public prominence and considerable talent, gave it valuable service. The presence and activity of a musician of your standing in Germany at that time lent those terrible criminals cultural and moral credibility, or at least helped them considerably in its acquisition.[5]

5

'You can expect some big surprises from the Jews in Chicago.
[signed] Israel Stern.' The aggrieved become the aggressors
in this anonymous threat, 1948

What lay behind Furtwängler's music-making, and what the value of
his contribution had really been, were questions which became sub-
merged in propaganda about collective guilt; pure emotion, which was
understandable then but now seems dated, hindered any careful analysis.
The novelist Fritz von Unruh played his part by reporting, as if it were
fact rather than pure invention, an imaginary poster for the Paris Opéra
announcing the guest conductor: 'Famous director of the Bayreuth
Music Festival and friend of Adolph Hitler: Professor Doctor Wilhelm
Furtwängler, Staatsrat [privy councillor]'.[6]

Von Unruh's Swiss publisher left that untouched, knowing he had
no need to fear libel proceedings. The conductor, who since his emigration from Germany in February 1945 had been resident in Switzerland, had obtained a temporary residence permit which was renewed
from time to time, but only on condition that he cease to attract so
much attention, in other words cease to make the headlines. This precarious situation continued for years; the Office Cantonal de Contrôle des
Habitants et de Police des Etrangers in Lausanne only finally gave him
permission to settle permanently on 19 January 1953. Had he taken any
libel action he would have been expelled instantly. It was an impossible

situation which certain journalists in this so-called haven of democracy exploited quite shamelessly:

> This musician is a typical example of those Germans who maintained loyalty right up until the collapse of the regime; they snapped to attention at the 'Führer's' order, and then afterwards claimed total innocence. [. . .] Furtwängler, who congratulated Hitler warmly on the invasion of Austria, who in the presence of Hitler and the whole gang of Nazi criminals conducted the 'Horst-Wessel Song' – 'When our knives are wet with Jewish blood' – Furtwängler, who under the Nazi regime was given a title and huge sums of money by the war criminals [. . .][7]

The Swiss Social Democratic Party made a crude attempt to use his case as ammunition against the 'bourgeoisie of Zurich', concluding:

> This is why Wilhelm Furtwängler, who used to be Göring's favoured Staatsrat, and Goebbels' general director of music, remains for us one of the most loathsome figures of the Nazi Reich. His presence in Zurich is something we never can and never shall find acceptable.[8]

In fact the accused, having fulfilled his duties as guest conductor in Zurich, did attempt in a private letter to set straight the most malicious misrepresentations and misunderstandings that were gleefully propagated by his contemporaries. But, as in all his other attempts to defend himself, he demonstrated little skill. The point was reached where anyone who felt so inclined could vilify him. No one had to pretend . . . anyway, impartiality and decency were just a nuisance. Even National Socialist vocabulary was taken from the Nazi regime and used to slander him.[9] Indeed, Furtwängler seems to have come to terms with his role as victim, even to have identified with it. He took the abuse, accepting vindictive character assassinations along with inane derision. The editor of a Basel newspaper got away with the following observation: 'Should you decide to answer this, your letter will be most warmly welcomed, as our telephone operators, who are great autograph-collectors, have told us they can get one "Ansermet" for two "Furtwänglers".'[10]

Humiliation was by no means all he had to bear. His opponents were not satisfied with unpleasant but essentially peaceful means. They boycotted his planned guest tour of America and, to show that they meant their rejection of the Nazis, they threatened him with violence – anonymously of course, even though in 'free' America they ran not the slightest risk:

You are not wanted in the United States of North America, particularly not in Chicago. The climate in this very well-known city would
be very bad for your health. It would cause fatal injuries, against
which the Ruyersons, Kuypers, Aarons etc. presumably could do
nothing to protect you. Do not ignore this warning. It is the only
one you will get.[11]

Bullying and cowardice go hand in hand; it is common knowledge
that bullies only attack the weak. Anyone who is strong might fight
back. Which is why his persecutors hid behind protective anonymity.
They stayed behind the scenes. Of course they could have established
more accurately what the conductor actually did under the regime. After
all, the US military government office, during proceedings in December
and January of 1947–8, gave clear reasons why they would not support
any objections to Furtwängler's stay in the United States. When such
information is available and easily accessible no one can claim ignorance,

so there can be little doubt that there was a purpose behind the proceedings. The Nazis had introduced 'collective arrests' whereby one person could become liable for his relatives' supposed crimes; their victims reciprocated with the equally unreasonable concept of collective guilt; both were merciless in their reprisals. After all, to attribute personal responsibility to each and every citizen of a country for the actions of that country's government naturally makes for even more interesting opportunities for revenge than did the policies of Hitler's Gestapo. It is therefore not surprising that the death of their victim did not put a stop to the activities of these assiduous revenge-seekers. Especially as the dead can no longer initiate court proceedings. They are quite powerless. That is why one obituary of Furtwängler could declare with no risk whatsoever:

> He conducted surrounded by a sea of blazing fire. While synagogues went up in flames around him he did not throw his baton into the flames; he carried on conducting, as the chosen Staatskapellmeister of Hitler, Göring and Goebbels. He was also a Prussian Staatsrat, a senator, a vice-president of the Reichsmusikkammer, the idol of Nazi arsonists and murderers, the musical henchman of their bloodjustice.[12]

It is an issue which has yet to be laid to rest. In 1983, Hirschmann, one of his most malicious persecutors, wrote a letter to the *New York Times* in which he reawakened the old thirst for revenge. What he wrote is a classic example of defamatory technique, made the more blatant by his claim that after the war he had had access to the American occupying authorities' official records in which he had found documentary evidence of 'Furtwängler's collaboration with the Nazi regime', evidence which was now in his possession. However he chose not to draw on these documents, but remained content with generalisations; at all events he first claimed to be appealing to the truth and then proceeded to make a mockery of it:

> The incontrovertible truth is that as conductor of the Berlin Philharmonic Furtwängler yielded to Hitler's anti-Semitic demands and fired the Jewish members of his orchestra. Some of them fled to Ankara, Turkey, where I was serving at the time as a member of the US diplomatic corps. Furtwängler remained at his post in Germany, while most of his colleagues, including Arthur Schnabel, Adolf Busch and Bronislaw Huberman left the country in a public act of defiance. A photograph was published in the *New York Times* showing Furtwängler

9

bowing down from the podium of the Berlin Philharmonic to Hitler and his gang seated in the first row of the auditorium.[13]

This is a mixture of hearsay and faulty information. Hirschmann's complete ignorance of questions of musical politics under the Nazis is embarrassingly obvious. Either he does not know – or is deliberately withholding – the fact that the conductor of the Berlin Philharmonic had no authority to dismiss musicians whenever he felt like it. Hirschmann further deceived his readers by trying to contrast his 'heroes of the resistance' with 'Hitler's servant'. Neither Adolph Busch nor Huberman nor Schnabel 'left the country in a public act of defiance'; Busch had already taken up residence in Basel in 1927, Huberman owned a flat in Vienna, and Schnabel, who was of Austrian nationality anyway, left Berlin quietly, but kept on his flat and secretary to facilitate return at a later date. Hirschmann was not serving in Ankara 'at the time'; that came later, in 1944, but this lie was supposed to give him the status of actual witness. The photo was one of a long line of press photos which caught, among others, diplomats and statesmen from the democratic countries in the act of bowing to Hitler and occasionally even doing the 'German salute'. It proves that the conductor was not actually doing a 'Heil Hitler', but was bowing in the conventional way. Obviously Hirschmann wishes to prevent the reader from imagining what would have happened if Furtwängler had failed to bow in the usual fashion, just because it was Hitler who was sitting in the first row.

Unfortunately editors were also to blame; it was thanks to them that at least two attempts to set the record straight were withheld from the public, including one by Joanna Graudan, the widow of a Jewish solo-cellist who had held out in the Berlin Philharmonic until 1935 before retiring voluntarily. Another was by the correctly informed musical historian, Daniel Gillis. It fits the picture that the allegedly incriminating documents in Hirschmann's possession do contain material which was widely known and was used in the de-nazification commission proceedings against Furtwängler; these, it will be recalled, led to all charges being withdrawn. Falsifiers of history, like frauds and adulterers, need a reliable memory. In Hirschmann's case it was lacking. He had forgotten that already, thirty-eight years earlier, he had admitted that 'this information was available to me but was too well known by everyone to labour the point'.[14]

Alongside private campaigns against the Furtwängler symbol there is the academic one, less crude and with pretensions to complete objectivity. Its originators are historians, musicologists, musicians, political scientists, all of whom seem to share a dislike of the discomforts of archival research. The views expressed by Michael Gielen in a television interview may be excused as opinions given on the spur of the moment; he found it sad 'that a man like Furtwängler, who after all could have had a great future abroad, and was in fact being courted by New York, decided to stay. Somehow, even though he did make gestures towards helping Jews, and did not accept the cars Göring offered him, the fact remains that he did stay, thereby lending his name to a shameful situation.'[15]

Other people, however, use their names, titles or publications to lay claim to providing the correct facts and judgement, and pretend authority in a way which can easily mislead the innocent reader. One of the authors of an extensive analysis of the Nazi regime produced by a well-known publishing house and edited by a very well-respected specialist in contemporary history was allowed to get away with only one sentence about Furtwängler under the Third Reich: 'Wilhelm Furtwängler conducted so-called "work-break concerts" to further National Socialist ideology.'[16]

The information itself is correct. However, in the rest of the book he is not mentioned at all; to focus on only a few hours out of twelve years of conducting is an unacceptable falsification of history. The author could have checked up on the facts. The programmes of the Berlin Philharmonic are after all reliably documented, and had he chosen to see for himself, the author would have discovered that there were just two such concerts: one on 21 December 1939 in the R. Stock & Co tank factory in Berlin-Marienfelde, the other on 26 February 1942 in the workshop of the AEG, the major electrical equipment and armaments factory. Such concerts took place all over the Reich, under various conductors and using different ensembles. Herbert von Karajan in fact conducted the Staatskapelle and the Berlin Philharmonic on several such occasions. Of course Germany's enemies also put on concerts in armaments factories, so one must question how well the phrase 'to further National Socialist ideology' disguises the fact that music was used on both sides of the Front to refresh and cheer the armaments workers. Doubtless the alert reader would like to know what Furtwängler did apart from conducting the two work-break concerts, seeing that he remained in Germany for almost the whole of the Nazi period.

Occasionally it is just not possible to obtain the information one wants. If for political reasons one cannot use the Berlin Document Centre's resources one is reduced either to analysing motives using the same old clichés or to holding one's tongue; musicology stands or falls by what it publishes, and so the (normally much better-informed) Russian music-lover is told:

11

He was able, even though surrounded by Nazis, to extend his brilliant and profound interpretations of Beethoven and Wagner to the limits of his musical taste and feeling, and at the same time to 'serve the regime' socially, psychologically and politically, promoting celebrations at the murderer's court. All the appalling events of the Third Reich took place to the pure sound of his orchestra. Furtwängler's Beethoven and Furtwängler's Wagner were just as much a part of that world as its swastikas, drums, parades and the exhausting screams of the Führer's speeches.[17]

These few examples have been given to demonstrate the factual inadequacy even of serious accounts of the conductor's political life. Of course this is countered on the other side by those 'genius cults' which out of possessive love refuse to acknowledge that there might be questions to be asked; they need not be considered here. In fact those who revered him were almost as blind to the facts as those instigating hate campaigns, but at least the former meant no harm, did not try to poison his good name, or to destroy him. His opponents on the other hand, by using him as a scapegoat, did not themselves accomplish anything worthwhile in the interests of the anti-fascist movement. Perhaps they wanted to avoid the risks which real action – including the assassination of the tyrant – would have entailed. At any rate Hitler was in many ways so distant that he hardly seemed real; Furtwängler on the other hand could not withdraw. He was right there in the limelight at each performance.

It seems worthwhile then to investigate why this man stood in for others and paid the price for the regime's truly monstrous crimes, even though no one would go so far as to claim he had had a hand in the crimes themselves. Why was he considered a Nazi even though he was not a member of the party or of any of its subsidiary groupings? Was he by any chance intoxicated by the National Socialist ideology? Did he worship Hitler or fill a post which a Jewish artist had to give up? Did he accept presents from those in power or profit more from Hitler's government than he might have been expected to under a democratic one? Did his concerts conceal the truth of the Nazis from the world? Did his musical activity prolong the war? Did the brown-shirted officials consider him a close friend and loyal companion in war? All these questions await a detailed answer; motives will be brought to light which may clarify the otherwise inexplicable; an investigation of the psychology of an above-average musician under the exigencies of the Nazi regime may yield new insights. A maximum of factual information should help to build a new and different picture.

What role was Wilhelm Furtwängler playing when he became the scapegoat? According to Jewish custom the people would, whenever a conciliatory sacrifice was needed, present the high priest with two he-goats. In order to ascertain which of the two would be pleasing to God, the high priest would cast lots. Having slaughtered the one chosen for God, he would then lay his hands on the other, which was destined for the evil spirit of the desert, Asasel; in so doing the priest was symbolically laying all the sins of Israel on its head. The goat would then be chased out into the desert, to bear those sins far away and so deflect God's wrath on to himself. The goat had no part in the guilt heaped upon him; he was the victim of a myth: a sacrifice. The opponents of the Nazis behaved likewise: they could not blame the whole German people so they sought scapegoats to take the blame for all the regime's shameful deeds. However, by force of reason they were limited in what they could say; it was after all obvious that in the case of Furtwängler, he had not formulated or revised the anti-Semitic Nürnberg laws, built any concentration camps, served as one of the terrible military judges or led an invasion, for example. So the accusation had to be subtler, allowing as few opportunities as possible for reprisals, laying charges against which no counter-evidence could be brought to bear. This did not require any very complicated scheming. It was enough to find one way or another to express the feeling that Furtwängler had, however one cared to look at the situation, 'gone along with it all' – by being one of the seventy or eighty million Germans who stayed in the country without being compelled to do so. When an action is inexplicable, especially where politics are concerned, a plausible explanation is usually quick to appear: in this case that he must have been bought off – because even though he was not a party member, he was so useful to the Nazis that they courted him as an accomplice and used his name to give credibility to their propaganda. A full consideration of all the facts concerning Furtwängler's artistic and political biography during the Nazi regime reveals on the one hand how unjustified such an attitude was, and on the other how he managed to avoid carrying out certain official requests by a hair's breadth. Because he continued his artistic activity in the 'new' Germany as if nothing had happened, many people accused him of being an accomplice to what was happening, an idea that persisted long after it was all over. This is powerfully demonstrated in the letter which the seventy-seven-year-old Anna Geissmar, whose Jewish daughter had been secretary to Furtwängler for many years, wrote in 1945 to her 'dear old friend' from exile in London:

As old and faithful friends we have followed your progress with fear and concern. I in particular could well understand how initially, filled

13

2 March 1945: the caricaturist incites Swiss readers against Furtwängler

with a love of your fatherland, you should have tried to help. We never lost faith in you. It was with horror however that we observed the worsening situation at home. Having been hounded from the country we loved so deeply, and, like plague-carriers, made homeless, we were aware of how bad things were in a way that you probably could not have been. [. . .] Then came the ever-worsening reports of horrific incidents, of murder and theft, of atrocities worse than any under the inquisition or during the Middle Ages. And so we always hoped that you would leave, show that you, one of the best, refused to stay in a place ruled by beasts in human guise, where a crazy fanatic was dragging our wonderful nation of thinkers and poets down into the abyss.[18]

There is in this, despite the respectful tone, also a note of disappointment that he had not made the hoped-for gesture: his reasons for not doing so were as inconceivable to the writer of the letter as they were to the artist's most violent opponents – and the latter did not restrain themselves unnecessarily by researching his motives. The scapegoat had to play his role; any recognition of his motives might have delayed his expulsion into the wilderness – and anyway, explaining a person's motives does not necessarily excuse them.

That Wilhelm Furtwängler liked to call himself a German musician is proved by his notes and correspondence. It was a trait he shared with the Nazis, but also with many nineteenth-century poets and

14

philosophers. To us today, the political abuse of the word 'German' is still repellent; for many years, even decades after the end of the Hitler regime, it was considered inappropriate to 'show one's true colours' in any sense of the word. From that point of view other nationalities were at an advantage: nobody would hesitate to call themselves British, French or Dutch. 'German' on the other hand had overtones of national chauvinism and stirred accursed memories of an unsatisfied thirst for greatness. The Nazis' misuse of the word has poisoned its use right up to the present day, in so far as our historic consciousness is still able to perceive cause and effect – an avoidable burden if one turns a blind eye to history. In all fairness, it has to be said that the Nazis were in no way the inventors of such misuse. They just exploited its ideological potential by encouraging its common usage. When I write 'Furtwängler, a German musician', the word German denotes nothing more than the man's place of origin: a musician from a particular country where a particular language is spoken. A person's birthplace is a matter of chance, and pure chance determines neither rights nor obligations. So it seems clear that 'German' cannot stand for any characteristics, but denotes only provenance. Anything more is ideology – such as is the verse from the much misused 'Song of the Germans': German women, German loyalty, German wine and German song . . . that this song still exists, and is even used to stir up feelings, is proof that people are remarkably thick-skinned in the light of recent historical experience.

For Furtwängler, on the other hand, it was quite usual to use the word in this broad sense, and it was not something he was likely to question, growing up as he had in a familial, social and political milieu which from 1890 until 1918 was untroubled by self-doubts, and in which the word 'German' was used not only to denote origin, but also to embody a set of ideal qualities and virtues which were further linked with noble birth. The expression 'German music' meant far more than just 'music by composers born in Germany': it was also understood in an ideological sense to mean 'music comparable with that of the great masters Beethoven and Wagner', the German masters; to describe a piece of music as 'foreign' was of course to imply the opposite, a measure of deficiency. To see through and break free from such ideology Furtwängler would have had to have been a totally different person. People from different social backgrounds providing a less fixed sense of identity were occasionally more open-minded, but the impressions Furtwängler absorbed at an early age seem to have remained with him. Although he appeared to be unruly, this Munich professor's son did not direct his *Sturm und Drang* against the apparently harmonious world of those adults who were almost his only companions, but against the

15

wholly different environment of school to the point where it was felt that educating him at school was of no advantage to him. He was put in the hands of private tutors, and from then on he was to feel that he was privileged and special, a member of a spiritual and cultural élite which imagined itself closer to God and the Kaiser than to the ordinary people, even if the ordinary people were German too.

Added to this was a heritage which carried its own obligations, the myth of Christian civilisation which this class had made its own, *Kultur*, a classical education, Wilhelmine codes of behaviour, a sense of values which left no room for doubts. One felt one stood for something and had to fight – chivalrously and according to the code of honour, of course – anything which seemed to threaten such values. That even this rather exalted world had its darker side became clear to the adolescent Furtwängler when he one day discovered his mother reading out loud the love-letters he had written to Bertel von Hildebrand, a girl of his age, the daughter of an art historian and sculptor who was a member of the Furtwänglers' circle of acquaintances. She was reading them out to some friends of hers, a betrayal which must have cut the sensitive youth to the quick. Soon afterwards he withdrew into himself, over-come with a distrust of women which he retained even many years later. As his reputation as a musician grew he became increasingly élitist in his thinking and indeed his whole upbringing conspired to isolate him, believing as he did that he was safeguarding moral standards.

As a result of the humiliation he had suffered for his first literary efforts Furtwängler only began to record his thoughts and impressions at about the age of thirty, writing them in an ordinary diary rather than in a journal, clearly for himself rather than with readers in mind. These notes begin at a time of his life in which he was directly confronted with a hostile world, a world in which pre-war certainties had disappeared. A spiritual and moral heritage had been shattered; an entire social class had lost both its financial and spiritual basis. The old order gave way to revolution, the Kaiser's rule collapsed, and the rule of the people – a dubious concept for someone brought up in the *ancien régime* – was heralded by the overthrow of monuments and myths. Was the fact that the Kaiser knew no Germans and fled abroad like a traitorous deserter not a shocking act of betrayal? Furtwängler stored it in his memory.

These events – tragic in the history of the world, for which several other European powers shared responsibility – in no way made the young conductor into a subversive. To have further undermined what was collapsing anyway would have gone against both his nature and the outlook on life which he had inherited. Preservation of what survived seemed to him to be the order of the day; havens of 'normality' were

16

necessary in the rush of events. At this time he frequently made a note of what seemed to be dangerous threats: Politics, Democracy, Progress, Technology, Theory, Intellectuals . . . and of course 'Bolshevism, that fashionable religion of hatred'.[19]

In contrast to these 'revolutionary' events his own conservative idealism seemed a source of existential security, a rock of peace, certainty, the very essence of the old and trusted values. It seems strange that such an outstanding musician should have needed the support of such an outlook, but it does demonstrate how much he feared the loss of his inherited and earned privileges in the general turmoil of the crisis. He wished to keep his societal and artistic status intact, both in his eyes and those of the world, and an undamaged value-system both maintained and enhanced this sense of élitisim. There was of course no place for the contemporary preoccupation with progress; such an ideology was merely repellent and reinforced the musician's conservatism, especially when adventurous experiments with 'progress' led to chaotic results. Anything which failed to fit his own ideological framework only heightened his gnawing fears of loss. It is hardly surprising that, untroubled by either scepticism towards his own values or the possibility of order offered by democracy, he came to the conclusion that democracy was the solution of 'those who had nothing to lose'.[20]

Although he might have been expected to eschew self-criticism completely, either because it simply did not occur to him or because he did not wish his well-developed self-confidence to be undermined, his notes contain passages in which he analyses his own behaviour critically – but they refer to his private life. His artistic persona, especially as the expression of an almost mythical artistic heritage, remained sacrosanct. He was above all concerned with its preservation, for reasons which his life makes clear. Furtwängler was clearly obsessed with the task of preserving many aspects of his culture other than just music: his wide interests and desire to accomplish something positive in all cultural spheres extended to pictorial art, literature, philosophy, ethics, and even to politics, loath though he was to admit it. Anyone believing himself in possession of a truth blessed by tradition eventually becomes liable to assume some sort of redemptive role, but Furtwängler's concerns found little echo among his contemporaries. After all, the installation of the Republic had changed the focus of power: questions of democratic procedure such as debate and majority decision-making were of immediate relevance, while the whole concept of authority was in some doubt. Thus Furtwängler was no stranger to differences of opinion, argument and division. He was rarely in a position to carry a particular task through from beginning to end, whatever the field of interest. He was frequently stopped half way, and tended to blame his disappointment on those who had blocked him, on those who would not accept his power and refused to recognise his authority.

His whole psychological make-up marked him as anti-revolutionary and conservative, as somebody who would be inclined to accept and defend the tried and tested, or at least what he believed to be tried and tested. Someone who derives so much of his energy from close involvement with tradition probably cannot do otherwise. He was one of the very few examples of a conservative intellectual. The point which he saw as bordering on the 'intellectualism' he hated so much was the point beyond which his own intellect was not prepared to compete; this was the ruthless intellectual dissection which seemed intent on undermining the traditional order, liquidating Western values and reducing the philosophy of life to a simple acceptance of reality. It constituted a prime threat to the foundations on which Furtwängler based his own outlook, and it was at this point that he began his counter-attack, not with the sophisticated and finely honed tools of dialectical argument which his opponents – mostly on the left – used with such skill, but rather with reasoning which he fully grasped and trusted. It was an ideologically circumscribed and methodologically somewhat unsatisfactory line of reasoning.

I do not wish to be misunderstood; Furtwängler was not in the least stupid, he was in fact endowed with great intelligence, but he would not use it to question his inherited certainties. He was certainly not unaware; he was only too aware. As far as he was concerned analysis did not offer the opportunity to disentangle complexities, but rather contained the threat of his own worthlessness, which is why all the words which were appropriated for propaganda purposes by the Nazis had a most personal significance for him; subversion, degeneration, German, nation, genius . . . He related each of these concepts to himself and incorporated them into his mosaic of values, judging some positively, some negatively, finding some uplifting and enchanting, others worrying and hostile. He thought in terms of polarities and analogies. His notes only rarely contain what one might consider examples of differentiation or deduction; philosophical abstractions are not present at all – each concept seems linked to a picture or a value. Such language, as he uses it, is more than just a means to communicate. It is an instrument of power, at least in all the places in his notes where he uses it so spontaneously and ingenuously. Unfortunately, by using such language, Furtwängler deprived himself of many opportunities to communicate.

He not only made demands on his readers' willingness to understand

18

him, he also missed the chance to benefit from the arguments of the 'intellectuals', even if only in the sense of being able to pay them back in their own coin on the occasions when they waged war. This may have been regrettable, but one must accept that such language was not his currency. New ideas did not enrich his outlook, they seemed rather to disorient him. There was thus every reason to distance himself from many influences, the more so as his whole being derived so clearly from a strong cultural identity. That he did so is evident from the books he read; like any well-educated German he was acquainted with the main works of the German classicists and romanticists as well as those of poets and novelists – leaving aside the detective novels he read for relaxation. Naturally he knew his Nietzsche. His reading of Baudelaire may have been a bold foray across self-imposed boundaries . . . but he had no motivation to go further and read the works of 'left-wing' writers such as Tucholsky or Brecht. He was more interested in writers as various as Stefan George, Ferdinand Bruckner, Erwin Guido Kolbenheyer and Ernst Jünger (with whose position as an outsider he may have felt some affinity). Hermann Graf Keyserling had already gone beyond the limits of what was acceptable and he seemed too shallow; Furtwängler noted in a sober tone in 1936:

The person who seeks to lead an inner spiritual life, as should everybody, must limit his openness to influence from the outside world. Keyserling long ago overstepped these limits and has become a master of the opposite attitude, which is why he provokes such opposition, despite his visibly great achievements. Above all such wordly minds misunderstand the importance of the inner self to the German people. They should ask themselves what would be left of their open-mindedness if everybody were as concerned as they themselves are with connections between things rather than with their real substance.[21]

However, when the officials from the Reich Propaganda Ministry who were responsible for literature managed to stifle Keyserling a year later, Furtwängler went in search of the forbidden fruit: 'Keyserling is on the list of "undesirables". Booksellers?'[22] Furtwängler did not now consider him one of the 'truly great', but he did adopt a friendly stance towards him. Keyserling would later take spiteful revenge on Furtwängler by letting it be known that he had been the one to persuade Furtwängler to stay in the Nazi state.[23] The sort of orientation from which Furtwängler hoped to confirm his own intellectual viewpoint was not one Keyserling could corroborate. In the post–1933 period any sort of corroboration was rare. The musician threw himself into difficult —

and most peculiar — studies in cultural history ranging from world history to psychoanalysis. He read or re-read whatever he could get hold of, from Johann Jakob Bachofen to Carl Gustav Jung, from Jacob Burckhardt to Ludwig Klages and Oswald Spengler's *Decline of the West*, all of which he judged as either affirming or contradicting his own opinions. He found no obvious explanation for the much-debated contemporary European crisis, although some attempts did stand out. As early as 1924 Rudolf Pannwitz had come to grief with his book *Krise der Europäischen Kultur* (The Crisis of European Culture), a breathless account lacking discussion, whose author exhibited a taste for sweeping generalisations and used punctuation which alternated between the chaotic and the non-existent. Furtwängler credited him with having achieved some profound insights, but overall felt he was spurious, and was critical of the undisciplined 'intellect' which could conceive such an ambitious project. His suspicious diagnosis that this work demonstrated 'intellect', shows how easily the musician was deceived by anything with 'literary' trappings. He was certainly very quick to pick up on anything with even a whiff of 'intellectualism' about it.

In the field of cultural history he was fairly undiscriminating, reading any new publication of substance – especially if a book's title touched on his own fear of loss. In 1940 he became acquainted with Edgar Dacqué's *The Lost Paradise*, a book which, while making a somewhat clumsy claim to contribute to the 'the spiritual history of mankind', provided some ideological justification for the many readers whose Christian convictions led them to resist Hitler's regime in some way or another. Dacqué's outline of a myth which would be universally valid in time and space was consciously opposed to Alfred Rosenberg's propagandist pronouncements; it very deliberately takes the thousand-year Reich as its starting point, but quite contrary to expectations ends by affirming the certainty of a Kingdom of God and Christian redemption . . . counter-propaganda for anyone who was reading closely. Furtwängler was certainly an alert reader, and understood that the writer and philosopher was an ally, but he disapproved of Dacqué's attack, because he felt defence to be more necessary. He felt the book concentrated overly on 'time-consuming polemic against modern intellectualism, something I too must try and avoid doing. People with a lively appreciation of deeply rooted values should put more time and effort into defending them, otherwise their appreciation is worthless.'[24]

At times his reading material served only to provoke him. For example Hans Künkel's *Schicksal und Willensfreiheit* (Predestination and Freedom of the Will) radically questioned the whole issue of *Kultur*, Furtwängler's very own specialism: this abstruse 'philosophy of astrology' (it is astonishing what areas his search led him to) had already appeared in 1924. It is not clear at what point the musician got hold of the book, but he discusses it in his notes of 1940, observing:

> Really the Socratic person of today realises as a result of all these enquiries that he no longer knows anything. From this point of view Goethe – or any artist – is truly in a better position. The performance and presentation of art are the means of access to our own personal 'myth' – no other means of access exists today, except possibly through a purely religious experience. [25]

Immersion in the literature of cultural history did prove to be useful. It no more provided final answers to his key questions than occasional visits to the fortune-teller would have done, but it did confirm the artist's previous opinions. He had doubtless hoped for more, and so it is possible that disappointment lay behind his sometimes brusque reactions to writers, as for example in the case of Richard Benz, whose love of music made him an easy target for the expert musician; Benz was damningly labelled a 'cultural windbag', a phenomenon Furtwängler elaborated on in his notes:

> Some people know what they are talking about, others just talk. The less attention one pays to detail, the easier it becomes to perceive the broad overview and the 'historical' connections. One then has an El Dorado for intellectual games of all kinds. There are very few histories of art written by people who really know something about their subject or have something original to say. In this situation it is still better to be absorbed in one thing, an approach which generally suits the artist better anyway. Then a genuine love-affair can develop. [26]

This love-affair – in the most general sense of the word – was a solution to the gathering confusion of the world as Furtwängler perceived it. He could use it as an explanation for why the artist reacts differently to the thinker. However, one work he read showed the problems of borderline cases. It was not another conventional cultural history, but a case of propaganda which unlike the publications of Hitler, Rosenberg or Ley, who made no bones about their propagandist intentions, turned up in the guise of an academic study of cultural history. The matter-of-fact title and the fact that it was published by the Reich's Institute for the History of the New Germany were deceptive. How could anyone know that the editor, the director of the institute Professor Walter Frank, was primarily a specialist in anti-Semitic propaganda? The book was published posthumously, its author, Christoph Steding, having died early in 1938 aged only thirty-four. As the golden boy of National Socialist historical research Steding knew what was wanted of him, and justified the deliberate imposition of a barbarian rule accordingly. His readers discovered that: 'It is only advocates of *Kultur*, in particular the non-Aryan race which counts among its most gifted exponents, who mistake the new freedom of the German Reich for a lack of freedom'.[27]

That was targeted above all at Jews, but also at *Kultur*. At another point Steding informs the reader that *Kultur* was initially a political artefact, and that Hitler's accession to power was coterminous with the solution to all ills, and of one in particular:

> The triumph of these forces in 1933 is the real refutation of Freud. [. . .] Founding the Reich was a political act which displaced the principle of 'diversification' with that of 'harmonization'. This refutes Freud in that it smokes out [literally 'sweats out' – *ausschwitzen*] the type of person who even today defines himself by how he differs from others, a process which threatens the annihilation of a great nation. Such people are compelled to emigrate, or find that the very existence of the Reich exacerbates their sense of alienation to the point of nervous breakdown or suicide; for anyone who seeks to be different for the sake of it finds that the objective power of the Reich is such, and its moral authority carries such force, that they must either yield to or be destroyed by it.[28]

Furtwängler read and pondered this in the spring of 1939. His notes do not go into Steding's anti-Semitism, but are sharply critical of his claim to be applying scientific principles and also of his scarcely tenable analysis with its ill-disguised intentions, especially in the 'crude way he links all his subject-matter to macho politics, which reveals the politician *manqué* behind the philosopher, and leads one to question the veracity of his statements'.[29]

At that time anybody reading Steding could not know that what he wrote was a dismayingly accurate foretaste of what was to come. Was it not with future atrocities in mind that he repeatedly made use of the word *ausschwitzen* in his references to the way Jews living in the Reich were to be singled out and forced to emigrate, or otherwise be eliminated? He coined the idea years before the Nazis' annihilation machine acquired a centre of operations at Auschwitz.

Furtwängler's choice of reading matter suggests the efforts of an educated person not only to keep up to date with new information, but also to broaden his horizons, or at least to consolidate his cultural heritage. He could never benefit fully because the barriers he constructed against what he considered 'intellectualism' seemed insuperable; his reading did however have a considerable effect on him. It convinced him that he really need not have made the effort in the first place. In his opinion all these authors had one thing in common; they lacked intellectual stature. He could not maintain any lasting interest in them because the fruits of their intellectual efforts were not worth the harvesting.

Furtwängler's metaphorical use of the term 'stature' as a distinguishing mark may seem naïve, given that he clearly felt himself to possess it in more than just a physical sense. However, for someone who has had to deal with so much public acclaim and artistic renown it is probably quite usual: critics, biographers, letter-writers and above all adoring women testified to his greatness in a seemingly never-ending litany. Only too often it verged on religious veneration. His admirers made an *Übermensch* of him; to them he was Prometheus and the Demiurge, a legend in his own lifetime, immortal. Greatness inspires invocations and faith, as can be seen from the celebratory tone of numerous tributes:

> Throughout a long period of demoralisation, emptiness and uncertainty Wilhelm Furtwängler was our leader; through music he guided us out of the chaos of the world to clarity; from unrest, noise and struggle to stillness, peace and reverie. It should be stressed again that he protected the great classic works through difficult times, and defended what for us are eternal values. At our darkest hour he strengthened our belief in a better and purer future.[30]

Anyone inclined to put this down to the outpourings of a rather dizzy lady admirer could, for example, take Oswald Schrenk, Furtwängler's second biographer, as proof that such tributes were the rule rather than the exception: 'It is also the current of the music which sweeps the conductor to a state of holy exaltation, leading him and his audience to the realms of unforgettable experience.'[31] A person who is the object of such powerful waves of sentiment – however undoubtedly justified and sincere – is surely not to be envied. All artists must have some idea of what they are capable of and who they are; but it can only be notional if, like Furtwängler, they eschew self-analysis or criticism for fear it might disturb them. Obviously any analysis might awaken doubts or create uncertainties which would be deadly for someone who needs absolute self-assurance. But such glowing and all-pervasive admiration is no less disquieting: it disorients the artist, deluding him about his own capacities and tempting him to succumb to delusions of grandeur. There is no record – at least, not a written one – of what Furtwängler thought of himself, but it can be said that he enjoyed praise and ovations to a point where they seemed indispensable. In his writings he referred several times to the problem of greatness, but he never made reference to himself. One fact of course required no special mention: the role of the conductor emphasises his physical presence. Not only does his position on stage mean that the public in the auditorium must perforce look up to him, but being on the podium he stands also above the level of the orchestra. Stature is one of the necessary qualifications of a conductor, as it is for an intellectual, a teacher, an actor or a politician. They are all automatically exposed and elevated when in the public gaze. The reality of this situation must have psychological consequences which are reflected in the way the members of these professions see themselves. Like priests, pedagogues, tragedians and politicians, the conductor is faced with an audience who cannot do what he is doing, even if it is perfectly possible to acquire certain of his skills. Thus 'those below' perceive 'the one on high' as so special and otherworldly that they are inclined to ascribe redemptive powers to him. To have to live with this and still lead a normal life poses considerable problems, which is as much as one can really say about the external effects of the rise to fame.

However, Furtwängler did outline his internal process in his notes. A list of the associations he made gives some idea of what he was thinking: he feels that modern man is not interested in greatness, and modern art correspondingly fails to express anything great: for greatness to give rise to heroism both human warmth and organisational abilities are required. He distinguishes the greatness of an age and that of an artist, but sees no place for objective measures of faith in human greatness or of true greatness: all such types of greatness are liable to attack by mean-spirited people. This conception of 'greatness' is then harmoniously joined with his individual élitism, a further means of self-defence. Clearly a great individual has to beware of smallminded and envious little people who may have it in for him because they cannot bear someone else to be successful, and so wait for a moment of weakness or uncertainty in order to attack from the rear. However, the greater one becomes the more secure one's position. To be at the top might signal the end of such fears.

Furtwängler was unusually uncommunicative about his own feelings. Only in exceptional situations did he give away any personal information, but even then nothing intimate. To infer so much about his ideas of 'greatness' is certainly to touch on a highly sensitive issue. Having no documentary evidence one is left to infer from circumstantial evidence, which is in itself a perfectly legitimate undertaking. The conductor definitely believed himself to be a new incarnation of the great composers whose music he conducted, with Beethoven, whom he considered the greatest, in first place. Once, and only once, Furtwängler did drop a clue, but even then he seems to have realised while writing that he was going too far, which caused him to break off in mid-sentence: 'I will both say and write that anyone who is not himself Beeth [sic] has no right . . .'[32]

It may be said that the conductor – so strongly shaped by his heritage (in all senses of the word), his conditioning and by public acclamation – was no longer free to act entirely as he chose, but was obliged to consider his status and image. Whatever he did, he could please neither his friends nor his enemies. This internal and external pressure gives the lie to the myth of free will, and for this reason Furtwängler's position was not one anybody could envy him. Force of circumstance is generally an acceptable excuse for one's behaviour, but the troubles of the soul are at best seen as weaknesses which should be kept from the public if at all possible. In fact Furtwängler did, in the written records of his defence after 1945, offer numerous explanations for why he had done one thing rather than another when the Hitler regime made its demands. The evidence can be found in the minutes of the de-nazification commission, and in his own notes. He did allude in a general way to the pressure of circumstances which bound him: primarily, the total constraints imposed by the National Socialist state. The fact that he was psychologically predisposed to close his mind to several alternative forms of conduct was not mentioned. The commission left it at that, looking no further than on the surface, because it was in the interests of the occupying powers, who pulled the strings and prevented the whole truth being known, that he should not be released unconditionally; a scapegoat was still called for as a trump against the Soviet Union which, in a rapid and humane move unclouded by political doubts, had tried to obtain the conductor for the revival of the Staatsoper in the Soviet sector of Berlin. For what other reason would the US military authorities have dealt with the Furtwängler question in such an obviously manipulative way, after years of costly war in the name of 'freedom and democracy', and while still in the midst of the difficult 'transition to democracy' in Germany?

The first irritating feature of his trial was its repeated postponement over a period of many months. Then one of the members of the commission, Karl Fischer-Walden, a decent man, withdrew in protest, claiming that customary access to the case files had been blocked, and that the commission had been called to an extraordinary meeting the day before the trial was officially due to begin, at which it had been made clear which way the case should go. As if this were not sufficiently farcical, Berliners were told at the end of January 1947 that concerts conducted by Furtwängler could only take place with the permission of the Allies, but that in any case, the commission lacked the necessary two thousand sheets of typing paper with which to apply for permission. The conductor's release could have been delayed for many more months if Boleslaw Barlog, director of the Schlosspark Theatre, had not had the bright idea of appealing to music enthusiasts to donate paper.

After even the proceedings of the commission had not revealed the motives behind his actions, Furtwängler did not disclose very much in other contexts either. He did plan a book by the title *Hitlerdeutschland und ich* (Hitler's Germany and I), which was to be an autobiographical sketch, but this got no further than the title and subtitle noted in his unpublished 1946 diary, and might not have contained any further information on the subject anyway. Furthermore, his collected works gave no hint that this much-criticised artist ever planned a general justification or an attempt to set the record straight in the form of memoirs or an autobiography. This may have been because in the last years of his life he felt he did not have the time, or because he had become resigned, and felt further defence to be pointless. So he submitted to the role of hated and doomed scapegoat, borne down – now much weakened by illness – by the burden of suffering until it killed him. Is it not true that grandeur, and delusions of grandeur, come before the farthest fall?

2

THE DYNAMIC STRENGTH OF THE
NATIONAL MOVEMENT

Although Hitler's initial accession to power was as legal as was possible within the framework of the Weimar Republic, he encouraged his supporters to believe that his appointment as chancellor of the Reich was the successful outcome of a National Socialist revolution. There is no doubt that he wanted parliamentary procedure to be overridden. He found it insufficiently combative, smacking of endless debate and the hated system of majority decision-making. For this reason the label 'revolution' was to be brought into use, intended to suggest overthrow, blood and violence; sacrifices had to be made if the 'higher goal' was to be attained – and it was alleged that there was no other way to 'save' the Reich. Thus, once power had been obtained it was extended and abused, in the absence of a 'ruling class', in a so-called 'revolution' against socialists, communists, Jews, even against certain books and ideas which were purported to pose a threat to the 'new' Germany. The Nazis were to be made to feel like courageous revolutionaries, real men who could sweep aside what was worthless, defend the mythical German Reich with life and limb, free the oppressed nation from the chaos of parliamentary rule . . . all under the unerring guidance of a genius who embodied everything that was great and good in the German character, and who would progress from being the chancellor to become the Führer. At least that was the official party line. While it is easy today for us to recognise it as the empty propaganda trick it was, political and economic circumstances in 1933 contributed considerably to its appeal. The yearning for some sort of relief, for a dynamic and strong-willed hero who could reverse the decline of a Reich which – despite being 'unvanquished on the battlefield' – had lost the war and been severely constrained by the Versailles settlement, and transform it into a glorious triumph, surely contributed much to the success of the National Socialists. So they set about clothing reality with their myth. Their methods – terror, demonstrations, proclamations – mobilised previously unsuspected forces within a very short space of time. Fear as well as shared convictions compelled people to participate, for participation was always good proof of loyalty at a time when renegades were setting the tone and tempo.

Initially musical life continued in Germany much as it had done under the Weimar Republic; a crisis situation had almost become the norm. Jewish musicians did come in for verbal abuse – usually from local party activists – but they themselves attached little importance to it; anti-Semitism was nothing new in Germany, and ironically the very freedom which during the republic had become a political reality for the first time in Germany's history also permitted the large-scale publication of anti-Semitic writings. Furthermore this had hardly aroused public anger, serving rather as ammunition in the fight between the right- and left-wing press. Anti-Semitism was after all a problem for individuals. The Germans appeared to have more pressing problems, not directly connected with the field of politics. Politics – and even today this is a widely held belief – was best left in the hands of the experts. As long as it did not affect one's job or intrude into one's private life, politics could be left well alone.

In 1933 Wilhelm Furtwängler, in his prime at the age of forty-seven, was possibly at the height of his artistic career: he had held the artistic directorship of the Berlin Philharmonic Orchestra for over ten years, and was much requested abroad as guest conductor: he enjoyed a devoted public, both in Berlin and elsewhere: he was considered the authority on his subject, Germany's musical guru – at least by those Germans who adhered to traditional values and felt themselves beholden to their cultural heritage, rather than considering it a hindrance to progress. His views on music were common knowledge, and he propounded them with an almost missionary fervour, having concluded after intense reflection – always closely linked to his actual musical activity – that they represented irrefutable truths, were some sort of higher revelation.

A personality of that cast of mind would certainly feel that to be involved in politics would be to lower himself. He was clearly not bothered that other musicians thought differently. He was aware that the conductor Hermann Scherchen cultivated socialist leanings, but he shut his eyes to this as resolutely as to Hans Pfitzner's anti-Semitism and xenophobia. He grew ever less compromising in his repeated assertion that music had nothing, absolutely nothing at all to do with politics. Instrumental music especially should be above the day-to-day wranglings of parties, a sanctuary for the beautiful, the true and the good, which the messy business of politics should not be allowed to disturb. This did not mean that Furtwängler was blind; the unpleasant reality of the situation must have struck him when the Berlin Philharmonic could no longer cover its running expenses, and so had to ask for public assistance, with its inevitable political implications. Already prior to that most of the opera houses at which he conducted were subsidised concerns under the thumb of the local or state authorities. He cannot have deliberately sought to deny the evidence of the critical state of the arts, but he saw the world as an idealised, fairytale realm of perfection which bore no resemblance to this shabby, tainted world, so he sought to deny any circumstances which punctured his picture and which showed the vileness and desecration taking place in everyday life. This was unfortunate, for although the people were incapable of sharing his idealism they might have grasped more fully what was going on had they had a first-class artist to help. Furtwängler was exactly the sort of person who, if he felt a cause was worthy, had the necessary persistence to see it brought to fruition. But he had great difficulty coming to terms with a reality which was so at odds with his carefully nurtured beliefs.

And yet he had already brushed with politics years before Hitler came to power. The Weimar Republic was also, according to its constitution, committed to nurturing and encouraging artistic activity; what this in effect meant was that it sought, by clever use of the apparatus of democracy and appeals to the will of the majority, to use art for its own ends. It was quite clear to those in power that music would be a suitable adjunct to public events, for example if used to open great state occasions, and it could also serve as a prop for political beliefs. The Democrats did not differ from the Nazis in using the works of the great composers on great occasions. These composers were German heroes, classic in the widest sense of the word, whose stirring and moving work could make the mythical unity of people and rulers seem believable, regardless of whether this was actually achieved. What the Reichstag wanted was symbols.

In the summer of 1927 Furtwängler was asked if he would like to take responsibility for the music and conduct the Berlin Philharmonic at the celebrations planned to mark the anniversary of the constitution to be held by the national government, the Prussian state government and that of the city of Berlin. Whichever way one looked at it this was a political matter. The ruling Reichstag was in fact composed of nine different parties, but every third delegate was a Social Democrat, in other words of a political orientation quite alien to Furtwängler. But the orchestra accepted state monies because otherwise it could not have survived – and so it was really obliged to do as the state requested. Faced with this quandary the conductor developed his maxim that music had nothing to do with politics, a maxim which he was to repeat many times while under the tight stranglehold of Nazi politics, if only to banish his own doubts. At the same time he tried to find out how the matter was viewed in political circles. During July 1927 Emil Berndt, the politician who could have provided an answer, was on holiday in Kampen, Isle of Sylt. Berndt was a lawyer, judge and alderman in Berlin, as well as head of the German civil service, and since the first elections had been the German National People's Party's (DNVP) delegate to the Reichstag. A written enquiry – Berta Geissmar had written to Frau Berndt, who was an acquaintance of hers – elicited the comforting response:

> My husband shares Herr Furtwängler's view that art has nothing to do with politics, and therefore considers that he need have no reservations about conducting at the constitutional celebrations. This can in no way be considered to demonstrate his political sympathies. The fact that my husband as a politician of the DNVP would not attend the celebrations is quite a different matter; given that the German Nationalists disapprove of the Republic and its constitution they have no reason to attend celebrations in its honour.[1]

That made everything clear. The conductor, who did not sympathise with the parliamentary politics of the DNVP but found himself in an awkward position, graced the constitutional celebrations of 11 August with music by Wagner, Schubert, and Beethoven, as well as Hugo Kaun's singularly appropriate 'Heimatgebet' (Prayer for our country). But he did not go one step further. When on 18 January 1928, the anniversary of Wilhelm I's ostentatious accession to the Kaiser of Germany in the Hall of Mirrors at Versailles in 1871, the Federation of National Associations celebrated the foundation of the Reich, Furtwängler left it to his colleague Julius Prüwer to create a suitably solemn and festive atmosphere with music by Beethoven, Wagner and Hummel, as well as a couple of military marches. However, at the Reich's next constitutional celebrations on 11 August 1928 he was once again on the podium. These two appearances in connection with undeniably political events staged by the government of the republic seem to have been the only ones; by contrast he frequently conducted social and charity concerts. But as time went on, political pressures increased.

In 1930 the government used a legal emergency ordinance to cancel a state subsidy to the Berlin Philharmonic Orchestra to which the Reichstag had just given its seal of approval. Unusually the Berlin city council refused to provide any more money. Furtwängler appealed to the chancellor of the Reich, Dr Heinrich Brüning, to save the orchestra. He made use – apparently for the first time – of a political argument which carried such persuasive force that he retained it for use with the new rulers after 1933. He underlined once again

the cultural importance which is attached to this one and only first-class concert orchestra in Germany – an importance which is perhaps even more clearly recognised abroad (Paris, London, Switzerland) than in Germany itself, as a result of the reputation we have built up through our many trips abroad over the last few years. [. . .] So I would like respectfully to ask you, Lord Chancellor, to bring your great and decisive influence to bear so that things just undertaken by the last Reichstag remain in force: that is a subsidy which will assure the financial security of the orchestra and thereby guarantee the maintenance of its current high standard. I am firmly convinced that you would be doing Germany's cultural interests a great service.[2]

It is an interesting case because a note in the files makes it clear that the ministerial officials wished the cut revoked 'because if it is put into effect the Reich removes all possibility of exercising its influence on the orchestra'.[3]

To the extent that promoting the country abroad was something which benefited both politicians and musicians, their interests overlapped, and the politicians accepted the authority of the musician's proposals. They felt that the enhanced prestige of the Reich abroad was worth 120,000 marks, and so the Reichstag's budget committee – at the suggestion of the Social Democrats – decided to restore the sum originally allocated to the orchestra and cut back on general police duties instead. At this point the conductor could still just about retain his belief that 'music has nothing to do with politics', but the experience that 'politics has a great deal to do with music', and concerned far more than just the Berlin Philharmonic Orchestra's tours abroad under its chief conductor, was equally correct.

The National Socialist 'revolutionaries' in no way took the Weimar Republic as a source of inspiration. They sought their political models elsewhere. But they saw as clearly as their deposed democratic

31

predecessors that linking art to politics was very necessary, perhaps supremely important. Marches and fighting songs alone would not suffice. Artistic greatness was required if one were to make an impression abroad. Hitler, who considered himself an expert in most matters, astutely included music in his political plans, beginning with Wagner's works, which he knew and loved as a mythical world which would complete and immortalise his revolution. Wagner, the creator of myths, was better suited than anybody else to do this:

Richard Wagner is more than a great artist. His personality and his work gave form to the German yearning for ultimate oneness. Thus when the united German nation reveres him today it honours the master in him whose magnificent example demonstrated that genuine creativity can overcome apparently insuperable obstacles.[4]

Hitler identified with this giant, who even posthumously was a usurper, and it is clear from the way he talked of the intellectual giants that he considered him to be one of them. It is an established fact that in the summer of 1932, Hitler, then a Reichstag delegate and leader of the Nazi Party, had talks with Furtwängler. It was a meeting of two very different minds, but they did share an interest in Wagner. Of course each had a different Wagner in mind. Hitler wanted to know why Furtwängler had cancelled his appearance at Bayreuth. Had Furtwängler's conflict with Winifred Wagner been motivated by a desire for prestige Hitler could have understood it, but to dispute who was to select the musicians, in other words to argue about artistic quality, was beyond his comprehension and he lapsed into a monologue. The conductor was taken aback but not very impressed by the grandiose plans Hitler hoped to realise at Bayreuth in the future. Various reasons for the rupture between Winifred Wagner and Furtwängler – which could only harm musical activity – circulated among their friends and there was a grain of truth in all of them – including the news that Hitler, although anonymously, had already stated his opinion on the matter:

A prominent personality initially expressed regret at Furtwängler's absence, but, after personal discussions with Frau Winifred Wagner, reached completely different conclusions and is now most decidedly on her side. Apparently Herr Furtwängler wanted to engage the soloists quite independently of Frau Wagner's advice. Furthermore he is reputed to be rather well disposed towards Jews.[5]

Thus it got around that it was not just a question of power but of ideology as well. Of Hitler's position there could not be the slightest doubt: someone who had for many years worked with a Jewish secretary, who was not ashamed to present Jewish soloists, and who was prepared to be 'used' by Leo Kestenberg, the head of musical affairs at the Prussian Ministry of Culture prior to 1933, could at best be of temporary usefulness to the Nazis, never their ally or soulmate. The musician had dedicated himself to music, that much was obvious; to try and ease him into following a different path, that of politics, would be a mistaken undertaking. And yet Furtwängler, despite his abhorrence at all forms of 'revolution', did show some faith in the new government. He was after all neither an 'alarmist', nor a narrow-minded critic, and was prepared to wait and see what authoritarian politics could accomplish. He continued in the following months – as Hitler became ever more forthright about his intentions – to express the hope that the nightmare would soon be over, or that everything would sort itself out somehow or other. As a musician he probably failed to notice that throughout this period the brown-shirts were penetrating the state and using public funds to make themselves invincible, because even towards the end of the year he was still expressing this short-sighted hope. It was the appeal to 'German' traditions and values which made the Nazi regime seem like a bulwark against the 'modern', by which he understood the manifold, contradictory, debatable and even chaotic phenomena which had accompanied the short-lived Weimar Republic, and which seemed causally related to it:

As a result of the renewal of Germany since the overthrow, moral forces have been unleashed on an unprecedented scale. That alone in no way guarantees the success of this renewal, because in life it is not intentions which count, however good they are, but actions and the realisation of those intentions. The awakening of the new Germany, and the fact that it has consciously laid claim to primary moral forces, also creates a responsibility which could hardly be greater. [. . .] We will not do justice to this responsibility while we just talk about it, especially if we continually try and assess, of ourselves and others, how close we are coming in reality to achieving the desired goal – which in the case of music would mean asking whether a closer relationship between music and the people really is being achieved, and if the chosen path is the best way.[6]

It is quite clear that the musician was living in a rather distant world of transcendental concepts, far removed from the day-to-day business of politics into which he lacked real insight. Generally he was only interested in information which was concerned in some way either with music or at least with the musical world. His driving ambition was to revive the art of music-making for the nation, and to this end he was prepared to cooperate with the new rulers, especially as he was as yet far from considering them criminals. His concern about the enticements of 'modernism' of all kinds was a part of the wider question about which approach was best. Initially he judged the regime on one matter alone:

> It is a decided merit of National Socialism which none of its opponents can deny that it has, regardless of world opinion, exposed the deep-rooted threat to the relationship between producer and consumer, between an artist and his public, between art and the nation.[7]

It was precisely at this time that Nazism was, regardless of world opinion, revealing its true face to anyone prepared to look behind the propaganda façade. At a certain point idealism makes people blind, and isolation becomes an absurd form of self-protection. But Furtwängler was not the only one to delude himself; he was one of a type. The fact that even in his concert programmes, much to the annoyance of Nazi officials, he failed to adapt to the requirements of the 'revolution', fits the picture. He would present an unchanged and almost canonic repertoire. There was something fundamentalist in his approach, in the way he performed certain classical compositions to his audience as if they were revelations – if not the word of God, then at least a spiritual breath of the sublime. Even before 1933 he had come under attack for not devoting enough time to promoting contemporary works, notably at the hands of the unforgivingly caustic and ironic Hans Heinz Stuckenschmidt.

Records – for the most part complete – suggest that he in no way sought to avoid coming to grips with contemporary modern music; but he did have rigorous criteria of quality, which were rooted in his 'metaphysical' relationship to Beethoven. 'National Socialist' music was quite out of the question. He showed not the slightest interest in the many hundreds of pieces inspired by National Socialism, including SS marches, songs for the SA and Hitler Youth, cantatas for the party, and 'Hymns to Germany'. At this time nearly every self-respecting composer who considered himself any good at all or who wanted to connect with 'the dynamic strength of the national movement' was contributing to the trend, which by 1945 had resulted in a correspondingly large *oeuvre* numbering some 15,000 items. Furtwängler's concert programmes remained unmarred by them; however well disguised they might be, he never conducted Nazi-inspired works. He also scorned instrumental works dedicated to Goebbels or any other member of the upper cadres, even the works of serious composers.

The Reich's propaganda minister saw this strict adherence to a set programme as Furtwängler's way of avoiding adopting an affirmative stance or recognition of the Führer and the Reich. Thus his angry statement concerning the programme for the opening of the second week-long theatre festival in Hamburg:

> It is not good enough to present the same old repertoire over and over again; the pieces may not have been written with intentions which conflict with the ideals of National Socialism, but they really contain nothing of the spirit of our times. Nor is it sufficient to just insert a few National Socialist pieces into a repertoire made up of pieces from the year dot.[8]

However much Goebbels may have liked the idea of total propaganda which would affect every sphere of activity, including the Philharmonie and the Staatsoper, he was unable to dictate to Furtwängler which pieces he should play. The powers of the brown dictatorship did not extend quite that far – at least not in this instance. The minister grasped early on that while the conductor was not a free spirit in all respects, he did have an obstinacy backed by an ideology which, although not directly counter to that of the National Socialists, was in some respects quite strongly incompatible with it. It was an uncertain and delicate situation from which the possibility of conflict or evasion could not be ruled out, which is why the minister tried to defuse the tension. On the one hand he denounced the 'reactionary' view that art and politics were not connected, on the other he had enough insight to be able to manipulate the artist's views so that even concerts featuring only classical music became vehicles for propaganda purposes, ensuring that there were no gaps left anywhere. Goebbels knew his artists, and the following argument could have been thought up specifically with Furtwängler in mind:

> It is not the case that artists are apolitical: serving the public's needs is political, and if anybody is in a position to do that it is the artist, having as he does the intellectual and spiritual power to give worth to people's lives, imparting values which are not just passing but eternal. The great bids which artists throughout history have made for immortality have subsequently entered the realms of the immortal, offering consolation and inner fortitude to millions in the hard struggle of life.[9]

35

It was a shrewd line of argument, and one which Furtwängler probably was exposed to in talks with the politician. The notion that as an artist he imparted consoling and strengthening values corresponded to what he was repeatedly told by members of his audiences. However, he obstinately persisted in his assertion that there was a distinction to be made between music and politics, as if his idealistic wish were a well-proven fact.

The day that Hitler came to power – 30 January 1933 – was a Monday. Bruno Kittel was rehearsing with the Berlin Philharmonic Orchestra and his own choir for a performance of Handel's *Messiah* on the following day. On Wednesday the orchestra was due to play for the business club in Magdeburg, to be conducted by Furtwängler. On that occasion the programme included the first performance of Günter Raphael's Divertimento op. 33, along with pieces by Wagner, and Tchaikowsky's Fifth Symphony. Collecting boxes were placed in the foyer of the town hall, and the programme notes ended with a reference to the bitter conditions outside and an appeal for donations to help the needy. A concert was planned in Leipzig for 2 February, and on 6 February Furtwängler was to conduct the sixth of the Philharmonic concerts that season: to provide a contrast to Beethoven's Violin Concerto and Tchaikowsky's Fifth he offered a first performance of the nineteen-year-old Gottfried Müller's 'Variations and Fugue on a German Folksong'. The next day saw the beginning of the orchestra's late winter tour of Belgium, England and Holland under their chief conductor. Thus in those days and weeks in which political decisions of historical consequence were being made the musicians' working life went on as usual, though the circulating rumours that the long-standing group was under threat of imminent financial collapse must have created a note of tension. Again and again they found their salaries being paid weeks after they were due. In such a situation it is hardly surprising that they did not have a lot of time to be interested in the wider political situation.

It was on the journey home from a guest concert in The Hague – next stop Bielefeld – that Furtwängler came into conflict with the 'brown revolution' for the first time. An SS commander eavesdropped on a conversation between the conductor and his secretary in the restaurant car. They were talking about foreign exchange rates and taxes; Willem Mengelberg, head of the Concertgebouw Orchestra in Amsterdam, had just acquired a property in Switzerland, which was a tax-haven for more than just the Dutch. The unnoticed eavesdropper pricked up his ears on hearing that Furtwängler had a holiday home in beautiful Engadin: sweeping accusations of 'Jewish tax-evasion and foreign currency smuggling' had long been a part of the right-wing arsenal, so it is

ZWEITES KONZERT

Mittwoch, den 1. Februar 1933, 20 Uhr, in der „Stadthalle"

Dr. Wilhelm Furtwängler

mit dem

Berliner Philharmonischen Orchester

★

SPIEL-FOLGE:

Günter Raphael
geb. 30. 4. 1903 in Berlin,
lebt in Leipzig

Divertimento (op. 33), Uraufführung
Allegro moderato
Vivace (Scherzo)
Moderato
Adagio
Allegro molto
Allegretto
Allegro moderato

Richard Wagner

Vorspiel und Liebestod aus „Tristan und Isolde"

Richard Wagner
(Zum Gedächtnis an den
50. Todestag Wagners:
13. Februar 1883)

Vorspiel zu „Die Meistersinger von Nürnberg"

Peter Tschaikowsky

Symphonie Nr. 5 in E-Moll (op. 64)
Andante-Allegro con anima
Andante cantabile, con alzuna licenza
Valse (Allegro moderato)
Finale (Andante maestoso-Allegro vivace)

Gedenket nach festlichen Stunden auch der Bedürftigen.
Sammelbüchsen für die Winternothilfe in der Vorhalle.

37

perhaps not surprising that the officer, in the belief that he was doing his duty to his country, got off the train at Bielefeld and tried to persuade the town authorities to cancel the concert. He was unsuccessful, but a report did go to Berlin, which Hitler also got to hear of, once again confirming his prejudice that the conductor was involved with Jews and their subversive activities.

The public remained unaware of what was going on behind the scenes. The Rudolf Oetker Hall in Bielefeld was filled to overflowing, so that several extra rows of seats had to be squeezed in between the orchestra and the organ. The press were united in acclaiming the concert as the event of the season, one critic declaring that the public 'was drawn into a clear and yet magical world of ideas, of deep and measured breaths: Wilhelm Furtwängler, the conductor, became the symbol and expression of profound intellectual depths'.[10]

This was not his first guest appearance, Bielefeld having long been part of the itinerary, lying conveniently as it did on the route to Holland and England. Yet the critic on the competing newspaper, as if he had some sort of premonition, wrote: 'Let us hope that this is not the last time that we get to hear the Maestro and his band!'[11] Yet nothing happened which could have given ground for such concerns. Furtwängler carried on giving concerts while the 'revolution' took place on the streets; self-appointed brown-uniformed 'cleaners' carried out the dirty work, seizing reds, democrats, Jews, and anybody else they suspected of falling into one of those categories. In the daily press the reports of 'unreliable' elements being dismissed multiplied; opinions were more important than actions; informers lived their finest hour, unearthing fearful political crimes committed during the previous era, which were then entered into the dossiers of various authorities, party offices and private blackmailers. As the terror grew so did uncertainty. For a time the concert hall and platform still appeared to offer sanctuaries into which the swastika-bearing rabble dared not break.

The Philharmonic in particular seemed to be a sphere unto itself, in which the Jews could hold their own. Furtwängler conducted as if nothing had happened. He was joined on 27 February by the violinist Carl Flesch and on 13 March by the pianist Lubka Kolessa; on 6 March the baritone Wilhelm Guttmann joined the soloists of the Singakademie and the Philharmonic Orchestra under Georg Schumann; a day later Prüwer conducted another concert with the orchestra, and on 10 March Felix Maria Gatz conducted it for the Bruckner Association, including a much applauded rendition of the Mendelssohn Violin Concerto. That things remained calm may have been because the capital city still served as a window on Germany for the rest of the world, and the Nazis were keen to avoid provoking any hostile reaction. Furthermore the 'revolutionaries' found themselves kicking against the solid and proven structures of the past.

Not by chance were the hallowed realms of the music world first invaded in the provinces, but this had a limited impact because the target in this case was not a Jew, but the German music director Fritz Busch. Busch had just returned from a two-week tour to Copenhagen and Hamburg, and was supposed to be conducting *Rigoletto* in the Dresden Staatsoper on 7 March. Two days earlier elections to the 8th Reichstag had left the Nazi Party with 288 seats, a success which encouraged the local party branches to be bold and even foolhardy. The rehearsal was interrupted when SA troops occupied the house. The actor Alexis Posse presented himself as the regional head of the National Socialist Workers' Party and authorised representative of the regional chief. He dismissed Busch but was generous enough to allow him to conduct the Verdi prepared for that evening. In the meantime the swastika banner was raised at the Dresden opera house. Pre-arranged demonstrators whistled and cat-called at the conductor: he did not wait for the end of the scandal but left the house. Naturally the press, which had been attacking him for months after his aspirations to the Berlin Staatsoper had leaked out, was full of the 'revolutionary' events the next day. What it was really all about is clear from the explanation of events offered by their per-petrator in response to Göring's urgent request. Göring, at that time still a minister without a ministry, thought highly of Fritz Busch and his brother Adolf, the violinist, and he thought Fritz – located in the capital Berlin of course – would be the right man to play a leading role in implementing the changes necessary in the character of German theatre. Events in Dresden hindered this as yet rather hazy project. Posse explained with the conviction of a fanatic Nazi:

> Busch has certainly never belonged to a political party. It is also a deliberate falsehood on the part of one particular newspaper to claim that Busch was urged to join the National Socialist Workers' Party. There was never occasion to do so. What is definite is that Busch is a member of the Rotary Club, and by his own admission an outspoken pacifist and democrat. [. . .] Busch moved primarily in the social circles of Jews, Democrats, and retailers.[12]

As though he was aware that such accusations would not carry much weight with Göring, the writer, all the while eagerly giving reassurances that he had never questioned Busch's capacities as a conductor, drew Göring's attention to a petition drawn up by the Staatsoper's board of directors and 'almost all' of its soloists. It was an appeal to Dr Paul Adolph, commissary-general and privy councillor, which, having cast aspersions on the musical director's organisational and professional competence, concluded: 'We do not feel that Herr Busch has either the artistic qualities or personal attributes necessary to be successful at the Staatsoper. His return would seriously destabilise and endanger the artistic activities currently being undertaken.'[13]

This petition dated 12 March was a stab in the back, orchestrated and executed in the space of a few days for that purpose, despite Posse's verbose reassurances that individuals had acted of their own free will, under no pressure from the Nazis – in such a climate of fear, full compliance was almost automatic. Not only the director of the opera, Hermann Kutzschbach, but also the conductors Kurt Striegler and Karl Maria Pembaur along with correpetitor Ernst Hintze gave their signatures, as did the whole cast and the majority of the soloists, among them Tino Pattiera, Maria Cebotari and Paul Schoeffler, the last to sign the hand-written text. Two absent singers – Erna Berger and Max Lorenz – agreed verbally, as did Viorica Ursuleac. At her own request her contract had not been extended, and now she did not wish to spoil her image by being seen to sign. Four courageous women did not take part in the campaign: Hilde Clairfried, Lotte Elsner, Martha Fuchs and Camilla Kallab.[14]

While this plot was being carried out behind his back Busch travelled to Berlin on 11 March to discuss his rehabilitation with Göring. Over the next few days Hitler twice telephoned Dresden to order Busch's reinstatement and forbid any further violence against him. The true situation is revealed by the fact that he could only persuade the provincial heads of state and party, the Reich commissioner Manfred von Killinger and regional leader Martin Mutschmann to carry out the second of his two demands. The 'revolution' had gone out of control. Even Göring had little to offer in the way of compensation. He hoped that once he himself had been appointed Prussian prime minister he would be able to see to it that the humiliated musician was recompensed with a leading position in the musical life of the capital. The politician envisioned a new order – which would of course have to be discussed with Hitler – in which the post of overall director of the Staatsoper would have to be filled, after which it would become the key attraction in *his* association of the Prussian state theatres. It was at this point in the vision that Busch's fate came into conflict with that of Furtwängler, with the result that, through no fault of his own, Furtwängler suddenly had a new enemy. He later gave the following version of what happened:

In the winter of 1932, just before the Nazis came to power, general intendant Tietjen and I had already signed a contract under which I was to take over the directorship of the Staatsoper. So when Göring approached Tietjen hoping to appoint Busch as director, Tietjen had to inform him that that was no longer possible because a contract had already been entered into with Furtwängler. Göring was very put out by this and even at his first meeting with myself and Tietjen in the spring of 1933, he still stated quite plainly that he had really had something else in mind, as I very well remember.[15]

This account is plausible: unfortunately surviving documents are insufficient to corroborate it. The archives contain no contract from the winter of 1932–3, whereas every other one Furtwängler signed is still available. Other questions also suggest themselves; why did the general intendant not follow usual procedure and inform the press of an agreement that after all augured well for the Staatsoper? Why is there no reference to the new position in the otherwise fairly detailed correspondence between the conductor and his secretary? Is it really very plausible that the music journalists, who particularly in the capital were inclined to hear the grass growing, were in this case completely oblivious for several months? The Prussian Ministry of Finance would have had to countersign such a contract because it fell into the theatre budget, yet even here the archives are uninformative. If one is unwilling to accept that the conductor was deliberately cultivating his 'image', one has to accept the unlikely proposition that by some trick of fate numerous widely dispersed sources of evidence just happened to be destroyed. Doubts give rise to myths.

While Busch in his memoirs recounted how Göring had been unable to keep the promise he had made because of 'arrangements made long before',[16] his widow created a mythical version of the story in which she declared that 'given that from one day to the next he found himself both morally and artistically ostracised, nothing left of the high regard in which he had been held, it would have been quite unnatural, even superhuman, if he had not fought back. And Fritz Busch did fight back against Furtwängler, but the latter enjoyed better publicity, as well as the assistance of Berta Geissmar, with all her connections'.[17]

Geissmar herself is ingenuous enough to suggest that the frustrated attempt to obtain a post of equal prestige counted as 'fighting back', and that as a Jew she was, even in the midst of an explosion of anti-Semitic feeling, nevertheless in a position to mobilise her 'connections' for Furtwängler's benefit. Characteristically she omitted several important details in her account of how the ostracised Busch, with the support of several well-disposed Nazi offices, was subsequently compensated – after turning down several offers.

During those turbulent weeks Furtwängler was also looking for ways to help his colleague. Given his concern for the state of musical activity, which had already been hard hit by economic pressures, and thus his desire to avoid political damage at all costs, this seemed to him a perfectly natural thing to do. But he had yet to find a friendly ear among the top officials. There was still confusion about who was responsible for what, and who held which powers. Only gradually was a sufficient degree of organisational stability achieved that one could begin to delegate responsibility for matters such as music. Chaos lower down meant that there were plenty of matters to attend to, most of which had nothing to do with conducting. From one day to the next Furtwängler found himself making decisions of political importance and dealing with their consequences. He was anything but free, even though his apparent disregard for his own well-being might have suggested that he was.

It was clear to him that he could not abandon the members of the Berlin Philharmonic to their fate – they were attached to him, and after so much time playing and rehearsing with him they had in a sense become 'his' orchestra. He knew that he was artistic director of a bankrupt undertaking, a fact which was nervously kept from the public, and which even the appropriate authorities only discovered two years later when the German audit and trust company carried out an audit. The orchestra had the legal standing of a limited company; each individual musician was a shareholder, and thus shared liability. Up until the financial year of 1931–2 the orchestra's share capital amounted to 48,000 RM, which increased to 66,000 RM with the incorporation of twenty-three musicians from the disbanded Berlin Symphony Orchestra. Reserve funds stood at a miserable total of 6,337.32 RM. The balance sheet for the financial year 1930–1 already shows a deficit which was to grow from then onwards. The management ignored the PLC law #64, which stipulated that 'every company upon becoming insolvent is legally obliged to enter, without undue delay, and at latest three weeks after said event' into legal adjudication proceedings and declare itself bankrupt. Neither directors nor shareholders seemed bothered by the 5,000-mark fine and year's imprisonment which they risked by non–compliance. Their behaviour was as illegal as that of any common crook, but if they had behaved lawfully the orchestra would have been finished.

It was one of those permanent exceptions; the attitude of the authorities after the investigations mentioned above suggested that where something of such cultural importance was at stake some leniency could be justified; whereas normally financial fraud and embezzlement, whether real or alleged would be ruthlessly exposed, in this instance such processes were not set in motion. Putting the whole Berlin Philharmonic in prison would, all things considered, not have done the reputation of the National Socialist state any good. But given this precarious situation Furtwängler could not afford to put his foot down, certainly not over political issues, especially as it was obvious that the National Socialist government was the only possible source of financial support. It was an awkward case, and becoming the subject of much heated debate that spring, but each government department on which it landed passed responsibility on to the next. The city of Berlin and the Ministry of the Interior were both giving monthly subsidies amounting to a few thousand marks – but also making it quite clear that they were reluctant to continue doing so. With these pressures in mind the management had placed a lot of hope in a planned series of 'popular concerts', which well-to-do and ambitious individuals with some measure of talent could pay to conduct – meaning that any old fool could hire the Berlin Philharmonic for an evening.

Furtwängler was aware of how grim the situation was, and how restricted room for manoeuvre had become. Yet every now and again he still showed a streak of independence, as for example when the sanctuary of the concert hall was once again invaded by the 'dynamic strength of the national movement': Bruno Walter had agreed to give five concerts in the 1932–3 season. In Berlin he had a devoted following, but once again the province of Saxony was up in arms with a strong expression of popular feeling against the Jewish conductor, fanned and coordinated by the Nazi party. His appearance at the Gewandhaus concert planned for 16 March was forbidden by the commissar for Saxony, on the grounds that it would provoke 'public disorder'. The Berlin concert, one of a subscription series arranged by the Jewish concert agency Wolff & Sachs, was to take place on 20 March. Four days prior to this Dr Goebbels took office as Propaganda Minister, but the question of whether music came under his purview or was to remain part of the education minister's responsibility had yet to be answered, and no official guidelines had yet been drawn up for dealing with 'non-Aryan' artists. Thus when the management's request for a couple of policemen to guard the concert hall was refused, Walter Funk, Goebbels' secretary in the new ministry, advised hiring an 'Aryan' conductor: Walter withdrew.

Should the concert be cancelled? Should the orchestra forego the income it would bring, thereby possibly accelerating its collapse? These were the difficult questions which had to be decided in the space of a few hours. Furtwängler resisted the political demand for moral

43

compromise, and refused to step in for Bruno Walter. Someone of Furtwängler's renown had to be found. There followed an intensive search by, among others, Hugo Rasch and Julius Kopsch. The former contributed articles on music to the *Volkischer Beobachter*, the official party newspaper, while the latter was a doctor of law, SA storm trooper, and conductor and composer who had taken to using the title of director general of music. Their efforts were rewarded when Richard Strauss stated his willingness to be the sacrifice – and it was a sacrifice in more ways than one. Quite contrary to his usual practice he donated the fee of 1,500 marks, which had been intended for Bruno Walter, to the orchestra, and refused payment for his services – although he did of course use the occasion to publicise his *Sinfonia Domestica*. The brown-shirts were thereby saved the political embarrassment of having to cancel under the eyes of the many foreign journalists stationed in Berlin. Rasch and Kopsch felt that Strauss's behaviour showed that 'Aryans' were more than just stop-gaps. Over the next few days however the public punished them for their lies: so many subscribers returned their tickets for the concert on 3 April, which was to have been the last of the season conducted by Walter, that it had to be cancelled.

After the débâcle of Strauss having to stand in, Furtwängler must have seen that political decisions were from now on going to be part of his everyday business, despite his intention to keep music and politics separate. This was proved by 'Potsdam Day': on 21 March Hitler made a great show of his concern for tradition and legitimacy by initiating a new state ceremony. He deliberately chose to stage it in the garrison church of Potsdam, where the Prussian kings William I and Frederick II were buried. The vast crowds were so overawed by the solemnity of the occasion, with its organ-playing, hymns and military marches, that they hardly noticed that the 'enabling Act' proclaimed two days later as 'a law to resolve the difficulties of the people and the state' in fact signalled the end of democratic legislative power and the beginning of the party's dictatorship. The ceremony at Potsdam was one of the first fruits of the Propaganda Ministry, which chose to crown the day with a performance at the Staatsoper under the baton of the most prominent conductor in the Reich.

The general intendant had made arrangements for a performance of Strauss's *Elektra*: Gertrud Kappel was to make a guest-appearance in the title role, with Margarete Klose as Clytemnestra and Marcel Wittrisch as Aegisthus. However, Goebbels at the last moment ordered that this be changed to Wagner's *Die Meistersinger*, because its mythical content was better suited to his propagandist intentions. It was more than just a ministerial request, it was an order from the government of the Reich.

44

So while torchlight processions wended their way through the streets of Berlin, the Staatsoper was playing one of its trusted 'repertoire' items: *Die Meistersinger von Nürnberg*. In the turmoil, the fact that Furtwängler was conducting received little attention:

> Chancellor Adolf Hitler was to be seen in the box of honour, along with the secretary of state von Bülow, and several ministers including Hugenberg, Göring, Frick, and Eltz von Rübenach. Vice Chancellor von Papen was present for the third act, together with the labour minister, Seldte, and the minister of justice, Dr Gürtner. There were also many SA and SS uniforms in evidence, and public personalities from the worlds of art, science and politics.[18]

At this point, the outward appearance of a constitutional state could still allay any fears an outside observer might have. The government still presented itself as a national coalition. Hitler, Göring and Frick represented the National Socialist Workers' Party (NSDAP); Hugenberg and Gürtner both came from the German National People's Party (DNVP); Seldte was a member of the 'Steel helmets'; Papen belonged to the Centre Party, and von Rübenach was an independent. Therefore the performance of *Die Meistersinger* was of no more or less political significance for Furtwängler than the concerts he had given at the Weimar Republic's constitutional celebrations. On that March evening everything seemed pretty much as it had been. However two very different diarists noted change. Goebbels enthused: 'The evening closed with a magical performance of *Die Meistersinger* at the Linden Opera. Everything is affected by the music. The joyous "Awake!" chorus has acquired a new meaning.'[19] Thomas Mann on the other hand drew a disquieting parallel between two separate musical events: 'Angry at Strauss taking over Bruno Walter's concert – and Furtwängler following the "government's" orders and conducting *Die Meistersinger* in today's celebrations. Boot-lickers.'[20] The two clearly had diametrically opposing views. The minister knew the background, while the writer did not.

Furtwängler could not and did not wish to put his entire energies into politics. He had to keep up his musical activity. The day after the state ceremony in Potsdam he conducted the postponed performance of *Elektra*, now with the 'non-Aryan' Rose Pauly in the title role. On 23 March he was in Leipzig with his orchestra, conducting the last subscribers' concert in Hamburg the following day. On 27 March he was once again on the podium in the Philharmonie, with Elly Ney as soloist, opening with the first performance of Arthur Honegger's third 'Symphonic Movement' followed by works of Schumann, Beethoven and

Havemann tangos with Hitler

Strauss. But perhaps this was just an attempt to flee the clutches of politics; what a musician wanted, even if he was the most prominent of the day, was of not the slightest interest to the 'revolutionaries' in power.

One of the keenest and most impudent of these 'revolutionaries' and himself a gifted musician was the violin virtuoso Gustav Havemann, a professor at the Academy of Music in Berlin. He initially acted with the support of the powerful state commissioner Hans Hinkel, and of the League for the Defence of German Culture (KfdK), an association propagating a particular brand of Nazi propaganda, but he was so wilful that he soon came into conflict with the party line. His opponents did not forget that although he was now conducting Nazi concerts in Berlin, he had as lately as October 1932 performed the Mendelssohn Violin Concerto with the Frankfurt Symphony Orchestra under Hans Rosbaud, provoking a storm of protest in the concert hall – and these opponents were not prepared to indulge such inconsistencies in his anti-Semitism; Havemann did think in terms of 'race', but made a clear distinction between Jews he considered friends and those he considered enemies. He even coined the phrase 'Jews of German origin' for those he was friendly with, and for this his enemies in the art promotion department added him to a list of 'music-Bolshevists' which was circulated in the National Socialist Cultural Association (NSKG) for orientation purposes. However in March 1933 he had yet to be blacklisted, and he took advantage of his position to send a letter to the management of the

Berlin Philharmonic Orchestra demanding that all the Jewish musicians, and above all Dr Geissmar, should be dismissed because their continued activity was unacceptable in Nazi Germany. On 13 March he repeated his demand during discussions with Funk, Höber and the conductor of the radio orchestra, Hanns Steinkopf; in addition he requested that the Philharmonic give a concert for the benefit of the KfdK . . . and could he please have an answer within forty-eight hours! Not only did he use the Interior Ministry's willing assistance to bring the German Musicians' Union (a body representing orchestral musicians) into line, he also at this time informed the German Union of Concert Performers that it should disband.[21] This was a union which made an energetic contribution to musical life, setting up concerts for its members for a yearly contribution of 12 RM. Its chairman was the Jewish pianist Georg Bertram, and the executive consisted of Bruno Eisner, Furtwängler, Hannah Hempel, Leonid Kreutzer, Kurt Singer, Richard Stern and Kurt von Wolfurt. Without exception they were well known in Berlin and elsewhere. But Havemann was not concerned with quality; he was fighting for a pure 'race', and as two thirds of the executive were Jews, none of whom he was inclined to protect, he said it was his duty to give warning that official steps would have to be taken. His intimidation attempt was unsuccessful, because the members of the executive, appointing Furtwängler their leader, insisted on official confirmation. As Havemann found himself caught up in internal disputes, the German Union of Concert Performers continued functioning for many more months. It was however eliminated during the reorganisation of musical life begun by the Reichsmusikkammer in November 1933.

Although both these attacks, which Furtwängler saw as directed at him personally, ran out of steam, he saw clearly that he required allies if he was to rescue whatever was left to be rescued. He managed to recruit one member from the other side, also in May, an altogether eventful month. As part of its efforts to eliminate all resistance to the adoption of 'nationalist' and 'anti-Semitic' politics the Nazi Party was appointing a commissioner to each of the more important organisations, who would serve as a contact to prepare the ground accordingly. Although the Berlin Philharmonic was legally a limited company, it was similar to a newspaper publisher, a radio station, or a transport company in having just the sort of links with the public which interested the party; furthermore those who accept subsidies are in a weak position *vis-à-vis* those subsidising them. For this reason it was possible to place a commissioner, who was officially supposed to counter Furtwängler, among the orchestra management. There were in fact already a few card-carrying members of the party among the members of the orchestra, and of those brought over from the disbanded symphony orchestra every other person wore the swastika badge. But they were 'insignificant' people who might not have been in a position to push through political issues in opposition to a leader who was convinced he could keep art free of all such 'mean and lowly' matters.

The party thus reasoned that the commissioner would have to be someone of similar social standing if he was to have any effect, and it is just an irony of fate that the commissioner's similar social background made him into an ally rather than an enemy of Furtwängler's. Rudolf von Schmidtseck, born 1901, a doctor of philosophy and sometime conductor, appeared from nowhere in the orchestra's offices in March 1933, to disappear again as unspectacularly a year later when Furtwängler lost his posts, to a place as nondescript as the one he came from, namely East Prussia, where he ran his estate, Woplauken, chaired the local orchestral society of Rastenburg and wrote music reviews for the local rag, *Der Beobachter*. From 1927–8 he had worked as a correpititor in Copenhagen. In 1930–1 he had had conducting jobs both in the Swedish capital and in some Swedish provincial towns, and thereafter had worked sporadically in Bremen and Königsberg before coming to Berlin with his party card, no. 1,118,274 – applied for and obtained from the local branch of the Nazi Party on 1 January 1932. This was the man without whom things would have gone very differently and probably far less to Furtwängler's liking. Schmidtseck immediately recognised that what Furtwängler was trying to do was to maintain and protect artistic resources and their quality, and he brought to the task the legal skills which his impulsive and occasionally explosive 'boss' was lacking. With this combination the process of ensuring the ideological soundness of the musicians in the orchestra became a dramatic conflict.

The first thing Furtwängler had to come to terms with in early April was that he had been defeated, simply because his musical authority had been overridden by political authority. Being party to the events detailed in the following dull but significant press-release confirmed his dislike of joint decisions:

> Discussions have taken place between the appropriate authorities, the mayor of Berlin and the appointed commissioner from Berlin's town council regarding the programme of events in the Berlin Arts Festival. The musical directors Max von Schillings and Wilhelm Furtwängler also took part in the discussions. It was decided that instead of a Jewish conductor the composer Hans Pfitzner will conduct the opera *Elektra*, followed by Richard Strauss conducting his opera *Salome*.[22]

The conductor found that despite sitting on the committee which decided the programme he was still unable to persuade others to choose by the criterion of quality rather than by the label 'Jewish/non-Jewish'. Max von Schillings was no help to him. The committee not only had to cancel completely the concerts planned for Bruno Walter and Klemperer, but also made such drastic cuts to a series of concerts with chamber pieces by Brahms, to which Arthur Schnabel, Paul Hindemith, Bronislaw Huberman and Gregor Piatigorsky were to have contributed, that they were only left with the Klingler Quartet to play Brahms's chamber music for strings. This incident so galled Furtwängler that he began to consider what he would have to do to obtain one single source of authority able to decide the content of music – throughout the Reich – without reference to political issues. It is quite likely that even at this early point he envisaged himself as the highest arbiter of musical activity in Germany. He must also have recognised how much power and politics would be involved in such a position. He still had private supporters working for him. For example the manager of the Bank of Dresden in Bielefeld appealed to the chief commissioner at the Prussian Ministry of Science, Art and National Education to use his office to clear up the deplorable state of affairs in Bayreuth:

> If Winifred Wagner, who is after all English, is so insensitive to this blunder and to the fact that by entrusting the direction of what is a German festival in Bayreuth to a foreigner on the fiftieth anniversary of his death, she is showing disrespect to the memory of the German poet and composer, then may I suggest that you, as minister, intervene? [. . .] At Bayreuth we should have a Strauss or a Furtwängler on the rostrum, not Toscanini – who is known to have indulged in passing defamatory comments about Germany to representatives of the foreign press.[23]

The ministry took two months to inform him that it was not possible to intervene because the Bayreuth Festspielhaus had never asked for state subsidies. This letter was dated 6 June; one day earlier Toscanini had withdrawn from taking part at Bayreuth for political reasons.

Furtwängler may well have aspired to being able to make an equally free choice. It is clear that he wanted to make up for the setback he had suffered as a member of the programme committee for the Berlin Arts Festival. An opportunity presented itself immediately, further proof that the conflict between the arts and politics was escalating. When it became known that several American musicians had approached the chancellor, concerning the boycott of Jewish and marxist colleagues, the commissioner-intendant for German broadcasting decreed that 'no compositions or records by the people concerned are to be broadcast by the German Broadcasting Company, nor can recordings of concerts, even if taken from other radio stations, be used if any of the concerned people are taking part in any capacity'.[24]

Furtwängler, who knew some of those musicians, read this announcement. He was seized with anger and at once sat down to write a letter to Mannheim, where, as part of the orchestra's great spring tour of Germany, France and Switzerland, a joint concert with the National Orchestra based there had been planned for 26 April. The chairman of the Mannheim orchestra, the trombonist August Sander, had written to request that on this occasion Furtwängler have members of the local orchestra at the first desk. The reasons were plain to see: as a result of the vehement anti-Jewish line taken by the party paper, *Hakenkreuzban-ner*, with headlines such as 'Down with the Jews in Mannheim!',[25] and the continual propagandist exhortations of Dr Reinhold Roth, regional head of the Nazi Party and leader of the local section of the KfdK, Mannheim had become a stronghold of anti-Semitism, especially where the arts were concerned. Therefore Sander wanted the Jewish leaders of the Berlin orchestra to disappear from the scene. Furtwängler roundly refused this request. In a letter dated 6 April he gave his reasons, which were primarily artistic, adding that if there were still any objections to having Jewish performers in the orchestra when it came to Mannheim, then the whole concert would have to be called off.

That same morning the Berlin newspapers carried a report from New York which gave further indication of how confused both sides still were in the debate about 'quality' and 'race'. Fritz Kreisler, a well-known violinist with an apartment in Berlin, was at the time touring America and had heard that a group of American musicians had tried, by dint of fairly intensive persuasion, to get Toscanini to cancel his duties at the Bayreuth festival. They had even, so it was said, threatened to cease performing with him if he did not withdraw. Kreisler, despite being a Jew himself, responded furiously to this story, saying that

> the musicians concerned do not understand the meaning and the dynamic strength of the national movement which the current German government has brought to life. The nationalist sentiments which now hold sway over the German people have overcome the lethargy and blank despair into which the vast majority of the people had sunk in the post-war period. Outbursts of nationalist fervour are as unstoppable and inevitable as the great upheavals which take place in nature and the cosmos. The causes of these events are manifest.

50

Everybody knows the tragic fate which the Germans have suffered in the last decade.

The violinist was convinced that applying such fierce moral pressure 'goes against all the principles which they purport to be defending: namely the principle that freedom of artistic expression should be unconditional and removed from the arena of political and racial conflict'. His appeal, which the Nazis welcomed gratefully, ends with the lofty pathos of an artist who was seeking to rescue what there was to be rescued: 'I would seriously entreat Toscanini to go to Bayreuth. At a time when nations are in such turmoil and threats to peace are to be heard everywhere, we cannot do without such a powerful ambassador of peace and goodwill.'[26]

Furtwängler read this report as well. Having been thwarted in his plans on an almost daily basis by the anti-Semitism of others he was aware that Kreisler was starting from the wrong premise. He himself welcomed foreign protests and boycotts because they gave him an almost unbeatable argument. Especially during the 'revolution' the new government worked hard to maintain the respectability of its image abroad, and to quieten foreign fears, in particular those concerning the aims and scale of its atrocities. Thus the demands of propaganda could be turned to good use by the music business. It was with this in mind that he wrote a second letter which arrived at the offices of the Ministry for Propaganda and Popular Enlightenment on 7 April. It was the day on which the Reichstag voted to pass a new law concerning the 'restitution of a professional civil service', which had the effect of excluding Jews from public service.

It is probable that Goebbels saw through the conductor's scheme immediately, and with all the means of influencing the masses which he had at his disposal, he was in a strong position to make the bold leap forwards which he saw was called for. What followed was a propaganda coup, an adroit mixture of worthy uprightness and skilful dissimulation, designed to set the world's mind at rest. He asked for permission to publish the letter in the papers.[27] Simultaneously he gave assurances on everything concerning the future of the Berlin Philharmonic in its present form – which could only mean including all its Jewish members – and all organisational matters. The short discussion in which the minister declared that he would act as a sort of patron of the orchestra took place on the Monday evening after Furtwängler's last concert of the season. That the politician took the trouble to go to the conductor's dressing room rather than asking him to come and see him was significant, as

A practical combination of music and politics, 1933

was the presence of many members of the government at this particular concert.

On the following morning – 11 April – Furtwängler's letter was in the headlines, swamping the telegraphed announcement of Hermann Göring's appointment as Prussian prime minister. To ensure maximum dissemination of the news, Goebbels had sent the letter via the Wolff telegraph office along with his own answer to it. For days – and abroad the discussion lasted for weeks – the letters were the subject of comment from journalists of all political persuasions. It was a sensation: the minister of a dictatorial regime was prepared to discuss art and politics with an artist, rather than having him censored outright. Goebbels basked in praise of the following kind:

> It is a welcome surprise to find that in the new Germany men of such dignity and standing can debate issues of cultural and political importance in public. Wilhelm Furtwängler showed admirable indifference to public unpopularity by courageously and openly defending his Jewish colleagues and fellow artists . . . and Propaganda Minister Goebbels was equally admirable both in his forthright statement of his own position and the way in which, where he felt able to do so, he was ready to acknowledge points of agreement. Above all however, one must laud the way in which neither man made use of political or artistic jargon or clap-trap, preferring instead to use those intellectual weapons of thesis and antithesis in what was truly an intellectual duel.[28]

There were others who were aware that this was no courtly joust

52

between two worldly and intellectual men. Thomas Mann, who was in Lugano, noted angrily:

> Yesterday's newspaper from Frankfurt – Furchtwängler's very appropriate but forewarning letter to Goebbels concerning culture – and that fool's response. These tyrants, so self-satisfied and vain, so free in their use of phrases like 'regained national honour'! Such a totally subjective 'honour'.[29]

The deliberate alteration of the musician's name to *Furcht* (fear) instead of Furtwängler was not so much a case of poetic licence as of psychological insight into a situation which was determined by fear alone. Mann could not know that for those few days after the letters had been published the conductor felt as if he had just won a pitched battle. Of course his defence of quality heedless of race came in for quite a lot of criticism. One particular analysis of the issues raised by the two letters is still worth reading today:

> The basis of such a viewpoint is the belief that art is a higher ideal than the state, that it is in fact the highest ideal known to man. Artists, regardless of who they are, should be treated with the greatest of respect by lay people. This belief first arose and was theoretically elaborated around 1800. Nowadays it is outdated. In modern thinking it is the state (or rather the nation, whose will the state is an expression of) which is the primary ideal, and art takes second place; logically therefore an artist who is personally hostile to the state will be deprived of all support from the state, however artistically valuable his work. Artistic talent should definitely not be used to excuse a lack of political conviction. Equally, political conviction should not excuse a lack of talent.[30]

The insinuation that Furtwängler really was just a rather inflexible old fossil who was automatically opposed to the demands of change is to be found in Goebbels' reply to Furtwängler's letter, in which he hypocritically assures him:

> You may rest assured that any appeal made in the name of German art will get a sympathetic hearing from us. Artists of real talent, whose extra-artistic activities do not conflict with the basic norms of state, society and politics, will, as was always the case in the past, receive our warmest support and encouragement in the future.[31]

While Goebbels prudently left it unsaid that what was at issue was a point of Nazi Party policy rather than a question of artistic excellence, he did allude to it indirectly, by way of warning. Those 'basic norms' defined the limits beyond which political involvement was not welcome. Any extra-artistic activity which went beyond them would be considered subversive. Organised total anti-Semitic hatred was the absolute norm intended by the party. How few people realised the monstrous implications of this is revealed by an Austrian contribution to the debate; Furtwängler had clearly lamented the existence of a dividing line between Jew and non-Jew. In Vienna this provoked the following response: 'Furtwängler states that one is drawing a mercilessly clear dividing line between the different faiths, even in cases where the political behaviour of the individual concerned is beyond reproach. Yet he wants to replace it with an equally sharp line between 'good' and 'bad' art.'[32]

Nevertheless many a critic asked what conclusions – ignoring questions of tactical concessions – were to be drawn from Furtwängler's largely mythical and uncritical world view. It was by no means the first time that he had had inconsistencies pointed out to him. In another letter from Vienna he learned that

. . . naturally nothing could be more desirable than that everything German should be automatically good. It is however not a matter of making the undefined concept 'German' signify 'all that is good'. It would be better to use terms such as 'responsible', 'able', 'aggressive', even though they describe only peripheral qualities. If something is 'very German' it does not automatically mean it is good art, because good art is autonomous, although it may be influenced by the national culture. It is not therefore a question of art becoming more 'national', but of the nation becoming more aware of art.[33]

In all the discussion on terminology, aesthetics and attitudes to art, the key political question was almost forgotten. Only a few people were aware that the mobbings and disturbances, including occasional incidents involving a death, were more than merely severe harassment; they were actually the tentative beginnings of a programme of racial extermination. Goebbels' ultra-careful avoidance of the word 'Jew' had successfully deceived people. Moreover he had cleverly heeded an astute warning from Furtwängler – that contemporary musical activity was already so weakened by the world crisis and the advent of the radio that it could not cope with any more experimentation, and that the criteria for music should not be made contingent – and then ingeniously twisted it to serve his own purposes. While Furtwängler had been referring to organisational 'experimentation', Goebbels responded as if he had meant artistic 'experimentation', and then claimed that he and Furtwängler were in full agreement in their criticism of 'the desire to experiment shown by unpatriotic and Jewish elements'. Furtwängler was caught out. It may well be that he was not terribly upset, having as he did a distinctly negative view of the uninhibited musical experiments of some of his contemporaries. Also concepts such as 'nation' and 'patriotism' had a very deep meaning for him. However, it is clear that race meant nothing to him.

This is why the flood of letters agreeing with him and thanking him gave him moral support. They came from all over Germany, from people who were affected on all levels: 'Your letter, which shows such human and spiritual nobility, helps us to maintain our faith and hope.'[34] People hoped that this one action by Furtwängler would serve as a symbol against a narrow-minded nationalism and racism which could only lead to the ruin of all intellectual life. One person for example wrote:

You are the only one to have summoned up the courage to oppose those who currently control Germany's cultural life. Neither Gerhard Hauptmann, nor Thomas Mann, let alone Richard Strauss or any other artist or scientist, has felt it worth the trouble to make it clear to those gentlemen that you cannot and will not share their view of what it means to have intellectual freedom.[35]

At any rate the conductor saw that many were in broad agreement with him. With this support he dared to hope that he could attain his ambition to disallow the politics of anti-Semitism in his own field, perhaps removing them from the musical scene altogether. Like a field-marshal he worked at what he hoped would be a successful strategy.

On top of this, the position of the orchestra had yet to be clarified. Goebbels' assurances of the Monday evening gave comfort but nothing concrete. At discussions about the orchestra's future which took place on the Wednesday there was no representative of the Propaganda Ministry to be seen. Furtwängler and the chairman of the orchestra, Lorenz Höber, sat opposite representatives from the Reich broadcasting company, the Ministry of Culture, the Ministry of the Interior, and the commissioner for the Prussian Ministry of Finance. The city of Berlin was represented by its mayor, Dr Sahm, but he was not eager to part with his money either. It was noted that the orchestra's debts had increased to 74,000 RM. When Höber detailed the budget for 1933, which included Dr Geissmar's salary of 6,000 RM – the equivalent of 100 RM per concert – faces fell. The meeting ended with no decisions having been taken.

A day later, by order of the mayor, Hafemann, a state commissioner at that time responsible for looking after the mayor's interests asked the chairman of the orchestra – in person rather than by letter – to act as an informant. He wanted a list of all the Jewish members of the orchestra, divided into 'fully Jewish' and 'half Jewish', along with their instrument and nationality. Furthermore, contracts were to be produced. Hafemann intended to find out who could be dismissed on racial grounds, and how soon. Höber protested, but ended up promising to do as requested; however, not being a party member, he did not feel a very strong obligation. But the musicians came to hear of the request, causing them considerable worry. At a meeting of the whole orchestra a few days later on 16 April they heard in grinding detail that things had got worse, because the subsidy which the Berlin council paid on a monthly basis was only to run until the middle of May. Bankruptcy loomed large.

With this gloomy prospect in mind the orchestra began its traditional spring tour, which was to last three weeks, beginning on 22 April, and taking in Essen, Düsseldorf, Cologne, Frankfurt, Mannheim, Saarbrücken, Karlsruhe, Baden-Baden, Paris, Marseille, Lyon, Geneva, Basel, Freiburg, Zürich and Munich.

3

TACTICAL MOVES

Among Furtwängler's papers there was a hand-written address book, which provides an accurate reflection of the social world he moved in during the period between 1922 and 1933. It may well have been used by his secretary Berta Geissmar in the course of her work. It contained the addresses of news agencies, hotels, travel agencies, concert management companies, music critics, editors, publishers, music societies, opera houses, record companies, artists' agencies, embassies and legations, motor clubs in both Berlin and London, and diplomats. Using this notebook one could contact the Inland Revenue and Bank of Germany, Lufthansa, booksellers, photographers, doctors, veterinary surgeons, garages, driving instructors, tailors, milliners (in Paris, an indication of the tastes of his Danish wife), photocopying and typewriter repair shops, and not least, because he was a keen horseman, the addresses of several riding schools in the Reich capital. It was a list for ordinary everyday use.

Also included are the addresses and telephone numbers of musicians with whom he came into contact socially and through his work. These included the singers Rosette Anday, Adelheid Armhold, Anna Bahr-Mildenburg, Marie von Bülow, Rudolf Bockelmann, Maria Cebotari, Carl Clewing, Fred Drissen, Marya Freund, Maria Ivogün, Sabine Kalter, Alexander Kipnis, Lotte Lehmann, Frida Leider, Lotte Leonard, Paula Lindberg, Marianne Mathy, Lauritz Melchior, Maria Müller, Delia Reinhardt, Wilhelm Rode, Helge Roswaenge, Heinrich Schlusnus and Lotte Schöne. This gallery of international celebrities contains every category of musician: among the instrumentalists are the violinists Adolf Busch, Carl Flesch, Gustav Havemann, Bronislaw Huberman, Georg Kniestädt, Fritz Kreisler, Arnold Rosé; the cellists Friedrich Buxbaum,

Pablo Casals, Eva Heinitz, Enrico Mainardi, Gregor Piatigorsky; the pianists Harriet Cohen, Alfred Cortot, Bruno Eisner, Eduard Erdmann, Evelyn Faltis, Edwin Fischer, Mali Frickhoeffer-Mathy, Margarete Klinckerfuss, Lilli Kraus, Marguerite Long, Mitja Nikisch, Arthur Schnabel, and the harpsichordist Wanda Landowska. The leading conductors of the day are also represented: Sir Thomas Beecham, Hans von Benda, Arthur Bodanzky, Gustav Brecher, Paul Breisach, Rudolf Cahn-Speyer, Robert Heger, Franz von Hoesslin, Bruno Kittel, Erich Kleiber, Otto Klemperer, Felix Lederer, Alois Melichar, Carl Muck, Kurt Singer, Fritz Stiedry, Heinz Unger, Felix Wolfes, Sir Henry Wood and Fritz Zweig.

Contrary to the imputations of his opponents Furtwängler is revealed as being in contact with contemporary composers including Béla Bartók, Alban Berg, Suzanne Bloch, Walter Braunfels, Max Butting, Alfredo Casella, Max Ettinger, Alexander Glasunow, Paul Hindemith, Arthur Honegger, Robert Kahn, Erich Wolfgang Korngold, Ernst Křenek, Joseph Marx, Hans Pfitzner, Ferdinand Pfohl, Maurice Ravel, Ottorino Respighi, Max von Schillings, Arnold Schönberg, Franz Schreker, Bernhard Sekles, Dame Ethel Smyth, Richard Strauss, Igor Stravinsky, Ernst Toch, Max Trapp, Edgar Varèse, Vladimir Vogel and Frank Wohlfahrt. Members of the press were, with a few exceptions, also included. The following names are all to be found in the address book: Adolf Aber, Edward Dent, Martin Friedland, Alfred Guttmann, Julius Korngold, Max Marschalk, Ludwig Misch, Ernest Newman, Robert Oboussier, Siegmund Pisling, Heinz Pringsheim, Henri Prunières, Hugo Rasch, Gustave Samazeuilh, Paul Schwers, Heinrich Strobel and Hans Heinz Stuckenschmidt; the conductor kept himself informed on who was writing what about him – so that he could answer back.

The wide range of his intellectual interests is evident from the addresses of scholars such as Wilhelm Altmann, Ludwig Curtius, Max Friedländer, Robert Hernried, Paul Hirsch, Ludwig Justi, Ludwig Karpath, Wilhelm Klatte, Hugo Leichtentritt, Wilhelm Pinder, Heinrich Schenker, Georg Schünemann, Hermann Springer, Fritz Stein, Karl Straube, Hans Weisse and Victor Zuckerkandl. Nor did he omit artists and organisations involved in the other arts, people such as Jürgen Fehling, Hans Flesch, Carl Hagemann, Rudolf Hartmann, Klemens Herzberg, Franz Ludwig Hörth, Ricarda Huch, Oswald Jonas – who was responsible for cataloguing the late Schenker's works, von Kalckreuth (Frederic Dunbar), Julius Kapp, John Knittel, Alma Mahler, Herbert Maisch, Emil Praetorius, Max Reinhardt, Max Slevogt, Heinz Tietjen, Winifred Wagner and Franz Werfel. This collection reflects an interest in theatre, literature and pictorial art that went well beyond what was necessary for his own immediate professional use.

Among the list of useful addresses are those of government departments, offices and advisers, including Franz Bracht (Prussian Ministry of State), Otto Benecke (German Assembly of Town Councils), Goebbels (work and home address), Göring, von Hindenburg, Leo Kestenberg, KfdK, State Secretary Otto Meissner (office and private number), Hans Esdras Mutzenbecher (German Arts Council), Edwin Redslob (secretary of state for the arts), the Ministry of the Interior, the Chancellery, Sievers (privy councillor, Foreign Office), Rudolf Vedder (concert promoter), and Count Albrecht von Bernstoff (German Embassy in London). Taking these names and the departments they represent, and knowing that they were not just jotted down for the sake of it, but were of use to Furtwängler in the many matters he dealt with, one is forced to question his proclaimed credo that 'music has nothing to do with politics'. From the spring until the early summer of 1933 the regular entries in the little address book stop, as if the conductor had suddenly begun to avoid making any new contacts; for the most part the pages are blank. One can only speculate as to the reasons. Is it possible that he deliberately withdrew this piece of very personal evidence concerning his social circles because danger threatened? He seems to have been adding names and numbers of key people and departments to the flyleaf, no doubt for quick and easy reference, until just before he stopped using the address book shortly after Hitler came to power: Hanfstaengl (foreign press-chief for the the Nazi Party, and a confidant of Hitler), the Reichstag, Hitler (under the number Flora A 2 6841), Frick and Metzner (Reich Ministry of the Interior), Goebbels, Sievers and Neurath (Foreign Office), Rust (both his number at the Ministry of Culture and his home number), Göring (office number), Hinkel (home number), Papen (vice-chancellor), Gürtner (chief justice), and another number for Göring at the Reichstag. This was clearly information to be used in case of emergency, and as in part at least the list included institutions whose link with music was at best tenuous, one can draw only one conclusion: he would ring such a number when a matter concerned, say, the Ministry of Justice.

Nobody would deny that the average citizen could only ever dream of having such connections. Yet the conductor must have feared that if the situation were to worsen dramatically then some of his addresses would not provide a very convincing alibi. If the book were to get lost, or to be seized – a very real possibility during the months of the 'revolution' – it would have provided a rock-solid basis for accusations that he was a 'friend of the Jews'. A large number of the addresses did after all belong to prominent Jewish personalities. Because from January 1933 onwards they had no choice but to become very mobile the list of addresses would only have been of limited use. Previously he had noted changes of address either by correcting previous ones or making a new entry, further proof that he made regular use of the book. Anyone confiscating the book might have chosen to ignore the Jewish musicians, but the three Warburgs were also in there; Erich in Hamburg, Paul and Felix (who died in 1937) in London. After the Rothschilds they were the Jewish bankers the Nazi regime most loved to hate; all party officials were aware, as one of their 'philosophers' wrote, that: 'All these Jewish brothers have only one aim, which is to "liquidate" the world, to empty it of meaning and content, to reduce it to the play of empty shadows.'[1]

Furtwängler read this quite some time after Felix had died and Erich's emigration to the USA in 1938. One wonders how he felt about such a stupid and arrogant obituary, given that he was in contact with them, as the address book proves. It also reveals another mysterious Jewish contact, without any further details: 'Loeb Synag J. London W2, 23 Cleveland'. A rabbi perhaps? No, just a careless copying error while writing it in. It was meant to say 'Sidney J. Loeb' – a son-in-law of the conductor Hans Richter who had settled in London and died in 1916.

After the orchestra had left Berlin to begin its long tour, State Commissioner Hafemann reminded them of his demand for the details of 'non-Aryan' musicians, this time setting a three-day time limit and making it very plain that he was serious: 'If my demand is not met I will not hesitate to use all available means to obtain the desired information.'[2]

The orchestra administrators asked for this to be delayed until the Philharmonic returned home, adding as a precaution that it was having difficulties obtaining the necessary records of descent. That was on 26 April, the day of the Mannheim concert. During rehearsals the chairman of the Mannheim orchestra, Sander, doubtless pressurised by the KfdK and the Nazi Party cell within the orchestra, had once again asked for the Mannheimer string players to be allowed to play at the front, at least from the interval onwards. Furtwängler again refused. To his satisfaction the concert passed without incident. Immediately after it had finished the leader of the Mannheim orchestra, Max Kergl, came up to him to tell him that he would not be coming to the planned post-concert party because there was such serious dissent over the question of who was placed where that a meeting of the KfdK was taking place. He was not the only one absent from the party. The morning papers on the following day reported: 'Regrettably Dr Furtwängler was unable to attend the party afterwards, owing to the stress of the tour.'[3] The conductor instead spent the evening at the house of his secretary's mother, Anna Geissmar, thus making a very clear political statement. In the meantime the musicians in the rose garden had a sociable evening of musical jests and droll sketches. Two trustees of the national theatre had been invited as guests of honour, the mayor and his deputy, August Zoepffle, who was responsible for cultural activities in the town.[4]

It was a simple social affair, not an elaborate reception. It was a shame Furtwängler had stayed away, but they made the best of it as the evening drew on with many loud outbursts of laughter. As a lasting reminder, the Berliners were handed a very good photo of the rehearsal – with Simon Goldberg clearly visible in the middle at the front. The following day they continued their journey to Saarbrücken. The day after that they gave a concert in Karlsruhe. It was here and in Baden-Baden the following Saturday that the storm which had been gathering broke. It was 29 April. The Mannheim party newspaper, which was available on the news-stands in Karlsruhe, contained an enthusiastic report on the joint concert on Wednesday by its music critic Hermann Eckert. But it was followed by an editorial comment:

> In connection with the above we cannot neglect to point to a very deplorable matter: we have already been given evidence of Furtwängler's lax attitude to the Jewish question in the well-known exchange of letters with Dr Goebbels. But what we saw on the present occasion was really going too far! Just think: the first desks of all the string sections are occupied by Jews, without exception. How can they still dare to offer us that here in Mannheim after 5 March! We will find ways and means to ensure that alien elements are completely eliminated from any orchestra subsidised by the German state. Under no circumstances can we put up with anybody presenting an orchestra containing dozens of Jews again. Let Furtwängler take heed for the future.[5]

The latter, who was staying at the Brenners Park Hotel, was absolutely furious and drafted a document to Goebbels, adding a copy of the explanatory letter he had written to the chairman of the Mannheim National Theatre Orchestra. As well as expressing his opinion on the matter he announced that any further appearances with the orchestra were forthwith cancelled for as long as they 'maintained such attitudes', closing angrily:

> The more general question of Jews working in the Berlin Philharmonic Orchestra is one which should be addressed not by you but

61

by the Reich government under whose jurisdiction the Philharmonic Orchestra comes. They know very well – whereas you seem to have forgotten – that 'being German means doing a thing for its own sake', and that in an orchestra which has to represent the height of German orchestral excellence not only at home but throughout the world, there can be only one criterion to choose by, namely merit. What we are concerned with here is the need to give the purest and most accurate renditions possible of the great German masterpieces, not the need to offer a certain number of mediocre musicians a way to earn their living.[6]

At the same time the conductor took the opportunity, using arguments which were to form the well-proven basis of his tactics, to voice his opinion strongly, as a professional who stood above any political wrangling:

> What I have seen of orchestral activity around the country (Cologne, Frankfurt, Essen, Mannheim, etc.) does not bode at all well for the future. I fear for the survival of the most spiritual and perhaps the most 'German' art-form our people possesses – by which I mean above all 'absolute' music – which by its very nature is more threatened by the current upheavals than almost any other intellectual activity. Unless free competition is reintroduced with the utmost speed, so that the public is in a position to make its opinion felt, then the upsurge of mediocrity which is currently taking place in our musical life will swamp everything and at that point Germany's standing as the home of music will disappear completely.[7]

That Sunday evening, orchestra and conductor travelled on to Paris. Here it quickly became clear what harmful political effects Jew-baiting in Germany was having. The people who sought to disrupt the Berlin Philharmonic's concerts in France and Switzerland – initially by harmless methods – had both understandable and honourable intentions, and they thought they knew everything. In Paris three organisations demonstrated jointly, namely the Association of Former Jewish Volunteers, the Committee for the Defence of Jews Persecuted in Germany, and the International League against Anti-Semitism. They almost managed to prevent a concert from taking place in which many Jewish musicians were taking part. However they eventually settled for a practical compromise. One side gave complimentary tickets, the other restricted itself to politely distributing leaflets during the interval. The text made much of the 'law concerning the restitution of a professional civil service'

62

as a result of which Jews in public service lost their jobs, but conceded that Furtwängler was something of an exception:

> You, the élite of the Parisian public, have come here tonight to be emotionally moved by the beauty of this music. But reflect for a moment that in a civilised country 700,000 men, women and children have been condemned to death by starvation: we entreat you to do all that is humanly possible to ensure that this monstrous crime is stopped! Despite our decision to continue and strengthen the boycott of Hitler's Germany, we did not wish to disrupt the performance this evening, which was organised before current events began, and whose leader has, in the name of art, protested courageously against this terrible oppression. Join with us and all people of soul who, in the name of honour and the human conscience, seek to preserve peace in the world by denouncing this return to barbarism.[8]

Obviously the initiators of this appeal did not delude themselves that the Paris concert-going public was in a position to change the course of events in the Nazi state, but they wanted to register their protest, however naïve it may have seemed. Their concern over reports from Hitler's Reich drove them to action, even if it could only be on paper. At any rate a copy of the leaflet made its way to Berlin, strengthening certainty there that the camouflage for the anti-Semitic programme which propaganda was supposed to provide was far from sufficient.

The Reich propaganda minister could not plead lack of experience on which to base his decisions, yet this problem was different from anything he had yet come across. Underlying it all were beliefs which one either held or did not, and Goebbels was left with the thankless task of undoing the damage done by Nazi beliefs. He also saw clearly that a nucleus of undesirable developments could crystallise around Furtwängler. The musician had to be won over, convinced, whatever the cost. Suddenly Goebbels saw it as a personal challenge which would test to the utmost all those propaganda and psychological skills which he had as yet used only for mass propaganda. If he could persuade this valiant, unbending individual, who had the courage to go on a lone crusade, to come over to the brown-shirts, it would be a feat by which to recognise a master.

On 5 May – the orchestra and its conductor were enjoying a day off work in Paris, in the way that only musicians who are far from home and family know how – a letter to Winifred Wagner was put in the post in Bielefeld. The sender was Albert Osthoff, a lawyer who dealt with the conductor's finances and taxes, and was also one of a crowd of ardent devotees. Osthoff was trying to counter slanderous lies which he

63

knew were being spread among certain circles in Bayreuth, by setting the facts straight. A week later – Furtwängler was at that point in Vienna at the eighth Brahms Festival to celebrate the composer's centenary, where he met with Huberman and Casals for an exchange of political views – Frau Wagner responded briefly but self-confidently:

> The claim that Dr Furtwängler has a favourable attitude towards Jews was proved once again by himself in his exchange of letters with Dr Goebbels. For the last sixteen years or so he has had Fräulein Dr Geissmar – a full-blooded Jewess – as his full-time assistant, and my first serious disagreement with him during the 1931 festival was provoked by our opposing views of the Jewish press.[9]

Such a man must not be allowed to 'desecrate' Bayreuth. Furtwängler himself saw clearly how dangerous it could be for himself, for the task he had undertaken, and above all for the Berlin Philharmonic Orchestra, if the party succeeded in manoeuvring him into the 'Jewish corner'. He recognised that his plans could only be carried through while he could not be charged with being an 'enemy of the state'. It was clear to him that he, more than anyone else, was the only person who enjoyed enough recognition, power and influence, and who was so indispensable as to have any hope of even a partial success in the urgent confrontation with the concentrated energy of the Nazi movement, and, in the larger sense, this was his task. He believed his plans were still far from being a forlorn hope and made unstinting efforts to deal with the brown-shirted functionaries, even from Vienna, where he was due to give a speech about Johannes Brahms as part of the festival. Counter to his usual custom and to peoples' expectations he used expressions in this speech which critics of Hitler took amiss. Thus he added Brahms to that 'long line of great German musicians' from Bach to Beethoven, stressed his 'typically German use of form', made a great point of attributing 'Nordic' qualities to him, and closed by declaring:

> Everything he was able to do, he was able to do because he was a German. Not, it must be said, because he wanted to be a German, but simply because he was one. He could do no differently; and even if his heart – which incidentally is also a sign of his German nature – was wide open to every stimulation from the non-German world, it was a world he saw through German eyes. In its bittersweetness, its outer reserve and inner abandon, its fantasy and exuberance, its self-restraint and severe greatness, his art is German. He was the last musician to bring forth once again with such unambiguous clarity

these aspects of German music which have world-wide value for everybody.[10]

Not knowing what had been done to Brahms behind the scenes in the Reich, foreign observers could only observe worriedly that such speeches signified 'in the first instance of course, a concession to the spirit which currently prevails in Germany'.[11]

In fact this was no concession, but a wholesale rejection of just that 'spirit'. Pressure had of course been brought to bear on the conductor because of the presence of Jewish soloists at the Brahms Festival in Vienna; the fact that it was an Austrian event did not bother those back in Berlin. They had just 'got rid' of the German Brahms Festival in Hamburg – for a few days. In keeping with the times one fanatic, probably let loose by Alfred Rosenberg and his KfdK, had made the staggering 'discovery' that Brahms was of Jewish descent, and that his grandfather had been called Abrahamson, which made it quite out of the question for a Brahms festival to take place in the Reich.[12]

The fanatic was quickly brought back into line by higher authorities, but there is evidence that there were consequences arising from his despicable story. Carl Muck, leader of the Hamburg Philharmonic Orchestra, gave up his position a short time later; at least one newspaper corrected the misinformation – clearly as a correction, but with due restraint and without actually mentioning the 'allegation':

> This leads to the real meaning of the surname Brahms, which was originally used to denote the origins of the first Brahms, who came from Brahmstedt. 'Brahmst' is an abbreviation used in dialect, like 'Lahmst' instead of 'Lamstedt'. Surnames such as Bramstedt, Bramste, Brahmst or Brahms are very frequent in north-west Germany. Other meanings are incorrect.[13]

In the same way as the critic Walter Steinhauer, whom the party had always regarded as an enemy, responded to the affair by praising the composer as 'exceptionally German',[14] and even emphasising that this was why Brahms had been played at the cultural symposium of the party congress after Hitler's speech, so Furtwängler sought in his memorial speech in Vienna to counter the fairy-tale of Brahms' 'Jewish descent' with – deliberately distorted – facts. The characteristic key sentence – 'not because he wanted to be a German, but simply because he was one' – was designed to challenge the insinuation that the composer's forefathers had been Jews who were aware of the need to fit in, and so had sought a 'disguise'. For the conductor this was, quite apart from

65

the question of historical accuracy, something of a duty, because he felt himself to be an invincible exponent of western morality and humanist civilisation. In comparison with his opponents, whom he saw as narrow-minded and spiritually impoverished, he felt he was a better German. Furtwängler versus Goebbels – it was a primal battle between the tall, shining hero and the small, malicious good-for-nothing. Yet although the two combatants were very different in physical size, they did have some things in common, for instance the urge somehow to break out of their own isolation, which caused them to suffer and yet gave them a sense of their own power. As regards weapons, the musician was at a disadvantage: he had to accept the wily and unfair Goebbels' foil, the intellectual's precipitate and pitfall-laden use of dialectic, which Furtwängler feared because it was so dangerous to him. His decision that despite all that he would wage war came in May 1933. Suddenly he was plunged into the politics which he had naïvely sought to avoid. At that moment he realised that if he wanted to achieve anything he could no longer afford to be naïve. Why then – before the de-nazification commission and right up to the end of his life – did he go on insisting that art and politics had nothing to do with each other? There is a plausible explanation: any admission that he was acting for purely political motives would have been misunderstood, even had he been able to clarify and document his actions in detail on behalf of his opponents and the commission. The claim to be nothing more than a musician was a kind of alibi which did not require complicated proof: and this claim to have served art and art alone was his last and boldest line of defence.

In the course of that month – and always implicitly referring to his letter to Goebbels on behalf of Bruno Walter, Otto Klemperer and Max Reinhardt – the first requests for help began to arrive, from those of his friends who, because the minister had deigned to discuss such issues with Furtwängler, had come to the over-hasty conclusion that Furtwängler had some sort of advisory influence, that secretly he had a mediating influence regarding the German music business. Did they realise that that was exactly what Goebbels wanted? One of the first calls for help came from Karl Straube, cantor at St. Thomas' Church, Leipzig. Straube, although he had been a party member since right back in 1926, was disquieted by the party's attempts to bring Protestant church music under its thumb, especially as they were using two 'insiders', namely the director of church music, Arnold Dreyer, and the twenty-four-year-old choir master and organist, Hans Georg Görner. He ended his letter as follows:

To prevent things getting worse I would like to try and encourage those in authority to use a different set of criteria. What I would ask you to do is to recommend to Dr Goebbels and Dr Rust that, whenever important decisions regarding evangelical music are to be taken, they should, in your opinion, listen to the cantor of St. Thomas'.[15]

This request appears to be a minor incident in the conflict which did lead to a *de facto* schism within the Church, between 'German' Christians and what was effectively a resistance church. In actual fact the attempt definitively to establish a party-based religious movement collapsed some years later, but the third point in the Thüringen 'Principles for the Church Movement of German Christians' demonstrates clearly what was planned, and it was to have been the same throughout the Reich:

God Almighty had a different vision of how each nation should be. In our country this has taken the form of the Führer Adolf Hitler and the National Socialist State formed by him. This vision speaks to us through the blood and toil which have made our people's history. Our faith in this vision demands that we fight for honour and freedom.[16]

By means of religious music – or even better its practitioners – church-goers were supposed to be drawn to a new 'militant' aesthetic, which would lay the ideological groundwork for the 'fight for honour and freedom'. Whether Furtwängler intervened successfully on Straube's behalf is not recorded. However, what took place was a showpiece of the tactics which Goebbels in particular was wont to use. If the principle of 'divide and conquer' was of no use, its reverse, 'conquer and divide', might still be. Straube became an accomplice. When the Reich formed an Office for Church Music in the Evangelical Church under the patronage of Bishop Ludwig Müller in October 1933, Straube proudly accepted the honorary chairmanship; on the advisory board, musicians sat next to party officials, such as Horst Dressler-Andress, head of the department of broadcasting in the Propaganda Ministry. The director of church music, Dreyer, was also given a seat and a vote. Within a few weeks Straube was not only in charge of those responsible for church music in the Reichsmusikkammer, but had even been appointed honorary president of the Reich Association for Evangelical Church Music. He now had to collaborate with a 'colleague' he had so visibly abhorred in his appeal to Furtwängler: the president of the association was the useful young Hans Georg Görner, already a functionary in the KfdK, and – of course an 'old' Nazi with the honourably low membership number 244,869.

If he had not known it already this should have taught Furtwängler that, and in what way, the different sides were blurring into one another, becoming ever harder to distinguish. This should have dampened his confidence, but for the moment he felt he was in a strong position: the Prussian prime minister had just engaged him in a five-year contract to the Berlin Staatsoper and named him the state's top conductor. This and the Great Golden Mark of Honour of the Republic of Austria which he had received at the Brahms Festival were, so to speak, 'badges' to mark his new-won status and growing political weight. Just at this time he needed this increase in authority. At about the same time as the cantor from St. Thomas', a teacher of theory and composition at the State Academy for Church and School Music turned to him, concerned not with music but with race: Robert Hernried, just turned fifty years of age, was an emancipated Jew whose family had only recently under the Kaiser regime changed their original name from Hirsch by Christian baptism. As a civil servant Hernried came under the *Judenreinigungsgesetz* of 7 April, the decree purging the Jews from the civil service. He had deceived himself about the situation having only just been named Professor Emeritus by the Propaganda Ministry on 6 March. Furtwängler requested his particulars and details. Hernried sent him a short résumé and at the same time indicated what he felt would be the best argument in his own defence:

Nationalistic activities: from my youth onwards a passionate protagonist of German music (research on Wagner, Brahms, Hugo Wolf, Hermann Goetz). At the Academy for Church and School Music I was the first to introduce the German folk song into theory lessons and into the state exam for trainee teachers. Since 1 April 1927 I have been a leading member of the national musicians' movement as secretary and editor for the Union of German Orchestras and Orchestral Musicians, one of the organisations recognised by the national movement.[17]

Furtwängler obtained a short reprieve for the professor. According to law, ex-servicemen from World War I – such as Hernried – were exempted from the measures taken; but as the authorities thought up the strangest of interpretations of the law, the case would have been lost without Furtwängler's intervention. Success builds confidence, although he can hardly have believed he would achieve total victory. He was not strong enough to prevent the state from carrying through its anti-Semitic laws, but he could do something about the methods of applying them. It was clearly a dilemma, and this is reflected in his tactics. In the first instance the trust of the Nazi leadership had to be won, in principle by showing positive acceptance of current policies, in so far as they had been drawn up in law; where to show positive acceptance went too much against his own morals, he would keep silent. Above all he must give no cause for doubt. If the brown-shirts were only slightly mistrustful then any possibility of success would be gone. The key problem was in what measure and when? Much as he suffered personally from the attacks which emigrants directed at him with increasing vehemence in the following months, he also needed them to give him political credibility in the eyes of his political interlocuters – who in reality were his opponents. It was like a spy film in which the agents swapped sides. When his critics abroad reviled him as a 'Nazi' the functionaries inside the country felt he was 'one of them'. For his part he found in Germany, depending on the circumstances and if no other way were possible, that he had to make a big show of being a 'sympathiser', a supporter of National Socialist policies, if he was not to forfeit his position as an arbiter. Unaware that they were doing so, leading Nazi functionaries and foreign anti-fascists worked hand in hand to help Furtwängler and his cause. Only as an 'accomplice of Hitler's barbarism' was he in a position to rescue Jews, and every voice from abroad – fortunately very rare – which counted him a member of 'the other Germany, the real one', endangered his chances of helping. He lived for years in a world of deception which put him under great strain and stretched his nerves almost to breaking point. In this position the musician was more than just a politician. He was a 'double agent' threatened with discovery at every moment.

One must also take into consideration that, unlike a normal secret agent, he did not work alone or under cover. As a guest conductor abroad he was always being watched. The musicians picked up on the fact that in certain towns he would hurry to the post office and hand over money to friends who had emigrated; foreign journalists on the other hand strained to catch any asides this impulsive man might let slip about the 'Nazis' back home. Security risks suddenly appeared, leaks had to be blocked, and sceptical reports sent by the foreign branches of the Nazi Party had to be neutralised with conflicting versions. Some nasty situations did arise. Furtwängler was occasionally a victim of his own temperament. On one occasion – in autumn 1934 – Berta Geissmar babbled a little too freely, and the damage was only just repaired, at the price of making an official denial which had the effect of making his secretary look untrustworthy. Right from the start it was a highly unstable situation, which would have made very great demands even on a master of subterfuge, which is precisely what Furtwängler was not. How must he have felt when for tactical reasons he had to pretend to be somebody he was not, and was so frequently unable to be himself? When reality and pretence were so indistinguishable? How must it have felt when he failed? He kept everything to himself, as if he possessed some great capacity to atone. He did not think it worth talking about how he really felt.

Goebbels seemed the most suitable person to approach with requests regarding music and politics, so Furtwängler turned to him. The Jewish question was the main problem. Given that he came from an upper class family of humanist sympathies, which would have used 'race' as an anthropological concept but not to express a permanent obsession, the imputation that in his heart of hearts he was anti-Semitic is scarcely tenable. Certainly he lived in an epoch which presented him with several uncomfortable experiences, especially during the ostensibly liberal and permissive Republic; of course, permissiveness and liberalism are not automatically virtues, they can quite easily, depending on one's opinion, be seen as tolerating barbarism. A letter from a colleague in the early days of the Republic is eloquent proof of the atmosphere prevalent at that time. He asked to be recommended in Frankfurt, and lest there should be any misunderstanding which might damage his prospects he explained:

I am not a Jew (although some people think that my nose looks Jewish). My mother's family were from Bohemia, my father's from Vienna. My cousins were all students in the corps and my sisters were all convent-educated – it appears that my admiration for Mahler and his kind, as well as my own temperament (which I myself am not worried about) are the cause of such 'suspicions'.[18]

Written twelve years before the National Socialist regime began, this letter, which Furtwängler requested be passed on to the relevant musical authorities of a town reputed to have the highest proportion of Jews in Germany, sounds like a precursor of the 'proofs of Aryan descent' which were to come later. The whole artificially created 'racial instinct' was encouraging new extremes of absurdity and irrational behaviour.

However, if the upper classes were by and large unmoved by coarse anti-Semitic rhetoric, the 'left' revolution in 1918 had roused considerable fears. Their privileges – social status, assured income and an intellectual ambience – seemed endangered, and by a type of climber who was competing with them by using the democratic mechanisms the upper classes found so disorderly and alien. These climbers were good businessmen with few scruples. They lacked tradition, were in fact lacking roots, yet they assumed rights and penetrated into areas which until

70

then had been the preserve of the upper class. They did not conform to the latter's comfortable notion of the 'honest businessman' or the 'genuine artist', but were often extremely good businessmen and artists for all that. There were many foreigners and Jews among them, some of whom had come to Germany precisely because the constitution guaranteed their freedom. These were the people the 'national' establishment feared and hated. It was not a case of simple 'anti-Semitism', but of social abhorrence born of the fear of being threatened – based on the experience that 'they' did react more quickly and more intelligently, did exploit their contacts to the full, did have the *goyim* up against the wall. Although the Republic's democratic motto was 'an opportunity for all', such people in fact were prominent in all the professions, becoming lawyers, doctors, artists and managers. They were seizing what had formerly been reserved for the élite, and which the revolution had made a free-for-all. They set about conquering musical activity as well, first of all light music, which was marketable, and an easy path to fame and profit, and then even set their sights on the 'classical heritage'. The establishment's fear of being superseded can largely be explained by a look at the statistics. If one correlated the 'non-Aryan' musicians in the 1929 *Deutsches Musikerlexikon* (Lexicon of German Musicians) with the two 'Jewish lists' of the Nazi period, one finds that about 280 were born outside the German Reich, 54 per cent of the total number. Thus every second Jewish musician who offered his services, or competed against others, was in the public mind a foreigner, an 'intruder'.

Quite apart from feelings of resentment, concern for one's own position was often aroused by one particular incident, normally when an 'intruder' came too close to a man of class – the conflict really did seem to be almost wholly restricted to the social pecking order. For example, three days after the proclamation in the Reich of the law boycotting Jews, Thomas Mann commented from Switzerland:

> The Jews . . . it is really no bad thing that something like Kerr's brazen and venomous attack on Nietzsche should no longer be possible; nor really is the removal of Jews from the judiciary. – Secret, turbulent, difficult thoughts. Adverse, hostile, base and un-German influences will certainly remain. But I begin to suspect that this question of rank could be one of those which has two sides to it.[19]

The writer, whom the emigrants prematurely identified as one of their own, thought the measures taken by the Nazis were acceptable. The Jewish critic Alfred Kerr had not only attacked the 'holy legacy' of Nietzsche, but had also frequently attacked him, Thomas Mann; the latter's bitterness caused him to generalise, and so, although by 1945 at the latest he had come to symbolise Germany's conscience, at this point he did not give a second thought to using the language of monsters: 'the removal of Jews'. He saw nothing wrong with 'cleansing' the press as Hitler decreed. His thoughts did not stop there. He does not seem to have thought it particularly important that at the burning of books in May 1933 he was symbolically cast into the flames along with his antagonist Kerr. A year later he still managed to suggest that at an ideological level the Jews were partly to blame:

> Thought of the irony of the current situation in which the Jews are being denied their rights and hounded from the country, when they did after all contribute a great deal to the intellectual ideas of which, although distorted, this political system is the outcome. They could thus be said to have played a large part in preparing the way for this anti-liberal turn [. . .].[20]

Mann remained intent on having 'honourable' and 'peaceful' ties with his country, because he did not wish to be considered a refugee; it was a situation which automatically brought susceptibility to moral incoherence with it. Musicians were no less susceptible, even foreign ones: Henri Gagnebin, the head of the Conservatoire in Geneva – perhaps to prevent his small German clientele from going to an 'intruder'? – made a great show of being extremely liberal when he claimed one could

> up to a certain point understand the German anti-Semitic movement, when one bears in mind the extent to which Jews have occupied places and made careers in music. By their activity, their flair, their sense of the moment, they have not only gained control of the majority of places in orchestras and publishing, but also become masters of composition, publishing, interpretation and criticism.[21]

Gagnebin expressed his opinion openly; Mann confided his to a private diary which was intended to be a source of material for future works, but which was published posthumously in original form – something the author could have prevented had he acted at the right time. Furtwängler was in a quite different position. His dislike of 'intruders', his fear of being superseded was hardly likely to be related to his own position as the leading figure in German music. He knew only too well how to deal with over-eager and critical journalists. But he did fear that

72

while his own position was secure, inroads were being made into the high quality of musical activity which he strove for. His concern was first and foremost with 'German music', and only very occasionally with his own reputation – although such was his identification with his material that the distinction between person and music must sometimes have been difficult to make.

It is possible to infer the nature of Furtwängler's thoughts on the Jewish problem from the notes he made. They are not to be found in his diaries, an indication of how unimportant he considered the question with reference to himself. But it was an issue he could not avoid if National Socialist leaders were to be his partners in talks and grant him concessions. Scattered sheets of notepaper were found among his papers on which he had sketchily and hurriedly jotted down a 'rough' version of the main strands of his arguments. Unlike Thomas Mann and Henri Gagnebin, he wrote not just his own opinions, but cogent arguments on a subject which was not strictly speaking his own field. From reading these – sometimes almost indecipherable – sheets, it is clear that he did believe the – Jewish – press had a harmful influence on musical activity, to the benefit of 'modernism'. No less striking is the way in which he tends to dramatise his thoughts: he fiercely denounced 'illegal' and ill-considered measures devoid of any higher purpose, in other words the use of crude terror. However, in his dialogue with the perpetrators he did not question the anti-Jewish laws, knowing full well that to do so would be to undermine his own effectiveness.

Many of these sheets are not even dated and are obviously drafts to be worked out later – he generally put his counsel on record in the form of memoranda. One sheet, probably his first on the subject, which has Goebbels noted as addressee at the top, may well have formed the basis of a discussion or of a memorandum to him; it may have been written in June 1933. Because of its significance for Furtwängler's standpoint, the text has been reprinted almost in its entirety:

The Jewish question in musical spheres:
A race of brilliant people!
As a percentage of the orchestra Jews are not over-represented. As soloists they should be defended. *Indispensable* as audience.
Should take responsibility for and spend the necessary *time* on all appointments – if dismissals cannot be avoided.
Infringements on the freedom of the arts which are not motivated by a concern for quality are unacceptable. If necessary will resign. Apply pressure where it's needed – among the opinion-formers, the Jewish press.

This requires:

1. Discreet surveillance of the existing Jewish press by *experts*.
2. The creation and subsequent support of our own media, which have hitherto not existed. Mobilisation of *Geist* which is *far more* available to National Socialism than they have yet realised.

[. . .] Points of view: Jews who are in service or are honestly self-employed should be allowed, but they should not be given organisational responsibilities or top positions. The views they hold should be kept under scrutiny. The boycott should be restricted to commercial activity, possibly including agencies. It should not apply to artistic activities; in this matter clear guidelines must be drawn up. If the boycott, by which I mean the measures which have arisen in the current political context, is extended to the supra-political field of art, then I shall resign from my post immediately. Any incursions into the autonomous field of art will prove to be a most disastrous move from the point of view of propaganda. [. . .] Jews who by their own abilities succeed as artists, singers, etc. and without the help of organisations or large networks, should not come in for discrimination. In this too one needs to be clear about what one is prepared to allow and what not. The influence of the Jewish press should be broken, above all by use of intellectual means. We must build up our own press, which – in music at least – we have been lacking until now. Quite apart from that, tendentious Jewish pen-pushers belong elsewhere, so far as it goes. They have no place in the administration, but in the free professions, at least where unusual talent is in evidence, they must be protected. At any rate to continue giving concerts would be quite impossible without them – to remove them would be an operation which would result in the death of the patient.[22]

The conductor conceded selection according to good conduct, which was anything but racist, and which doubtless reflected a wish to see the use of objective professional and political criteria. As it was, the law passed on 7 April prescribed a 'Jew-free' civil service or administration. He remained adamant about the question of 'tendentious Jewish pen-pushers', even though journalists did not count as civil servants and so were not subject to the law – a problem which the Reichskulturkammer solved with a law passed in November of that year. Whether or not he considered Theodor Wiesengrund (Adorno) – who, quite in keeping with Nazi ideology, condemned superficial operettas but actually praised some of the resounding pieces written in homage to Hitler, to be one of the 'tendentious Jewish pen-pushers', remains an open question, because Furtwängler was not in the slightest interested in political music. The text nevertheless suggests that in principle he was prepared to resign. His references to stepping down were more than just paper threats. Goebbels took them seriously. But the matter of which minister had which powers had yet to be clarified.

The musician knew this and did not want to waste his breath, which is why in the first instance he turned to the Ministry for Science, Art and Popular Education. From Paris, where ironically enough, as part of the annual opera festival, he was conducting *Tristan und Isolde* and *Die Walküre*, with Lotte Lehmann, Frida Leider, Lauritz Melchior,[23] Alexander Kipnis and Sabine Kalter – a 'racially' very mixed team – he sent Dr Rust, the minister, a list of suggestions concerning musical activity, elaborating on them in an accompanying letter. His demand was that the government should make it clear that in future every artist, regardless of race, would be given a hearing in Germany. Failure to do so would result in any international exchange being killed off and a strengthening of the boycott. Furthermore, a quasi-official supervisory body should be responsible for control of musical activity. He added the warning:

If the government continues to shy away from adopting such an unequivocal stance at this point in time, then it will certainly be too late to organise even a half-decent set of public concerts in time for next year. Such a declaration, recognising unconditionally that artistic merit is the sole principle by which distinctions are to be drawn, is indispensable if the currently poisoned atmosphere within German music-making circles (especially in the provinces) is to clear, and if we wish to fight the latent terror which is having such a disastrous effect on our concerts.

Included with the accompanying letter were recommendations for a number of cases in need of attention such as those of Hernried and Straube. He dressed up his case for Arnold Schönberg with a warning about a possible negative international response, because 'among the Jewish international community [this composer] is considered clearly the most significant musician of our time. I urgently recommend that you do not make a martyr of him, and that now that he has been dismissed – which I also would not have considered right – you should be generous with your financial settlement.'[24]

In a letter dated 23 May 1933, Schönberg had found himself dismissed forthwith from his position running a composition master-class. The letter deemed that his case fell under the law of 7 April and was signed by the president of the academy, Max von Schillings. Schönberg was left on the street almost destitute, and while making arrangements to emigrate he appealed to Furtwängler for help in sorting out the money he was owed by the Prussian Academy of Arts. Furtwängler intervened several times but the authorities dragged their heels so much over coming to a decision that he had reason to complain. Busch is also mentioned in this letter to Rust. Without Busch's being aware of it Furtwängler had tried to counter some of the discrimination Busch had suffered by seeking a position of equal status for him. He saw several possibilities, because as a result of the merry-go-round of posts set in motion by the persecution of Jewish conductors there were plenty of vacancies; the 'Aryan' Busch ought to have stood a very good chance. In the first instance Furtwängler ensured that he was, as it were, brought in from the cold, by mentioning his name at discussions on a replacement conductor at the Gewandhaus now that Bruno Walter had been boycotted. Busch however did not wish – and this speaks for him – to 'displace' a Jewish colleague or to help cover up the boycott. So his untiring sponsor made a fruitless request for further information on the status quo, adding as a precaution:

> I am wondering how one could find Busch a job in Berlin, regardless of that [the Gewandhaus job]. In any event I will arrange for him to be guest conductor of a concert series with the Philharmonic Orchestra in the Philharmonie, much as I did with Bruno Walter last year. I will tell you the rest of my thoughts on the matter when I see you (but all this is not meant to detract from the main concern, which is that the Gewandhaus matter should be sorted out satisfactorily).[25]

A successor for Busch in Dresden had been decided on at the end of May; after a guest appearance Karl Böhm had been offered the contract, and although releasing him from his long-term contract as general director of music in Hamburg caused several problems, such contractual considerations were swept aside by Hitler's personal intervention. This opened up a morally acceptable solution for Busch; the Hamburg and Dresden Staatsoper were in practical terms of equal standing, even if the institution in Saxony could lay claim to greater repute. Busch's widow was quite right when she observed: 'Furtwängler said at the time Busch was expelled from Dresden: "Well, Busch can go to Hamburg." '[26] In saying this however, she seemed to suggest that her husband was being palmed off with some paltry job out in the provinces. In actual fact Busch was already engaged elsewhere; although it was not the contract for the Berlin Staatsoper, which Furtwängler had already won, nor a very long-term contract. It was still very spectacular and was set up as a result of the concerted efforts of Göring, Commissioner of State Hinkel representing the Prussian Ministry of Culture, the Foreign Office and the Nazi Party's department of foreign affairs, without which a German opera season in the Teatro Colón in Buenos Aires could not possibly have taken place. Ernest Ansermet brought the invitation from Argentina. At that time Busch was still hoping to be given the conductorship of the Berlin Staatsoper which Göring had prematurely promised him, and so, although arrangements with the German Pro-rata Theatre Recruitment Agency, which was dealing with the requests of management in Colón, were already fairly well advanced, he somewhat hesitantly turned the offer down. In his report to Hinkel (which may also have been a request for help) the manager of the recruitment agency, a party member, informed him that he had the impression that 'because if he commits himself to this tour he will be absent from Berlin throughout September, the first month of the new season, Busch is afraid this will again count against him, just when he had hoped things would be in his favour following the review of the Dresden affair'.[27]

In personal discussions which followed, Hinkel did not succeed in setting Busch's misgivings at ease, even though he emphasised how important it was for the Reich to have a German presence in South America. Shortly afterwards Busch, who was staying at the Hotel Knie, informed him by letter that he could not accept the responsibility, because at this late stage in the day he could no longer hope to get together a first-class ensemble. It was a plausible but trumped-up excuse. The Argentinians acted quickly, engaging Erich Kleiber instead, sorting out all the prior arrangements, printing posters and publicising a German 'Temporada' with Kleiber! But he suddenly cancelled. The Colón management sent a cry for help to the Reich embassy, which in turn cabled to Berlin:

The agency has once again proposed very welcome Fritz Busch, however final decision only mid-May because of cultural matters at home. Urgently request in interests of avoiding damage to the opinion here of German opera you arrange Busch's availability for guest performances in Colón and inform us by beginning of next week at latest. In very undesirable case that alternative is needed only world-famous names such as Richard Strauss, Furtwängler, Klemperer, Knappertsbusch possible.[28]

None of those named had to step in: when Göring said that he regretted the 'cultural matters at home', Busch made up his mind. Now it had become an overseas task; now he suddenly found it possible, despite the fact that time was even shorter, to take the responsibility. Nobody – not even the best organiser – could have gathered together the forces required for opera, equipped them and set things going, if all obstacles had not been cleared from his path. The recruitment agency, Hinkel, Göring and the Foreign Office were all involved, the last because there were also financial matters to be resolved. The musicians were recruited partly from those who were available as a result of having been thrown out under the 'Aryan clause' – for example in Dresden – and partly of singers who were under contract but had of course been granted special release: Anni Konetzny, Edith Fleischer, Kerstin Thorborg, Lauritz Melchior, Paul Seider, Walter Laufkötter, Karl Wiedemann, Walter Grossmann, Michael Bohnen and others were all among the artistic personnel, with Carl Ebert as stage director.[29]

The target of this foreign publicity was obvious. It was addressed less to the German colony in Argentina – where the Nazi Party was already carrying out 'nationalist works', with the result that German firms and branch offices, such as that of IG Farben, were turning Jewish workers on to the streets – than the politically important local establishment around President General Justo. The Nazi Party had a number of very concrete proposals: trade and foreign exchange agreements, an exchange of military attachés and subsequent armament deals. This was why it was necessary to use German arts to prove that everything was fine in the Reich; if it were not how could they dispatch an ensemble in which 'Aryan' and Jewish musicians performed side by side in such great works as *Parsifal, Die Meistersinger, Tristan und Isolde, Der Rosenkavalier* and *Fidelio*? Although the modern opera which had initially been promised had to be cut, this would not detract from the value of these performances for Germany's foreign standing. This was the tenor of the report to Hinkel from the party leadership in Argentina. He in turn put Göring in the picture. Melchior, a Danish tenor, was not the only one who was aware that they were acting as ambassadors for Hitler.

Just how unfree Busch was while performing his conducting duties during this tour is shown by the fact that he was under discreet observation – but not only by the embassy in Buenos Aires and secret agents of the party's department of foreign affairs who were stationed there: Hinkel had appointed the theatre and party official Peter Unkel as an assistant organiser on the trip and charged him with reporting back to him, it being generally agreed that everything should be done to rescue such a useful artist for 'the German nation'. Afterwards the Reich propaganda minister complained to Hinkel that he had had no knowledge of this tour, and stressed 'that I consider it very important that I be informed in good time of any propaganda tour abroad undertaken by German musicians'.[30]

Hinkel denied responsibility and informed him that the tour had been decided on at a time when the Propaganda Ministry was not yet in existence. It was an excuse. Goebbels had already moved into his offices on the Wilhelmplatz on 22 March. On the same day Hinkel received a detailed report on the Busch affair in Dresden from the Saxony branch of the Nazi Party, signed by Gaukunstwart Posse. Buenos Aires was first discussed weeks later. Apparently they wanted to keep Goebbels out of it.

Furtwängler did not hear the details of the whole story, but his impression was strengthened that propaganda tours abroad offered special opportunities because the party did not yet take them very seriously. He decided to make full use of this chance both in his arguments and in practice. In the first instance, though, there were internal matters to be resolved. Inner tensions between the members of the Berlin Philharmonic surfaced in open conflict after they had been relieved from immediate financial worries by a reluctantly granted increase in the Reich subsidy, which guaranteed their finances for the next few weeks. At a meeting on 8 June – three days after Toscanini's spectacular withdrawal from Bayreuth – politics were discussed. The musicians demanded an improvement in working relations. The main trouble was the merger with a part of the Berlin Symphony Orchestra the year before, which had led to the formation of a strong cell of Nazi Party activists by 'imported' party members; Furtwängler's attempt to prevent this happening had failed because the authorities refused to undo the merger. Some of the musicians were now demanding the election – which was really overdue – of a new executive committee. What was bad was that accusations of 'Jewish predominance' were also voiced; these were naturally aimed at Berta Geissmar, also at the violinist Richard Wolff, who was co-leader with Höber and had a Jewish wife. Even the concert agency Wolff & Sachs which arranged some of the Philharmonic's concerts was suddenly in the firing line. Several ardent members made it their job to act as the mouthpiece of the 'national' forces, and addressed themselves to Hitler as representatives of the orchestra:

Party members who have worked very hard for clarity and order are now called trouble-makers. Dr Furtw. appears to have been misinstructed. His statements on the Jewish question are to the effect that after consultation and by agreement with Herr Reichsminister Dr

Goebbels they are to remain in the orchestra in the future. He claims the press have been instructed to that effect too. Dr Furtwängler treats any further attempts to raise the question as a personal affront.[31]

The unrest had its consequences. The municipal council dispensed with the services of Wolff because of his 'non-Aryan' ties, and demanded the election of a new executive committee. Fritz Schröder, a party member, temporarily became general secretary, ostensibly to provide a replacement and counterweight, but actually to ensure that the Berlin Philharmonic was at last brought into line politically with the party. Furtwängler was disappointed, even embittered. Sobered by the knowledge that a group which had worked together for more than ten years had fragmented at the first hint of political pressure, he returned to Paris for the second half of his guest appearances at the opera, while his musicians prepared for the summer holidays, still internally divided.

Berta Geissmar suffered even more. The undisguised hostility had opened her eyes. A resolute, highly educated and strong-willed woman, who was enthusiastically devoted to her boss, and to some extent in his thrall, she decided to fight. She did not think much of his by no means perfected tactics, and so, to catch up on political experience, she flung herself into an extraordinary adventure. On 11 July, a Sunday evening, she appeared in London and moved into a suite in the Park Lane Hotel together with a plenipotentiary of the Reich. This man – who, as she always refers to him by the abbreviation Fr.[32] in her detailed reports, must have been known to Furtwängler as well – had been sent by one of the government authorities in Berlin on a mission to sound out British politicians and to play down the Jewish question in German politics. Frau Geissmar officially accompanied him as secretary and interpreter, but because of the circumstances and their liking for one another they spent a lot of time talking, the diplomat spending hours on end discussing his negotiations with her. Thus in London she served two masters at once, because on the side she was seeing to musical matters for the conductor; she of course wished her newly acquired political experience to be of use to him too, if only indirectly:

There are purely tactical lessons which you in particular could learn. From what he tells me our situation is very complicated; externally one retreat after another, internally – extreme tension. Your position, seen purely from a political point of view, is quite difficult and yet necessary. It is not very likely that there is anything in the world which can harm you, but you must remember constantly to reiterate where you stand. Because the new Germany's spiritual image is 'unspiritual'.[33]

As an emancipated Jewess with family in London, she enjoyed English 'fairness' and contact at the highest levels; a meal at the house of the son of Lord Justice Jessel at which she met the daughter of Baldwin, prime minister for many years, was one among many invitations. There was no sign of racial discrimination, and she reflected:

> When one talks with all these people it makes one quite wild to think that a certain Sellschopp can advise one to not make oneself too obvious at the glass door lest Dr Metzner see one, and that one has to suffer inner torment because one is so afraid of harming a man like you just by one's presence. One realises just how grotesque the things taking place in our country are, and how necessary a man like yourself is. You too, although you are no politician, really should be talking to world leaders, in fact you should be playing a quite different role in politics, with people coming to you rather than always thinking they know best.[34]

The plenipotentiary was indefatigable; in the space of three days he had talks with half a dozen top British politicians of all sides, including Chamberlain, and began drafting a memorandum in support of the German line of argument. His assistant learnt astonishingly rapidly and easily; she after all was not 'rootless', in fact she felt herself to be a German national, with an obligation to help maintain the cultural heritage of the Reich, even if at that moment in time it was suffering the unavoidable misfortune of an anti-Semitic leadership. She soon produced a first attempt at a piece of 'diplomatic' thinking:

> People here make an absolutely clear-cut distinction between Germans and Hitler people. I regret this for Hitler's sake, who surely does not wish it so. But you, Dr Furtwängler, should really be proceeding quite differently. There are certain things which must stop. The dismissal of Jews from the Staatsoper which has appeared in all the papers here has stirred everything up again. Speeches and such like should not be printed in the press; things which have to be done must not be allowed to create a stir. The emphasis on the masses in our country must stop. The respect in which we are held by the whole world is at risk.[35]

She was naïve in her belief that it was public revelations and declarations of intent which were ruining Germany's honour rather than the evil deeds themselves; but on the other hand there is no doubt that the foreign press reacted more vociferously to the Nazis' inflammatory Jew-baiting speeches than to their actual deeds. Many of those in a position to do so still hoped that, in some way or another, they could achieve something, and that the regime was no more than a short nightmare. Berta Geissmar shared in these hopes. She laid her bets on Furtwängler's moral authority:

> You are the only person who has managed to combine service to the Nazi government with world-wide popularity. You are walking on a knife-edge. But people such as Pulay are adopting too narrow a viewpoint. They should see things in a broader perspective. However it will probably be necessary for you to speak your mind to Papen-Hitler and at the same time somehow make sure that you are well covered. Having done this you will be in a position to begin. Everything so far has really been little more than dabbling. They will have to concede quite different functions to you.[36]

Doubtless inspired by this experience of a diplomatic mission, she tried to cajole the musician, whom she considered too slow and cautious, into 'high' politics. The respect which had accrued to him abroad as a result of his intervention with Goebbels on behalf of Jewish musicians seemed a good basis. She also managed to strengthen Furtwängler's political self-confidence. It was at that time clear that Toscanini's abrupt decision to pull out from Bayreuth despite a personal appeal from Hitler, after he had both come to a cordial agreement and accepted, with expressions of 'deep gratitude', the freedom of the city of Bayreuth, was bound to have repercussions. Already the press was hinting that the Italian would not have made a very good exponent of Wagner, but they did not fail to add – and in this they were in agreement with Furtwängler – a dig at Winifred Wagner's thirst for artistic power:

> That Frau Winifred does possess qualities of leadership and the corresponding organisational capacities, is no longer a matter of serious dispute among musicians today. But the absence of an overall artistic director in Bayreuth, a suitable replacement for Richard, Cosima and Siegfried Wagner who provided the overall artistic direction of the festival in the past, is still painfully obvious. It was obvious while Toscanini was there, and it will remain so even if Richard Strauss, who is thankfully standing in the breach by taking on *Parsifal*, is only allowed to function as a stop-gap or at best as first conductor.[37]

82

Still in June, Furtwängler reaped the reward of what seemed to be a breakthrough in musical politics. First of all one of the government authorities, the Prussian Ministry of Culture, adopted a stance on organisational practice within the music business, including the Jewish question, in the form of a dispensation whose most important parts had been written by the conductor himself. Its contents offered hope that under the given circumstances he could achieve a compromise between political and musical interests:

On the assumption that the people best suited to give support and advice on musical activity in the new Germany are well-known Germans whose reputation rests on a long record of high achievement, the Minister for Sciences, Art and Popular Education has called together a commission consisting of Wilhelm Furtwängler, Max von Schillings, Wilhelm Backhaus and Georg Kulenkampff, who are to examine the programmes of all public concerts (whether subsidised with public funds or not), and will advise those responsible for the programmes where necessary.

The guidelines to be used are as follows: the prime concern of our music making must be the safeguarding of our own great German music. This does not mean that non-German music should not be played; we should continue to listen to and be stimulated by music from the non-German world, just as has traditionally been the case in Germany.

From among contemporary works special consideration should be given to German composers, but again this should not be taken to mean that the most significant and representative achievements of foreign music are not to be suitably introduced and encouraged.

The principle that German artists who are competent to further and preserve a German musical life should always be used in the first instance applies equally to performing musicians (soloists, singers etc.). However it must be stressed that in music, just as in every art form, a person's abilities must always remain the decisive factor, and this principle of merit must come before all others. All real musicians should be able to perform in Germany and be rewarded in accordance with their abilities.

This committee which the minister has set up will in future be the only body authorised to decide questions of programme content in Prussia's musical life.[38]

Minister of State Rust had handed the draft version, which landed on his desk on 8 June, on to his advisers for their opinion. They wanted to supplement the commission of four with representatives from the two concert agencies, Bote & Bock and Wolff & Sachs – apparently it did not matter that these were both Jewish-owned. In addition they wanted programmes to meet a quota requirement: works by German composers should form two thirds of any concert. There is no question that the officials at the ministry knew which was the politically explosive issue, ending their report with a *nota bene*: 'The word "German" should be replaced by "of Aryan descent".'[39]

Their wish was not met, perhaps because the result would have been rather too obviously open to interpretation. Furtwängler wanted 'the principle of merit to come before ALL others'. The editors however, in order not to have to forfeit racism, shortened this demand to 'others', which effectively meant only some other principles. Still, Furtwängler now believed he could do as he liked, and he must have spent the last days of June almost uninterruptedly at his typewriter. He firmly believed that Prussia had benefited German musical activity by honouring his authority and experience.

This was why on 29 June he acquainted Rust with a list of urgent cases, not all of which were new. This time though his obstinacy showed through; he wanted results and he insisted. Prof. Dr Georg Dohrn, conductor of the Silesian Philharmonic in Breslau, had just turned sixty-six and was having problems with his pension. Furtwängler brought the case to the minister's attention – and not just because Dohrn was distantly related to him on his mother's side. Ten months later the deserving professor went into retirement. Professor Bernhard Sekles, who had been dismissed as head of the Hochsche Conservatory in Frankfurt, had applied for an unprecedented severance payment. To further his case Furtwängler stressed that Sekles 'is one of the few Jews who, ever since I have known him (about fifteen years), has acted in a consistently constructive manner, and who has always manifested a genuine inner affinity with German music. I believe it is the duty of justice to settle this case generously.'[40]

Schönberg's case was also still up in the air. In response to a despairing telegram appealing for help which reached Paris on 29 May where he was appearing as a guest conductor, Furtwängler had looked him up at the Hotel Regina at the beginning of June and offered to approach the authorities on his behalf. He repeatedly reminded them to consider the matter, and later even approached Hitler; throughout the turbulent November days of 1934 the composer still trustingly brought his requests to Furtwängler to pass on to the appropriate place. Later Schönberg's widow would state in evidence: 'How very different from Richard

Paris, den 4. Juni 1933

Sehr geehrter Herr Schönberg!

Ich habe Ihre Angelegenheit bei dem Minister
R u s t anhängig gemacht und hoffe sehr, dass sie in Ihrem
Sinne erledigt werden wird. Da wir zur Zeit in der selben Stadt
sind, würde ich mich sehr freuen, wenn es einmal möglich wäre,
dass wir uns sehen könnten. Sobald ich etwas Ueberblick über
meine Zeiteinteilung habe, werde ich versuchen, Sie im Regina-
Hotel telefonisch zu erreichen.

Inzwischen verbleibe ich
mit den besten Grüssen

Ihr

Paris, 4 June 1933

Honoured Herr Schönberg!

I have raised the matter concerning you with Minister of State Rust, and
hope very much that it will be settled in our favour. As we are currently
both in the same town I would be pleased if we could meet, if that is
convenient. As soon as my timetable is a little clearer I will try and contact
you by telephone at the Regina Hotel.

In the meantime I remain yours sincerely

Wilhelm Furtwängler

Strauss's ironic retort to Otto Klemperer: "Just the right moment to go
putting oneself out for a Jew!".[41]

Carl Flesch, the eminent violin virtuoso and teacher, actually owed
his life to Furtwängler's efforts – even if it was not obvious in the short
term. The violinist, blind to all warning signals, scornfully rejected
suggestions that he should emigrate. Although he had been born in
Hungary and worked in several countries, he had finally found a home
and employment in Berlin and Baden-Baden. When it had been decided
to expel him from the Berlin Musikhochschule because of the unavoid-

85

able 'Aryan clause', he notified the conductor, who decided to play on its importance for foreign affairs:

> Even if the law offers no pretext on which to keep him, I would think it advisable to make an exception in this very important instance, in order not to increase further the already catastrophic extent of Germany's isolation. As the land of music, Germany should at all costs find ways and means of retaining its top teachers.[42]

The dramatic sequel to the fight for this famous musician came some years later. Furtwängler's influence was sufficient to allow him to carry on teaching undisturbed until 30 September 1934. When it became clear that in general the foreign protests against German anti-Semitism restricted themselves to paper, the Nazi Party began to clamp down and enforce the restrictions. Flesch also had to give way. He initially went to England, before seeking refuge in Holland with his wife. In 1940 Hitler's armies caught up with him. At the end of the year he succeeded in coming to an agreement with the Curtis Institute of Music in Philadelphia which allowed him to obtain an entry visa to the USA. And yet the commissioner of the Reich for the occupied territories of Holland refused to grant him permission to leave. Again Furtwängler intervened, but by this time he was definitely no longer in the Nazi authorities' good books, and even his repeated efforts brought no success. In the process a year went by. The USA entered the war and shut their mission in Holland. Cuba seemed the next best possibility. Again the German occupiers refused their permission. Flesch once more turned to Furtwängler, who gave him a letter of recommendation to one of the commissioner's leading officials. There he was in the middle of the war asking for soft treatment for 'Jewish enemies'. It is not surprising that nobody had the courage to pass the letter on to the functionary. More time passed with nothing happening. The visa from Cuba expired. In September 1942 the Germans arrested the two Fleschs and transported them to the Scheveningen prison. His 'crime' was already on record: 'He belonged to that category of Jews who were aiming to instil Germans with an inferiority complex so that they could then manipulate them to their own ends more easily.'[43]

As they entered the prison they had to give up their passports. The officer registering the elderly couple, a woman, told them that they would be moved to a Dutch concentration camp the next day. When she found a letter of recommendation from Furtwängler amongst their papers she was taken aback; just to be sure she made enquiries with the addressee at the offices of the commissioner and must have received specific instructions: the Fleschs were allowed to return home. After a lot of red tape and further help from the conductor, they were allowed to leave, going first to Hungary and from there to the security of Lucerne, Switzerland. Even as he fled, his persecutors were still trying to ensure his total ostracisation; silencing precedes murder. This is demonstrated by their response to what they considered an unforgivable slip: 'Through an oversight, quotes from a review of the Hungarian violinist Flesch from the *Pester Lloyd* were printed in the music column of the overseas section of *Kulturspiegel* No. 93, page 8, 19 March 1943. This review must on no account be used or evaluated by the press.'[44] Without Furtwängler's efforts it seems certain that Flesch's life would not have been worth a ha'penny, even though his wife was considered 'Aryan'; although mixed marriages between members of the German Reich were 'privileged' so long as the partners' loyalty was demonstrated, such considerations were dropped in cases of foreign nationality – in this instance Hungarian. Yet even at the de-nazification commission the conductor did not make a great issue of his successes in helping people, and so, like many a good deed, they sank into oblivion.[45]

At the end of June 1933 Furtwängler was occupied with more than appeals for help. He was putting his plan into action, intending to cut through the brown-shirts' anti-Semitic prescriptions and make the functionaries look fools on their very own ground: ideology. This plan, which must have taken a lot of forethought, was cleverly contrived. Protected by the general licence offered by the Prussian concert dispensation, which he himself had formulated and seen enacted with this future strategy in mind, he wanted to fetch Jewish musicians into the country to appear in the next concert season with the Berlin Philharmonic. It would be a spectacular coup to pull off in the very heart of the Reich, a sure sign for all to see that quality came before race, and that art really was a free realm. This would undermine the boycott of the Jews, thus weakening the main plank of the Nazi Party programme – in view of the whole world, represented in Berlin by foreign correspondents. His idea was that if musical life continued as if there were no Nazi regime the hollowness at the heart of Hitler's ideological proclamations would be shown up and his political theories would be revealed as lies. He certainly let no one in on his plan, apart from his secretary. He had no use for witnesses. He briefly informed the Prussian minister for culture that he had invited soloists for the 1933–4 season, and gave their names. It must have been immediately obvious that here was someone who was trying to reverse the expulsion of the Jews. Dr Rust bided his time.

Furtwängler put letters of invitation in the post to the violinists Huberman, Kreisler, Menuhin and Thibaud, to the pianists Arthur

Schnabel, Cortot and Josef Hofmann, and to the cellists Casals and Piatigorsky.[46] He hoped that the musicians – especially the Jewish ones – would not cause his plan to come to nothing, even though he could not explain it to them properly. He could only give hints, hoping that their penetrating Jewish intelligence, which both fascinated and frightened him, would grasp the idea and draw the necessary conclusions. In order to make the situation clearer he added a copy of the press report on the Prussian concert dispensation to every letter. Would he be understood? He knew that people might have reservations. During the Brahms Festival in Vienna in May he had discussed the situation in detail with Huberman, who did not seem against the idea of performing in Germany again, but would not give a definite 'yes'. Since that meeting the government dispensation had been granted. The conductor tried to entice him: 'Someone has to be the first to break through this dividing wall.'[47]

A number of people wrote letters to Furtwängler on 1 July. One of them was the widow of a renowned music teacher and critic. She had heard 'that the name of Wilhelm Klatte and the memory of his work are still alive in your heart. In honour of this man please help his worthy son, who is being pursued as a non-Aryan, as you have already helped countless others who were being pursued.'[48]

Her son Arnold, a junior barrister, had been suspended without notice by the president of Berlin-Charlottenburg regional court III, despite the fact that – strictly speaking – he did not come under the 'Aryan clause', because his genealogical tree was 'marred' only by a Jewish great-grandfather. Furtwängler at once spoke to Commissioner Hinkel about the case, leaving for a holiday on the Baltic a few days later. A week later Frau Klatte telephoned Berta Geissmar, who briefed herself on the case by writing to her boss, after which she advised intervening 'with the right person at the Ministry of Justice'. The right person was the secretary of state, Roland Freisler.

Another letter dated the same day came from Fritz Kreisler. Under the impression that there was almost total anti-fascist solidarity among his fellow Jewish colleagues, he had had a change of heart and was cancelling. He either did not understand that the invitation was the beginning of a political campaign for a common cause, or he may have wished to compensate for his eloquent appeal to Toscanini in April. Whatever the case, he offered his regrets:

> I believe that if you call back only artists such as Bruno Walter, Klemperer, Busch, etc. it could do a great deal for the way art is viewed by the public both at home and abroad. It is a matter about which I feel as deeply as you do, but I fear that if I were to perform it might be seen as a compromise solution.[49]

Furtwängler was nonplussed at being reproached for trying to take things one step at a time, but of course the violinist was unaware of his overall plan, which was perhaps a good thing given that such information could quite possibly have reached the wrong people, as in fact happened a year later; the British prime minister told Kreisler in confidence that a coup was in the offing in Germany, whereupon Kreisler's 'Aryan' wife – having been sworn to secrecy – spread the story, until it eventually reached the Nazi Party's department of foreign affairs, which was able to organise counter-measures with which to destroy the 'Röhm revolt'. In the first days of July, looking forward to his holidays in Bansin and still hoping that his invitation would receive a positive response from the other musicians, Furtwängler nevertheless found that as usual he had to make time for orchestral politics in his busy schedule.

To begin with he settled various loose ends. He wrote a letter to Fritz Busch, who was unwillingly or unsuspectingly contributing to the Nazi regime's propaganda plans in Buenos Aires, and suggested that they should share the Philharmonic concerts that coming winter season between them. Busch, who was now getting more lucrative offers for guest appearances than he could take on, declined with thanks. There were many other matters calling for Furtwängler's attention, most of them urgent. Fearing that he might not get away on holiday he hurriedly scribbled to his secretary a list of things to be done:

> I am sending you letters from the following to deal with:
> LEIST: Please (possibly together with Schmitseck) sort out the text. Urgent.
> SCHÖNBERG: Now really need to get things moving.
> HALLER: Sort out by 'phone.
> FIEDLER: Perhaps now is the moment to show this to Busch etc.!
> COLOGNE: What should we do? What stance should we take? It will be the [same] wherever the resident conductor is not particularly popular. On the other hand cannot recommend too much competition![50]

The first of these was from Dr Ernst Leist, senior adviser at the Prussian Ministry of Culture, who had been dismissed on political charges, and was now working privately as a lawyer and associate in the banking company Berger & Co.[51] The significance of the Haller affair is still a matter of debate; given Furtwängler's frequent interventions in other matters, it is quite possible that he intervened on non-musical grounds. The retirement of Max Fiedler, general music director in Essen, on grounds of age – he was seventy-three – had opened a vacancy for the autumn; Furtwängler was still thinking of Busch. About the disputes in Cologne he could do nothing. Just how many requests for help he was able to settle by telephone, and which therefore are not documented, can only be a matter for conjecture. Even from Bansin he was involved in sorting out actual cases. Meanwhile Frau Geissmar and Schmidtseck in Berlin dealt with problems relating to cultural policy; the two complemented one another to perfection in preparing Furtwängler's next *coup de main*. He wanted to have more influence on the management and the supervisory board of the Berlin Philharmonic Orchestra, to make it his weapon and his guarantee against the Nazi regime. And of course there was also work to do concerning the Staatsoper. Just how indispensable his office in Berlin was is indicated by one of the reports Frau Geissmar regularly sent him:

> Intendant Hartmann visited me yesterday. He is only interested in one thing at the Staatsoper. It turned out that Hinkel at the commission knew nothing about the case, so will have to find someone else to deal with it. Maisch rang up and is coming tomorrow. Felix Wolfes too. I spent a long time with Kapp. I have been on a good footing with him for years now, and so he was quite forthcoming. What he said sounded quite plausible, but it would not be wise to

write about it. I went through all the applications for the Staatsoper with him. There were doubles of some, some had already been seen to, and he gave me the lowdown on several others. He told me what he thought about the room question, and I was able to pretend with a good conscience that I knew nothing. It might be a good idea to let him have his way, given that he has worked at the opera house for ten years and really means well. He is quite sceptical about what will happen when T. is here, and thinks it absolutely necessary that you should make your own position clear.

In the same report she informed him that Pablo Casals had refused the invitation, out of loyalty to his colleagues and because he wanted to be quite sure that the concert dispensation really was reducing the tensions. Because Furtwängler was away his mail went to the office, which meant to the flat she lived in; she forwarded only the most important items, took care of the replies, thus ensuring that 'business' continued under her attentive eye. That as a Jewess she should be banned from attending official meetings pained her initially, but she soon managed to gain access even to confidential information, which she then immediately forwarded to Bansin. Those were days in which important and high-level decisions about the future of musical activity were being taken, and Furtwängler had to be kept up to date:

As far as the meeting is concerned, apparently it was none too pleasant to begin with, until Hi shut up Ha by saying that there were always people for whom things were not fast or mindless enough. With the best will in the world I cannot understand why they keep a man like that, especially as the moment he has the opportunity in such meetings he speaks so rudely to his superiors that they have to shut him up in mid-sentence. Trapp was there, and Graener, who is supposed to have spoken very well. Kulenkampff was careful to say nothing, even though when it came to foreign affairs he was supposed to report that Holland had cancelled. It still seems to be the plan, if all musicians have to become part of the German Labour Front, to apply the 'Aryan clause' even to private tutors, even though there may be the possibility of some exceptions, as in the law for officials. But this is still at the negotiating stage. All the same, looked at objectively, the fact remains that even in the free professions race would be considered more important than ability, which would be further evidence that ability is no longer the prime consideration in Germany. If the free professions are to be restricted then the 'Aryan clause' should not be the basis on which to do it.[52]

Generally such meetings were attended by Schmidtseck, and he always had something to contribute. Whether it was a meeting with the commissioner of state, or the Propaganda Ministry, or Göring – his wartime flying companion – or Rust or the Berlin City Council, he was always there, and if they could not come to an agreement during the meeting he would go and have a meal with the functionaries afterwards. His clear thinking relieved Furtwängler of a great deal of the day-to-day organisational and juridical details. He had become indispensable.

In a letter written on 10 July from Castelveccana on Lake Maggiore Huberman was the next to decline the invitation. He lamented that the principle of merit should only apply in music and not in general, as if it were in the conductor's power to overturn racial politics at once and in all areas of life. On the other hand he was pessimistic about what a single person could achieve, and was convinced that 'the natural force of the collective conscience, once awakened, will tear down all resistance like paper walls'.[53]

Much romantic language but little understanding for a 'conspiratorial' undertaking within a racial war; Huberman was unable to fulfil Furtwängler's intentions, because he had already succumbed to sentiment. The conductor received his letter forwarded to Bansin; Frau Geissmar had prepared a carbon copy and – as with Casals' letter declining the offer – she gave a copy to Schmidtseck, who immediately informed Hanfstaengl, his direct line to Hitler. She added a note:

I do not wish to say any more in writing, but we are becoming increasingly isolated. If Menuhin decides to decline your offer (and it has occurred to me subsequently that he almost certainly will, out of consideration for Henry Goldmann, who after doing so much for German universities etc. had to leave Germany again in the spring in such unhappy circumstances), then your plan is no longer feasible. What the consequences will be for Germany is anybody's guess. Schmidtseck took Huberman's letter very seriously, he knows more of what is going on than we do. So that you can get a better overview I have included your letter to Huberman. Schmidtseck thinks it would be a very good idea to publish the exchange of letters. Of course some things would have to be changed I think. Schmidtseck has just come back from Hanfstaengl, whom he only told about the arrival of the letter. Now he has read it, likes it, but thinks it would be very dangerous to publish it.[54]

To make up for the disappointment Berta Geissmar and Schmidtseck tried to persuade Hitler's adjutant to arrange a meeting between

92

Furtwängler and the Führer. The conductor began jotting down preliminary notes for the discussion. At the same time he was occupied with a call for help from the university of Heidelberg, where he was an honorary doctor. Prof. Dr Ernst Hoffmann, a member of the Academy of Sciences, had brought an urgent case to his attention. The person concerned was the twenty-seven-year-old Dr Raymond Klibansky, an unsalaried lecturer in philosophy who had come unstuck over the 'Aryan clause' and been suspended; already a brilliant scholar despite his youth Klibansky was working on a critical edition of the collected works of Nikolaus von Cues, and the university boasted that 'he is probably the only scholar at the present time who has a complete grasp of all aspects of research into the history of philosophy in the fifteenth century, from the deciphering of texts right through to their exegesis'.[55]

The conductor thought the résumé of the professor's achievements unsuitable for a successful appeal. It was too academically dry and oppressively fact-laden. So he formulated his own version which he felt was more likely to unsettle any functionary who might read it. He gave it the eye-catching title 'Nicholas of Cues and Meister Eckhardt', followed this with seven brief lines in praise of the young scholar, and then brought in his argument, which focused on the planned publication of the collected edition:

> France is very eager to be the country which publishes these editions, and would put it in Dr Klibansky's hands if the Akademie had to let him go. If the Akademie were then obliged to continue publication without K., then France would still try to get Klibansky and use him to produce the only valid version. This means that the works of both these highly important German philosophers would further the glory of France instead of that of Germany.[56]

Once again he was playing the international hand which he thought seemed likely to win, and he sent the note to Hinkel asking him to take further action, which he did, sending it on to the Ministry of Culture as coming under their jurisdiction. Klibansky, who had not only had his permission to teach withdrawn but had also by special decree been forbidden access to his study in which lay the material and results of seven years' work, did not know that Furtwängler was defending his case. He only found out about it after the war by way of Colonel Nicolas Nabokov, who as a commissioner for the military government in Berlin had been made responsible for rebuilding cultural activity:

Herrn Staatskommissar H i n k e l .

Sehr verehrter Herr Pg. Hinkel!

Können Sie mir einen Juden nennen, für den Furtwängler
nicht eintritt? Aber im Ernst, auch wenn ich es wollte,
könnte ich für diesen Dr. Raymond Klibansky nichts unter-
nehmen, weil er ja Privatdozent an der Heidelberger Uni-
versität ist und somit mir nicht untersteht.

H e i l   H i t l e r !

Jhr sehr ergebener

Gerullis.

When I met Nabokov in the early autumn of 1945 he informed me
that a file had come to light in Furtwängler's dossier, which showed
that he had (1933) made considerable efforts to get my dismissal
revoked; in the margin there was a cutting and a very angry comment
in Goebbels' handwriting. This immediately proved how empty the
allegations concerning Furtwängler's behaviour were, and how different his behaviour was to that of Karajan and many others.[57]

The remark allegedly made by Goebbels – 'There isn't a single dirty
Jew left in Germany whom Furtwängler has not yet stood up for!' – has
appeared in all the literature since Boleslaw Barlog first quoted it in
1947,[58] because every author since has avoided going back to the documents. In actual fact the propaganda minister knew nothing of the case.
On the contrary it was Prof. Dr Georg Gerullis, ministerial director at
the Ministry of Culture and a close associate of Rust, whose signature
is really nothing like that of Goebbels' (see illustration). His answer,
which arrived at Hinkel's office on 20 July, was a little more civilised
in tone: 'Can you name me a Jew on whose behalf Furtwängler has not
intervened? But to be serious, even if I wanted to I could do nothing
for this Dr Raymond Klibansky, because he is an unsalaried lecturer at
Heidelberg University and so does not come under my jurisdiction.'[59]

It was true that Heidelberg came under the Baden Ministry of Culture, but Furtwängler's attempt did not fail for that reason alone. This was unfortunately a case occasioned by the law of 7 April, which allowed no exceptions: full-blooded Jews had to give way.

While Furtwängler was expending a great deal of energy in seeing to individual cases, he had to concede that his great plan to use Jewish soloists was threatened with failure; they did not want to appear in Germany as matters now stood. Berta Geissmar cheerfully advised him not to worry. She added: 'I had a long talk today with Hindemith, who was charming and said he had thought it over and would probably write you something different after all. I spoke with him about this whole question, he said he knew all of their points of view but thinks that our stance is quite justified as regards responsibility etc.'[60] There were some successes, such as a dispensation 'that artistic activity of foreigners and non-Aryans in the free professions, [. . .] i.e. disregarding the legal rights of officials, should not be hindered in any way'.[61]

Almost at the same time, and yet unexpectedly, his image was given a boost. The Prussian prime minister, apparently on a whim, rang Furtwängler to tell him he had been appointed to the Prussian Staatsrat. This came right in the middle of discussions about money for the orchestra; such a title could perhaps be useful. Frau Geissmar reported to Bansin: 'Generally people are putting a great deal of hope in your influence, and as it is said that the members of the Staatsrat are intended to support the government and are therefore highly trusted men, it does make an enormous difference. The office is very busy and we have just opened a new file, "F. Staatsrat".'[62]

The appointment was made public on 20 July, and it was now clear that he had obtained the advisory position for which he had been striving for so long. At this time no one saw what Göring was trying to do, namely to strengthen his dynastic power *vis-à-vis* his opponents by creating a harmless but impressive 'advisory body' – whose advice he would never actually heed – made up of assorted famous names. Furtwängler certainly did not let the title go to his head, although he was wide of the mark in his estimation of the responsibility which would go with it. This was why he still stressed 'the state's sense of cultural responsibility', possibly in the hope of convincing one foreign musician or another to change his mind; this sense of responsibility was so great, he claimed,

> that men who are completely apolitical representatives of cultural spheres and who furthermore are neither required to be members of the party, nor in fact are, are being called to join the new Prussian Staatsrat, formerly a purely political body. They are at the

government's disposal in an advisory capacity, and I too have been called to this body in such a capacity, in order to be listened to as an artist giving professional advice.[63]

As it actually turned out he was offering advice which Göring, Goebbels and Hitler did not want to hear at all. They cannot have remained blind to whose side of the conspiracy the musician was on. He in the meantime had thrown caution to the winds. He still hoped to be able to carry out his plan to break through the anti-Semitic front. To do so required the help of the musicians who were being discriminated against. So once again – from Berlin and under the suspicious eyes of the Gestapo – he turned to the one he thought most clear-headed and strong-minded, and that was Huberman. He now also confided his strategy to him:

For the politician – and how much more so for the artist – there is only one thing to do in this situation: take the given facts as foundations and build anew on them. This is the light in which the step I have taken and my invitation to you should be seen; and I am convinced that if you had grasped the hand I offered and accepted my invitation, then it would have had far-reaching consequences. Whatever is possible in Berlin would become possible in all the other German towns, and anything you did, all your colleagues would do in imitation of you. The things which happened in the world of concerts would affect all other areas of artistic activity, and more besides.[64]

At the same time – contrary to Goebbels, who preached the opposite – he pleaded the case for 'keeping the pure domain of art free of politics'; but as this contradicted the plan he had just told Huberman about for using music and musicians in a conspiratorial fight against the party's anti-Semitism, Huberman could make little of the letter. That was the end of the planned politico-cultural coup. This must have affected Furtwängler's self-confidence. There was soon a good opportunity to try this out.

Until then the Berlin Philharmonic had had to scrape along from one subsidy to another, always just avoiding financial collapse. Faced with a new crisis the conductor took action in two directions. One was the reorganisation of the orchestra administration. Schröder, the newly elected chairman, bothered him, not least because he was an ardent party member, but above all because he defended the unhappy merger, which was causing so many interpersonal and artistic problems which the 'boss' then had to deal with. The other worry was the economic one. Without a moment's hesitation he condensed all the important issues into one memo, gave it to the cooperative Herr von Schmidtseck, and sent him off to a meeting with Hitler in Bayreuth on 26 July. The commissioner was to seek help at the highest level regarding three questions. These were organised in the same order of importance as he had put them in on 4 July. At the top stood one name: Tietjen.

The general intendant of the Prussian state theatre had been prominent on the hit-list for a long time, even though he was 'Aryan'. He was so inscrutable that it was difficult to find any chinks in his armour. But because he wanted to put on good theatre productions he did now and again have to compromise with the brown 'revolutionaries'. A year earlier they had already told him 'that the German people not only want to hear and to see the works of its poets and composers, they also want them to be performed by German artists, because logic tells them that a Jew, however good a musician he may be technically, for spiritual reasons cannot be in a position to understand German works at their deepest level and to bring out their true content in performance'.[65]

This was sent by a retired ministerial councillor, a lawyer with party membership no. 244,930, whose wife described him as having a 'northern wife and northern beliefs'; after their marriage on 1 May 1930, she, princess zur Lippe, quickly adopted the modest title of Frau Marie Adelheid Konopath. Konopath was very active as a member of the KfdK and as head of the Nazi Party's department of culture and politics in Berlin, and was also author of several speeches on the question of race, and of 'Is Race Destiny?', a tract dealing with the fundamentals of the national movement, published by the notorious J. F. Lehmann publishing house (Munich 1926). He had early on sensed the forth-coming change in the political climate and so, in the course of 1928, had 'Aryanised' his Polish name Konopacki before it became a hindrance. He had demonstrated his party's use of music for political purposes by encouraging the formation of a Nazi instrumental ensemble, the German Concert Orchestra in Berlin which then gave rise to the KfdK orchestra. In other words he was an 'expert', and many others like him agreed with such criticism. As Tietjen had, within two weeks of assuming the post, dared to put on an unorthodox modernist *Tannhäuser* produced by Jürgen Fehling and with Klemperer conducting, he had to deal with the following question:

And what is Heinz Tietjen's response to this scandalous production? He is after all responsible for it since the opera house has been entrusted to his care. I fear that not a few competent judges and influential witnesses to this artistic outrage will voice their feelings in the demand 'Give us the general intendant's head on a silver platter!'[66]

97

When it became clear that the brown 'revolutionaries' could do nothing against the clever Tietjen, the critic continued his attack:

> So when is the Berlin Staatsoper going to be sorted out? Just about everything in the place, from head to toe, seems to need changing. It would be the devil's affair if it were not possible to make this institution into a show-piece theatre of the sort which we must categorically demand to have at the centre of the Reich.[67]

Of course even the slightest alleged lapse on the general intendant's part was entered into his dossier. His position became precarious. Three weighty accusations in particular counted against him: firstly the *Tannhäuser* production: secondly, relations with Jewish artists, as shown in a letter which Kammersänger Wilhelm Rode, a party member, had sent to Commissioner of State Hinkel on 25 April: thirdly, the Boerner affair. Charlotte Boerner, a young dramatic soprano who had worked at the Staatsoper in 1928, had then given guest performances in the USA, mainly in Philadelphia, and was now trying to get back to Berlin. Because Tietjen had other plans this resolute young lady began to pressure him. By threatening suicide and then actually disappearing without trace she set off a much-publicised series of interrogations, investigation of records and – above all – a sensational press scandal, which quickly died away after the headline which appeared on 25 April: 'Charlotte Boerner found unharmed'. The actress abandoned the battlefield, allegedly spending the 1933–4 season in Milan, and the following one in the Magdeburg municipal theatre as the press took malicious delight in pointing out. When the commissioner appointed to investigate the Tietjen case presented witnesses' reports that during the Weimar period he had even worked for the 'reds' and given money for a red flag, it seemed the last word had been spoken. By the end of May it was an open secret:

> The almighty Tietjen still holds the position of general intendant of the state theatres, but his days are numbered, and there can be hardly anyone who will shed a tear at his departure. [. . .] He was given all the prerequisites and the necessary authority with which to bring about great politico-cultural achievements, but what he leaves behind him today is a scene of destruction.[68]

This over-hasty journalist underestimated his readers; it would have been obvious that at issue were not great politico-cultural achievements but National Socialist, in other words narrow-minded, cultural policies.

For all that Tietjen weathered the storm. Behind him stood Furtwängler. On 4 July he had drily informed Rust at the ministry:

> If there is really nothing more which could be brought against Tietjen, then I would consider, given my knowledge of the theatrical mentality in general and more specifically of the aspersions in question, that to settle this case against Tietjen just in order to accommodate some general but not necessarily very well-justified feeling, would be an unforgivable perversion of justice.[69]

He was himself hoping for a constructive partnership with the Staatsoper – and with Tietjen, a difficult and unconventional producer and organiser at the best of times. Rust however did not wish to respond to the hard-pressed Tietjen's demand for a full apology, giving the usual reason that Tietjen could not really be treated as equal to a member of the party. Tietjen responded to this new affront by threatening to resign. In the memorandum which von Schmidtseck, acting as Furtwängler's 'ambassador', made known to Hitler in Bayreuth, the conductor cautiously supported the theatre director, pointing to the ultimately fruitless results of the enquiry and letting slip the word Bayreuth, a deliberate move, because Hitler was so keen on the festival there that he could well picture to himself what Tietjen's absence would mean. The long and short of it was that Tietjen stayed. And Furtwängler had made himself another – initially disguised – enemy, for Tietjen was by no means one to feel uncomfortable if he could not immediately repay one good deed with another.

The second point on the memo was the troublesome matter of the orchestra. Hitler discovered to his astonishment that the Prussian state wished to sacrifice the Philharmonic Orchestra to compensate for the financial burden which the upkeep of a state opera brought with it. Furtwängler described the maintenance of great absolute instrumental music as an honourable duty, and stressed this with his request: 'So I would like to ask the chancellor of the Reich to exercise his authority in this case, to the effect that firstly the Philharmonic Orchestra must be maintained under all circumstances, and secondly that an agreement on the distribution of resources and the reorganisation be reached as soon as is at all possible.'[70]

It was after all a matter of some 450,000 RM. Shocked, Hitler mobilised the propaganda minister, who had already given certain assurances. But Goebbels seemed in no hurry, as soon became clear. His slow response may have been intentional. He may have thought that this pro-Jewish conductor should be kept on tenterhooks a while; perhaps that would be the way to make him see that there quite possibly was a connection to be made between the Jewish question and the continued survival of the orchestra. At any rate one could frighten him by keeping him in the dark as to whether or not the regime considered his particular ensemble necessary, and obviously this was worsened by Goebbels' open lack of eagerness to help. As had been previously agreed Robert Ley of the German Workers' Movement (DAF) added to the situation by accusing two – unnamed – musicians of 'behaviour hostile to the state'. Havemann wrote to Hinkel in outrage: 'I have received about twenty telephone calls from different towns, asking what is really happening with Furtwängler and myself. People in the musical world think we are the ones being referred to.'[71]

Months later the accusation reappeared in a politico-cultural report from Rosenberg's office, providing further material for the day of reckoning if things had reached that point: 'Even the first conductor of the Berlin Staatsoper, Staatsrat Dr Wilhelm Furtwängler, does not seek to further National Socialist interests. Even today he still has the Jewess Fräulein Dr Geissmar as his secretary.'[72]

And yet Furtwängler would not leave off. Hitler read the title of the memo's third point with a feeling of self-satisfaction and was already almost sure that he would succeed in converting Furtwängler: 'How to fight the Jews in music'. A number of drafts have survived whose numerous additions, crossings-out and corrections show just how carefully the conductor chose his wording; not a word was left to chance, unlike in his spontaneous reflections on aesthetics and philosophy. Here his desire to be understood had a further goal; it becomes quite clear that Hitler was at last to be drawn into the very strategy that was aimed against him. Was Furtwängler possessed? Was he deliberately ignoring the difference in their respective strengths? To suggest that he was a naïve man who did not understand day-to-day reality is to miss the point. Such a man could hardly have reached such an exposed artistic peak. Besides relying to some extent on his secretary's help he himself needed to be fit enough to manage the struggle to reach the top in the artistic world. Is it illogical to carry what one has learnt in the professional struggle over into politics?

That title, 'How to fight the Jews in music', would be terrible if considered in isolation. But he was using it as a screen with which to disguise some of his most important attempts to help, knowing full well what would go down with Hitler and what would attract his attention. As the complete text proves, it was honey with a bitter aftertaste:

The accusation that we are barbarians because in our fight against the

Jews we have not shown sufficient respect for knowledge and art has grown to such dimensions abroad that in the case of music especially it has led to an almost total – but unorganised – boycott, to Germany being wholly cut off from abroad, which at one blow has destroyed Germany's world reputation as the land of music. If anywhere it is here that the fight against the Jews should be properly conducted. If for example a violin teacher such as Carl Flesch – who is today recognised to be the top teacher in the world – were to be thrown out of Germany now, it will not only be damaging materially (because all the best young violinists from all over the world will go elsewhere to study instead of Berlin), but also will give further support to those who accuse us of not being interested in art. I believe this case to be of the utmost importance for external affairs. Equally, I believe it necessary on the grounds of external relations that a man of such standing as the composer Arnold Schönberg should be given decent financial compensation. It is to be desired that such exceptional cases should be settled outside the framework of the law and all the usual channels, perhaps by the chancellor himself, bearing in mind the effect these cases have on our foreign standing.[73]

It is clear that what he was talking about was not how to fight the Jews but how not to fight them, using an argument which was bound to carry some weight in the early years when the regime was sensitive to external opinion. At this point Schmidtseck had to act as herald, informing Hitler that Furtwängler wished to know if he 'could' – though protocol would have suggested it, saying 'might' seemed to be going too far – speak to him personally about the preservation of what was now 'a completely run down concert-life and how this is connected to the Jewish question'.

The office had been trying to organise this audience for months, but in vain; now Schmidtseck was able to get a short meeting, which was only delayed once. And that was not all. Hitler made him certain promises concerning the orchestra. At least the troubled musicians heard from their 'boss' that things would carry on, and how: 'The Führer and the government of the Reich have given me their assurances that the Berlin Philharmonic Orchestra will be preserved whatever the circumstances. Dr Goebbels added to this assurance the condition that I am to have absolute control of all artistic and personal matters regarding the orchestra.'[74]

For the moment at least he could delude himself with the hope that the 'Führer principle' had been brought to bear in favour of himself and his plans, and that he could now use his authority to stop all internal

101

quarrels, and eventually make Germany's most prominent instrumental ensemble count on the political scales. He hastily prepared himself for his meeting with Hitler, elaborating and sharpening the arguments Schmidtseck had already introduced, organising them without a thought that they might be off-putting to a busy politician who was prejudiced and not very interested anyway. On the morning of 9 August he took the nine o'clock flight to Munich. From the main station there he caught the 13.40 for Berchtesgaden. When he arrived at about five o'clock in the afternoon he dialled 443, the telephone number of Hitler's house, Wachenfels, and was collected in the Führer's official car.

4

IN TIME, OUT OF STEP

A series of statements made in early August 1933 prove just how offended Furtwängler was by the rejections to his invitation. He was set on his plan to the point of obsession. Now his disappointment turned to anger, into bitterness at being so misunderstood. In his impulsive way he tried to overcome this by generalising and by shifting his political stance. If Hitler had only let him speak at their meeting on the Obsersalz-berg he might almost have been convinced that this was a convert standing in front of him – even allowing for possible tactical ploys. The conductor had intended to outline his attitude to the Nazi Party and its politics more or less as follows:

> I am a supporter, not a member, as I feel I am a musician rather than a politician.
>   The selection of musicians is impossible while public opinion remains subordinate to party doctrine. The most important task is to restore value to public opinion. Just as much a question of attracting real intellect as of removing Jews.[1]

A carbon copy of a typed and elaborated version based on the above was found in his papers, with a hand-written note beside it 'Drafted by Furtwängler alone for Hitler 8.8', an indication that he would usually have asked Schmidtseck and Berta Geissmar for their moderating and diplomatic advice. In this instance he wrote down his thoughts on the Jewish question without consulting them:

> In principle I share this view. Question not so simple when consider-ing higher intellectual activity. Essential: there is a conservative strand

in Judaism – the long preservation of their identity is proof of it and signifies an unusual strength, the tendency to define well-known works in intellectual terms. To us this often seems too intellectual. However I have reached the conclusion that this strength must at all costs be preserved and put to good use.[2]

Again he used the argument about publicity effects abroad to support his case:

Politics should be used in our external relations; it is here that we must appear to cooperate, without abandoning our intentions. *Suaviter in modo* should be our motto, which musical relations are particularly suited to putting into practice. Above all we must take care not to let ourselves be considered as something we are not because of this whole Jewish question. Propaganda concerning the Jewish question should cease to be obscure and blind in character. In so far as the Jew is an intellectual enemy he must be fought with intellectual weapons. Written guidelines by which to fight Jews must be abandoned – and only you can cause that to happen. Laws on their own cannot solve the problem because the problem lies in their application. [. . .] This and the fact that we are attacking innocent people puts foreign propaganda in a powerful position. This is inevitable, given the situation of the Jews as it now stands, and consequently we must be on our guard not to yield an inch over the fundamental principle. All the more reason though to employ every possible means to lessen the outward appearance of conflict. And I must say that much of what has happened in the realms of cultural activity has been quite unnecessary, and the removal of intelligent people has gone too far; intellectual matters cannot be solved by biology alone.[3]

A reading of this memorandum shows that – still with his plan in mind? – he wanted to do more than co-determine policy concerning cultural matters, he wanted to pre-determine it. He demanded to be heard before anybody else; he wanted, in addition to his position as Staatsrat, a sort of commissarial function between ministries which would give him automatic access to the Führer at all times. The tenor of his argument was that he or some supreme body of professionals should have this power, because there was currently a general state of confusion with people giving conflicting orders. He was not wrong in his appraisal. Goebbels, Rosenberg, Ley and Göring were still arguing about their share of responsibility for cultural policy; each wanted as much as possible, because each thought it would benefit his image.

104

The most pressing problem seemed to Furtwängler to be that of teaching appointments to music colleges and conservatories, because there was a lack of suitable people amongst the 'Aryans'; next most urgent was the question of the press. The memorandum mentions by name the music critics Zuckerkandl and Zschorlich, but an error had slipped into the typed version; instead of Zuckerkandl – the Jewish music expert from the *Vossischen Zeitung* who shortly thereafter emigrated to Vienna – he talks in the handwritten draft about Stuckenschmidt, and this would make sense. The names suggest that he wished to see the press moderated, marking as they do the two militant poles of the profession, both of which were equally irritating for practising artists: Stuckenschmidt so to speak on the 'left' and Zschorlich on the 'far right', both polemical, the latter in the *BZ am Mittag*, the former in the *Deutsche Zeitung*. Furtwängler was no less concerned with the 'brain drain' taking place in the Reich as a result of emigration:

> How serious the consequences of this great exodus of the most intelligent members of our society (which includes non-Aryans) will be, can hardly be gauged with any accuracy at present, but must of necessity lead to an impoverishment of that intellectual activity which formerly, even before 1914, lay at the heart of our nation.[4]

Furtwängler was still striving towards his goal of reversing Nazi policy towards the Jews. This was why he had wanted to bring a series of cases – which were far from being resolved to his satisfaction – into the discussion, skilfully stressing their significance: Flesch, Schönberg, Sekles, Klatte and, a recent addition to the list, Prof. Dr Curt Sachs, an expert on the history of musical instruments at the university and the Musikhochschule in Berlin, and Jani Szántó, a Hungarian violinist with a flair for contemporary music, whose teaching post at the Munich Academy was under threat. Not surprisingly he occasionally misdirected his efforts to helping people who did not merit it: for example Anna Bahr-Mildenburg, an 'Aryan' Wagner heroine and singing teacher who had been denounced for her relationships with Jews such as Bruno Walter, and who then, after the Austrian government expressed its hostility to the Nazi Party by making it illegal, joined Pfitzner and several musicians who were party members in demonstratively withdrawing from an appearance in Salzburg as a mark of their protest.

From dealing with these matters to dealing with the question of Jews in the Berlin Philharmonic was a small step. Once again Furtwängler stressed the effect the issue had abroad:

Significance for foreign affairs. Avoid risk of isolation. An art institute at which each individual is chosen according to merit. [. . .] I have already discussed the continued presence of the Jewish leader and members of the orchestra (6 Jews and 2 half-Jews) with the ministers Goebbels and Göring, and they were basically in agreement with me. There is however the risk that the Aryan clause will be brought to bear on the basis of the law concerning professionals, because the Philharmonic Orchestra is subsidised from public sources. (??) Must make it possible to make an exception. The Berlin Philharmonic Orchestra is at the present time the only institution to export culture and to serve as a propaganda tool for the German spirit which is still in demand abroad.[5]

At the end of the ten-page memorandum he lamented the 'isolation of the Führer', and suggested that it was necessary for Hitler to write to Toscanini about Bayreuth again after all. The conductor however had no opportunity to present even half his ideas; Hitler interrupted him and launched into a monologue. Furtwängler persisted even though he must have noticed that he was getting nowhere. The volume rose. Encountering resistance Hitler became abusive, digressed from the theme and pontificated on political matters. Agreement was out of the question. On the journey home, in Munich, the conductor rang up his secretary and gave her a report; he ended with an unambiguous statement of his view of the Führer. She later wrote that this conversation had been tapped.[6] At all events, the meeting had served in some way to draw up the lines of battle.

There can be no doubt of Furtwängler's enormous strength of will; showing not the slightest inclination to compromise he repeatedly set to – despite failures – to see his vision realised. He could not stop thinking about his invitation being refused. He still had his overall plan in mind. With great patience, acting as if he had never received a refusal, he renewed his invitation. It looks as though he either considered Huberman especially important or hoped that he would be more easily persuaded. A handwritten draft for this second invitation, which is really more of an entreaty, still exists today:

Personally as I said, I was striving, then as now, to keep art as pure and as independent of political influences as I could. It is not that I am not strongly conscious of how deeply rooted in the nation music is. There has never been music which did not have the nation as its source; but however firmly the tree of art is rooted in the worthy and inexhaustible soil of that mightily inspired collective we call the

106

nation, it must be able to stretch its branches and foliage to the sky, unhindered by any contrived pressure.

He advised Huberman not to 'become a mere tool of the politician in him'; what was at stake was the capacity to unite the people, to create a 'popular sense of identity derived from art but going beyond it'. The violinist's equanimity must have been ruffled at the point when Furtwängler angrily reminded him of the responsibility 'which you take upon yourself if you persist in declining the invitation, if you push away the very hand which through me is offering you the new Germany. It will not be possible to hold out this hand to you again in this way.'

In this draft for his secretary he had underlined in red the text he wanted copied into the finished version. Some arguments were to be left out, including the following:

> The performer has to overcome the terrible feeling that there are members of the audience who automatically assume that he is incapable of performing German music just as he has always had to reckon with the existence of hostile critics. And if you are concerned that the principle of merit is only applied to those performing in public concerts and not to other cultural activities, then you should be reassured by the example of your colleague Flesch, who is still working as Joachim's successor at the state musikhochschule in Berlin.[7]

He could not know that his key example would have to leave his job at the musikhochschule only six weeks later. But Huberman would not let himself be convinced anyway. In order to make this clear once and for all – to the point of being offensive – he sent a barely altered version of his first refusal from Vienna on 31 August. There were a few corrections to the text, and one informative addition; he now included 'the Busch brothers' in a list of positive actions taken against the racist 'purgers'. Despite Huberman's rejection the thwarted host did not give up his idea, he just decided that he would try putting pressure on Hitler again as he had not let him have his say at Berchtesgaden. In order to comprehend Hitler and his tirades properly he read *Mein Kampf*. There is no record of what he thought of this book – apart from one single sentence laden with double meaning: 'It was only when I read your book that I really understood everything.'[8]

In order to make his views heard he began writing a letter to Hitler at the beginning of September which contained all that had previously been left unsaid.

In the meantime his opponents were not inactive either. They were not going to be intimidated by his growing authority in questions of cultural policy. A second line of resistance arose. On 18 August a denunciation was sent to Rosenberg in his capacity as overall head of the KfdK. Its originator was Walther Rath-Rex, chairman and chief organiser of the cabaret group within the Greater Berlin branch of the KfdK:

> It is a common topic of conversation in artistic circles that Furtwängler still has a tendency to favour Jewish artists, as is particularly clear at this moment.
>
> 1. Through his invitation to the Galician Jewish violinist Huberman, who is well known for being a fanatical Zionist and has refused all concert invitations for a year in order to devote himself wholly to pan-European propaganda.
>
> 2. Through his invitation to the Jewish pianist Arthur Schnabel. It is an open secret that the driving force behind his favouring Jewish artists is Furtwängler's Jewish secretary, who together with her mother is said to use the opportunity of frequent personal contact to influence Furtwängler completely.[9]

Rath-Rex's tactic is obvious: as the conductor himself seemed impervious to any attack, it was necessary to go for his weakest point, his Jewish secretary, possibly also with the intention of distracting her boss; worrying about his indispensable assistant would clash with making further efforts on behalf of 'unknown' Jews. On the same day as Rosenberg received this report the chairman of the orchestra Höber signed a letter to the ministerial adviser von Keudell at the Ministry of Propaganda. In order to sort out the orchestra's finances Goebbels had drawn up a contract with the wealthy broadcasting service which – as in the previous season – was supposed to pay a certain amount for transmitting concerts, with an advance of some 30,000 RM. What was the contract?

> As I know him Dr Furtwängler will not accept Paragraph 3 of the new version under any circumstances. Herr Donisch's comments suggest that he fears Herr Furtwängler might engage Jewish soloists. This objection is groundless as Herr Furtwängler will definitely not engage Jewish soloists without the agreement of the Reich government. He will only do so if it is reconcilable with the general conditions.[10]

The governors of the broadcasting service knew that situation of course. The 'general conditions' still allowed freelance Jewish artists to perform; on the other hand the orchestra needed every mark it could lay hands on – and as soon as possible. Which was why they attempted to use this situation to muzzle Furtwängler politically. Furtwängler, with Hitler's words still in his ears, resisted this pressure and threw himself into work with the opera once his contract – which was still only verbal – began on 1 September. The highpoints of his programme were Zemlinsky's *Der Kreidekreis* which had already been accepted, *Der Freischütz*, Strauss's new version of *Ägyptische Helena* and Rossini's *Wilhelm Tell* reworked by Julius Kapp and Robert Heger. He also thought the Staatsoper should be given its due, namely by the inclusion of some representative items from the traditional German repertoire, but he added:

> It is the duty of the Berlin Staatsoper to nurture contemporary art. In connection with this it must be said that just because in recent years a somewhat one-sided and over-intellectual form of art has been predominant, this does not mean that all those who as a consequence were somewhat overshadowed were all great artists. Now, just as in earlier times, there are those who profiteer from the tide of events.[11]

Naturally in the fiftieth year after Wagner's death the repertoire – which in the 1933–4 season comprised sixty-five performances – gave prominence to the work of the Bayreuth master.[12] Furthermore, Furtwängler loved conducting these scores, which are complicated and demand such an exact sense of drama and timing if they are not to drag, and he conducted *Die Meistersinger, Tristan und Isolde, Das Rheingold* and *Die Walküre* throughout the whole season.

Two days after the first of the season's performances of *Die Meistersinger* he called the members of the Philharmonic to a meeting, at which, like a true 'Führer', he annulled the latest election and reinstated the previous management, forbidding any further discussion of the matter:

> He repeated his declaration that the Jewish question had been settled by agreement with the Reich. Any worries unnecessary as the Berlin Philharmonic Orchestra is guaranteed in its present form having been approved by the Führer and government. Staatsrat Dr Furtwängler presented Dr Schmidtseck as his representative. The latter after a short speech in connection with the election made all party members stand up and accused them of being ambitious climbers behaving in an undisciplined way.[13]

Schmidtseck, who suddenly saw himself as professional adviser and second man in the 'leadership', had – despite being the Nazi Party's representative in the orchestra – forgotten his original task, and was

Bln. 9.9.33

Sehr geehrter Herr Staatskommissar,

es war bis jetzt noch nicht moeglich ein
groesseres Vorsingen hier einzurichten, desshalb sind die von
Ihnen dafuer vorgeschlagenen Kuenstler noch nicht aufgefordert
worden. Selbstverstaendlich werden Ihre Wuensche in dieser Hin-
sicht genau beruecksichtigt werden,und ich werde veranlassen ,

dass ein Bescheid ueber den Verlauf jeweils an Sie weitergeleitet

wird.   Ihr sehr ergebener,

Berlin 9.9.33

Dear Commissioner of State,

It has so far not proved possible to arrange larger-scale auditions, which is why the artists you suggested have not yet been called upon. Naturally your wishes in this matter will be taken into consideration and I will make sure that you are informed of the outcome.

Yours faithfully,

Wilhelm Furtwängler

---

working, as one can see, against attempts to bring the orchestra into line. He had no difficulty warning people against denouncing their colleagues for political reasons.

After the irksome bother of the ceremony held to open the Prussian Staatsrat – which included an oath of 'unswerving loyalty to the nation and the Führer' – Furtwängler delegated his representative to a press conference at which the orchestra's programme was to be made public. The press reacted with alacrity:

Should the possibility of playing with the Philharmonic be withdrawn on principle from all conductors who come from abroad, even those of considerable standing? And what is supposed to happen with well-known soloists who would like to have an orchestra available? Do we want to and can we afford to cut ourselves off completely from all foreign contact? Would that be in our own best cultural interests? Surely we also wish those of our conductors who are well known to continue spreading Germany's reputation for cultural prowess abroad as they have done in the past.[14]

The programme for the 1933–4 season was obviously meant to prove something, namely that the absence of Jewish soloists was a loss which the music world could little afford. Melchior, the 'non-Aryan' Dane, was calculated to refresh memories; moreover Furtwängler was presenting the wholly or half-Jewish members of the orchestra Goldberg, Schuster and Bottermund as soloists. By way of contrast he also engaged the 'Aryan' Rudolph Schmidt, pianist and party member. In Hamburg – no less ostentatiously – the Jewish harpischordist Edith Weiss-Mann was allowed to step in at the 'last minute' to play the continuo in Bach's concerto for orchestra and double violins. The only great foreign instrumentalist on the season's programme was Mainardi. Apart from the renowned British conductor Sir Thomas Beecham, the 'boss' deliberately fetched in lesser artists: Sidney Beer, Henri Busser, Ebbe Hamerik, Odd Grüner Hegge, Hidemaro Konoye, Ottorino Respighi; but pointedly chose only individuals from northern and 'friendly' countries, or individuals concerned only secondarily with conducting. From Germany he made an equally studied choice of conductors who either came from the farthest provinces or were party members, and all of whom were members or supporters of the KfdK: Richard Jäger, Richard Richter, Edwin Lindner, Hans Hörner, Hellmut Kellermann, Werner Richter-Reichhelm and Hellmut Thierfelder. They played along unsuspectingly. He filled the gaps with worthy and long-time favourites of the public such as Max Fiedler, Robert Heger, Hermann Abendroth, Ernst Praetorius, Eugen Papst, Ernst Wendel and Schuricht, as if to show what was possible. As if this were not enough, the programme contained reminders of talented Jewish composers, namely Goldmark and Mendelssohn-Bartholdy. Schmidtseck of all people, a party member and commissioner, gave dazzling performances of music from the *Midsummer Night's Dream*. Some of the music critics and members of the public must have understood what this was all in aid of; at least one review was ringing with sarcasm:

It must be said that this is a noble and imaginative programme which

111

will bring those who made it possible the respect and thanks of all real music-lovers. It is a programme worthy of Adolf Hitler's strong and well-considered cultural initiative, which sadly has not hitherto been followed as eagerly as it should be. The fact that Furtwängler is watching over and monitoring all this beauty and that his highly developed artistic sense has joined with the Führer's artistic will in an eminently fruitful union, means we are guaranteed the best possible execution of this broad and historically suitable programme.[15]

The head of the Berlin Philharmonic Orchestra gave further hints as to what he thought about the musical policy of the NS officials, by himself conducting all the tours that season – except one in nearby Magdeburg, at which Eugen Jochum conducted.

Days and weeks passed. He had to correct mistakes on all sides. Göring had rewarded a performance of *Carmen* by the Italian diva Gabriella Besanzoni with a special bonus of 2,500 RM, and now Dusolina Giannini was asking for the same favour. Then the German Association for the Arts demanded a 20,000-RM government contribution towards an absurd music festival they were planning in Egypt. Furtwängler offered suggestions on all these matters. The German Association for the Arts, which did in fact subsidise the Philharmonic's foreign tours and guest appearances by foreign conductors, was only somewhat offended when Furtwängler blocked a concert tour through Latvia, Estonia, Finland, Sweden and Denmark, planned for autumn 1933. However Mutzenbecher, one of the managers, did not bother to ask for permission before going to the Russian embassy and discussing a cultural exchange between the two countries, suggesting to a wary diplomatic secretary, Hirschfeld, that 'one could and should be able to separate politics and culture. If for example one were to send Furtwängler one could surely be certain that he was purely a musician who would have nothing to do with politics.'[16]

Institutions and individuals – both political and cultural – were scrambling after the famous musician. Hinkel invited him to the preview of the propaganda film *Horst Wessel*, alongside Erich Kleiber and Georg Kulenkampff; poets and writers such as Hanns Johst and Werner Beumelburg, the actress Käthe Dorsch and numerous members of the party and government were present, including Prof. Dr Gerullis from the Ministry of Culture – one person who had assessed the conductor very shrewdly. When on 12 October Furtwängler introduced Strauss's new opera *Arabella* at the Staatsoper, Hitler and Goebbels' presence was almost taken for granted.

The future of the Berlin Philharmonic Orchestra was now

organisationally and financially secure; on 16 October the mayor of Berlin, Dr Sahm, and Funk, the secretary of state for propaganda, met for the purpose of settling what to do with the musicians who had been taken on from the disbanded Berlin Symphony Orchestra – it had become clear that the conductor was not to be crossed in his energetically defended determination to clear away this particular trouble spot. Three days later Schmidtseck informed the musicians of the latest development: all but a very few of the ex-members of the Symphony Orchestra would have to go, and the Philharmonic Orchestra would be taken over by the Propaganda Ministry and raised to the level of 'national orchestra', which in plain language meant that in future only the Reich would be paying subsidies. This disguised takeover by the state meant security for the musicians, but those who had to go protested. Dr Sahm tried to intervene on their behalf at the Propaganda Ministry, but he met with a rebuff from the secretary of state responsible: 'After consultation with Dept. 1, I have informed the orchestra (via Schmidtseck) that the minister sees no reason to try and influence Furtwängler's decision to retain only eight members of the erstwhile Symphony Orchestra.'[17]

The fifteen musicians affected by this would not let the matter rest. Many of them insistently pointed to their membership in the Nazi Party and took exception to the fact that they had been dismissed rather than the Jews. Worse still; places which should have gone to them had been taken by less able players – café musicians for example. It is true that the Berlin Philharmonic Orchestra contained erstwhile members of resort orchestras, as well as the former café musician Erich Bader, viola, and the cinema musician, Hans Kloska, viola, but these players had all long since reached the high standards demanded by Furtwängler. The legal adviser to the dismissed musicians brought matters to a head when at a meeting at the Propaganda Ministry he asked the representative from the ministry, Dr Schmidt-Leonhard, whether Hitler knew of the dismissals and claimed that as a result of them,

front fighters and party members are being affected while non-Aryans remain in the orchestra. At this the ministerial adviser jumped up from his place and declared that should that question be repeated he would declare the meeting closed. He stressed that the chancellor of the Reich was pressing for a decision and that we would have to abandon the positions we have held up till now immediately. If we tried to resist the ministry would have sufficient means at its disposal to force us. It would be of no consequence whether we were in the right or not.[18]

In the end the town took responsibility for relocating those who had been 'rationalised out'. One of them, the violinist Willy Bogenhard, who since 1 May 1933 had been party member no. 2,010,266, in fact advanced his career rapidly, even if not as a musician; he became the regional leader of the Reichsmusikkammer department XX in Pomerania in Stettin, also working for the Reich propaganda office there, and in February 1942 turned up in Riga as cultural adviser in the general commissioner's main propaganda department. Two years later he was on the salaried list of the Danzig propaganda department. As one can see, Furtwängler had been a key player in an 'act of liberation'.

Meantime untoward things were happening behind his back. One of the innumerable and unavoidable arguments about the parts for singers at the Staatsoper signalled the start of another page in his dossier, which at that time consisted in separate files in various offices. The Swedish soprano Nanny Larsén-Todsen, who was quite renowned and had already sung in the ensemble of the New York Metropolitan Opera and at the Bayreuth Festival, made a complaint to Hinkel, who promptly handed the case to Rust, adding of his own accord that 'Furtwängler and his Jewish secretary Frl. Dr Geissmar respectively are causing us a great many problems'.[19]

In the meantime the regime's cultural policy had been consolidated – organisationally at least. Music was to come under the roof of one single Reichskulturkammer. Membership of the Reichsmusikkammer would be obligatory and give automatic right to work professionally. Because such a form of corporate self-representation had long been talked of, and moreover had previously been familiar through the chambers of industry and commerce, the musicians' long-standing dreams seemed to have come true. That Goebbels had created himself an instrument of control and discipline was apparent only to critical observers. Because it was essential to have a man like Furtwängler in this centralised decision-making body, the minister included him in his calculations – perhaps even with the intention of channelling his irksome extra-musical energy yet further; he was not afraid that the prominent musician might outstrip him, because as president of the Reichskulturkammer and a politician he was the supreme authority, and for all eventualities he had arranged that the leadership of the Reichsmusikkammer should be shared by two colleagues, who if not exactly hostile to one another were definitely mutually suspicious: Richard Strauss as president and Furtwängler as vice-president. The latter received the news of his appointment on 15 November – the day the Reichskulturkammer was founded. Now he was simultaneously vice-president of the Reichsmusikkammer and a member of the presidential council. He accepted this – after consultation

114

Richard Strauss, 'Musikgeneral'

with the minister – as a tribute to his significance for musical activity in the country, and as an opportunity to increase his power to correct what he believed to be negative developments. It was quite a relief to know that in future he would no longer have to deal with lots of different subordinate officials who continuously contradicted and fought one another; henceforth he would only have contact with the minister responsible for art. The possibilities for propagating his cultural policy convincingly and successfully seemed to have improved. So he filled out the Reichsmusikkammer questionnaire no. 12,291, but left it until the following year to pay his Reichsmusikkammer contribution, which was supposed to be 1 per cent of income.

While the solemn opening of the Reichskulturkammer was taking place in Berlin and positions and responsibilities were being shared out at the first high-level business talks, the German Embassy in St. Louis, USA found itself with a politico-cultural problem which involved Furtwängler. The North American – 'expatriate German' – choral society was planning a song festival which was to include several orchestral concerts. Initially they wished to use conductors such as Walter

115

Damrosch from New York or Vladimir Golschmann, head of St. Louis' own first-class orchestra. The embassy advised against this on grounds of race and nationality, and recommended bringing over great artists from the Reich:

> We should like it best if you could arrange for Furtwängler to come over, as he enjoys a particularly strong reputation here. In discussing it with him it should be pointed out that he would both be doing the new Germany a great service and of course would himself benefit from the very great publicity he would receive, given that music-loving Germans, German Americans and Americans from all over the States will be gathering in St. Louis. I would be most grateful if you would be so kind as to get in touch either with Furtwängler or with another conductor.[20]

In fact the responsibility for using art for publicity purposes abroad still lay with the foreign office, but the consulate had heard about Strauss' and Furtwängler's appointments, and as time was short and there was the prospect that one of the 'American, generally non-Aryan conductors' might get the job, the Propaganda Ministry seemed better suited to solving the problem. Official adviser Klaus asked Furtwängler. He turned the offer down. He did not wish to appear as a musician advertising the Reich under such spectacular circumstances. So the Propaganda Ministry instructed the German Association for the Arts to recruit Busch. The association, which declared itself to be a 'non-profit making association for Germany's cultural relations abroad', and was legally registered as such, with the producer Hans Esdras Mutzenbecher as its managing director, was in fact a cover organisation used by Goebbels on occasions when the real promoter had to be concealed for political reasons. This was only one of a whole series of such organisations, which claimed to be wholly 'unpolitical' but were in fact supported by the Propaganda Ministry. The president – His Royal Highness Prince August Wilhelm of Prussia – enjoyed the same level of popular trust as the majority of the internationally renowned board of trustees. How could anybody know that 'Prince Auwi', as he was familiarly known, was not only a member of the party but even an SA-Oberführer? The public were equally unaware that while there were a number of personalities who served as frontmen, the board of trustees also contained people with definite ties to the party. A notable figure among these was a member of the Reichstag, Hugo Bruckmann, publisher of 'nationalist' literature, member of the KfdK executive, presidential adviser from the Reichsschrifttumkammer and, with party membership no. 91, a man who had been there from the very beginning. But who abroad would be likely to suspect it?

Mutzenbecher sent a telegraph to Busch – at Erich Engel's address in Zürich – making a confidential offer; the prospective honoraria amounted to $2,000. On 12 December Busch sent his 'most sincere thanks for your trouble and friendly greeting' but informed him:

I have had an exceptional number of offers for guest appearances abroad, and am at present waiting for the decision on a repeat series of concerts at the Teatro Colón in Buenos Aires which should arrive any day now. If that season does take place it will, as the follow-up to the last one, represent unusually successful publicity for German art. I would then have to go to South America mid-April, which would not allow time for St. Louis.[21]

Busch clearly did not wish to give a flat refusal, which would have demonstrated his anti-fascist stance. He asked them to wait for two weeks. The Propaganda Ministry was of course keen for him to go and tried to wait for Busch's decision, but it was too slow in coming for the American choir organisers and they engaged Damrosch, a Jew, perhaps particularly because the Nazis' racial doctrine found little favour abroad, even among expatriate Germans. In the meantime Busch arranged a second season of German opera at the Teatro Colón.

On 16 January 1934 Furtwängler belatedly signed the contract with the Staatsoper, to be retroactive to the beginning of the season and to last for five years. Now he had his positions in black and white: senior conductor for the Staatskapelle and director of the opera, with a yearly income of 36,000 RM. The Prussian prime minister, Göring, was party to the contract, having signed it with his own hand. The reaction abroad was much as might have been expected as foreign observers found it difficult to understand why the Staatsoper was linked directly to such a senior member of the party and the government. Ignorance of what lay behind such connections was a recurrent theme in the boycott of artists resident in Nazi Germany. Even in England, where the Berlin Philharmonic went the day after the contract with the Staatsoper was signed, the first signs of serious opposition were beginning to show. In order to lessen their impact Sir Thomas Beecham sent a public letter to one of the main London newspapers. He said appeasingly: 'People seem to be under the impression that this excellent ensemble has been robbed of its traditional independence and its conductor forced to renounce his life-long principle that art and music are to be kept separate from politics.'[22] Under the subtitle 'No racial discrimination' the prominent British musician continued:

> Nothing could be further from the truth. From my own personal observations and inquiries in Berlin I can safely say that the orchestra, which is due to appear in London next week, will, as far as its composition is concerned, be the same as the one which visited us last year. There have been no changes and racial discrimination has not been allowed. Such outstanding musicians as the orchestra leader and the two first cellists, all three of whom are Jewish, have retained their places.[23]

Berta Geissmar, who had travelled on ahead of the orchestra, was relieved to find that anti-fascist actions – not least thanks to Beecham's testimony – were kept within very narrow limits. At the same time she observed correctly how sharply hopes of any normalisation of the situation had dropped. Once back in Germany, Furtwängler conducted the Philharmonic as if everything were completely normal, playing among other things three excerpts from Mendelssohn's *A Midsummer Night's Dream*, in explicit recognition of this German, and also Jewish, romantic's 125th anniversary. Initially Goebbels had been expected to attend the occasion, but he was just in the process of defending his Reichskulturkammer against Rosenberg, a party ideologue who saw his field of jurisdiction as being narrowed by the Kammer, so Goebbels could not compromise. He would have witnessed for himself the very deliberate way the public applauded the Mendelssohn pieces. While the press did not go overboard in its praises it did make it clear that it thought this had been the last opportunity to hear Mendelssohn performed 'live'. The journalists clearly had not reckoned with Furtwängler's obduracy; he was still the one – faithfully assisted by Frau Geissmar and Schmidtseck – to draw up the concert programmes and he made sure that Mendelssohn continued to be played. So it happened that Hans Chemin-Petit conducted the same 'Jewish' pieces again on 7 October 1934, without even the slight protection offered by Nazi Party membership, being merely a member of the NSBO, the NSV, the Reichsluftschutzbund and the National Socialist old boys' association: 'harmless' organisations one joined if one did not wish to adopt a strong political position. At least one newspaper did report that the Mendelssohn and several other pieces had been performed in a 'singularly lacklustre fashion', and that the Philharmonic had unfortunately played as though 'their heart was not really in it'.[24] This may have just been due to the conductor's obvious unease. The official party press went somewhat

Mendelssohn ignored, *Der Angriff*, 14 November 1934

further; the music correspondent for *Der Angriff* was deaf to the Mendelssohn and passed over it in silence, as if it had never featured on the
programme, or even in Furtwängler's programme either.[25] This cavalier
behaviour was repeated towards the well-known violinist Georg Kulenkampff on the last occasion the Berlin Philharmonic's programme contained Jewish music; he played Mendelssohn's Violin Concerto under
Max Fiedler on 11 March 1935, and although the critic enumerated
several other pieces, he 'forgot' Mendelssohn and thus Kulenkampff as
well.[26] The latter had been given lengthy applause, with one non-party
critic giving special mention to 'Mendelssohn's Violin Concerto which
used to be such a popular and much-played part of the repertoire'.[27]

In the meantime Furtwängler continued giving one concert after
another, including part of the concert on the first German Composers'
Day on 18 February 1934, at which Paul Hindemith amongst others
mounted the rostrum to conduct his Concert Music for brass and strings.
Although this piece evoked a mixed response from the public, some of

whom applauded while others showed their displeasure, there seemed to be much fellow feeling among the creative musicians – no doubt encouraged by the idea of a musicians' union (Musikkammer) – which could bridge all differences of style and direction. Didn't Hindemith sit on the executive council of the Reichsmusikkammer? At this festive occasion appearances were certainly deceptive. Problems had already appeared before the Christmas holidays; different authorities came into conflict with one another. Strauss wanted to make the Reichsmusikkammer an illustrious body representing the interests of musicians, and so thought it would be fitting for it to have its own official newspaper. He let himself be persuaded by Mahling and Havemann that this could only be *Musik im Zeitbewusstsein* (Music in Our Time) – it did not seem to matter that Mahling happened to be its editor. Only the vice-president opposed it on organisational grounds and called upon Goebbels to settle the issue. But he had left for his Christmas holidays, despite having previously made an appointment to meet. As there were more important matters to be seen to, Furtwängler did his usual thing of noting down a few key points for later talks with Hitler and Göring. These notes are some proof of how very much he was concerned with the entire spectrum of musical activity as well as his own narrower field. He took his advisory function seriously.

In his own field danger-signals were becoming ever more frequent. To sound out where best to begin 'repairs' to the orchestra, the Propaganda Ministry had given one of the Reich's financial commissioners the task of formulating an expert opinion on it. One of his conclusions was that 'there seems to be no justification for making use of the conductor's private secretary, at the expense of the company, in preparations for concerts'. It is probable that the commissioner knew that Berta Geissmar did the work of two ordinary people, if not a bit more. But maybe an 'expert opinion' could be used to get the Jewess out of the way? The management complained to the Propaganda Ministry:

> The so-called 'private secretary' of our chief conductor, Dr Furtwängler, does not actually work on his private business. Much of her work consists on the one hand in the wide-ranging task of preparing the orchestra's concert tours; on the other in dealing with all matters which arise when a conductor in this top position works with his orchestra. It involves some eighty to ninety concerts both in and outside Berlin.[28]

Furtwängler responded on the same day, with nineteen pages of detailed counter-evidence which revealed the financial commissioner for

120

what he was, a witless bureaucrat who knew nothing of orchestral organisation. The threat passed over. Once again an attempted attack had been thwarted. Unimpressed, the unyielding conductor picked a quarrel with the Cologne Gauleiter. Staatsrat Josef Grohé – influenced by Walter Trienes, party commissioner for the political reform of the music college, and a writer on matters musical – had suspended the director of the college, Hermann Abendroth, on the grounds of 'political unreliability', and was threatening to withdraw his conductorship of the Gürzenich orchestra. Furtwängler responded harshly to the Gauleiter's arguments. He suggested that he was 'acting according to unassailable National Socialist principles, which naturally must remain the starting point of all debate. It may be though that he has been one-sidedly and inaccurately informed by his advisers and informants.'[29]

Despite the conciliatory tone of the introduction, he used his nine-page broadside attack on Trienes to tear those principles to shreds, supported by a letter of some days earlier from the government to Abendroth asking him to conduct in Russia again after all, as the Reich considered it important to have good relations with the USSR. Furtwängler was fully behind the now threatened Abendroth; should Abendroth lose his position, 'I hold it to be my duty as Staatsrat to insist that the other well-known musicians who are currently to be found in important positions should be subjected to an investigation into their past prior to the overthrow, and into their connections with left-radical circles or regimes.'[30] This was intended to include himself; had this been done there would only have been a few party members left who had sufficient musical experience to be able to represent German music. The top-level officials could well imagine this horrific scenario. Shortly afterwards Göring declared that the special commissar was no longer necessary. Trienes desisted from Jew-baiting and Abendroth resumed his teaching and conducting activities at the musikhochschule.

However, the enemy regrouped, again trying to move up on Furtwängler's flank rather than attacking him frontally. In this case the flank was Hindemith. The circle around Rosenberg and his KfdK were especially angered by the attention given to him by the Reichsmusikkammer and which he had attracted as the most significant of the Reich's younger composers at the German Composers' Day: they also hoped to be able to deal a blow to the hated Goebbels. The attack began in a music periodical with a feature article purporting to analyse the press's response to the Composers' Day, before then coming to the real point:

We have gone into such detail over the Hindemith story because we see it as a symptom, a case which will have fundamental and far-reaching consequences for the future development of our music. What is at issue is obviously not Hindemith personally; greater things, namely the well-being of German music is at stake! Should Hindemith be used to prepare the way for other composers of his ilk?[31]

As the composer was already announced with a première for the ninth Philharmonic concert, Furtwängler scarcely paid attention to the 'purgers', especially as he had prepared well in advance and made sure that the work which he wished to present for the first time in the Prussian Staatskapelle on 12–13 March, was kept out of the more politically sensitive Staatsoper. He could well do without demonstrations in the 'hallowed hall', and the Philharmonie was a safer place to accommodate novelty items; so this is what happened, with a change of programme one week before the concert was due to take place. Hindemith's symphony *Mathis der Maler*, first performed on 12 March, excited a great deal of attention.[32] Stuckenschmidt declared it a 'triumph for contemporary music'[33], for which he was of course labelled a 'cultural bolshevist'.[34] But praise was the order of the day. One critic even wrote: 'Furtwängler should today be thanked for a deed which gave vivid and emphatic proof for all to see of the new state's intentions for the future and of the respect in which it holds creative personalities.'[35]

Even the party press almost went under in all the clamour of acclaim. *Der Angriff* itself showed no restraint;[36] the perplexed music critic on the Nazi Party's main paper had to admit that 'there was no excuse to talk about a "Hindemith case" in the past, and certainly not on this occasion'.[37]

But it was just at this point that the 'Hindemith case' really took off. One of the co-authors of the original dispute had set the ball rolling:

It is difficult to find any contemporary music which is less linked to the German nation that that of Hindemith. There is not a trace of the German spirit to be found in it. It stands in sharp opposition to all the requirements which, as the Führer and his subordinates have so emphatically pointed out, determine the musical ideals of the new Reich.[38]

At the beginning of February the public had learnt from the press that Hindemith was working on a new and full-length opera about Matthias Grünewald. This was no longer just the object of general concern, but also of the 'tactical plans' made by the clique around Rosenberg, who, because of Hitler's well-known dislike of the composer, felt in a strong position. The surprisingly positive reception accorded to the symphony

aroused fears in this circle that it might provide a starting point from which Furtwängler, Hindemith and like-minded colleagues could soften up Nazi ideology. At that moment however, the conductor was clearly not concerned with undermining ideology; he once again found himself with his back to the wall. While the press still resounded with praise of the symphony, a new problem had suddenly arisen with the orchestra. At a meeting in the Propaganda Ministry on 14 March he made the unpleasant discovery that nothing was happening as he had wished. The real 'Führer' of the Reich's orchestra was not himself but a strong executive committee; in order to set this up and make it of some use the ministry had let the orchestra retain its status as a limited company. Furtwängler was allowed to remain first conductor, as per contract – with personal responsibility for a certain number of concerts at home and abroad. The committee would appoint two managers, one business and one artistic, the latter also to be the second conductor. Greiner and Funk wanted to get rid of both Höber and Schmidtseck, proposing to replace the former with a 'Herr Müller' and the latter with Schuricht.

Max Müller, the son of a church organist and choirmaster, had joined the Nazi Party in 1931, membership no. 690,992, and now, at the age of fifty, held office in the party. He had been trained as a salesman and had worked for many years as managing clerk for Steinway & Sons, organising the office and sales, before being sacked despite his three languages and relevant knowledge. He made himself known by sending applications to every conceivable official department. Even Hitler got to hear that this worthy National Socialist expected to be considered when it came to allocating jobs. Might this man have been deliberately placed in Furtwängler's path? Perhaps a surprise blow was intended, because since 1 March he had been working as the 'Aryan' manager in the offices of the famous concert agency Wolff & Sachs, which was threatened with an 'Aryan' reform. Funk at any rate was sure that Furtwängler would come to terms with this Herr Müller, should the ministry decide to appoint him. Müller, had in fact, at the party's recommendation, already applied for the position in January 1934, but had immediately been denounced as a 'paralytic' and as politically unreliable; the denunciation was the work of his enemy Rudolf Vedder, who wanted to shut him up, because he knew about a youthful crime.

A second possibility for Höber's replacement appeared towards the end of the month. Paul Wehe applied to the Propaganda Ministry. He was fifty-nine, the son of a goldsmith and himself a very skilled goldsmith, and since 1 September 1930 had held party membership no. 297,700. He had been an export manager, later both technical and sales director for a charcoal and peat works in Holstein, and most recently

124

had been involved in a company extracting fuel from indigenous mineral resources. His knowledge of the music business was zero. The ministry repeatedly bothered Furtwängler with references to 'the chosen two', but kept the final decision hanging in the balance for two months, plainly as part of a war of nerves. Only at the end of May did Wehe hear,

> I am sorry to have to tell you that your services as manager of the Berlin Philharmonic Orchestra plc are not required. Herr Furtwängler had such strong feelings on certain matters that we did not feel we could ignore them. I am therefore sincerely sorry to have to return your application. I do hope, in view of the difficult circumstances relating to this matter in particular, that you will accept this and not take it personally.[39]

Meanwhile it had been decided to give Schmidtseck a last chance by appointing him business manager; hardly a great comfort to Furtwängler, who was left with two inescapable problems as Secretary of State Funk had made clear to him: Berta Geissmar could not remain an employee of the Reich orchestra, and while he remained at liberty to continue employing her personally there would be no special remuneration forthcoming from what was now the Reich's own company. Secondly, he no longer had a place or a vote on the supervisory board, although of course his advice would always be considered. Effectively he was being stripped of power. Goebbels wanted to keep the reins in his own hands, and this was reflected in the membership of the executive committee. It comprised four representatives from his own office; Secretary of State Funk as chairman, the director of the Ministry, Dr Greiner, and the ministerial advisers Dr Ott and von Keudell in addition to State Secretary Pfundtner from the Ministry of the Interior and the ministerial adviser von Manteuffel from the Ministry of Finance; only one representative was allowed from the orchestra: Höber. The members of the Berlin Philharmonic had sold themselves for about 50,000 RM – the personal liabilities which the Reich had returned to them. As a nationalised company they made no decisions any longer and could only listen.

In the meantime Frau Geissmar was busy setting up a counter-move in defiance of the brown-shirts. During an almost month-long concert tour of Germany, France, Italy, Switzerland and Luxemburg she engaged in diplomatic activity. On official letterhead from the Hotel Scribe in Paris she informed the Reich's ambassador in Rome, Herr von Hassell, that 'the Italian head of government will receive Herr Dr

HOTEL SCRIBE
PARIS

PARIS HOTEL SCRIBE
       HOTEL ASTORIA
       HOTEL MODERNE
CANNES CARLTON HOTEL
ANTE CARLO HOTEL DE PARIS
       HOTEL HERMITAGE
       BEACH HOTELS
MEGEVE HOTEL DU MONT D'ARBOIS
TROUVILLE HOTEL DES ROCHES NOIRES

17. IV. 34.

Sehr geehrter Herr Botschafter,

Herr Minister Stiewe hat
mir einliegenden Brief gegeben.
Ich schreibe Ihnen schon von Paris
weil ich die Nachricht heute erhielt
daß der italienische Regierungschef
Herrn Dr. Furtwängler empfangen
wird. Obwohl in dem Schreiben alles
nähere enthalten steht, möchte ich
in Rom doch erst bei Ihnen vorsprechen.
Ich komme Samstag abend an,
Herr Dr. Furtwängler kommt Montag abend mit dem Orientexer
an. Dürfte ich um eine Nachricht
im Hotel Eden bitten, an wen
ich mich wenden darf, oder ob ich
mich bei Ihnen sehr geehrter Herr
Botschafter selbst melden darf –
Mit den besten Empfehlungen
Ihre sehr ergebene
Dr. Berta Geißmar

Furtwängler. Although all the details are dealt with in the letter I would still like to call on you first.'[40] Just to be sure she asked the German Embassy in Paris to second her request and to recommend her in Rome, which the diplomats did willingly, as they did not identify with their regime's racial policy: 'I am complying with her request, even though as I said to Fräulein Geissmar it is unneccessary, as I am sure you are aware how much Herr Furtwängler values her as his assistant.'[41] By the time the letter arrived ambassador von Hassell had already spoken with Frau Geissmar. The meeting with the Duce took place a few days later. In a report to Berlin the ambassador emphasised: 'Even Mussolini, who received Furtwängler on the occasion of his visit, expressed his great satisfaction to me. The king honoured Furtwängler by bestowing a mark of distinction on him.'[42]

This spring tour by the orchestra, although a great success, demonstrated still more clearly the position the Jewish musicians were in. They were the object of ever more violent racial hatred. A report from Mülheim even complained to the government

> that we have just had to put up with the Jewish leader Goldberg in the first desk for the nth time. We do not understand why it is that Furtwängler, who as a Staatsrat has accepted the guidelines of the National Socialist state, in this instance has not yet made the thorough changes necessary, nor why a scarcely believable exception should have been made for him, after all a musical representative of the Third Reich, or for his orchestra, which is supposed to be the Third Reich's most representative ensemble.[43]

By the time the paper carrying this article appeared, the conductor was already in Paris, but he read what the 'purger' had written a few days later. How long would he be able to keep the Jews in the orchestra? Had he not done everything within his powers?

That spring a mysterious chain of events occurred, the consequences of which would come back to trouble him shortly before his death. In 1954 Dr Curt Engelmann, a doctor who was married to the singer Violetta de Strozzi, wrote to him from New York as part of his attempt to obtain reparation payments for his wife. He had found out from Tietjen that her 'dismissal' at the end of March 1934 on grounds of 'marriage to a non-Aryan' had been signed neither by the general intendant responsible, nor by his managing director, but by the state's senior conductor. Now Furtwängler, who could no longer remember, was supposed to verify that the dismissal had had to occur because of the Reichsmusikkammer's laws, as the singer was married to a Jew. Dr

Engelmann added that he suffered from a heart condition and that his wife had had to go into a sanatorium: 'She never recovered from the shock of Göring threatening to arrest me. In my absence Göring twice managed to send his adjutant, Captain Müller, to my flat, with the following suggestions; that she divorce me, accept the title of 'Kammer-sängerin' for a salary of 60,000 RM and be more "friendly" to him!'[44]

The fact of the matter was that Furtwängler had nothing to do with personnel matters either at the Staatsoper or at the Reichsmusikkammer; at the Reichsmusikkammer it was the responsibility of the manager Heinz Ihlert, who had been given power of attorney by the president Richard Strauss – which included removing 'non-Aryans', while at the Staatsoper the managing director Franz Josef Scheffels was responsible. As the singer was engaged on a one-year contract which was renewed as and when necessary, it could not possibly have been a case of 'dismissal'. On 10 July 1933 the minister for science, art and popular education had given his written assent to a list of people it proposed should be hired for the 1933–4 season – including Violetta de Strozzi; the fact that Göring wrote 'OK' at the bottom of the estimate is some indication that everything was in order.[45] It is quite correct that the singer had already been denounced as a 'Croatian' on 9 February 1933 by the theatre and film section of the KfdK, and so if she had once been removed by the Reichsmusikkammer or the Reichstheaterkammer on racial grounds, she could no longer have been employed, unless that is she had complained and obtained special permission from Göring, which he sometimes gave in individual cases. As Göring was prepared to protect even 'full-blooded' Jewish members of the Staatsoper who seemed indispensable to him, it may be that there was some personal animosity at work here. But even then she could have been excluded by not renewing her contract rather than by a 'dismissal'. What Furtwängler was supposed to have to do with it is not clear, unless he was to be drawn into a late settling of accounts which Tietjen made possible by denying all blame. In not one of the archives is it possible to find any such evil documents signed by this man who fought for the preservation of 'non-Aryan' musicians with so little thought for himself.

On 9 May the Propaganda Ministry received a request from the leaders of the exiled Austrian branch of the Nazi Party to call a halt to Strauss' and Furtwängler's participation in the Salzburg Festival because of the political situation: '. . . the festival has considerable propaganda value for the Austrians' foreign relations, and it is for that reason that our party comrades in the country are using all available means to boycott it'.[46]

The official adviser laid a note regarding the problem on the minister's desk, just in case. On 20 May Goebbels wrote in the margin: 'Should not take part! Dr G.'. Five days later two identical letters were sent to the composer and the conductor, in which Funk informed them that the minister had asked him to inform them that guest appearances at the Salzburg Festival 'would be contrary to the Führer's policy towards Austria, and so he requests that in the interests of the political situation you do not participate at the Salzburg Festival'.[47]

That is what then happened, a further example of the way art can be used 'negatively' for political purposes, namely by not allowing it at all. This was an extreme case in that it meant a lost opportunity for publicity. In view of the conditions prevailing in the Reich it is not surprising that Furtwängler did not dare to spite the Führer's 'request'. Such unaccustomed compliance strengthened his politico-cultural status in Berlin – despite his liking for Hindemith – as did a pamphlet which he brought back from his guest appearance at the Paris Opéra. It was a document of slanderous hatred which wounded him deeply, even though he immediately recognised what a political gift had come his way; among other things the pamphlet contained the following:

We accuse Staatsrat Dr Furtwängler of aiding and abetting crimes such as murder, arson, robbery, theft, fraud, torturing the defenceless and, above all, keeping silent about the truth. Staatsrat Dr Wilhelm Furtwängler has proved in word and deed that he wishes to 'beautify' and 'defend' Hitler's bloodied and tyrannical regime with his art, and by abusing the great works of the classical composers. His membership of the Staatsrat is a favour from Göring and Goebbels. Staatsrat Furtwängler made no protest when Germany's best musicians, including Otto Klemperer, Bruno Walter, Arthur Schnabel and Arnold Schönberg were driven out of Germany, their own country.[48]

The author of the pamphlet was a composer of what the conductor would have regarded as propaganda songs, and such things lay outside his demanding and bourgeois tastes. Eisler championed what he saw as the working class, as well as promoting himself – an emigrant in Paris with moderate commercial successes in cinema and theatre. Furtwängler was conducting a short summer season in the French metropolis. He began with *Tristan und Isolde* in German; Melchior and Frida Leider played the title roles, and their performances were not interrupted. Eisler's pamphlet had most effect in Berlin. At the Propaganda Ministry they must have shaken their heads at such ignorance and intellectual confusion; after all they knew their Furtwängler, the 'Jew-helper'. And yet, as often happens with such absurd accusations, something stuck. If

129

German musicians march in time, as seen from Moscow in 1933

this man were attacked by an émigré left-wing Jew who really ought to be able to distinguish friend from foe, then there might well be a grain of truth in the accusation, and if that were the case it would make sense to trust Furtwängler, his victim – although always with a grain of caution, of course.

On 1 July Simon Goldberg and Joseph Schuster retired from the Berlin Philharmonic Orchestra; they were neither dismissed nor thrown out, but went of their own accord because they could not stand the psychological pressure any longer. Their position had been truly 'impossible'; as Jews were not wanted in the Reich they had obviously been 'protected', or at any rate privileged. Furtwängler lamented their departure, because now it would be harder to demonstrate how stupid and corrupt Nazi ideology was. On the other hand, was it really necessary to prove it?

Eisler's pamphlet certainly set an example. Already in early spring a very unlikely authority, the Commission for Economic Policy at the Nazi Party's headquarters, had issued a statement on rumours concerning Staatsrat Furtwängler, possibly in an attempt to implicate him in financial crimes – such as tax-evasion for example. On 27 April a police inspector in Essen drew up the minutes of a conversation. Ludolf Schmidt, administrative director of the Volkwang Schools and a party member, had come to help the former director, Kurt Jooss. Jooss had since emigrated and was on his way from England to Vienna. Schmidt

130

wanted to apply on his behalf for exemption from the thousand-mark tax with which the Reich was curtailing traffic with Austria. The policeman asked Schmidt

why he was so keen to help Jooss. In my opinion there was no reason why anyone should so much as lift a finger for him as he seemed to have been unable to separate himself from Jewish capital and the Jew Cohen and so had put himself outside of German society. To which party member Schmidt responded that I was too harsh in my judgement, and asked whether I was aware that Staatsrat Furtwängler still has Jews in his orchestra and even now still employs a Jewish secretary.[49]

The official was clearly thrown; he had discovered something which should not be possible in the Third Reich and yet clearly was. Disturbed, he sent his report through the official channels. After several detours it landed on the desk of von Keudell, ministerial adviser, causing him headaches too. He drafted an ultra-smooth answer in which he said that the non-Aryan Goldberg had left the orchestra, and that he did not consider the other Jews worth mentioning. He was reprimanded in a memorandum from his colleague Rüdiger: 'I consider any answer futile for the simple reason that the assertions in the police report that Furtwängler still employs Jews, and even today has a Jewish secretary, are true. The evasive character of the answer is immediately obvious, given that the police report does not mention Herr Goldberg once.'[50] And so no answer was sent. The inspector in Essen and the various official channels he had followed, including the Nazi Party's racial policy department, were left to their uncertainty.

Furtwängler took similar chances in his talks with the Propaganda Ministry concerning a new contract. After long discussions with Schmidtseck, followed by talks with the newly appointed deputy manager, Karl Stegmann, a draft proposal was drawn up. In order to consolidate his power further Furtwängler had had a paragraph 9 inserted, which reveals what he was hoping to achieve: 'If public bodies fail in any serious matter to act in accordance with Dr Furtwängler's intentions concerning artistic direction, then he has the right to withdraw from this contract without giving prior notice.'[51] This was intended as a warning. The people in the Propaganda Ministry understood and they returned a modified draft as a counter-proposal. It no longer contained a paragraph 9, but a completely new paragraph 7 instead; this granted the conductor the right to choose the soloists for his Philharmonic concerts, but no others. There was only one condition: 'It is however not possible to engage non-Aryans.'[52]

Furtwängler, who had ostentatiously installed his Jewish concert-master as soloist for the first and third Philharmonic concerts – contractually acceptable because he was already under contract rather than being contracted for specific occasions – signed neither this nor a later version drafted on 16 October, which was for a three-year contract. It contained several novelties, such as – astonishingly – a grant of 10,000 RM for his personal secretary, in other words for the Jewess Berta Geissmar; the ban on engaging non-Aryans was replaced with an altered version of paragraph 7: 'In exceptional cases the permission of the management must be sought' – really only a cosmetic improvement given that the Propaganda Ministry firmly controlled the managers. He was even more upset by the newly incorporated obligation to give 'free concerts on special occasions when so required by the minister of the Reich'. In fact he had avoided the request to conduct the music for the funeral of President of the Reich von Hindenburg, and for almost the whole of August had been unreachable on the Górzno Post Garzyn estate near Lissa in Poland. Although von Keudell agreed to the contract on 8 November, Furtwängler refused to sign and continued working without a written contract. The ministry assumed, as was legally perfectly correct, that a contract had been arrived at by mutual compromise and verbal agreement.

That he had no intention of giving in over the Jewish question is proved by his choice of a successor for Goldberg. He decided on Hugo Kolberg. When the bureaucrats at the ministry learnt that the violinist had been offered – with the minister's permission – a very high monthly salary of 1,000 RM, they took the precaution of enquiring whether this was correct. Goebbels himself wrote: 'Yes!'. The draft of the five-year contract – which was also an unusual length – contained a sentence, probably formulated by von Schmidtseck, which could not have been clearer: 'The contract is entered into in the full knowledge that Herr Kolberg is married to a non-Aryan.'[53] Funk did actually ask for this to be removed, and so, when the violinist joined the Berlin Philharmonic Orchestra, the Nazi authorities were obviously fully aware that he was married to a non-Aryan. Not all plans were executed so successfully.

Difficulties were beginning to appear at the Staatsoper. Some were trifling matters which were easy to deal with. When Georg Wollnick, assistant manager and the leader of the NSBO cell, tried to get involved in questions of whom to hire and how to stage things, Furtwängler quickly decided to deal with him on a political rather than an artistic level, and so complained to Goebbels. In the meantime he was making

---

To Herr Hanke, Ministerial Adviser.　　　　　Berlin, 19 October 1934

The Philharmonic Orchestra intends to appoint a leader by the name of
Kolberg. The manager, von Schmidtseck, informs me that the minister
has given Staatsrat Dr Furtwängler the authority to offer Kolberg a monthly
salary of 1,000 RM.

I would be grateful if you would confirm that this is so.

---

no headway on the matter of the Hindemith opera. The composer, the
director of the Staatsoper and Tietjen were all agreed the Staatsoper
would be responsible for the première. And yet problems of all sorts
were developing. The press reported that the Hamburg State Theatre
was also negotiating for the opera even though the business side of
things had already been discussed in Berlin; Hindemith – or his publisher
– was to receive a 10,000 RM honorarium and 10 per cent of takings, a
normal arrangement.[54] Those concerned knew that the composer was
the object of a politico-cultural dispute; the prime minister, Göring, was
also informed of it, but when his opera director reported on the matter

133

to him at a meeting in July, he initially withdrew from the whole business, saying that he regretted that he was unable to give his permission without the Führer's agreement. Furtwängler correctly inferred that the whole thing was being turned into a political matter and stressed that he was competent 'to deliver an objective and professional judgement on the value of the work, and that furthermore, as one of those who decided on programme content for the Reichsmusikkammer according to the laws of the Kulturkammer and as Staatsrat for Prussian cultural concerns, he was in a position to give a considered decision'.[55]

He stated his point of view once more in a letter and suggested postponing a decision until the autumn, obviously hoping that things might have changed by then. Unfortunately times were against him. So he decided to adapt to the times. The opportunity to do so came with the death of Hindenburg, and Hitler's attempt to use a plebiscite on 19 August 1934 to legitimise the office of Reichspresident which he had 'inherited'. On the day before the plebiscite a 'proclamation by all artists' appeared, in which among other things they declared:

We believe in this Führer, who has fulfilled our strong yearning for concord. We trust his work, which demands sacrifices which go beyond all carping and hairsplitting, and we place our hope in this man who believes in God's Providence over men and things. Because the artist and the poet can only create if he also has the same trust in his people, and because he has the same deep conviction that the people's holiest right consists in the right to self-determination, we belong to the Führer's followers.[56]

The names of the thirty-seven who signed reflected a cross-section of intellectual circles and political categories. Among those who participated were Ernst Barlach, Rudolf S. Binding, Gustav Frenssen, Erich Heckel, Georg Kolbe, Agnes Miegel, Emil Nolde, Hans Pfitzner, Richard Strauss, Heinz Tietjen, Erwin Kolbenheyer and . . . Furtwängler. The connection with the Hindemith opera strikes one immediately. At the beginning of July he had heard from the prime minister's office that its performance at the Staatsoper 'is not at present permitted'. The opera director obstinately asked Göring to arrange an audience with Hitler, stressing:

You will understand that my sense of responsibility does not allow me to turn down a work which I am the only person to know, and which I think is good. Furthermore my sense of responsibility to art is of course the only criterion on which I base my judgements, and which must guide me in the posts you have put me in.[57]

The prime minister, however, did not reply immediately, and when he did, on 26 August, he was placatory with regard to the decision Hitler had taken, requesting Furtwängler not to see the matter as so important and decisive, but also saying that he would do what he could to arrange an audience with the Führer. Before this letter reached Furtwängler he had been alone with his problem and the conviction that he could do nothing without support from the very top. For a man who had found that the trade-off of achievement and counter-achievement was a useful principle in political negotiations the opportunity to try and win over Hitler after all was very welcome. Furtwängler's signature on the proclamation was what he was offering to barter. In the meantime it was becoming clear that the *Mathis der Maler* symphony, which the functionaries had classified as political, was a success. It headed the programme planned for 1934–5, which was being announced in Baden-Baden, Breslau, Chemnitz, Dresden, Frankfurt am Main, Kassel and Leipzig; various conductors enthused about it: Eugen Jochum in Hamburg, Johannes Schüler in Essen, Werner Gössling in Bielefeld, Wilhelm Sieben in Dortmund, Hero Folkerts in Gelsenkirchen, Karl Elmendorff in Wiesbaden and Erich Seidler in Königsberg. The fact that even party members were taking up the work showed the Rosenberg group how soft cultural policy had already become. More than forty engagements or performances, of which eight were in Holland alone, were enough to alarm them into taking countermeasures.

In the meantime the KfdK had been incorporated into the Nazi Kulturgemeinde (NSKG), retaining a similar proportion of leadership positions and still very much an instrument for Rosenberg's politics. As 'the Führer's commissioner for the supervision of the overall intellectual and philosophical education of the Nazi Party', he had created himself a position of considerable power against Goebbels and Göring, a position from which he could attack. In the first instance he was intent on engaging the Berlin Philharmonic to play for the party, which would allow him, as it were, to 'pocket' them. So he suggested to Furtwängler that he should conduct at the party congress in September. This would have allowed him to separate the Jewish musicians from their 'Aryan' colleagues, because of course with Hitler present a state of racial 'purity' would have to prevail, at least on such an occasion. But Rosenberg, chief ideologue and anti-Semite, suffered a severe setback: the orchestra's secretariat directed him to Frau Geissmar of all people. Finally Schmidtseck informed him that according to instructions from Dr Goebbels the

135

orchestra was a unity which could not be divided, that the honorarium would be 3,700 RM, and that the payment of expenses would have to be guaranteed in writing beforehand. Rosenberg and his colleagues were left dumbstruck. Schmidtseck informed Furtwängler by telephone, who enjoined him to consider his argument about foreign affairs:

> He said both the Philharmonic Orchestra and he personally were primarily interested in the export of culture, and that over the last few months negotiations with France and England among others had demonstrated that the possibilities for such export were seriously endangered. Even at the time when Furtwängler was appointed Staatsrat the French press were already talking of him as a 'Hitler minister', an indication of how difficult things had become.[58]

Schmidtseck further explained to the NSKG's chief music critic, Friedrich W. Herzog, that Furtwängler should at all costs remain neutral, as his appearance at a party congress would make it still more difficult to perform abroad; thus he could only undertake to conduct at Nürnberg under express orders from the Führer. Rosenberg was offended and turned to Hitler, only to discover that he felt the musician's presence abroad to be more important. Herzog decided to take action. As his opponent so clearly had protection at the highest levels he redirected his attention to attacking Hindemith. The pressure on Berta Geissmar also increased. What the situation was like is clear from one of the conductor's letters in which, in reference to political concessions, he declares that anyone who wants to retain their position must 'come to some sort of agreement with the ruling party', unless they can afford to leave altogether:

> If you do not wish to do that you have to forbear from doing certain provocative things, such as hiring a Jewish nanny for your children. [. . .] It is somewhat different for me as I am not tied to my positions here and have deliberately decided to act as a free man (I have similar difficulty with Berta G.). It will shortly become clear whether or not I shall be able to stay in Germany. At least I am aware of what I am doing and that there is the possibility of leaving Germany for good.[59]

The beginning of a major attack on Hindemith was signalled by a music periodical which had only come under the control of the NSKG in July. In an article dealing with some minor issue the following quite unconnected piece appeared:

136

Paul Hindemith: Ability and natural artistic talent are not one and the same thing. Hindemith undoubtedly has great ability, but he is an imitator, and divine inspiration will always be denied him. If the people reject his ability it is not because this newcomer makes use of new materials, but because his ability shows no genuine originality. Hindemith is a craftsman who knows every trick there is to know, but even the most rigorous adherence to particular styles is of no use if originality is lacking.[60]

That might have passed as just another example of 'right-wing' musical criticism, but action followed swiftly on, again not in Berlin itself but in the province of Saxony. The Stadtrat for Leipzig, F. A. Hauptmann, who combined the functions of leader of the culture section of the Leipzig Nazi Party and of the NSKG's regional branch, forbade the performance of the *Mathis* symphony which Abendroth had planned for the first of the season's Gewandhaus concerts. Furtwängler appealed to Goebbels, who either could not or would not intervene, although strictly it was his responsibility. In the light of this incident the conductor decided to resign from the committee which decided programme content.

A second article in the NSKG's music periodical was an overtly political attack on the composer:

Even if Hindemith does appear in a more positive light as a result of his *Mathis der Maler*, this in no way proves that this man who, as defined by Germany's national socialist laws, is closely related to non-Aryans, has really changed. The fact that even after the National Socialist Revolution he agreed while abroad to make a recording together with two émigré Jews is clear proof of his unsound character, which has already been demonstrated to be a 'standard-bearer of decadence' by the convictions he shares with one Bert Brecht.[61]

For Furtwängler it was now a matter of rescuing the première of the opera which was due to take place in May. For weeks Hitler had been unavailable to discuss the matter, but the musician had just received an appointment to meet him. The decision was to be made on 30 November. Having read the above article he was under little illusion as to what it would be: Hindemith – politically intolerable.[62] He was, however, still certain that the NSKG was not responsible for music in general, which strengthened his view

that the Kulturkammer law had affirmed the autonomy and freedom of artists, and therefore if another organisation took a condemnatory line on artistic questions, as had happened in the case of the cited allegation that Hindemith was 'politically intolerable', then this would contradict the government-created Kultur- or Musikkammer. As vice president of the Musikkammer F. believed very firmly in defining its remit.[63]

To prevent Hitler from being prejudiced by one-sided information Furtwängler decided on a rescue plan; his opinion of the worth of the opera, the correct opinion, must be publicised *before* reaching Hitler's desk and their meeting together. So he drew up a letter to set the record straight and gave it to Robert Oboussier, music critic on the *Deutsche Allgemeine Zeitung*, to pass on to the chief editor. When the latter checked, Furtwängler assured him 'that he knew the risk he was taking. He was concerned not only about Hindemith and the new music, but about the freedom of the artistic personality'.[64]

At this point he sought to bring the full weight of his authority to bear. He was not taking up an anti-state position, but was making a clear distinction between state and party institutions. He considered Rosenberg and the NSKG as trouble-makers who were acting against the best interests of the state. It was a fact that they had no authority to rule; it is however questionable whether the musician ever fully understood the meaning of the law proclaimed on 1 December 1933 securing the unity of party and state, which was really the legal guarantee of the party's power over the state. Because of this he was moving on dangerous ground. He unwittingly sabotaged the party's claim to control when he commented sharply:

Hindemith has never been politically active; where on earth would we be if the practice of political denunciation were to be extended to all areas of art? There can be no doubt that amongst the younger generation there is nobody who has done more for Germany's musical standing in the world than Paul Hindemith. [. . .] I would go so far as to say that – and we should be clear about this – in view of the deplorable world-wide dearth of truly productive musicians, we cannot afford to discard a man like Hindemith without further consideration.[65]

This unleashed a storm. The inflammatory article, which appeared on the Sunday morning, not only excited general attention, but also drove so many people to the Philharmonie, where Furtwängler was rehearsing for the Monday concert, that there were demonstrations both on the streets and in the concert hall itself. On the Monday a furious Rosenberg went to see the Führer and showed him the article. Hitler gave his permission for the National Socialist press to lay into the troublesome Furtwängler, and had his governmental adviser Meerwald cancel the planned audience. The press war began, opened by *Der Angriff* with an aggressive banner headline and four columns of first-page coverage. Erich Roeder gibbered on about a conspiracy:

That all those who were formerly artistically connected would one day get together with their intellectual string-pullers to try and capitalise on Hindemith's nomination was no surprise given their ambition and egotism. [. . .] It is said that approaches were made to those in the highest positions, with no success. The indications of an explicit power struggle were beginning to appear.[66]

The NSKG's review was quick to agree with him, emphasising still further:

It is not permissible that reactionary currents, which we thought overcome, should be allowed to dominate the extremely important field of cultural policy as a result of silent sufferance or sheer carelessness. This is why we attribute such fundamental and central importance to this particular case and repeat: the party's cultural organisation should not and cannot act any differently in the fight for intellectual and philosophical renewal, from the way the political wing acted in the fight for political power.[67]

Not all the papers joined the polemic against the composer and his 'accomplice'; several did make sure that the reader was not lacking objective information by giving both sides of the story.[68] Foreign journalists were quick to recognise what could be made out of the affair and began by reprinting Furtwängler's article. Thomas Mann read it on Thursday 29 November in the *Neue Zürcher Zeitung*, his diary showing that he was less interested in Hindemith than in how he himself was affected by it all:

No 'colleagues' raised a voice at the treatment those brutal mob leaders in Munich allowed to be meted out to me – not a single individual or group. And yet if they had it would have brought German literature international recognition. It would have been an easy opportunity for them, given that their works are not really of a suitable standard otherwise.[69]

As what was at issue in Berlin was not real estate or printed works but ideology and reasons of state, the case escalated. Late on Thursday Furtwängler discovered that a standard report was being prepared for the whole press, and so, in an attempt to ease the tension, he tried to contact either Goebbels or Funk to discuss the wording; however, he failed to achieve contact and the press department of the ministry had no authority to stop publication. Thus on Friday morning the offices of the NSKG trumpeted:

We object to the NSKG being pejoratively referred to as 'certain circles' and accused of political denunciations when it has openly and honestly expressed its justified objections to Hindemith. It should be made quite clear to Herr Staatsrat Dr Furtwängler that statements made by an organisation within the National Socialist movement have nothing in common with political denunciations. We therefore unconditionally reject the attempt made by Furtwängler and the *Deutsche Allgemeine Zeitung* to use such methods to attack us for criticising a controversial artist. Whether the composer's musical achievements have value or not is not even at issue in the NSKG's criticism of Paul Hindemith, as their originality has yet to be verified. The fact that even years before the seizure of power Hindemith deliberately adopted an un-German stance, and already then, according to Furtwängler, did this because it fitted the mood of the times, makes him quite unsuited for the movement's task of cultural reconstruction, especially as one can assume that his current stance is also adopted to suit the circumstances, which means that he is just changing external appearances.[70]

In the light of this latest blow it seemed advisable to seek a meeting with the prime minister with a view to persuading him to take his opera director and Staatsrat under his protection. At the meeting, which took place on Sunday evening, Göring censured him for having taken the matter to the public and thereby provoked a press campaign. Hearing this, Furtwängler – excessively sensitive even to a political reproof – offered his resignation, by which he meant resignation from all political offices. Göring calmed him, saying that was out of the question, that the affair was not important enough to merit such action. However as things now stood, Hindemith had become a political issue and so the performance of his music would be forbidden from now on. They agreed to continue their talk on the Monday. The public, which heard nothing of the behind-the-scenes dispute, concentrated all its hopes on Furtwängler; victory seemed within his grasp:

These words whisk away the last unpleasantness like a fresh breeze. It has been a liberating moment because we know that Furtwängler is no blind advocate of change, and that he has shown great strength of character in taking a stand against the excesses of those who are. The fate of German music in the future has now been decided – in an affirmative sense. Full of hope and in high spirits we now move towards this future.[71]

On the Sunday after these lines appeared the conductor knew that he had left the realms of apolitical music behind him. When he conducted *Tristan und Isolde* that evening at the Staatsoper the public gave him an ovation before every act; Goebbels and Göring witnessed – doubtless with mixed feelings – this spontaneous surge of political support for the artist.[72]

On Monday morning he sought a meeting with Goebbels, believing that Hitler would be more easily reached by way of the propaganda minister; worry about rehabilitation had pushed everything else into the background. For the politician it was a welcome opportunity to take the musician down a peg or two, and this was why he refused to see him. Almost panic-stricken Furtwängler turned to Tietjen to ask him to mediate. His position on 3 December at midday was as follows: he was prepared to continue working as an 'apolitical' artist, but had decided to give up his position as vice-president of the Reichsmusikkammer . . . From Tietjen Göring learnt that the conductor, now that he found himself in opposition to official cultural policy, no longer felt able to accept the responsibility of being at the head of the Reichsmusikkammer. Göring was loath to make the decision himself and so he spoke with Hitler, who reacted angrily because the quarrel was beginning to have unpleasant ramifications. In the afternoon the artist was brought an ultimatum by the general intendant: if he made a personal apology he would be allowed to retain his position. No move toward Canossa – no politico-cultural function. Deadline the following day at twelve midday.

He was now under double pressure because the anniversary celebrations of the Reichskulturkammer had been scheduled for 6 December in the Sports Palace, and he was due to appear both in his official capacity and as conductor. There was thus no question of postponing the decision; if on the other hand he were to be granted several weeks of leave immediately the problem would solve itself, because he would then be able to retire discreetly as part of the re-shuffle of the Reichsmusikkammer presidential functions which had been planned for a long time – Richard Strauss and others were to be moved

141

5.Dezember 1934.

Sehr geehrter Herr Dr. Furtwängler!

Ihrem Wunsche entsprechend, entlasse ich
Sie hiermit aus Ihren Ämtern als Leiter des
Philharmonischen Orchesters und als
Vizepräsident der Reichsmusikkammer.

Wegen der Abwicklung der geschäftlichen
und finanziellen Angelegenheiten bitte ich
Sie, sich mit der Abteilung I meines
Ministeriums in Verbindung zu setzen.

Heil Hitler!

gez. Dr. Goebbels.

Herrn Min.Rat R ü d i g e r

zur Kenntnisnahme.

I.A.

Herrn
Staatsrat Dr. Wilhelm Furtwängler,
Berlin W 35,
Bürnbergstr.6.

---

5 December 1934

Honoured Herr Dr Furtwängler!

As you requested I hereby release you from your duties as leader of the
Berlin Philharmonic Orchestra and as vice-president of the
Reichsmusikkammer.

May I ask you to contact department no. 1 of my ministry to settle
administrative and financial matters.

Heil Hitler!
pp. Dr Goebbels

142

around as a result of Rosenberg's many complaints. Once again Göring consulted with Hitler; Goebbels was also drawn into the discussion. Late that afternoon at around six o'clock the artist was informed by the prime minister that the Führer would not wait beyond eight o'clock for his resignation. If he did not offer it he would be dismissed. At this point Furtwängler was still convinced that, as the conflict was a politico-cultural one, only his official positions would be at stake, and so he rather casually said that in that case he requested to be discharged.

It must have come as a terrible shock when Göring informed him that this would apply to all his positions, in other words to his musical ones as well; he could, however, formulate his resignation himself in which case the press would be forbidden to comment, because the Führer desired a peaceful and amicable separation. Shortly before eight o'clock Tietjen handed the prime minister two resignations from the deeply upset conductor; one was to Goebbels and concerned his positions as chief of the Berlin Philharmonic Orchestra and vice-president of the Reichsmusikkammer, the other to Göring concerning the position of director of the Staatsoper. At this point no decision was taken about his membership of the Reichsmusikkammer's presidential council or of the Staatsrat,[73] an indication of their lesser importance. On 5 December the minister for propaganda granted his request, also seeing to it that his membership of the presidential council was annulled a week later. The prime minister only authorised the request on 10 December, because it was only then that he was sure that he would not have to refuse the request and keep his opera chief on for lack of a successor. After urgent entreaties a successor had travelled up from Vienna on 9 December: Clemens Krauss. Krauss agreed on the spot. When he conducted *Falstaff* at the Vienna opera house two days later, there was a sense of outrage in the audience; in order to avoid demonstrations – many in Austria now considered him to be a political traitor – the general intendant immediately released him from his contract.[74] On 10 December, knowing full well that he had played one off against the other, Göring dictated a press release about Krauss's appointment and the following letter to the dismissed opera director:

I would like to take this opportunity to tell you how painful I find this separation. I had hoped that we could clarify matters and come to some sort of agreement by which we could continue to collaborate. It was not to be. I personally wish sincerely to thank you for all the work you have put into building up my institution. I would like to thank you for the many wonderful hours which you have given me as an artist and conductor. Even today I still comfort myself with the

Der Preußische Ministerpräsident.

Berlin W 8, den 10. Dezember 1934
Wilhelmstr. 63.
Fernspr.: A 2 Flora 6341, 7071.

St. M.

Herrn

Staatsrat Dr. Furtwängler

B e r l i n W.
- - - - - - - -

Sehr geehrter Herr Staatsrat !

Generalintendant Tietjen überbrachte mir Ihr Gesuch,
in welchem Sie um die Entlassung aus Ihrem Amt als Operndirektor
der Staatsoper nachsuchen. Ich bewillige Ihnen hiermit das Gesuch und entlasse Sie aus dem Verband der Preussischen Staatsoper.

Ich möchte die Gelegenheit benutzen, um Ihnen zum
Ausdruck zu bringen, wie schmerzlich mich die Trennung berührt
hat. Ich hatte gehofft, wenigstens in grossen Zügen zu einer
Klärung und Einigung und damit zu einer weiteren Zusammenarbeit
zu gelangen. Das hat nicht sein sollen. Es ist mir aber ein
inneres Bedürfnis, Ihnen aufrichtig zu danken für all die Ar-
beit, der Sie sich beim Aufbau meines Institutes unterzogen
haben. Ich möchte Ihnen danken für die vielen wundervollen Stun-

den

THE PRUSSIAN PRIME MINISTER

Berlin W8, 10 December 1934
Wilhelmstr. 63.

Herr Staatsrat Dr. Furtwängler
Berlin W.

Dear Herr Staatsrat!

General Intendant Tietjen has delivered your request to be released from the position of director of the Staatsoper. I hereby grant this request and release you from the Prussian Staatsoper Association.

I would like to take this opportunity . . . [for continuation see p. 143]

---

hope of seeing you again, perhaps as guest conductor, at my opera. There is nothing in life which cannot be set right. I have asked General Intendant Tietjen to inform you that I am leaving your full salary unchanged until further notice. Please see this as a sign of my gratitude and recognition for your achievements at the Staatsoper. With every hope that your further artistic career will be a fruitful one, I am convinced that your path cannot but complement that of National Socialist Germany.[75]

The politician's moving and sugar-sweet phrases could not for a moment disguise from Furtwängler the fact that his ambitions, including those for art and freedom, were hopeless. Force, necessarily masked by empty phrases, had triumphed. He stood alone.

5

A GUEST IN HIS OWN COUNTRY

The loneliness of the great is the outcome of incompatible and conflicting social desires; people in such a position have a status at odds with the needs of human nature. While many people are inhibited about being open with others, one might suppose that the figure who could reign far above the 'masses' and yet still be happy could only exist in fiction. Yet Furtwängler's personality was split between these two types, the tension between which drove him to the point of exhaustion. For him 5 December 1934 was like being cast into hell. He might well have been able to cope with the loss of his political functions, but Hitler, no doubt with the intention of breaking this difficult man once and for all, had torn away from him his orchestra and with it most of what gave meaning to his life. He could either bear the suffering or try to effect a cure by emigrating. Could he turn his back on Germany? It is not really the right question to ask. We know that even before this crisis he had expected or feared that at some point he would *have* to go abroad for political reasons. Now he knew he would have to make a decision. He was certainly not primarily concerned with 'Germany' or with crude patriotism or any of the other concepts which at that time were so highly valued. Furtwängler was a widely travelled man who, while his roots were in the land of his birth, could if necessary have felt more or less comfortable in Switzerland, Austria or even in England or the USA. The idea of changing his country, home, language and culture was completely alien to him, but it could not be said that he was bound to the Reich by patriotic sentiment.

For this reason he wrote to John Knittel, the Swiss writer who had taken up residence in Egypt, to ask him if he might not take up an earlier invitation to come and visit. That was on 10 December, in other words before he had received Göring's permission to resign. This journey could easily have been the first step towards emigration. He had already made a note of the connections to Alexandria via Munich –Zürich–Genoa, and also that Cairo time was two hours ahead; his diary contained a reminder to take an English and a French grammar with him. He was held back by two things, however. Hitler, who wanted to avoid drawing undesirable political attention, urged him to forego his journey abroad for the immediate future, and to emphasise the point also had his passport withdrawn. Strange as it may sound, this in a sense 'rescued' the outcast. For there were psychological reasons preventing him from emigrating. Even if he found a way of crossing the border it was very clear to him that despite the many possibilities he had of taking well-paid work abroad, he would go into a decline if he were forced to stay away for an extended period. The problem was thus a psychological rather than an economic one.

The stock of musical phenomena by which Furtwängler judged all other music, and which he also used as the basis for his whole artistic philosophy, was essentially limited to the 'classical' and 'romantic' repertoires, though with occasional forays back into the music of Bach and forward to such works of contemporary composers as served him in his arguments against 'intellectualism', 'atonality' and the like. There was no place for the vast field of light music, nor did he have any conception of 'world music'. As far as he was concerned music could perhaps just about be considered European, but was primarily a German achievement. That many compositions – 'classical' ones included – serve as entertainment was a notion his musical mythology could not encompass, because he thought that such historicist perspectives were useless; if faith ranks higher than knowledge and thinking counts for less than feeling, then the most noble function befitting art is that of redemption. This myth gave Furtwängler an existential handhold which he clung to lest he should have to question his actions or even his whole existence; only thus could he remain certain that the music he was conducting was brilliant, and that the works he served were those of great masters.

The myth provided him with a firm footing in the 'chaos' of modern times, because it set clear limits, allowing him to consolidate a system of thought which always led to coherent conclusions because it forbade any subtleties which might undermine the overall argument. Thus, for example, he succeeded in refining concepts like 'symphony' and 'symphonic' to such an extent that, contrary to the reliable evidence of musical research, he eventually felt able to declare that they were

148

'German'[1] and that 'a genuine symphony has never ever been written by a non-German'.[2]

Questions such as what, other than being a member of the state, made one a 'German', or what made Haydn as German as Brahms, or what effect the political differences between Mannheim and Vienna around 1780 had had on music making, did not come under consideration. As if it were a mistake to differentiate at all, he reduced his concepts still further: Germany was 'the true creator of pure instrumental music' . . . 'a real symphony'. This mechanism ranked composers such as Berlioz, César Franck or Tchaikowsky as mere 'semi-symphonists' who 'in all important respects were completely under German influence',[3] which led almost automatically to the conclusion that 'German music had world-wide validity'.[4] His definition of what it was that he felt gave this music its German quality came at a time which was politically ripe for such a far-fetched question.[5] At that time – not content with striving for economic autarchy – many musicians and theoreticians were grappling with the problem, without however obtaining any provable results. The conductor was thus one among many who slipped into an unreal world, in which considered reasoning gave way to mythological fantasy . . . as one can read in the writings he left behind. Anyone who acted as he did, on the basis of the three virtues — the good, beautiful and true — did so for the sake of his own resoluteness.

If music has a redemptive function, then it is the conductor who mediates this transcendence. At the same time he represents the immortalised genius; the public then also recognise him as a representative, and through their veneration and admiration they effect a growth in his stature, or at least in his real power, which he can then utilise for the benefit of what is good, beautiful and true. The stronger the affective ties between the public and the conductor on the one hand, and between the conductor and the orchestra's musicians on the other, the clearer the effect. Furtwängler lived in a very pronounced interplay of affective relationships. The public loved him. The podium in the concert hall, that raised point between orchestra and auditorium, was his 'German' Reich – 'German' signifying close to home, trusted, familiar and indispensable. He knew his roots were here. He knew that here he could exercise a determining influence which extended far beyond merely being a conductor, and this certainly reflected his ambitions. He could achieve this only in Germany. Going abroad was fine for guest performances but if he stayed in a strange land for any length of time he would perish. Once his passport had been taken away the temptation to leave disappeared as well. He stayed in Germany.

Initially it seemed it had been not just the only possible decision but also the right one. Remaining in Germany he experienced a great deal of solidarity. Kleiber immediately cancelled the concert he had been due to conduct on 5 December in the Philharmonie. The public understood this gesture of sympathy. When Arthur Rother stood in for him the hall was only half full; young people were demonstrating in the foyer and the public remained restless throughout the concert. The foreign press was almost unanimous in its condemnation of the Nazi regime's outrageous actions, leaving several diplomatic missions somewhat helplessly requesting the official government 'protocol' from the propaganda ministry. This included the embassy in The Hague, which complained that 'German cultural propaganda has suffered a noticeable loss of prestige as a result of this affair, especially given that only the most outstanding artists are suitable exponents of any such cultural propaganda. The public repeatedly voices doubts about the publicly given grounds which are supposed to have led to Furtwängler's retirement.'[6]

That public opinion was in support of the outcast conductor is documented in a flood of private letters – to both the conductor and the minister – and countless offers of jobs from all over the world. Huberman sent him a three-page letter wishing him luck, which he showed to the government. Even more effective was the reaction at the box-office. The audiences which regularly attended Furtwängler's concerts, in Hamburg as well as Berlin, began returning their season tickets in the hundreds. Goebbels was given occasion for serious doubts. In Berlin a third of those eligible to do so claimed their money back, which came to 16,044.40 RM, while in Hamburg the amount was 13,397.05 RM.[7]

Even Rosenberg came to see what a key asset this artist could be in the politico-cultural balance, and while on the one hand he still criticised him, on the other he quickly sought to re-establish contact. This conflict and its embarrassing repercussions abroad must be laid to rest, and so, having put him in his place, he now beckoned to Furtwängler:

National Socialism is about far more than just politics; it embraces all aspects of our lives, and if it did not do so it would not be a great revolution. But as we also know that for people to change spiritually takes many years, we are prepared to wait for it to find its expression in art. National Socialists therefore feel they must try to bring together all serious artists, including those who are perhaps still somewhat bound to the old ways of thinking but are now sincerely seeking to change, to break away from that past, and to serve through their own work this new world, whose ideals must move all people capable of feeling.[8]

150

A music lover pleads on Furtwängler's behalf, December 1934

This meant that the Nazi leadership would accept those who conformed and welcome those who changed their minds, and it was written specifically with Furtwängler in mind, which was why they did not want any public debate on the matter. Goebbels gave instructions to tell journalists at a press conference

that this is not a signal to the press to take up the issue. It is, so to

151

speak, a confidential talk between two people, namely Rosenberg and Furtwängler [. . .] Dr Goebbels will give his response to Furtwängler in his speech today at the Reichskulturkammer's anniversary celebrations, although without mentioning him by name. That also should not be taken as a signal to take up the debate.[9]

It seemed advisable to wait till the excitement had abated; this was the course adopted by both sides, both of whom were also noting every little indication of their own success. For Goebbels this included a telegram: 'Congratulations and my full support for your marvellous culture speech. You have my admiration. Yours faithfully, Heil Hitler. Richard Strauss.'[10]

Furtwängler enjoyed renewed declarations of loyalty from his supporters, which reached him either directly or indirectly; some he clearly remained unaware of, such as a risky action taken by some music students: on 10 December Assistant Detective Kraft recorded that the unheard of had occurred, namely that at the Berlin-Charlottenburg Musikhochschule 'lists of signatures had been collected from amongst the music and orchestral students with the intention of having the dismissed director general of music, Furtwängler, re-called. [. . .] Who began this collection of aforementioned signatures is not yet known. Cannot give further information about who currently holds the lists.'[11]

The people's clear endorsement and their visible admiration for him strengthened the musician's certainty that he was in the right and must continue to fight. He immediately began to use his 'unemployed' days to write at least two drafts of a memo to Goebbels, one of which he gave the title 'Problems in German Music', the other the rather less dangerous one of 'Recognition'; both however contained a rebuke for the politician. Furtwängler, who had just learnt what mass solidarity could accomplish psychologically, immediately converted this experience into a lesson on the role of the people; he declared himself convinced

> that every decision must be taken for the right reasons, i.e. intellectual decisions can only be taken with intellectual justification. Therefore such decisions – if they are to be effective – must have the support of the general public, or rather of 'the people'. Of course atonal ignoramuses should be rejected, but the less easily resolved question is whom to count as an atonal ignoramus. As we know from history Beethoven, Wagner, Strauss etc. were regarded in a similar light by some of their contemporaries, and so today we should beware of making over-hasty judgements and, in so far as is possible, we should involve the people in such decisions; the people are after all the artist's

152

'other half' to whom he turns, and whose silent assistance as judge and evaluator is plainly essential to the creation of works of art. The people – in day-to-day musical life represented by 'the public', although they are not one and the same – may often be mistaken about individual cases, but in the long term are always right.[12]

It was a clever attempt to trap the minister with his own arguments, shored up as it was with set pieces of Nazi propaganda, including phrases from Goebbels' own mouth. The latter next discovered why it was that politically motivated interventions ultimately violated the people's rights:

One can thus say that every artistic decision is a sort of 'people's decision' in miniature. For the state to try and anticipate this by the use of authoritarian means – when it is not obviously dealing with either complete trash or anti-state cultural Bolshevism – is just to defer the real decision. The works and artists under discussion will in no way disappear from view simply because they are banned. We in Germany are after all not alone; culturally speaking we have always, ever since antiquity, been a part within the whole of Europe. On the contrary we are today discovering that works and artists who are banned more or less explicitly receive more attention than they may by rights deserve; in other words one ends up with the opposite result to the one intended.[13]

The minister understood immediately from this that the musician was far from ready to come to heel, and he was even somewhat embarrassed by the line of argument, having himself – as there is much evidence to prove – his own reservations about censorship and bans; on the other hand he could console himself that no formal and official ban had been issued against Hindemith. There had only been Hitler's own statement, which furthermore had infringed on his, Goebbels', area of responsibility. The target was not so much 'atonal' music, which neither he nor the majority of music reporters could even define, as suspected 'anti-revolutionary' developments concealed under the guise of art. As it was undesirable that Germany's musical activity – which somehow also seemed to symbolise the Reich's internal organisation – should remain disrupted, Goebbels had an active interest in settling the crisis; the fact that Furtwängler had been prevented from emigrating and so had been retained for the Reich opened up several lines of political action which would not involve a loss of face. It was definitely an annoyance for the politician that the case was still making the international headlines and strengthening the regime's opponents. He could cope with the reaction from Moscow however, even if they did give a more pessimistic account of the conductor's situation, because linguistically and politically they were still very isolated:

> These are methods of terrible oppression, of strangulation and threats – including torture in concentration camps. Even worse: he is threatened with being sent to a concentration camp! This is how the few representatives of German culture who have dared to remain in fascist Germany are being removed and hounded away, one after the other. They are then replaced by untalented but 'reliable' agents of the fascist party. Need one say more about the short-sightedness of 'National Socialist culture'? It is a path which leads quite inevitably to total degeneration and disgrace.[14]

Besides, from a propagandist point of view Goebbels was justified in taking steps to divert the press's attention. First of all the name Furtwängler must be made to disappear; this could be arranged within his own immediate area of authority: when the commercial manager of the Berlin Philharmonic Orchestra wanted to issue a calming notice to stop the return of tickets, he sent a proposal to be approved by the Propaganda Ministry:

> We would not bother you with it if we had not already, due to the way people are reacting currently, talked about the possibility of Dr Furtwängler conducting one of the Philharmonic concerts in the course of the season. As we are led to believe that discussions are still to be held at the beginning of January between Herr Staatsrat Funk and other ministers, we would like to suggest the return of Herr Dr Furtwängler if there is any possibility at all of that occurring.[15]

Nothing came of this. The director of the ministry, Dr Greiner, crossly rang the manager and put him back in his place. Any mention of Herr Furtwängler was quite out of the question. In other places such insistence on protocol was unnecessary. Slowly Furtwängler's awkward name was dropped from circulation. One of the few relevant publications to completely ignore the matter was Vienna's *Anbruch*. Readers searched in vain for information on this politico–cultural scandal which was being discussed world-wide; instead they found a report by Willi Reich, which had nothing to do with music, about how he had translated Mussolini's *La Dottrina de Fascismo* into German and sent a copy to the Duce: 'I experienced great happiness and profound satisfaction at being able while working to witness a stirring period in the life of a unique and almost larger-than-life person, and in the life of a whole people.'[16]

As early as January, Rosenberg's faction already expected that the musician, having been cold-shouldered, would give them a signal, and they made a visible effort to make such a political conversion appealing to him:

A new music which can combine freedom and order, feeling and form, which is genuine and has developed naturally, will always find a response. When Wilhelm Furtwängler conducts in future he too will be able to count on this response, once he has recognised that his tasks in National Socialist Germany are a duty and a *sine qua non*. Artistic achievement cannot be commanded; one has to feel it. Anyone who swears by Adolf Hitler knows the path which must be followed if at the end of it we are to find the fulfilment of German thought.[17]

This was no doubt meant to be the sweetener; it was followed immediately by a warning drum roll:

The purification of German art has only just begun. German musical life has such a wealth of talent that the loss of a number of so-called international figures cannot affect the overall standard of our musical culture. It is in fact to be hoped that this will break the unhealthy fascination with star performers which is so detrimental to musical activity. The practising musician should once again become a servant to his art whereas in recent decades the opposite has been the case: art seemed to provide the background against which to glorify those performing. Even if musical activity in some of our larger towns does suffer a temporary set-back as a result of weeding out undesirable artists, this should not be seen as a disadvantage, because here as in all things National Socialism is working with a long-term perspective.[18]

The conductor took note of all such signals and made preparations for his return to musical activity, but not to the posts he had lost; rehabilitation had to be more than reinstatement. To apologise as Hitler had wanted was out of the question. Yes, he wanted to conduct, but only under conditions which he himself could dictate. And so, initially in rough form, he outlined his thoughts on the Staatsoper. He no longer wanted to be director of the opera; he wanted more:

1) An independent position directly under the prime minister.
2) A title which will make this unmistakably clear to all and sundry (some sort of honorary title).

3) As the prime minister's personal professional adviser to be entrusted with all matters concerning the Staatsoper.[19]

This memo was intended for Göring, overall head of the Staatsoper, from his special adviser and artist '*in spe*', who – despite having just been thrown out – was demanding a rank equal to that of general intendant, above that of the opera's director, Krauss, and barely below that of Göring. This draft, of almost surreal boldness, would in fact later prepare the way for a new agreement. Matters took a similar course with the propaganda minister with regard to the Berlin Philharmonic. Even before leaving for Munich at Christmas he had talked with Göring who asked him to remain chief conductor of the Berlin Philharmonic but was promptly snubbed; as he could not have 'everything' Furtwängler preferred to have 'nothing'. In his talk with Funk shortly afterwards he stated confidently that after a while tempers would cool and he would be able to return to Berlin – as a private individual. The state secretary suddenly found that this was a different person he was talking to; when he brought the conversation round to the orchestra's planned and politically crucial tour of England, for which they had been unable to find a replacement conductor because of the rush, Furtwängler, to the ministerial official's chagrin, once again said no, but then wrote to him from Munich as if nothing had happened, gave suggestions and offered his experience (his own contribution to a battle of nerves?):

> Moreover I would like to repeat what I have already said to you personally, namely that I am of course now as ever at your disposal if there is any advice I can offer pertaining to the orchestra; it is after all a matter of maintaining an artistic ensemble for which I myself have made great sacrifices over the last fifteen years in order to bring it up to its current standard.[20]

However, it was primarily organisational decisions which were at issue rather than artistic ones. On 22 December Funk had revoked Schmidt-seck's appointment as manager; this was not surprising given that the latter had hardly fulfilled his task of representing the orchestra's National Socialist concerns, but had instead spent most of his time supporting Furtwängler's politics. The Propaganda Ministry presented the conductor Hermann Stange as his successor. A party member since 1 May 1933, No. 3,471,440, Stange had worked for several years at the Sofia opera and then in the KfdK, and was now at a loose end and in need of a new job; Goebbels protected him – even after he had to leave the post of commercial manager on 30 September 1935 due to incompetence.

Hermann Stange, merely the manager

business considered the appointment an unfortunate one because Stange, 'despite the many qualities he may possess (I have know him for many years) is inclined to a rather pathological self-importance and to wrongly estimating or rather to underestimating his colleagues'.[21] This was a mildly expressed but telling assessment; almost on his first day Stange, as the new general director of music, demanded no less than to take over the Furtwängler concerts; he considered second-class concerts beneath him. Supported by their former chief, who remained in the background, the orchestra turned against the arrogant upstart and made life difficult for him.

During these days and weeks Furtwängler did entertain some hope, but he was not happy. The circle of people immediately around him – more to him than just the foundations of his power – had fallen apart. Schmidtseck, who had become more than just an assistant, was no longer available. Berta Geissmar finished instructing her successor and

157

was then gone, although they remained in frequent contact – in her subsequent capacity as secretary to the British conductor Sir Thomas Beecham she arranged several meetings – as she continued to work discreetly on Furtwängler's behalf. Goebbels had taken the opportunity to settle the whole matter in one go, actually by making use of the Reichskulturkammer's law. When the organisation was founded Frau Geissmar had filled in the relevant form for the Reichsmusikkammer and thereby acquired provisional membership as well as automatically being given a work-permit . . . as did the other Jews working in the music business. Obvious 'non-Aryans' were then singled out and lost their licences within the first few months. Thanks to Furtwängler she enjoyed – until the Hindemith affair – a special but revokable licence. The president of the RKK did then revoke this important paper with effect from 31 December 1934; as her contract was based on the orchestra's financial year, in other words was only due to end on 31 March 1935, this amounted to dismissal without notice.[22]

On the one hand her boss missed her devotion and dedication, on the other he distanced himself from her rather freely expressed political opinions. When she reaffirmed, to all who wanted to hear, her conviction that the separation was only temporary and that Furtwängler would work with her again later abroad, his opponents naturally assumed that the conductor intended to emigrate and so gave free rein to their mistrust. The authorities conducted a war of nerves against Frau Geissmar[23] which can in part be put down to official uncertainty about the intentions of the conductor, whose reactions were neither predictable nor as they wanted. In addition to this the Berlin Philharmonic Orchestra now lost Kleiber. Since as conductor of the Staatsoper he had not felt able to register his protest by resigning on the spot, but only with effect from 1 February – his solidarity with Furtwängler was not sufficient to justify withdrawing from his contract without notice – he looked for another opportunity which would be formally valid. The threats which his support for contemporaries provoked, as for example when he conducted Stravinsky's *The Rite of Spring* and Berg's *Lulu*, did not impress him, but then after the Hindemith affair he did not expect anything different. On 10 October he had agreed on six concerts with the orchestra, of which the first took place that very evening; he had – with the manager's consent – dropped the second concert on 5 December because of Furtwängler's 'resignation'. But 9 January saw him back on the podium. The pretext for resigning was not long in coming: in their frustration at the return of season tickets, which completely upset all their budget calculations, the management had sent out a circular promising the following: 'In order to offer you some compensation for the

158

fact that other conductors are leading the Philharmonic in place of Herr Dr Furtwängler, we are prepared to allow you admission to one of the final Kleiber concerts free of charge.'[24]

The Propaganda Ministry had let this wording pass without noticing the hidden legal trap. Kleiber put his lawyer on to it. He took the precaution of cancelling with immediate effect the agreement on guest appearances by appealing to paragraph 626 of the Civil Code – for misuse of name and damage to both his client's reputation and the appeal of the concert his client was to conduct; the wording 'some compensation' was also held to detract from his artistic personality. He could not be made to budge from this, which made the need to resolve the conductor problem still more urgent. The following replacements for Furtwängler were found for the Philharmonic concerts; Jochum, Schuricht, Abendroth, Fiedler and – for the final concert and more by way of trial – Stange. And yet there were still aggravations. The ninth concert on 10 March, to be repeated the following day, had initially been offered to Pfitzner. He did not have the time and so it was offered to Strauss who was also supposed to be taking over the concert in Hamburg on 8 March; for the three concerts he demanded 5,000 RM instead of the 3,000 RM on offer. So the concert went to Fiedler instead. The state secretary commented peevishly: 'Fiedler was very good. It is well known that Strauss asks fantastic prices. It's his way.'[25]

A number of people thought a new chief conductor was needed, with the result that applications arrived from various musicians who all had one thing in common; they vastly overestimated their own ability. One person, namely the conductor and choirmaster of the Berlin Liedertafel, Friedrich Jung, a party member who had also conducted the chorus at the Bayreuth Festival the previous year, thought he would be very clever and asked Goebbels for a personal interview. The Propaganda Ministry made enquiries with the Reichsmusikkammer and gave him one chance only. Jung was allowed to conduct the Berlin Philharmonic's chamber orchestra at the celebrations on the fifty-second anniversary of Wagner's death.

The German concerts which Furtwängler was to have conducted did more or less continue under various replacement conductors, but were not very satisfactory because the public scorned these stop-gaps. Jochum began in Breslau on 15 January with the national anthem, so that people had to stand up, arms raised in the 'German greeting', and sing along – the occasion for this was the vote in the Saar district which was to lead to *Anschluss*; and yet the press was wistful:

The hallmark of all great orchestral performances, and especially of

German ones, was lacking: that metaphysical, otherworldly, elusive quality of sound which the Berlin Philharmonic always used to be so good at producing for us, like a gift of the Holy Grail. To try and hide this would be a serious mistake, precisely because the members of the Berlin Philharmonic are the nation's best, and as first-class cultural representatives must have first claim to the very top conductors, especially if one also considers that their artistic achievements abroad reflect praise and honour on the German name. Let us hope that there will soon be an artist at the head of this orchestra who is suitably equipped for the task, and able to dedicate all his time and energy to his ensemble rather than indulging in naïve and out-of-place digressions into musical politics for the sake of some ungrateful phantom.[26]

A few days later Jochum found only a sparse audience at the hall in Hamburg. The press voiced regret and criticism because 'the Berlin Philharmonic has already been sufficiently hard hit by the recent course of events, and now deserves every possible support on the part of the German public'.[27]

The tour of England, already confronted with the passportless Furtwängler's 'no', was encountering further difficulties. In former years it had been a costly yet profitable undertaking; in return for its investment the orchestra could expect a profit of 20–30,000 RM – which meant foreign currency for the Reich Ministry of Finance. The English public was now of course insisting on Furtwängler. Furthermore, a number of English conductors had politely declined to step in for him and Harold Holt, the concert agent in London and the other party in the contract, was asking for a definite answer. The musicians would have liked to go. On 5 January Holt contacted Furtwängler by telegraph in Munich, wished him a happy new year, mentioned the threatened financial loss and disappointment of the British public, and asked him for a positive reply . . . by Monday, because it would be necessary to make an announcement. This wording suggested that he had written with the official account of the resignation in his mind, the protocol version he had convinced himself was true because he did not want to believe the opposite: nobody could throw out someone like Furtwängler, not even Hitler! Furtwängler thus found himself in a serious dilemma. He had to correct Holt's belief that his resignation had been a free decision, as otherwise he would continue to hold the associated expectation that this decision could easily be reversed for the purposes of the England tour. Furtwängler had to send some sort of signal. He had to go against the

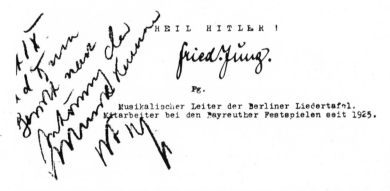

6. 3. 35. Über den Herrn Staatssekretär   18. 9 2007 9. 7. 25. Jü 1/13.

Friedrich J u n g   Berlin,den 3.Januar 1935.
Berlin Lichterfelde
Tulpenstrasse 6.
Tel: G 6 Breitenbach 1144.

Reichsministerium
f.Volksaufkl. u. Propaganda
4 - JAN 1935 Va   100   **112**

An den Herrn

Reichsminister Dr. Josef G o e b b e l s

in B E R L I N
=====================
Propaganda Ministerium
Wilhelmplatz 8-9.

Hochverehrter Herr Reichsminister!

        Ergebenst Unterfertigter bittet Herrn Reichs-

minister Dr. G o e b b e l s   höflichst um eine persönliche

Unterredung. Grund: Bewerbung um eine Dirigentenstellung beim

Berliner Philharmonischen Orchester.

        H E I L   H I T L E R !

            fried.Jung.

        Pg.

Musikalischer Leiter der Berliner Liedertafel.
Mitarbeiter bei den Bayreuther Festspielen seit 1925.

Berlin, 3 January 1936

To Herr Reichsminister Goebbels

Highly respected Minister,
Your humble servant requests a personal interview.
Reason: application for the position of
conductor of the Berlin Philharmonic Orchestra.
Heil Hitler!
Friedrich Jung   Party Member

161

interests of those covering up the awful truth and – even if only for a moment, in a flash, so to speak – let the truth shine through.

He did this with the skill of a secret agent sending forbidden information. 5 January was a Saturday. Holt had asked for an answer by telegram, and was prepared to wait 'until Monday next', which would leave enough time to check by telephone with the Propaganda Ministry first thing Monday morning; it was advisable to do this because responsibility for matters concerning the tour lay with the ministry, or more precisely with State Secretary Funk, chairman of the supervisory board of the Berlin Philharmonic. However, Furtwängler quite intentionally read Holt's telegram as saying not 'Monday' but 'Monday morning'. Thereby the deadline was drawn so much closer that there was no time to check. He could therefore – by force of circumstances – send an unauthorised text to London, and did so the very same day:

> As you know my demission was asked for and accepted. My lost position included conducting the concerts of the Berlin Philharmonic in Germany and other countries. Therefore I really regret to be unable to conduct the Orchestra this Season in England. I hope the Public of the concerts will understand these facts and keep its sympathy for the future.[28]

In order that he would not be found out in Berlin he wrote – also on the Saturday – to the secretary of state and guilelessly informed him of the content of Holt's request and his own answer. This letter lay on Funk's desk on Monday morning, and around this time he received a telephone call; Schmidtseck, the dismissed manager, was on the line. Furtwängler had rung him from Munich and asked him to deliver a message, namely that the letter concerning the exchange of telegrams with England contained a translation error. By mistake he had written 'As you know my demission was asked for and accepted'. This had since been corrected to 'As you know, I asked for my demission and it was accepted'. Funk passed his minutes of the conversation on to his colleagues Greiner and von Keudell; none of these busy officials, all of whom were trained lawyers, noticed that the correction merely concerned the letter and not the original telegram. What is more, instead of using the word 'resignation' the conductor had – perhaps deliberately – used a word taken from the French which was never used in normal English and which definitely suggested 'dismissal'. The telegram's addressee can hardly be blamed for not making a big thing out of it, but at least there were a few people in the English music business who knew what brown-shirts had managed to bring about in Berlin. Holt

162

calculated the damages from this cancellation at 3,478 RM – which he asked for in hard sterling; Goebbels ground his teeth, but he had to allow the payment to be made.

In that week the conductor did several other things which could have been considered conspiratorial undertakings. As it was still unclear whether he might not after all have to leave Germany, he had taken the precaution of making contact with the American concert agent, Arthur Judson. It was actually Judson, president of the Colombia Concerts Corporation, who had given the incentive. He was interested in arranging guest appearances with the New York Philharmonic and the Philadelphia Orchestra. Hans W. Heinsheimer in Vienna was the middleman, using a friend as a go-between and coming to the capital of the Reich himself once a month. The conspiracy, which included 'secret codes' and cover addresses, did not however come to anything because of the uncertainty of the whole situation.[29] The idea of sending information by code was one which the conductor played with at other times as well. His 1936 diary contains – alongside many other notes – a key to the names of twenty-nine places and people; it is in Berta Geissmar's handwriting and was clearly intended to be used in the correspondence which it was hoped would develop between Berlin and her new home in London; Sir Thomas' new right hand could not know that it would only ever be sporadic. What they expected to be writing about is shown by the uncoded names: America, Berlin, London, Paris, Vienna, New York, Potsdam, Munich, Bayreuth, Stokowski, Toscanini, Koussevitzky, Klemperer, Bruno Walter, Kleiber, Clemens Krauss, Beecham, Bodanzky, Judson, New York Philharmonic, Hoboken, Berlin Staatsoper, Vienna Staatsoper, Covent Garden and the like; Göring was called 'Max' and Goebbels 'Pica'.[30] It would have enabled the transmitting of information secretly if Frau Geissmar wanted to arrange the conductor's emigration or even just to arrange guest appearances at the most important foreign music venues.

In these weeks Furtwängler was always haunted by the fear of separations. Past and future were in the balance. The work of building up the Staatsoper seemed lost for good; and what he considered his life's work, creating an artistic association with the Berlin Philharmonic Orchestra, had been brutally destroyed. He longed for his normal self-imposed isolation . . . he felt uncertain on all counts while he waited for strange and senseless decisions. It was a frightening situation. He was automatically isolated socially as a result of his central role in the music business. Although he was admired, sought after and venerated it was like being a memorial, a demi-god, unapproachable, always surrounded by an invisible wall. Of course he had a lot of 'human' contact, but as there was always the likelihood that it would be abused he had to protect himself by keeping his distance both inwardly and outwardly, generally more than he would have liked. Those who crowded around him wanted to share in his image, seize some of the reflected glory, be given advice, help or often just money, and it was they who drove him into ever deeper isolation. Even his numerous and generally short affairs with women seem to have been merely a form of compensation. Success brings sex with it, and women made it available to the point where he no longer wanted it; but even a temporary relationship symbolises a normal 'relationship' to others, to the mass of ordinary people. It was only very occasionally possible for him to achieve permanence in his involvements with his social surroundings. Every break – and of course every professional conflict – increased his fear of separation and isolation. His spontaneous readiness to listen to others and to help them, even with great expenditure of his own time, energy and money, can be at least partly explained by his need for contact. He sought a response from people for many reasons; not just in answer to his questions, but also to confirm his position within society.

It was vitally important to him to know that there were invisible links between him and the world of other people. Although he had no part in National Socialist party affairs he did keep up 'social activities', however indirectly, even if in some cases, where he was no more than a name on the membership lists of associations and organisations, this really verged on the illusory. He did in fact belong to a large number of associations, many of which were not directly linked to his profession: the Society for Free Philosophy, Darmstadt; the Goethe Society, Weimar; the German-Italian Society, Berlin; the Nordic Society, Berlin; the Association of Berlin Friends of the German Academy; the new Bach Society, Leipzig; the Society for the Support of Retired Artists, Berlin; the Society for the Protection of Authors' Copyright; the German Music Society; the Young Ring; the Society for Arts and Sciences, Bonn; the German Brahms Society, Berlin; the Hans Pfitzner Society, Berlin; the International Bruckner Society, Vienna; the Germany-Denmark Committee (part of the Nordic Twinning Association), Berlin; the Committee for the 40th Jubilee of the Cultural Morphologist, Leo Frobenius; the Committee for Wilhelm Kienzl's 80th Birthday Celebrations; the Carl Schurz Association, and others.

He was an honorary member of some, in others he did no more than pay his subscriptions – and they alone came to a considerable amount each year. Membership of the Reichskulturkammer – pass no. 3899 – could not be avoided as it was obligatory, and the contract which he signed on 1 April 1937, giving the copyright association STAGMA sole rights to his work, was expedient in view of the extent of his *oeuvre*. After all, in six months spanning 1938 and 1939, STAGMA paid him 19,950 RM in royalties for radio performances alone. Some of the associations did – more or less incidentally – serve the Nazi regime's politico-cultural purposes; but as he did no more than obtain formal membership, he did not get involved. His interest in motor sports is reflected in the list. He was member no. 248,752 of the German Auto-mobile Club in Munich, and was even on their board of trustees. Hardly had the Union of National Socialist Stage Artists been re-formed as the New German Film and Theatre Club than he was asked to join the honorary committee, together with (among others) Max von Schillings, the conductor Hans Trinius, the actors Hans Albers, Emmy Sonnemann and Willy Fritsch, the composers Clemens Schmalstich, Paul Lincke and Paul Graener, and the singer Margarethe Arndt-Ober.

It is not hard to understand that, having been given the cold shoulder after his so-called resignation, Furtwängler should have found it difficult to come to terms with his new situation. He saw clearly the need to renew contact where it had been broken. Without some forbearance and a certain amount of sympathy from Hitler, Göring and the Propaganda Minister, the situation could not be resolved. This was why he had to make his concerns understandable to those in power. He still hoped for their insight and respect for his professional authority as a music expert. As he – undoubtedly correctly – held Goebbels to be the most intelligent and tactically most experienced of those with whom he had to deal, he turned to him. It was an astute move. Despite their great differences in character and occupation each could almost have been the other's second self. Both in their own ways were 'conquerors of people'; both compensated for their isolation with their public appearances; both found reassurance in the company of women. One controlled people's 'souls' by means of music, the other controlled their minds and beliefs by means of politics. Both believed in their own genius and mission and recognised only one master, although each a different one: for Goebbels it was Hitler, for Furtwängler it was God. They even spoke similar languages. Goebbels spoke that of the politician interested in all things artistic, especially literature – though not himself particularly gifted – while Furtwängler spoke that of a politically skilled musician convinced of his own charisma. Their differences and similarities stimulated an antagonistic relationship which could never lead to liking, based as it was on a struggle, but which did awake mutual respect and even occasional sympathy. Both were in the business of conquering others, but both now turned their efforts to conquering one person above all others, namely each the other. Goebbels wanted to get Furtwängler on his side, while Furtwängler tried to be a missionary to the minister, winning him over to the good, the beautiful and the true.

This attempt to fish for each other only promised to produce the hoped-for catch if there were suitable enticements. The correct 'lures' had to be chosen. Rhetorical language was to be the bait. Goebbels spoke fluently of 'art' and 'eternity', 'the German nation' and 'immortality'; Furtwängler countered with the 'Jewish–Bolshevist influence', 'atonality' and . . . 'the people'. Without elaboration, and taken out of the context of the original argument, some of the texts he wrote with the minister in mind can be regarded as 'incriminatory', especially if the observer is unaware that at that time such tactics were a necessary adjunct to intelligence. And so the musician slipped into the role of cultural politician. It is noteworthy how even now – after all his experiences with the mindless power of the state and the party – the fight against racism forms a central point of his action, in connection with which he tried to build up something like a 'positive German identity' as a counterforce to the Nazi doctrine. At times Goebbels seemed the political bungler: 'The moment one is led to reject Schiller's "*Brüder, überm Sternenzelt*" [Brothers, Beyond the Canopy of Stars] or Beethoven's "*Seid umschlungen, Millionen*" [Embrace, ye Millions] by one's racist point of view, one is rejecting the very best of what is German. That is literature, or if one prefers, "orthodoxy", but it has nothing to do with politics.'[31]

The minister was not always told everything of what the musician noted in his diary in preparation for their next meeting. But once the dialogue had achieved a certain regularity he even came to hear criticism of certain holy principles. Originally written with Hitler in mind, Furtwängler had the following warning to give:

Nowadays, when *Bewusstsein* and *Geist* are so widespread – which is both in marked contrast to earlier times, and the precondition for the Jewish–Bolshevist success – a people can no longer be one-sidedly politicised by the use of force. The task is to politicise the unpolitical. It cannot be accomplished through oppression and force. To seek to carry out racial policy with force and to exterminate all supra-racial tendencies: that is the beginning of the end. National Socialism is in danger because of its own blind brutality.[32]

The musician saw himself as representing a moral standpoint, and despite the apparently blinkered use of the catch-phrase 'Jewish–Bolshevist', his penetrating gaze saw what was really going on; even if he had been interested in political science and the history of ideology he could

166

at that time hardly have seen that 'Bolshevism' had nothing to do with Jews, and that ideologists of all persuasions black-listed *Bewusstsein* and *Geist* as soon as they suspected that they might contain even a trace of criticism. It is noticeable, however, that he more and more frequently expostulated on matters outside his area of knowledge, lacking the relevant criteria by which to make judgements. When at the party congress Hitler publicly awarded the propagandist poet Hanns Johst and the 'race researcher' Professor Hans Günther with lavish Nazi Party prizes for the arts and sciences, the musician blithely denounced the donor's action:

> A narrowing-down is taking place. You as a politician must keep the reality of National Socialism in mind. The artist is rooted in the nation, but goes beyond it. From a political point of view he should be a tool of foreign policy. To give a prize for National Socialist arts and sciences is to surrender both fields to literary and scientific dilettantism. False intellectuality – Rosenberg, Goebbels – is alienating and dividing the real minds of Germany. [. . .] There is a danger of premature intellectualisation leading to the trivialisation of art – with the party's blessing. It is no pleasure to be an artist in Germany today.[33]

In the first few months of 1935 Furtwängler – if one disregards a few errors – achieved far greater clarity of mind regarding many political matters which he had previously not got to the bottom of; at the same time he built up an impressive supply of ammunition for future discussions. In all innocence he demanded that

> in principle those works of living artists which cannot be classed as either complete trash or as examples of cultural Bolshevism ought to be made available to the general public for their judgement, even in Germany today. I believe I know the Führer's various statements on this matter well enough to be able to say that in principle he shares this viewpoint. It is after all, in so far as I have understood correctly, one of the fundamental principles of National Socialism.[34]

As in this example he repeatedly returned to the Hindemith case; not having realised just how deep Hitler's dislike of the composer went, he placed hope in his own powers of persuasion and racked his brains as to how he could reach something akin to rehabilitation for the composer. He repeatedly appealed to one – decidedly democratic – function

167

Was heute in Deutschland vor sich geht, ist folgendes:
Die Kulturpolitik des Nationalsozialismus besteht haupt-
sächlich darin, den jüdischen und allgemein-zersetzenden
Einfluss im kulturellen Leben niederzukämpfen. Dieser Kampf
macht es nötig, dass auch die öffentlichen kulturellen und
Künstler-Institutionen nach politischen Gesichtspunkten
von seiten der Partei durch- und umorganisiert wurden. Der
zu erreichende Zweck ist im Ganzen erfüllt; der Kampf ist
schon seit einiger Zeit in der Hauptsache abgeschlossen.
Er erforderte allerlei Kleinarbeit, war aber im Kern nicht so
schwer, da abgesehen vom Verschwinden der Juden und Haupt-
bannerträger usw. sich der Futurismus und Bolschewismus
auf kulturellem Gebiet eigentlich schon vor der Machtübernah-
me mehr oder weniger abgekämpft und für alle ernsteren
Deutschen gleichsam selber ad absurdum geführt hatte.

Nun hat die Durchorganisierung des kulturellen Lebens
von seiten der Partei,die für die Kampfziele der Partei notwendig und richtig war, auf künstlerischem Gebiet Begleit-
erscheinungen , die geeignet sind, Fortschritt und Grösse
des bereits Erreichten von einer anderen Seite her in Frage
zu stellen. Um mich verständlich zu machen muss ich weiter
ausholen:

Richard Wagner hat in den Meistersingern einem für
jedes reale Kunstleben stets aktuell bleibende Problem
Gestalt gegeben. Hier die Meister, die Zunft, d.h. die
Künstler selber, die die Kunst repräsentieren, dort das

Volk

MEMO

What is happening in Germany today is as follows: The main thread of
National Socialist cultural policy consists in overcoming Jewish and other

generally demoralising influences in cultural life. This struggle means that it is necessary to organise or re-organise public cultural and artistic institutes according to the party's political standpoint. The stated goal has been achieved, and the greater part of the struggle has been over for some time now. It demands all sorts of detailed work, but overall was not really so difficult, as apart from getting rid of Jews and ringleaders etc. futurism and Bolshevism in cultural circles had already been more or less overcome before the take-over of power and had been seen by all the more serious Germans as having degenerated 'ad absurdum'.

Now the organisation of cultural life by the party, which was necessary and correct for attaining the goal of the struggle, is having side-effects on artistic activity which will tend to undermine the recently achieved state of progress and greatness from another angle. To make myself clear I must elaborate:

Richard Wagner's *Die Meistersinger* tackles a problem which is ever-present in day-to-day artistic life. On the one hand you have the Masters, the association, i.e. the artists themselves who represent all art, and on the other the people.

---

of the people: 'In order to break the Jewish and subversive press, the role of the press has effectively been destroyed altogether. This has however simultaneously removed any possibility for the people to regulate or correct things which are happening. Because even though the press did not exactly represent "the people" it was still a mouthpiece for them.'[35]

There is no doubt that he was referring to the people who he knew supported him, and whom he considered a counterweight to the party, disregarding the fact that every third German was a member of the Nazi Party or one of its branches or affiliated organisations. From these he discounted the average artists, seeing them as a danger to geniuses – who he thought were always positive, even politically. It is a line of argument which he was still using in 1944 as the basis for an article.[36] It is the cry for help of a genius who has yet to be rehabilitated, telling the regime it should be strong enough to allow itself the luxury of a genius – together with all his wilfulness and protests:

The thoroughgoing politicisation of public life often lays great emphasis on the importance of even artists acknowledging the party philosophy. Mediocrities, whose mentality and activities have very little to do with the deeper ideals of the party, are, precisely because they do not act in a fashion befitting National Socialism, all the more

169

inclined to make it their business to make much of such acknowledge-
ments and to reinforce them. Especially as, lacking any sort of deeper
roots in the life of the nation, all forms of hypocrisy and deceitfulness
come easily to them. Genius by contrast, the more it is conscious of
acting and working according to the true spirit of National Socialism,
will generally scorn giving such a facile account of its life-philosophy.
It may even be the case that because of its deep commitment and
genuine sense of responsibility to the national cause, genius will feel
occasion to support that cause with constructive criticism. Mediocrities ought not to feel inherent hatred for all independent action, ought
not immediately to mobilise the party at every instance of such action,
and use its help i.e. the help of glib political denunciations, to damage
or even wrong the genius.[37]

It is a telling indictment of conditions within the Nazi state; but the
musician used this accurate picture of the situation to bring to people's
attention the fact that his case urgently needed to be settled. By rehabilitation, he meant more than a triumphal reinstatement to his artistic
functions. But that was where the difficulty lay. Clemens Krauss was
now in charge at the Staatsoper, and Göring had tellingly approved a
ten-year contract with him. This meant that all possibility of return was
blocked. But Furtwängler felt particularly strongly about the musical
stage. Some sort of solution had to be found if his talents were not to
lie fallow. Whether in the intervening period Göring or – even more
likely – Goebbels dropped him a clear hint, is not documented. But in
February the conductor drafted a statement in which he clearly outlined
what he felt should happen:

> I am currently making arrangements with Vienna and New York;
> despite this I wish to remain a German while abroad, and attach the
> greatest importance to being able to carry out my activities outside as
> a German [. . .]. This means that, even if in future I am not to have
> a position with fixed responsibilities in Germany, I still wish to have
> the option of conducting as a guest, in other words as a free man in
> my own country, just like any other German.[38]

Shortly afterwards a part of this draft text was included in a letter to
Goebbels which signalled the resumption of dialogue over his continued
artistic activity in Germany. Both sides definitely sought a *rapprochement*.
No sooner had her predecessor told her her responsibilities and the
current situation, the conductor's new secretary, Ingeborg Mörschner
approached one Herr Brückner and asked for a short meeting, because

'it now seems necessary to me to talk with you about Furtwängler's situation'.[39]

Frau Mörschner-Figdor was acting informally and counter to protocol; Herr Brückner was no other than SA-Obergruppenführer Wilhelm Brückner, Hitler's adjutant. So it is not surprising that in the first instance he telephoned to decline the request. At about the same time Hans Sellschopp, a party member, decided to take action. Sellschopp, a product of the KfdK, was a wine merchant and proprietor of the firm Engelhard & Sons in Lübeck and not a musician, but he headed the department of the Reichsmusikkammer which dealt with concerts, and was among other things responsible for tours abroad by German performers and for concerts given in the Reich by foreigners; he had financial backing from the Propaganda Ministry. On 8 February he had dealings with Brückner and must have convinced him that Furtwängler's unavailability for artistic propaganda abroad was doing damage to external affairs which could not be overlooked, because the adjutant suddenly took an interest. Sellschopp informed Furtwängler's secretary. It was a successful mediation. Shortly afterwards Frau Mörschner-Figdor was telling Hitler's adjutant what she believed was required in this situation. In the meantime the manager of the Berlin Philharmonic Orchestra had also had an idea.

With touching zeal Karl Stegmann had developed a completely megalomaniac plan which he handed in to Goebbels. He proposed pulling down about forty houses around the Philharmonie, to make room for a new and enormous House of German Culture, which would accommodate the entire Reichskulturkammer, as well as large concert halls, a new Philharmonie and a new summer garden with restaurant; estimated cost a 'mere' twelve million RM. And the purpose of this proposal? Quite simple:

> As the Berlin Philharmonic Orchestra would be deprived of its concert hall while the new one was being built, it could use the time to carry out a world propaganda tour under Germany's best conductor, as has already been talked about in the past. This could cover – depending what position Germany is in regarding her foreign affairs – the Balkans, Egypt, India, Japan, the Dutch East Indies, Australia, South America, perhaps North America and back. According to earlier calculations the subsidy required for such a journey would not be very great – if what is easily still Europe's best concert orchestra were conducted by a conductor of world-wide renown.[40]

Although his name was not once mentioned it was perfectly obvious to

Goebbels that this costly detour was intended to get none other than Furtwängler back on to the podium. Something had to be done, that was certain, as there was far too much confusion in Berlin's musical life and that of the Reich in general. The Philharmonic was constantly asking for business loans to cover their running deficit, a development watched with unease by the Reich finance minister. On 28 February the propaganda minister granted the conductor an interview; it inevitably turned into an argument. Goebbels played his cards carefully. He told the conductor that as he had been retired, he was free to leave Germany whenever he liked, but that this would then be final and irrevocable; as long as the Nazi state continued to exist no emigrants would be allowed back. Furtwängler declared that he had decided to stay, in so far as he could reconcile doing so with his own honour and principles. The minister immediately put him under pressure by demanding his signature to a document which was an undisguised declaration of loyalty to Hitler and would signal his complete submission. The musician refused, saying he had left because of Hitler's cultural policies and so could not recant. After further altercation he made moves to end the meeting. Goebbels held him back and said: 'Herr Furtwängler, you surely do not wish to deny that it is the Führer who determines cultural policy in Germany.' He received the answer: 'I never tried to deny it; after all any child knows it is true.' Goebbels: 'If you are prepared to confirm that I would be satisfied.'

The musician noted that his opponent had abandoned his original demand, and took this to be a trap. Then he saw the possibility of a compromise, because this confirmation would contain exactly what he wanted to express; that he was not the one responsible for music policy – and its mistakes – but that the leadership was: in other words, Hitler. Lest there should be any doubt, he assured the minister that he was only prepared to remain in Germany as a completely apolitical artist, and therefore asked that he should not be used in connection with political propaganda. Goebbels conceded, saying that he was primarily interested in maintaining a high standard of musical interpretation for the German people.[41] They ended by agreeing on the wording of a communiqué which was to be published; the details of Furtwängler's return to the music business in the Reich had not been mentioned. The minister subsequently sent news of the agreement to the agencies, but not the full version of Furtwängler's declaration, just a short report that his article on Hindemith

had been written as a musical expert intending only to deal with a musical matter from a musical point of view. He regretted the political consequences and inferences which resulted from his article, the more so as it had not been his intention at all to use this article to interfere in the formation of the Reich's cultural policy, which in his opinion too could obviously only be determined by the Führer and the appropriate minister appointed by him.[42]

The report referred correctly to the content of the discussion. And yet Furtwängler's point of view was seen by certain circles as a 'capitulation': within Germany by those who – without considering the power relationship – had expected a great show of resistance, and abroad above all by emigrants who wanted confirmation that they had done the right thing, and so could not admit that the decision to stick it out and fight was even an option. The German press welcomed the agreement as of one voice, commenting hopefully that one might infer from this 'that the great musician could once again take up the position which befits him in the National Socialist State'.[43]

This anticipation of future agreements was based on the concrete information that it had been the pressure brought to bear by a discontented public which had induced the government to make peace. Foreign agencies – for example the Associated Press – were talking of a 'public strike'.[44] There were two people of consequence who found it hard to be well disposed to the course events had taken. The newly appointed director of the Staatsoper Krauss secretly feared he would sooner or later have to return the post to his predecessor – despite his ten-year contract and the soothing assurances of Göring, he made sure he was on his guard. Furtwängler's great political enemy, Rosenberg, was no less discontented because he felt he had been passed over completely.

On 5 March Goebbels received a letter sent by the Nazi Party's department of foreign affairs; simultaneously, and also delivered by messenger, a copy of this letter together with a cover note arrived at the desk of Reichsminister Hess, the Führer's deputy. Rosenberg was complaining about the wording of that 'peace' report, which he considered a 'direct provocation':

Furtwängler does not apologise for his political attacks on a National Socialist organisation, he only expresses regret at the consequences and inferences which have allegedly been drawn from his article. And a National Socialist minister allows him to get away with such a statement. I would therefore ask you to demand of Herr Dr Furtwängler that he apologise in exactly the same way to me, but for his political attacks on the NS cultural association, not for the inferences drawn.[45]

This complaint produced an effect. The conductor had still not been given the permission to resume his responsibilities which he so anxiously awaited; dates agreed for concerts abroad were drawing ominously close. An audience with Hitler had already been agreed, but it did not take place as planned. Furtwängler had suggested beginning his return to the podium with a charity concert in aid of the needy in winter – a good cause which as far as he was aware had no political overtones. This was to have taken place on 8 April, but nothing was done about it. Almost at the last minute he sent a reminder to Hitler, pointing out that, since making his 'declaration of loyalty to you which I gave to Dr Goebbels', he had already signed contracts for two concerts in Vienna, one concert in Budapest, two opera performances in Covent Garden on the English king's jubilee and for four performances during the Wagner *Ring* cycle at the Paris Opéra; he unashamedly stressed the demands for damages which would ensue if he did not go:

> As a self-employed man I cannot legally renege on a contract I have entered into. Is it your wish that I should appeal to *force majeure* – the only option which would remain to me in this case – and does the government wish to take full responsibility (of both a financial and a moral kind) for this step, or will I be allowed to keep to the contracts I have made? Is it not possible that I would otherwise be turned into a martyr abroad?[46]

Even Hitler would not have liked that; embarrassing attention abroad was to be avoided. But there was still one formality to settle – although no evidence survives to prove whether or not it really was only a formality. According to *Der Führer*, on 9 April a meeting took place between Furtwängler and Rosenberg on 'matters concerning German art and culture'.[47] The report is not in itself terribly informative, but it is probable that the Reichsleiter Rosenberg, as he had made clear in his letter to Hess, still felt it important that there should be an apology for political attacks on an official party organisation, the NSKG, and that Furtwängler did then condescend to say something, no doubt hidden behind a mass of protective clauses but formally correct, which appeared to satisfy this demand. Furtwängler's main aim was to manoeuvre in such a way that he would not be stuck on the sidelines where he could not bring any influence to bear on politico-cultural matters. Having made these preparations he hoped that the meeting with Hitler on 10 April, in the midst of the excitement of Göring's wedding, would clear the way for him. And this is what happened. Someone who did not understand the motives behind the artist's actions had observed uneasily of this outcome 'that the successful master conductor has knuckled under after all'.[48]

At any rate the following afternoon Furtwängler began rehearsing the Vienna Philharmonic in Vienna for the Sunday concert, and the musicians, who understood that the 'capitulation' had been a political success, gave him an enthusiastic welcome. It was no different in Berlin at the beginning of the rehearsal for his first concert together with the Berlin Philharmonic since his withdrawal from public life. On 24 April he mounted 'his' podium once again; the orchestra's director Höber delivered a speech saying,

We can now continue on this path of great achievements, the only path, which we must pursue, not merely to satisfy our sense of artistic responsibility, but also to discharge in our jobs our duty as citizens of the new state. You were previously our proven and unique leader. We know exactly to whom we owe our deep gratitude for being able to work together again.[49]

Although the orchestra may have been waiting impatiently for the restoration of a situation which had for many years seemed their ideal, it was now obvious that the day-to-day atmosphere had changed. This was not a declaration of sincere friendship, but a speech of thanks to someone one took the precaution of treating as an official. Had Höber even informed Furtwängler that the management had invited Hitler to the first concert? This invitation was addressed directly to the Chancellery; when there was no response State Secretary Funk was asked to mediate, and at the same time the invitation was extended to include Goebbels, the 'patron of our orchestra':

We have already invited the Führer and chancellor of the Reich to the concert on 25 April conducted by Wilhelm Furtwängler, but now take the liberty of asking you if you would kindly give your support to our invitation to the Führer. We hardly need to point out how much the orchestra would appreciate the great honour the Führer would be doing us by attending, as he has unfortunately not yet found the time this winter to attend any of our concerts.[50]

Funk, who knew that Hitler was not in Berlin and would not be back until after the time, made a note of it and informed Stegmann by telephone – the day after the concert.

It was a sensational event. A crowd of people had already begun collecting at 7 p.m. outside the Philharmonie, which was sold out to the

175

Regarding the use of the German greeting by the conductor at symphony concerts

From the Minister for Popular Enlightenment and Propaganda

29 January 1937

To Herr President of the Reichmusikkammer
re letter of 21.12.36

It has hitherto not been customary to greet the public using the German greeting. But the German greeting is now desired on such occasions. However under no circumstances should conductors be forced to greet the public in a particular way.

(signed) Walter Funk

---

last seat. The stream of cars arriving seemed never-ending. Furtwängler arrived shortly before eight o'clock and entered the building through a side door in Köthener Strasse, to the accompaniment of enthusiastic ovations in the street. On the podium the applause surged around him for so long that he had to lower his baton several times before he could begin. Between pieces the applause was like the thunder of the elements; in the main interval the public showered their long-lost hero with hundreds of flowers. After the concert the Philharmonie resounded for a further half-hour with the enthusiasm of music lovers. Those representatives of party and state who were present – Rosenberg, Funk, the mayor Dr Sahm, Reichsminister Dr Frick and probably several others – understood that this was without doubt a political demonstration, and this must have been apparent to the foreign diplomats, above all to the French ambassador, François-Poncet. The press were almost lyrical in their unanimous acclamation, testifying to the worth of the regained conductor. Eight days later, on 3 May, he repeated the well-proven Beethoven programme to a similar response. This time Hitler, Göring and his wife, and Goebbels were present. When they entered the hall, the orchestra having already taken their seats, the public and the musicians stood up and offered the 'German greeting'. At almost the same moment the conductor sprang on to the podium, and now the politicians could see for themselves the flush of enthusiasm which his appearance unleashed. All attention was on him and all hearts were on his side; the politicians were just members of the cheering public. The foreign press were alert to what was going on: 'One could hear several calls of "Heil Hitler!" when Furtwängler stepped on to the podium immediately after Hitler's arrival. He thanked them for the applause but then turned immediately to the orchestra.'[51]

For readers today there may be nothing so special about this; but at that time it had a hidden meaning and was a signal to people that Furtwängler had not changed. What was at issue was the 'German greeting' to Hitler; it was not actually the custom for a conductor to offer it, but master conductors who were also members of the party thought it their duty, even if it did go beyond the requirements of etiquette. Who exactly had demanded that he raise his arm in front of Hitler is not clear,[52] but it was the orchestra's attendant, Franz Jastrau, who gave the enraged chief the tip which solved the problem, namely to go out holding the baton in his right hand.[53] Hitler had doubtless not expected that the musician would snub him, but he put a brave face on it and after the concert made his way on to the podium to shake Furtwängler's hand and hand him a bunch of roses. Göring also thanked him with a hand-shake, as if he had to demonstrate that this was really 'his' artist, whom he had discovered for the Staatsoper; perhaps at this moment he was already regretting that he had made such a definite agreement with Krauss. At any rate this 'reconciliatory' concert in many ways presaged future developments. Only a few days later the telegraph wires between the German news agency and editors' offices were buzzing with the news of a further – apparent – peace treaty: 'The management of the Bayreuth Festival announces that Wilhelm Furtwängler will be chief conductor at the 1936 festival.'[54]

There is no doubt that Hitler had given a nudge here, because Winifred Wagner had not forgotten her old grudge; in addition a politically important date, which would be useful for canvassing support, had been fixed: the year of the Olympic Games in Berlin. Only those in the know could interpret what lay behind the announcement by the management of the Berlin Philharmonic that Furtwängler would only conduct four or five of the Philharmonic concerts in the coming season. The papers rejoiced prematurely: 'With the reinstatement of Furtwängler as the central pillar of our German musical life, the survival of a great spiritual tradition of live performances through which the great masterpieces become a part of us and through which we develop, is once again assured.'[55]

However, Furtwänger could not be counted on to serve the purposes of cultural propaganda, making himself scarce even for the routine round of repertoire concerts. He would not be misused for political purposes! That was the condition he had set. He really did reduce his activity with the Berlin Philharmonic in Germany – and probably elsewhere too. Until the end of the war the number of concerts he gave remained without exception below that reached in the 1930–1 and 1931–2 seasons. On the other hand he increased his activities abroad, not least so that the credibility of his argument would not be put at risk, namely that domestic politicisation had a prejudicial effect beyond the border. It is debatable whether he ever really believed that it was possible to use music for propaganda purposes, but to further his own aims he acted as if it were.

Totalitarian regimes – but others also – like to make world-champion boxers, conductors, ballet ensembles and national football teams conform to the same rules, because they feel it in their interests to chalk up their victories as if they were victories for the nation. The fact that a concert is not the same as a sports match because there are no teams competing with one another does not bother them. Most politicians see the possibilities for using music – like sport – as a weapon in the competition for international prestige. If artists make a lot of good music, then the state whose passport they happen to carry in their pockets considers itself an 'artistic and intellectual world power'. However the quality of music-making manifestly does not depend on the morality of the government which happens to be in power, nor even on the subsidies it gives; it depends on quite different factors. Even a high level of financial input cannot buy lasting quality. Money produces neither good composers nor brilliant interpreters of music. Those in power have no right to use their country's music at political events. However, they would really like artistic achievement to belong not to the artist who creates it, but to his state, and they therefore nationalise not only musical institutions but also individual artistic achievements. It is to this illusion, that the state can 'appropriate' art, that the idea and practice of using music as propaganda owe their existence. A veil must be drawn over the fact that instrumental music is 'useless' for this because it publicises itself only and nothing else . . . which explains the love of dictators – and also of brown-shirt ideologists – for Plato, and their panic-stricken hostility towards 'formalists' such as Hanslick and

178

Stravinsky. This belief in the political effectiveness of music forms current ideology – although there is not a trace of factual proof. Of course music does certain things; it distracts, even if only temporarily, from reality; it calms or excites, makes people aggressive or peaceful; but it has neither a moral impact nor does it work in the interests of any party, because for it to do so requires the listener to have a continuity of will which exists for more than just the moment itself. Beethoven, when played by the Reich's brown-uniformed symphony orchestra, could strengthen the ideological beliefs of a party member. Furtwängler with his Philharmonic in London or Paris, with the same Beethoven in the programme, would convince not even the most stupid of listeners that Hitler could be considered a sort of cross between Albert Schweitzer and Abraham Lincoln.

People did after all read the papers. That is why it is absurd that extremely anti-fascist emigrants should have appropriated this – considerable – chunk of Nazi ideology; only such an ideological infection can explain their firm conviction that Furtwängler really did effect publicity for the regime. Not one voice of doubt or critical reason was raised. Nobody asked why or how he would want to carry out this political publicity, nor how many of his listeners he turned into 'Nazis'. Does everyone who listens to Beethoven become an ardent supporter of Hitler? What was the connection between this great master and the dictator? The various 'cold wars' of our own times have unfortunately strengthened the misconception that artists are representatives of those in power and as such may be persecuted and harassed.

Furtwängler drew clear distinctions. For example, in June 1935 he refused to conduct at the summer solstice celebrations at which the leader of the Hitler Youth, Schirach, was to give a 'torchlit' speech to 20,000 youths. Nor would he conduct at the second congress of the Nordic Society – he was a member – which was to include a celebratory concert and the inauguration of the Lübeck Holstentor as a 'site of honour in the military history of the Hanseatic town of Lübeck'; but he did agree to do the subsequent Nordic Music Festival which was co-organised by the federation of Scandinavian composers, and so conducted the opening concert. At this time international plans were facing numerous difficulties. For example the exchange of soloists with Vienna suddenly came to a standstill. Frau Mörschner enquired whether the stoppage was of an official nature:

What is the Führer's basic position regarding the exchange of soloists with Vienna? a) Krauss has been behind it until now because he wants to ruin the Vienna opera – and a total prohibition on going to Vienna

179

has been issued to the people at the Staatsoper. b) We have been exchanging for more than fifteen years now, regardless of all political tensions. c) These soloists are required by Furtwängler.[56]

The secretary had touched on a highly political and sensitive area, which brought her into a conflict of interests with Alfred Frauenfeld, who had not only been appointed manager of the Reichstheaterkammer, but was also a Nazi Party Gauleiter and had had to flee from Austria.

Initially everything remained calm. Hitler honoured concerts given by Furtwängler with his presence more often than usual; for example at the Munich festival in June, he attended a performance of *Tristan und Isolde* at the Bavarian Staatsoper and a Beethoven concert in the Exhibition Hall the following day. He had plans for the famous musician and the musician had plans for the Berlin Philharmonic Orchestra, although it was only 'his' in a metaphorical sense now that it came 'under the supervision of the Ministry for Popular Enlightenment and Propaganda', and shortly afterwards it was made one of the latter's 'subordinate departments'. In his capacity as a member of the supervisory board Höber acquainted the minister with the orchestra's historical principles, obviously in the hope that something at least might be rescued:

> Team spirit, total commitment and enthusiasm for an artistic vocation together with the highest standards of personal achievement were the demands above all others. Personal freedom could not be abused because however free an individual was, his duties to the collective were greater than his rights. [. . .] The high quality of our orchestra is proof that it was a system which worked. Even Wilhelm Furtwängler demanded no privileges in this respect, because he valued the cooperation of the orchestra on such an important point. [. . .] This ideal working collaboration in artistic achievements brought the most superb results. In the mind of the world the great conductor and his orchestra have become inseparable. Hard work, great ability and love of music brought about achievements which placed both the conductor and the orchestra at the very top of musical activity throughout the world.[57]

This was more than merely information for the minister; it was a hint that tradition could not just be swept away and replaced with a 'new spirit' and commands from above, tactically clothed in the empty phrases of a declaration of loyalty. Or maybe not totally empty; the musicians had reason to be grateful as the subsidy from the state treasury increased year by year, finally amounting to 1,100,000 RM.

The Staatsoper was similarly concerned with money. Box-office takings made it clear that Furtwängler's dismissal as musical chief had disgruntled the public to the point where they boycotted the opera. The finance minister noted this with great concern, bearing Göring the bad tidings that

> since the beginning of the calendar year 1935 there has been a constant decline in the takings. In the last few months the Staatsoper has not even been breaking even. [. . .] While not technically in a position to express an opinion on the reasons which have led to this unfavourable financial development, the finance minister does however feel he should point out that it is not the season or the general economic situation which are to blame.[58]

Some lines further on the finance minister made it clear how well he saw through the whole situation; he suggested that Göring should take a stronger grip on the management of his theatres than he had done hitherto, economise on the position of opera director and engage 'one or two particularly highly qualified conductors' instead, with the general intendant to provide musical direction. An attached statement of monthly takings allowed the prime minister to see for himself how serious the situation was. From the moment the public had understood that Furtwängler was not coming back, they had stayed away. In February 1935 there was still a surplus of 34,407 RM; by March this had already become a deficit of 8,144 RM, reaching 24,444 RM by June. Göring acted on the spot and behind Krauss's back, although probably not without obtaining approval from Hitler first. He asked Furtwängler to put down his thoughts on their future collaboration in a draft contract.

Furtwängler sketched out the text of a five-year contract in which he wanted not only to guarantee his financial security, but also to stipulate directive functions, stating that 'should the extent of his influence as outlined by this contract be insufficient to allow him to determine the artistic standard of the Staatsoper as he wishes', he would insist on modifying the contract to give him the title of 'director of the opera with overall responsibility for music'. The first paragraph ran as follows: 'With effect from 1 January 1936 the Prussian state appoints Herr Staatsrat Dr Furtwängler to the post of the state's chief conductor at the Staatsoper in Berlin.'[59]

His desire for complete rehabilitation is impressively documented in this draft. Of course the fact remained that Göring had changes of mind, and it did not remain a secret for long who was most likely to be affected by them. Tietjen feared for his own power and began to intrigue, and Krauss too could already see himself on the street; he could well imagine how little his ten-year contract was worth if Göring no longer wanted it. So he called on powerful friends and political associates; firstly Gauleiter Frauenfeld, a trusted brother-in-arms from the Vienna period who valued the musician precisely because, as he was not officially a member of the Nazi Party, he could agitate unrecognised. The Gauleiter had after all witnessed Krauss's departure from Vienna, after he had been put on the list of suspects there, 'primarily for political reasons; his pursuit of the fight against the Austrian system of government, begun by us two years earlier, also extended to culture'.[60] The functionary was now able to demonstrate his gratitude. He sent the heads of the Reichskulturkammer an eight-page memorandum in which he discussed the tactics of the campaign of politico-cultural destruction against Austria, and pointed out a tiresome problem: there were certain artists who had the nerve to try and sabotage this campaign, led by one person in particular:

> Dr Wilhelm Furtwängler has been engaged for a series of guest performances at the Vienna Staatsoper for the coming autumn. Amongst other things he is supposed to be producing a newly staged version of *Tannhäuser*. The new staging is not being done by the Vienna opera's resident theatrical director, the Jew Dr Lothar Wallerstein; a second Jew has been engaged at Furtwängler's request, namely Dr Herbert Graf, who emigrated from Germany and whose father is art critic on the Vienna weekly *Der Morgen* and the daily *Der Tag*, both Bolshevist-Jewish-run papers.[61]

What irritated the exiled Gauleiter above all was the distinctly positive reponse to this by the Viennese press; he of course read deliberate malevolence into the remark that Graf's appointment was 'particularly noteworthy, as in making it without consideration for the racial policy of the Berlin regime Furtwängler has made it quite clear that artistic quality is the only criterion he will work by'.[62]

Everybody understood that the conductor was demonstrating abroad what by 'force of circumstance' he was prevented from demonstrating at home, that he was definitely acting for political reasons, and that in so doing he was exposing the Nazis' racial theory to ridicule. In the Reich those 'circumstances' were worsening day by day. In the Berlin Philharmonic Orchestra there were no actual dismissals, but the psychological pressure was more than sensitive artists could bear. The Jewish

MAI

8 Dienstag Stanislaus

1 Furtwängler's diary, 8 May 1945:
'When I am in Switzerland and observe the people's behaviour towards Germany, how they judge them in their defeat, I think of two verses from the Bible: ' "Vengeance is mine," saith the Lord' and 'He that is without sin among you, let him first cast a stone'. The willingness of a whole nation to pass facile judgements is unchristian and unsound. It is terrible when it is so widespread; there is a hardening of souls which is just as much the devil's doing as the National Socialist (devil, which they think they are fighting).'

2 Everyone working in the music business was on the files of the
Reichsmusikkammer

3 Goebbels the music historian: speech during the Bach–Schütz–Handel year, 21 March 1935

4 The Berlin Philharmonie

5 German Week of Culture, Paris 1937. Honouring the dead at the Tomb of the Unknown Soldier: 'The Government official raised his arm good and high, Tietjen did so satisfactorily, but Furtwängler stood with his arm held awkwardly pressed against his shoulder. Later I discovered that Tietjen showed this picture to the relevant authorities as proof of Furtwängler's treacherous anti-Nazi feelings' (Friedelind Wagner).

6 Hans Pfitzner in 1942

7 Symbolic of Furtwängler's situation: 'Big Brother' Adolf Hitler was always present in one way or another

8 A welder listens to Wagner, 26 February 1942

9 A work-break concert at the AEG in Berlin, 26 February 1942

10 Armaments workers listen to classical music during their – extended –
lunch–break, 26 February 1942

i) Guests of honour at Hitler's birthday celebrations

ii) The minister is displeased because he has had to threaten Furtwängler

iii) Furtwängler conducting between speeches, against his will

iv) A brief handshake – frozen smile

v) His expression gradually becomes stonier

vi) The public applaud, unsuspecting

| 4 | | 5 |

| noch I. Angaben zur Person | IIa. Musterung |

10	Schulbildg. (nur Abschluß)	*Gymnasium*	
11	Kenntnisse in Fremd- sprachen*) (keine Schul- kenntnisse)	*engl. franz.*	
12	Berufliche, techn. oder sportl. Be- fähigungs- nachweise **)	*Fahrschein Kl. 2*	
13	Anschrift des nächsten Angehörigen bzw. der bei Verlust- anzeige zu be- nachrichtigen- den Person (nur im Kriege auszufüllen)	Vor- und Zuname: *Elisabeth Furtwängler* Verwandt- schaftsgrad: *Ehefrau* Ort: *Potsdam* Straße, Gebäudeteil, ggf. Untermieter bei: *Hiltlerstr. 36*	

| 13 a | **Nachträge** |

IIa. Musterung

Gemustert Ärztlich untersucht	als *Dienstpflichtiger* (Dienstpflichtiger, Freiwilliger für R. bewußt, W.. u. §§ GAB.*)	
	Wehrbezirkskommando, Truppenteil, Kommdtr.	Tag, Monat, Jahr
I	**Wehrmeldeamt Potsdam 1**	**7. Dez. 1944**
II		
III		

Entscheid

Tauglichkeitsgrad	Wehrdienstverhältnis
14 **arbeitsverwendungsfähig**	**Landsturm II**
I Kriegsdienst(schrift)/Kommdtr.	Unt...	Wehrbezirkskommando
	Fischer	
	Major und ...	...beamte
II		
III		

*) Nichtzutreffendes durchstreichen

*) Dolmetscher, Übersetzer oder Sprachkundiger – Prüfungsdatum.
**) Reiter-, Führer-, Pionier-, Nachrichten-, Sanitätsschein, Bescheinigung des deutschen Alpenvereins, Ausweise über seemännische und fliegerische Betäti- gung, Seefahrtzeit.

12 Furtwängler's military service card

13 Dr Wilhelm Furtwängler and his wife Elisabeth, 1954

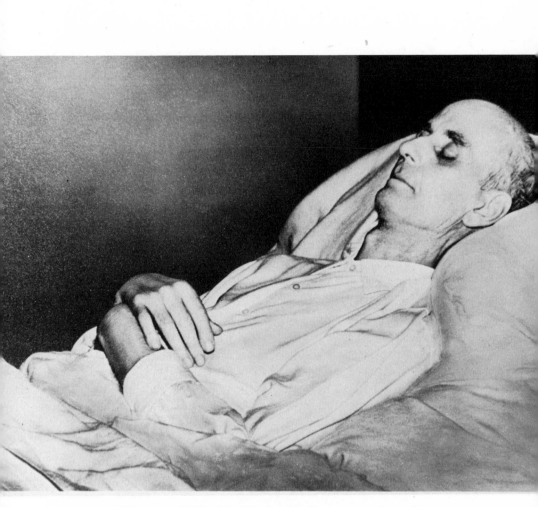

14 ' . . . on his deathbed in the shirt he wore to rehearsals,
his hands as I had arranged them. Then the dear nuns came, dressed him in a
satin shirt and folded his hands. Truly death and transfiguration . . . '
(Elisabeth Furtwängler)
30 November 1954

Jüdifchen Mufikfchule. Komponift hebräifcher Mufik. — Vater:
W o l f g a n g   G r a d, Mutter: R o f a   I f r a e l e w i t z. —
Verh. mit R a c h e l   H a l p e r i n. — A. / Philo. / Mü.

Gradenwitz P e t e r, Dr. phil., geb. 1910 zu Berlin. Komponift
und Mufikfchriftfteller in Berlin-Pankow, Breiteftraße 44.
Nennt fich P i e t   G r a n d o. — A.

Grätzer-Jacobfohn F r i e d a, geb. 1899 zu Berlin. Mufiklehrerin
in Berlin, Bambergerftraße 60. — A.

Graf M a x, Dr. jur., geb. 1873 zu Wien. Mufiklehrer und Mufikfchriftfteller (u. a. für „Das neue Wiener Journal", „Wiener
allgemeine Zeitung") in Wien, Eifengaffe 30. 1921/1922 Her-
ausgeber der Zeitfchrift „Mufik-Kurier". Vater = J o f e f G.,
Mutter = R e g i n a G. — SV. / Nat. B. / Ei. / Mü.

Gramatte S o n j a, g e b. F r i d m a n n, geb. 1892 zu Moskau.
Geigerin, Pianiftin und Komponiftin (u. a. Violin- und Klavier-
mufik) in Berlin. — ABC, I.

Grand E d g a r, Mifchling, geb. 16. 7. 1902 in Leipzig-Gohlis.
Schlagzeuger in Leipzig. — A.

Grando P i e t = G r a d e n w i t z   P e t e r; fiehe daf.

Granichftädten B r u n o, geb. 1880 zu Wien. Operettenkomponift
(u. a. „Der Orloff", „Evelyne", Brettllieder) und Kapellmeifter
in Wien. Seine Libretti fchrieb z. T. Robert B o d a n z k y. —
H 39. / SV. / E 3.

Grau M a u r i c e, Imprefario in Paris. — SV.

Graudan J o h a n n a, geb. 18. 5. 1905 in Libau. Pianiftin in Berlin-
Schöneberg. — A.

Graudan N i c o l a i, geb. 24. 8. 1896 in Libau. Celift in Berlin-
Schöneberg. — A.

Green L u d w i g, M o f e s, D a v i d, geb. 1897 in Öfterreich.
Liederlibrettift in Brooklyn. 1920 verh. m. Anna von Hinken.
— Nat. B.

Gregorowitfch C h a r l e s, geb. 1867 zu Petersburg, geft. 1926.
Geiger in Berlin. — Kohut. / SV.

Grift E m i l = G i f t   E m i l; fiehe daf.

Grinbaum K u r t, Mifchling, geb. 1914 zu Berlin. Mufiker in Ber-
lin-Spandau. Wörtherftraße 17. — A.

Grifi C a r l o t t a, geb. 1821 zu Haute Iftrie. „Wunderkind". Tän-
zerin und Sängerin. — Nat. B.

Grifi G i u d i t t a, geb. 1805 zu Mailand, geft. 1840 zu Cremona.
Opernfängerin in Paris. 1833 verh. m. d. Grafen Barni. —
Nat. B. / SV. / H 39. / P.

The cellist Nikolai Graudan is among those denounced in the first *Judenlexikon*,
1935

solo-cellist Nikolai Graudan went at the end of August, despite having a new year-long contract dated March 1935 in his pocket; at the end of the year the first violinist Gilbert Back, also a 'non-Aryan', left with severance pay of 15,625 RM and emigrated to Ankara. The evidence of Furtwängler's combatting racial madness at home was becoming thin on the ground. Hugo Kolberg did stay, it is true, though a rather comical disappointment which befell him had nothing to do with politics: one day in August the orchestra's management gave him the use of a supposedly extremely valuable violin, which according to the label was a Jacopo Brandini, made in Pisa in 1816. It was a donation from one Frau Hedwig Wolff of Dahme-in-der-Mark, which she had sent to Goebbels. He passed the priceless gift on to the orchestra. For insurance purposes one of the managers, Stegmann, had it valued by an expert and it turned out that it was a fairly elderly example from Saxony, worth at most 500 RM, though slightly enhanced by the fact that its source of origin had been falsified.

Nevertheless these changes, both of personnel and otherwise, created unrest and tension among the musicians. On 31 July Goebbels dismissed Hermann Stange as manager and as his successor appointed – on Furtwängler's recommendation – the conductor Hans von Benda, who had been music reviewer at the Reichsradio. Furtwängler also suffered from these machinations, in so far as they restricted artistic possibilities, and he found the ever-increasing amount of paper-work so repugnant that he even sent back one of the Reichsmusikkammer's questionnaires without filling it in. Frau Mörschner was promptly informed by Hinkel that 'every member of the Reichsmusikkammer is obliged to fill out the form'.[63]

In the meantime he was receiving disquieting intimations; the gang of Austrian Nazis who had 'emigrated' was still agitating, which ensured that all official channels were kept busy. The details of his 'lapse' in Vienna were being circulated around the various departments; different bits of information crossed and multiplied; the outlines of a denunciatory statement began to appear. The similarity of the wording clearly points to one source: Frauenfeld, as Krauss's spokesman. The Propaganda Ministry informed the Reichskulturkammer who were however already aware of it; the direct links to the Nazi underground movement in Vienna are unmistakable:

Graf's political and ideological opinions are ones which have been rejected by the National Socialist state. He is an emigrant of the worst sort. The rumours currently circulating here are to the astonishing effect that a Prussian Staatsrat is working at an Austrian cultural institution together with a full-blooded Jew. Please inform me whether any action should be taken from here.[64]

His denouncers were particularly bitter that Furtwängler had voluntarily engaged the director off the street after discovering that Graf was currently unemployed. However, Hinkel remained unconcerned. He filed away the letter without taking any further action. Even though the case involved those holding high office, it did not yet concern the state. The conductor was still needed, as Hitler's adjutant made clear: 'By request of the Führer, Furtwängler is to conduct the première of *Die Meistersinger* at the opening of the Party congress.'[65]

Although it was beyond the comprehension of a retired captain that it was not the première which was at issue, and why not, the factual content otherwise was more or less correct – apart from the confusion of 'opening' with 'the evening before the opening'. There was more to come. Hitler also wished him to conduct Beethoven's Fifth in Nuremberg's Apollo Theatre for the party congress's cultural symposium. The promise not to use him for propaganda purposes had been forgotten, but such requests made his importance clear. He agreed to do the opera in the town theatre, even though the Nazi Party's national organisers rather than the usual board of management were responsible for the event. But he would do no more than this; *Die Meistersinger* was to take place the evening before the political event rather than being a formal part of the programme. The party congress was ceremonially declared open the following morning. In fact in that year's official programme the opera was still listed, haphazardly reserved for the diplomatic corps and various high-ranking members of the party; but the legally decisive point was the timing of the official opening, and it could thus be argued that the opera was not a part of the congress. For us today this may seem rather feeble, but at the time it made a statement. Regarding the performance of the Fifth during the congress, Schaub, Hitler's adjutant, was then informed that Furtwängler,

sticking very carefully to protocol – as I would particularly wish to stress – has asked to be excused. His reasons are as follows: he needs the time prior to *Die Meistersinger* for thorough rehearsals of *Die Meistersinger*. *Die Meistersinger* itself lasts five hours and puts extraordinary demands on him as a conductor which would affect his capacities the following day. [. . .] In short he declares that he is very aware what a distinction it is to be chosen for this, but that for the above reasons it is almost impossible for him to meet the request.[66]

185

Although diplomatically phrased, it was a definite refusal on plausible and irrefutable grounds; those attending the cultural symposium heard the 'Egmont' Overture instead of Beethoven's Fifth, played by the Leipzig Gewandhaus Orchestra under Peter Raabe. Furtwängler was still welcomed despite having declined to conduct; as an honoured guest at the party congress he stayed at the Deutsches Haus Hotel in Nuremberg, and it must have struck him that there was a purpose behind the regime's newly awakened affection for him. It was the purpose Goebbels supported: namely a 'foreign mission' for the benefit of National Socialism. The Reich's congress organisers had arranged the evening of opera for the same purpose. Hitler was clearly the one giving the orders in artistic matters; it was at his request that Kammersänger Karl Kronenberg sang the part of Hans Sachs in place of Jaro Prohaska, who had fallen ill. National and regional leaders, the chiefs of the SA and SS, representatives from the different branches of the armed forces, the ministers of the Reich and Hitler, accompanied by Gauleiter Julius Streicher, all took their places on the tiered seats. The press was rather heavy-handed in its praise of this political event:

Wagner's *Die Meistersinger* is the musical expression of our race. The whisper and the vitality of our blood which we hear in this music is similar to the quiet rushing we hear when we hold a shell to our ear. [. . .] The very thing which was held against Wagner right from the beginning and which his malevolent (usually non-German) opponents claimed was a lack and a sign of the low standing of his art, is what we today consider the greatest merit of that art: its overwhelming and irresistible sensuality, which sweeps us along with it, filling and bewitching all our senses.[67]

This response was a warning to Furtwängler that his participation in this occasion had endangered and even detracted from his artistic integrity, especially as the evening of opera had certainly been seen as part of the congress, in other words he had indirectly played a role in a party rite; at that point he must have decided he would have to act even more cautiously to avoid being compromised in any way.

Because of the public attention he received and his success in Nuremberg his enemies mounted another attack on him. This time it began anonymously, with a middleman delivering a – 'strictly confidential' – letter (p. 187) to Hinkel's address:

A leading personality in Berlin's cultural life, who does not wish to

Berlin, am 17.September 35.

An Herrn S t a a t s k o m m i s s a r
H a n s   H i n k e l
Geschäftsführer der Reichskulturkammer

B e r l i n .

Streng vertraulich!

*Eine führende Persönlichkeit des Berliner Kunstlebens,
die nicht genannt sein möchte, für die ich aber mich ganz
verbürge, kam vor wenigen Tagen aus Wien zurück.*
*Dort traf sie auf der Strasse zufällig mit dem jüdischen
Schriftsteller Franz W e r f e l zusammen. Werfel erkundigte
sich eingehend über die Zustände im Kunstleben des dritten
Reiches und fragte nach seinem guten Bekannten Wilhelm Furtwängler, der bekanntlich in Wien in diesen Kreisen verkehrt.*
*Der Befragte gab Herrn Werfel zur Antwort, dass Furtwängler
zurzeit beim Parteitag in Nürnberg weile, dort die"Meistersinger" dirigieren werde. Werfel konnte das nicht fassen und
sagte immer wieder, dass dies ein Irrtum sein müsse. Das sei
bei der Einstellung Furtwänglers ganz unmöglich. Nach wieder-
holten Beweisen des anderen Herrn, der Herrn Werfel auch nahe-
legte, sich in den Radioprogrammen davon zu überzeugen, ent-
gegnete der jüdische Dichter, dass Furtwängler sich in den
Wiener Kreisen als ausgesprochener Gegner des neuen Deutschlands
deklariere und die Zustände aufs Abfälligste kritisiere. So
sagte er zu dem jüdischen Emigranten Schriftsteller Zuckerkandl:*
*" Man müsse die Machthaber alle miteinander
abschiessen (beseitigen oder umbringen -
einer dieser drei Ausdrücke war es -), frü-
her werde es in Deutschland nicht anders werden. "*

be named, but whom I will vouch for completely, returned from
Vienna a few days ago.

While there he happened to meet the Jewish writer Franz Werfel
in the street. Werfel asked him detailed questions about the state
of artistic life in the Third Reich and then asked after his good

187

acquaintance, Wilhelm Furtwängler, who as you know mixes in those circles in Vienna.

The person being asked told Herr Werfel that Furtwängler was currently attending the party congress in Nürnberg and would be conducting *Die Meistersinger* there. Werfel found this hard to believe and repeatedly said that this must be a mistake, and that given Furtwängler's opinions it was quite impossible. After repeated assurances from the other gentleman, who also urged Herr Werfel to look at the radio programme if he was not convinced, the Jewish writer responded by saying that in Viennese circles Furtwängler had repeatedly declared himself an out-and-out opponent of the new Germany and been very scathing in his criticism of the current situation. For example he had told the émigré Jewish writer Zuckerkandl: 'Those in power should all be shot (removed or killed – it was one of those three), and things in Germany would not change until this was done.'[68]

This was one of those cases where political naïvety causes great mischief. Why didn't Werfel, who had just finished writing *Die vierzig Tage des Musa Dagh* (The Forty Days of Musa Dagh), learn some political and human wisdom from reading his own book? Or was he, contrary to all the reports in the Viennese press, convinced that the person he was talking to was harmless? Or was the idea to make life in Germany impossible for the conductor and so force him to emigrate?

The denouncer was Oskar Jölli, a party member and oratorio singer, who because of his 'brown' orientations in Austria – he was founder and leader of the Association of National Socialist Artists and regional adviser on cultural matters – had been boycotted and therefore emigrated to the Reich. He was now writing radio plays and acting as the reporter on Austria for the producers of the Reich radio service, as well as belonging to the group around Frauenfeld. He vouched for the veracity of his informer and even stressed that the latter had asked him not to tell anybody. However he felt it was his duty to lodge the information. The air of secrecy surrounding the informer was a farce; anyone who wanted to could use the evidence to put two and two together: the man had visited Vienna, was a member of the same circle of acquaintances as Werfel and Furtwängler, and played a leading role – probably of a musical nature – in Berlin. Anyone in the picture would know that like Jölli he came from the circle around Gauleiter Frauenfeld. Hinkel can hardly have doubted for a moment that Clemens Krauss was the person in question. The latter had deliberately targeted his indiscretion at Jölli, a fanatical believer in the Führer, so it would have maximum effect. Asking Jölli not to blab anything was no more than an alibi. Of his own accord Jölli added the transcript of an interview with the 'Jewish-Bolshevist director Herbert Graf from the most notorious communist paper in Vienna' to the denunciation. But to begin with even this denunciation came to nothing. The commissioner of state made sure the letter disappeared, neither putting it into the files nor giving it to his office to deal with.

On 30 September Ingeborg Mörschner ceased working as secretary to Furtwängler, who immediately engaged Elisabeth Müller-Horstmann. Had Mörschner been allocated to the conductor because she was seen as a catalyst? And what was Captain Wiedemann's interest in her? He seemed keen that she be put to use again fairly rapidly, this time – no doubt not by chance – in the Reichstheaterkammer of which Frauenfeld was manager. He then let it be known that 'on 1 December 1935 the lady will take up a post as secretary at the Pro-rata Stage Recruitment Agency, and will probably be given work suited to her skills in the foreign department which is to be opened there'.[69] Furtwängler must have suspected or noticed that certain things were happening which he could not explain, but which were serious and dangerous, and he reacted – once again – by falling ill; the psychological burden laid him low. Between 16 December 1935 and 15 January 1936 he did not conduct the Berlin Philharmonic at all. This did not stop his opponents from letting the avalanche gather pace.

When Jölli did not receive an answer to the letter he had given to Hinkel and there was still no report of Furtwängler's arrest in the papers, he approached one of the authorities which seemed to offer a greater likelihood of success, because there was already a dossier on the suspect in existence there. He sent a message to the person appointed by the Führer as Reichsleiter of the department which supervised the Nazi Party's intellectual and philosophical education, namely Rosenberg, and it was put into his file on cultural politics. Since the beginning of 1935 the equally fanatical Dr Herbert Gerigk, party no. 1,096,433 as of 15 February 1932, who had recently become a member of the SS, had been in charge of the office dealing with the collection and evaluation of incriminating material against individuals from artistic and cultural circles. Gerigk took immediate action. He passed a copy of Jölli's denunciation on to the Gestapo, commenting:

Furtwängler's statements, and the fact that he engaged Herbert Graf, the Jew, prove not only that he has learnt nothing from what has happened to him in his time, but also that he is apparently just waiting for the moment at which he can publicly espouse a differently oriented politico-cultural line. In this connection it is noteworthy that the

189

newly appointed chief concert master, Hugo Kolberg (formerly at the Frankfurt-am-Main opera house) is married to a full-blooded Jewess. Furtwängler is thus continuing to seek out people whom we cannot countenance according to our principles.

In order to facilitate the Gestapo's investigations Gerigk added, 'for strictly confidential official information only', that 'the leading personality in Berlin's cultural life described in the second paragraph of Jölli's script is probably Clemens Krauss, the opera director. Krauss, who is supposed to have been discriminated against with rumours spread both by Furtwängler's circle and by Tietjen and his people, has always made an exceptionally good impression on us'.[70]

The succeeding months were torture to Furtwängler. His customary assurance began to crumble. He could not understand why politicians suddenly cut him, why doors were shut which had previously been open, and why Hitler refused to speak with him. It gradually dawned on him that he was living as a stranger in his own country. Notes in his diaries show what he would have wanted to say if only anyone had been prepared to listen, and how he would have liked to dispel the agonising distrust which he believed that some, such as Hitler, held him in, after hearing

> that it is not, as I had assumed, your work-load which is causing this delay, but rather dissatisfaction with my recent behaviour. I find that hard to believe. However, if it really is a case of distrust again, which can only rest on mistaken assumptions, then that would be another reason to repeat my request that you grant me this audience.[71]

Hitler however was silent, because he trusted the informers who provided him with incriminatory material. However he continued to act as before, not in order to deceive Furtwängler, but because the occasion demanded it for reasons of protocol: the conductor's fiftieth birthday. The press had prepared a triumphant celebration:

> Furtwängler is and remains for us a great guardian and incomparable guide to the powerful heritage of monumental German music. He was and remains for us the conscientious and sober character who emphasises, and where necessary defends, the need for unhindered creativity relevant to the changing ideals, artistic materials and social structures of our times. These are the beliefs and hopes which link us in gratitude to the fifty-year-old.[72]

190

Was there anything shameful about accepting this reprieve from on high? Hitler sent a silver-framed picture of himself together with a dedication,[73] Goebbels an ornate baton made of ivory and gold along with a flattering card; as part of his laudation the minister expressed

> my deep and sincere thanks for the great services which you have rendered in your many years of musical activity, both to the development of German music and to the invigoration and furtherance of conducting in Germany. I would also ask you to accept my personal thanks for the many hours of pure and wonderful artistic enjoyment which you have given me by your incomparable interpretations of the musical masterpieces.[74]

Was this a signal that the difficulties had been put aside? Possibly the conductor overestimated the significance of these birthday gestures. He had actually asked that there be no great show to mark his fiftieth, and yet State Secretary Funk had been commissioned by Hitler and his ministers to travel to Potsdam to bring greetings and presents to his house. Goebbels even offered him a lifelong honorary pension of 40,000 RM per year, but received a polite 'no thank you' in reply, as a matter of principle. There is no doubt that the artist believed the inexplicable conflict settled and that he once again applied for a meeting with Hitler. The orchestra – which of course had noticed that something was up – supported him in this; the new manager, von Benda, even suggested suitable dates to the Chancellery: Furtwängler was to conduct the *St. Matthew Passion* in Berlin and would therefore be 'at the Führer's disposal on Friday 21 of February – and probably for three to four days after that'.[75]

By way of a reminder Stegmann one day later sent Hitler's adjutant an excessively laudatory birthday article which had appeared in the *Musikwoche*, written by Werner Buchholz, a member of the orchestra. The Chancellery did not react. And yet Furtwängler once again felt so confident that he gave his assistance in a difficult case in a way which probably did nothing to put him in a good light. It had – still – to do with the rehabilitation of the music critic Stuckenschmidt. Even prior to 1933 this militant and sometimes quick-tempered correspondent on the *BZ am Mittag* had already come under attack from the right; shortly after the take-over of power Hinkel, as chairman of the KfdK, had tried to get the editors to remove this difficult individual. The newspaperman knew that some musicians, whom he had sweepingly categorised as 'right-wing' and then attacked venomously, did not love him; he saw himself as the victim of a personal intrigue and even picked a quarrel with Hinkel:

> I was particularly interested when your secretary told me that you were acting by request of all German musicians, and that they reject my work as a critic. The names Schillings and Furtwängler which he mentioned in this connection really say it all. Honoured Commissioner of State, I cannot but reproach you with having let yourself be used as a tool in an undertaking based on purely personal motives, without informing yourself of the real reasons for the hostility which Messrs. Schillings and Furtwängler entertain towards me.[76]

Naturally such boldness did more harm than good; in December 1934 Stuckenschmidt, faced with closed ranks, lost his permission to work by being struck off the list of professional writers. A year later he applied to be reinstated to the Reichsschrifttumskammer; Furtwängler heard of this and tried to help, despite having sufficient grounds to hold a grievance against him. As he had heard that he was to be used to give evidence against the outcast, and as the experience of being an outcast himself was still fresh in his mind, he now voiced support for Stuckenschmidt, informing Hinkel that the applicant

> at the time of his retirement possessed all the qualities which made a good critic – a fluent pen, good knowledge of his subject-matter, and experience (and it is experience which is absolutely indispensable in this profession) – in a measure which raised him far above the average. Given the acute shortage of really good minds in Germany, which is currently affecting journalism as well as other areas, I could only welcome the rehabilitation of St. [uckenschmidt]. I would ask you – if the matter is still under discussion, as I very much hope – to throw my opinion in this matter on to the scales.[77]

How did he sign off? Not 'Heil Hitler', but 'with very best wishes' . . . He had still not learnt, but even had he used the appropriate niceties this was an altogether inauspicious moment for successes; Hinkel must have suspected the conductor of trying to introduce a 'cultural-Bolshevist' into the musical world with plans for future subversion in mind. This was why – after a whole year – he refused the application, but declared himself ready 'to give permission for the publication of individual items once they have been checked'.[78] By keeping him on a short rein Hinkel hoped to bring the critic to his senses. Stuckenschmidt preferred to leave for Prague instead.

192

Zur Haupt- und Nebenausfertigung sind
je 1¹/2 Reichsmark in Stempelmarken
entwertet worden.
26.Februar 1936.

Zwischen

dem Preussischen Ministerpräsidenten
vertreten durch den Generalintendanten der Preussischen Staats-
theater zu Berlin
und
Herrn Staatsrat Dr. Wilhelm F u r t w ä n g l e r
zu Berlin
ist folgender Gastspielvertrag abgeschlossen worden:

§ 1 .

Herr Dr. Furtwängler verpflichtet sich, während der
Spielzeit 1936/37 eine Mindestanzahl von 10 (zehn) Abenden als
Gast an der Staatsoper zu dirigieren; er verpflichtet sich,die
hierfür nötigen Proben abzuhalten.
Über die Besetzung und die Anzahl der Proben ist vorher
mit dem General-Intendanten Übereinstimmung hergestellt worden.

§ 2 .

Als Honorar erhält Herr Dr. Furtwängler 2000 RM (Zweitau-
send Reichsmark) für den Abend.

§ 3 .

Der mit Herrn Dr. Furtwängler unter dem 16. Januar 1934 ab-
geschlossene Vertrag gilt mit dem Beginn des vorstehenden Vertrages, d.i. 1. September 1936, im beiderseitigen Einverständ-
nis als aufgehoben.

§ 4 .

Die Kosten des Vertrages an Stempelgebühr tragen beide
Parteien je zur Hälfte.

Berlin,den 24.Februar 1936.
Der Preussische Ministerpräsident: gez. W. Furtwängler.
gez. Göring.

Für die Richtigkeit der Abschrift:

Reaktivierung vorste-
henden Vertrages s. umS.

CERTIFIED COPY

A stamp duty of 1 Reichsmark each has been deducted for the original and
copy.

The following contract for guest appearances has been agreed between the Prussian Prime Minister represented by the General Intendant of the Prussian State Theatre in Berlin and Herr Staatsrat Dr Wilhelm Furtwängler in Berlin:

1. Herr Dr Furtwängler undertakes to conduct a minimum of 10 (ten) evenings as a guest at the Staatsoper during the 1936–7 period; he also undertakes to hold the necessary rehearsals. The timing and number of rehearsals has been arranged by prior agreement with the General Intendant.

2. As honorarium Dr. Furtwängler will receive 2000 RM (two thousand Reichsmark) per evening.

3. With effect from the beginning of the current contract, i.e. 1 September 1936, the previous contract with Herr Dr Furtwängler agreed to on 16 January 1934 is considered terminated by mutual agreement.

4. Both parties accept responsibility for half the cost of the stamp duty on the contract.

Berlin, 24 February 1936. The Prussian Prime Minister:
signed; Göring

signed; W. Furtwängler

To certify the correctness of the copy:

For renewal of contract see over.

For Furtwängler the case seemed settled for the time being, especially as he had to solve the problem of his own rehabilitation: his return to the Staatsoper. The draft contract he had drawn up in the summer, involving negotiation, plenty of cuts and postponement until the following season, because there was nowhere else for Krauss to go, had come to form the basis of an agreement. On 24 February he signed a contract which booked him – as a guest only – for ten evenings at the Staatsoper: the honorarium per performance came to 2,000 RM, and he had no further guaranteed rights. It was a first step towards rehabilitation and of some importance, as was shown by the fact that it was countersigned not, as planned, by General Intendant Tietjen, but by Göring himself. The conductor noted – despite everything – 'a light and pleasant feeling'.[79] There was another reason for his high spirits. After much debate – and on the recommendation of Toscanini, who had resigned as musical director of the New York Philharmonic Symphony Orchestra – the committee had approached Furtwängler; an agreement had been reached which booked him for the New York season on condition that he did not take up a permanent conducting position either in Germany or elsewhere. The appointment was announced in the American press on 28 February. The German press noted the conductor's return to the Staatsoper one day later, reporting that 'a contract has been agreed under which Dr Furtwängler will resume his conducting activities at the Berlin Staatsoper as a guest'.[81]

This report, which for unknown reasons reached the USA in garbled form, provoked the press to a storm of protest against the 'Nazi' Furtwängler. Strong opposition to the artist had spread immediately after 1933, and effective boycotts had been organised. Now the opposition unleashed a new campaign. The pretext was the Associated Press report from Berlin that the conductor was once again director at the Staatsoper; owing to circumstances this could not be verified because Furtwängler had already left Vienna for Egypt and his long overdue holiday visiting John Kittel. The Associated Press claimed to refer to official sources, even though the German press official announcement had quite clearly and correctly stated 'as a guest'. At least one cannot accuse Göring of having had an interest in sabotaging the guest trip to the US with false information. At any rate the American papers went beserk on 1 March. The initiator of the protest was a twenty-nine-year-old business man called Ira Hirschmann, sales director and publicity manager for the company Lord & Taylor. He was a Jew from Baltimore,[82] a climber by nature, with boundless ambition and the sort of character to stop at nothing. His connection to music was initially limited to his marriage to the pianist Hortense Monath, a pupil of Schnabel, but then widened when the exiled pianist came to New York and encouraged the pair to found a chamber-music society, the 'New Friends of Music', which in its first season – 1936 – put on sixteen concerts in the New York Town Hall; emboldened by success they expanded to form a chamber orchestra under Fritz Stiedry, moving immediately from the Town Hall to the huge Carnegie Hall, which has 3,000 seats. This proved to be a mistake because potential sponsors wanted nothing to do with this 'vulgar Jew'; the deficits, increasing from season to season, dampened Hirschmann's artistic fervour.

When he divorced his wife he also dissociated himself from the 'New Friends of Music'; it had not been a successful undertaking. Hortense Monath tried to rescue it on her own. The orchestra declined, the artists demanded payment in advance. Before the last concert she pawned her fur coat and after the concert she took poison. Hirschmann kept silent about it all and made a career as a manager in many different lines of business; warehouses, television, universities, politics and anti-fascism, wherever access was easiest; he even misused the guileless Schnabel as co-author of a 'Survey of Music'. Because his frenetic activity left no time to worry about the truth his boycott of Furtwängler was a great success; definitely helped by the timely invasion of the Rheinland by Hitler's forces, which began on 7 March and showed the treaty of Versailles, which had created a demilitarised zone west of the Rhine, to be not worth the paper it was written on. This disturbing demonstration of power, the first, did not actually result in counteraction by the future Allies in the world war, but it did strengthen propaganda against the Nazi regime.

For his campaign Hirschmann did not scorn to involve even the strangest of bedfellows; protests came from the musicians' and teachers' unions and also from the American Federation of Labor (AFL), the Federation of Professional Businesses, the Carl Schurz Association and, strangest of all, from the German-American League. All in all it was a united front made up of capitalists, officials from left-wing associations, Jews and American fascists! The 'League', which was highly subsidised with dollars from the Reich to fight communists and Jews and to use publicity to further a good understanding of the Nazi regime, did actually wear grey-black uniforms, preach a racist ideology and have contact with the Ku-Klux-Klan.[83] It only began to go downhill when its 'Führer', Fritz Lieber Kuhn, was called to court charged with embezzling the league's money, as for example when, although married and blessed with two children, he spent 711 dollars from the league's coffers telephoning a woman he had met on a trip to Europe; he had also spent money on another lady, heedless of the fact that she had already been married and divorced nine times. It is quite possible that the league was given a tip-off from the capital of the Reich, and because of the financial support alone had to do as it was told. This German-American connection was not within the prime minister's remit, falling instead quite naturally to his competitor, Rosenberg, by way of the Nazi Party's department of foreign affairs; the latter – with Furtwängler's dossier to hand – had a moralising interest in punishing this 'enemy of the state' by hindering his foreign success, even if such action cost the regime considerable political prestige.

It was thus a strange medley of string-pullers who made the conductor into their scapegoat, and the press tuned into this discordant concert of intimidation by reiterating the lie that he had been reinstated as director of the Staatsoper.[84] The atmosphere was becoming heated. The fact that half the sponsors of the Philharmonic were Jews restricted the committee's freedom to manoeuvre, as was pointed out by the music critic William J. Henderson:

It is manifestly impossible that the sons and daughters of Israel can dissociate their feelings from their artistic judgement at a concert conducted by a man whom they regard as an enemy of their race. To avoid painful experiences they will take the simple and logical course of staying away from these concerts. And if they abandon the Philharmonic Society, it will perish. There is no musical enterprise of any kind whatever that can prosper in this great Jewish town without the support of the Jews . . . [85]

On holiday in Cairo and Luxor, Furtwängler only heard some of what was happening. He guessed that these were political attacks, for which he just happened to serve as a target, and he sent a telegram to New York to cancel. On the other hand the uproar could benefit him, as it created a sort of alibi in Berlin, where there was still no official prepared to speak up for him, although in the long term the echo of this affair from abroad, which gradually ebbed away, was no great help to him in his difficult situation. He needed to do more, to give a clearer signal. The opportunity to do so came a few days later.

In order to give evidence of his political success and credibility, particularly in view of the Olympic Games planned to take place in Berlin that summer, and also to obtain mass consensus for far more rabid undertakings, Hitler had called for an 'election' to take place on 29 March – in reality just an opportunity to show the acclamation there was for the Führer. For weeks now the papers had been publishing extracts from election manifestos and from individual speeches made by well-known public figures. Musicians were also harnessed to the campaign, whether party members or not. These included among others the composers Hans Pfitzner, Paul Graener and Hermann Blume; the directors of the music colleges in Berlin and Weimar, Fritz Stein and Felix Oberborbeck; the performers Heinrich Schlusnus, Wilhelm Backhaus, Michael Raucheisen; the conductor Karl Böhm; the chairman of the Berlin Philharmonic Orchestra, Wolfram Kleber . . .

The Reichskultursenat issued its own proclamation for the elections, signed by any of its members who were available, which did not include Furtwängler who was still in Egypt. Goebbels had created the Reichskultursenat intending it to be a prestige-giving body in imitation of Göring's Staatsrat, only less self-important and, because the senators were paid nothing, cost-free. He wanted to add the conductor to his circle of illustrious personalities, and so had appointed him a 'cultural senator of the Reich'. Obtaining the full declaration of loyalty which the proclamation contained required organisation, and a wire was sent to Luxor. Furtwängler thought that by making one move he could escape his dilemma; he answered with a telegram 'in which he agrees with the sentiments expressed in the proclamation made by the Reichskultursenat and adds his name to the vote for the Führer contained therein'.[86]

Following tried and trusted methods, a news report was distilled from the contents of the telegram rather than it being cited word for word, and this went out not only to the German press but also abroad, where it aroused much attention – because it was open to many possible interpretations. As the conductor passed through Switzerland on his way back from Egypt he was already able to observe some of the consequences: 'There have been comments on my "election propaganda" in all the papers here. If the same thing happens in America – given the current situation there – I still do not know whether our concert in Paris at the end of the month will be possible!'[87]

From an awkward position, he had hoped that making this advance commitment would retrieve the situation; this would not only benefit his own artistic work, but also enable him to continue to exercise influence in politico-cultural matters. But he miscalculated, and in the first week of April Hitler annulled the contract with the Staatsoper. This was clearly intended as a form of retribution, because he simultaneously ensured that a new one was drawn up dated 12 April, which set back the starting date to the beginning of the 1937 season and doubled the honorarium per performance to 4,000 RM. It was a signal. If an artist is on our side it said, he will do well out of it, and by this means the dictator hoped that this obstructive man would finally understand his place.

Furtwängler did not understand. He was a bundle of nerves; everything he had wanted seemed suddenly to have fallen apart. In his frustration he renewed, more urgently this time, his request through Captain Wiedemann for an audience. He impatiently followed this up with a letter; his employment and arrangements for the next musical year were after all in danger:

> I hear that there are always people busy trying to cast doubts and suspicion on my unconditional commitment to Germany. I do not know whether these allegations have come to your hearing, and if so how many. I can only say this much, that these are all a matter of poor misunderstandings resulting merely from difficult situations, which not everybody is in a position to understand fully.[88]

If the addressee was reading this carefully he must have noticed that once again there was mention only of Germany and not of National Socialism, and that the sender had not been able to bring himself to

198

write 'Heil Hitler!'. Furtwängler's mood is betrayed by the notes in his diary: 'Sorrow – not hatred.'[89] and, 'Hitler! You do not know the things which are being done in your name.'[90] The political reality of the Nazi regime encroached on him more and more as he saw that his morals were determined by power after all. One bastion fell after another. No sooner was Tietjen told that he would be one conductor short because Hitler had postponed Furtwängler's engagement for a year than he began negotiations with Werner Egk, who happened to be in Berlin for the first performance of his opera *Die Zaubergeige*, and did not know what had hit him.[91] As if by coincidence *Der Angriff* suddenly began to express reservations, if not serious doubts about the artistic achievements of the already besieged Furtwängler. On 20 April he had included Beethoven's 'Eroica' in the programme, a piece much loved by himself and his public, and a welcome opportunity for critics to find fault with the deteriorating quality: 'Furtwängler's considered and sensitive interpretations were once the hallmark of his fame at home and abroad. Together with the members of the Philharmonic he used to become as one with the music. It is just that through overuse it has now lost its shine. Which is why it will shortly require something of a "thorough overhaul".'[92]

Shortly afterwards Hitler finally granted the audience at which the worried conductor hoped to settle everything. Doubts about the soundness of the conductor's political views were definitely on Hitler's agenda; on the one hand the dictator wanted to keep him for the Reich, on the other he wanted to make clear just who was in charge. As he knew what the podium means to an artist, it was here that he brought pressure to bear; the American Jews may have managed to do the same thing, but their arch-enemy was a long-time expert at it: he talked of boycotting the conductor. Furtwängler took the hint and moved on to talking about his plans as a composer. Nevertheless, their talk ended without any clear decisions having been taken; Hitler's wishes had been expressed between the lines. One thing was clear and that was that the Bayreuth Festival would remain in well-tried hands – not least because of the Olympic Games. Furtwängler understood. A short while later he sent a letter requesting temporary release from all conducting duties, offering two alternative formulations of a text with which to announce this to the public, one with and one without the explanation why, namely that he wanted time for his own work. Should Hitler consider it necessary to publish this explanation, the following version was to be given to the press:

The Führer and Chancellor of the Reich has, until further notice, released Wilhelm Furtwängler, at his own request, from all conducting duties within Germany. Wilhelm Furtwängler, who wishes to dedicate himself to personal work, will conduct nowhere next winter except at the Bayreuth Festival. Once the coming season is over he will resume his work at home and abroad.[93]

Hitler could deduce the persistent obstinacy of the man from the last paragraph of the letter:

Just how important it is to me to be able to be fully active in Germany again once this period is over, is something I have already had opportunity to explain to you. I hope – and you yourself, my Führer, have said you expect this to happen – that as a result of further developments in your foreign policy a more relaxed and calmer atmosphere will gradually prevail, with regard to cultural policy as well, as this is necessary if those of us in the artistic professions are to produce of our best.[94]

Once again the sender signed himself 'your obedient servant' and omitted the Hitler greeting; would this be generously excused as artistic wilfulness? On Hitler's orders the version of the announcement giving his reasons appeared in the press, this time unchanged. It appears that Göring was also party to the decision, because contrary to usual procedure the Chancellery was not involved and was only told afterwards by the prime minister's chief adjutant that the Führer had already read the letter and ordered the publication of the second version, and that he, Captain Bodenschatz, had already ensured that this was taken care of. The musician seems to have believed that by this – politically extorted – arrangement he had covered himself somewhat. Not to have to curry official favour all the time for a year was after all at least something. But this was not recognised overseas. Those who had emigrated could not or would not take due note of the fact that here was someone who was risking ongoing conflict with the brown-shirts and yet staying in Germany; without knowing the facts this stance must have seemed abstruse and incomprehensible. This was why when he came across the musician at a performance of a play by Knittel in Zürich, Thomas Mann reacted as he had learned to do, even noting himself doing so: 'Smoked with the author in the interval. Avoided Furtwängler.'[95]

He did actually talk with him at a social event the following evening at which it would have been ill-mannered to do otherwise, but it was the musician who made the first move. They discussed Wagner. But the writer felt uncomfortable. Only eight days later did he regret not having entered into the conversation more whole-heartedly. There had however been no mention of politics. And yet in recent times Mann had been becoming more outspoken. Two years earlier he had still agonised over the question of whether or not he should 'stand up for the unfortunate Ossietzky who is rotting in a concentration camp',[96] without ever actually doing anything about it; now however his publisher, Bermann, had moved to Vienna, which meant that he could speak more freely and adopt at least the beginnings of a viewpoint, namely by challenging the Nazi regime and expressing solidarity with those who emigrated. But even at the beginning of December of that year Mann postponed sending a nasty letter to the Reich's Interior Ministry lest it prejudice Bermann's Christmas sales in the Reich. Such economic considerations would have been incomprehensible to Furtwängler; trading one concession against another, yes, but corruption for the sake of financial gain, no.

At this time another blow was struck behind the conductor's back, aimed not at him personally, but still in such a way as to strengthen suspicions. It was a new denunciation. Alfred-Ingemar Berndt, ministerial adviser and leader of Division IV (Press) at the Propaganda Ministry, and at that time an SS-Standartenführer, alerted Franz Moraller, the manager of the Reichskulturkammer; it seemed there was a danger that 'Fräulein Geissmar will very soon be trying again to gain a foothold in Berlin's artistic circles in order to be able, for reasons of competition, to betray the Philharmonic Orchestra's foreign arrangements and other useful information to her future foreign employers.'[97]

Moraller informed Hinkel, who in turn put his very efficient adviser, Walter Owens, on the job: 'Confidential: Take this in hand, but do not decide anything without me. Enquire at 1 Albrechtstrasse etc. Try ringing up Berndt, the SS-Staf. and talk to him. Why he gives such things to Mo [Moraller] heaven only knows!!!'[98] The proceedings show how in certain cases the relevant state authorities, in this case the Reichskulturkammer, could be circumvented and the matter dealt with through party channels. SS-Sturmbannführer Hinkel entrusted SS-Standartenführer Owens with settling it – with agreement from Berndt in his capacity as SS-Standartenführer rather than as ministerial adviser; this would ensure that nothing would escape notice. Owens immediately warned the Reichstheaterkammer and Reichsmusikkammer, and for good measure the Gestapo headquarters in Berlin as well.

The denunciation originated from a stenographer at the Propaganda Ministry, who had astonishingly exact information regarding Frau Geissmar's movements; journeys, contacts, plans . . . the comprehensive appointments diary of a 'culture spy': 'In America, Frl. Geissmar, "true to type", spent time with, among others, the Jewish banker Jakob

Goldschmidt and at the house of Lachmann-Mosse, the exiled emigrant she has been friends with for many years.'⁹⁹ This informer dutifully accused Furtwängler's former secretary of devious machinations,

> firstly to make German artists dependent on her in order to then use them as objects of her Jewish business intrigues and politics; secondly to make those artists who fall into the trap dependent on the favours of world Jewry abroad, and thirdly to ensure that German musicians participate in events taking place abroad under Jewish management, which fourthly is then claimed to prove the 'affinity of the exponents of German art with Judaism'; fifth, systematically to poison the minds of sensitive artists, who mostly have a weak character, and thereby, together with clerics and reactionaries, to sabotage the Führer's cultural policy.¹⁰⁰

Anyone who thinks this is the product of a sick mind is mistaken; it is just one of the innumerable proofs of the persecution mania which characterised Nazi Germany, as a result of which it did not for one moment seem crazy to assume that a secretary working from abroad, quite probably 'in the pay' of other members of her race, could pose a threat to the Reich which should be taken seriously. This aside, there was a grain of truth in the denunciation. Frau Geissmar was working as Sir Thomas Beecham's secretary, and had met in Switzerland with Furtwängler, who was on a guest tour with the Berlin Philharmonic to Lucerne, Basel and Zürich from 5 to 7 May; she had discussed performances by the German Staatsoper in London in 1937. The Gestapo may have found out that, although she had been denounced, the Propaganda Ministry sanctioned her precisely because of her involvement in foreign cultural relations. Thus she had no difficulties re-entering the Reich and staying in Germany, not only on several occasions in 1936, the last being the tour which Beecham made with the London Philharmonic in November, but also for a holiday in July 1937 when she visited Bayreuth, Heidelberg, the Starnberger See and Mannheim, and even as late as her six-week holiday in July and August of 1938.

Furtwängler suspected nothing of the constant agitation. He conducted abroad, continued composing, appeared at the Bayreuth Festival, which he opened with *Lohengrin* – in front of a seasonable audience which this time contained more foreigners than usual; the Olympics also attracted music lovers. Hitler sat in the balcony box flanked by Frau Winifred Wagner and Frau Goebbels; Göring and his wife were in the adjoining box. Ministers, military figures, and diplomats from home and abroad completed the picture. In passing, Tietjen, who was involved as a producer, received his appointment to the Prussian Staatsrat.

The Reich Radio Service blew this opening performance into a politico-cultural event of world importance:

> The whole of Europe, Africa, North and South America stayed by their speakers from afternoon till evening, and we hope that you all enjoyed the same technically excellent reception as we were fortunate to experience here. [. . .] The whole atmosphere of ceremony was wonderfully transmitted: the fanfares at the beginning of each act, the presence of the Führer and the government of the Reich. All this made one appreciate the technology serving these great cultural works, and while thanks are due to all the artists, they are due especially to these artists of technology, who fought and won a battle for peace.[101]

Just how much of this was bluff is shown by the fact that the journalist said nothing about the different time-zones of other parts of the world, mentioning simply afternoon and evening. Listening to *Lohengrin* on the radio in Switzerland, Thomas Mann summarised his reaction as follows: 'One should not have listened, should not have lent one's ears to such fraudulence, given that in principle one despises all those participating.'[102] As his books were still being printed in Leipzig he kept this political criticism quiet, but he need not have been afraid of saying out loud that the quality of reception had been poor – even Furtwängler got to hear criticism of the transmission quality. This only served to strengthen still further his dislike of wireless as a 'musical instrument'.

In the summer of 1936 the Jewish problem as defined by National Socialist policy had still not been solved. Yes, there were the 'Nuremberg laws' which legalised a radical, if bureaucratically complex policy of racial segregation, and new orders were continually being issued further to circumscribe the Jews' means of survival, such that any of the more or less enthusiastic support given to emigrants was almost superfluous. Yet there were still areas of doubt, which also touched on the music business. The continuing presence and activity of 'non-Aryan' artists aroused concern because the party faithful saw it as a punishable inconsistency, even as a betrayal which demonstrated ideological unsoundness. Of course Furtwängler had not been alone in his insistence on the integration of 'non-Aryans', both in his own field and beyond, but he had been the only one to do so ostentatiously and in doing so to send out a signal. Now, with the Olympics over, the time seemed right for a propaganda campaign which would smother any inconvenient conclusions others might draw from his example.

This happened in August. Hinkel thought up a plausible sounding declaration, and gave instructions to the press at a politico-cultural press conference given by the Propaganda Ministry. He asked – although of course really it was an order – that

> the few individual cases in which there has been a departure from the rule forbidding the employment of Jewish or non-Aryan artists should not be given too much attention. It would do no harm to mention them once so that people abroad realise how solicitous and generous Germany is, but it should be taken into account that these exceptions have only seldom been made, and even then only in order to have a 'token conductor' who can be produced when necessary, as well as the odd 'token actor'. These can be very useful for effective counter-propaganda abroad.

The functionary did not mention the numerous but scarcely renowned singers and instrumentalists of Jewish origin or with Jewish relations, because this would have destroyed his own argument about 'token' cases. It was evident – although certainly unintentionally – from what he said next, that the regime only gave its special permission under extreme pressure, rather than voluntarily or for political reasons: 'Those of mixed blood, who according to the laws have the option of becoming citizens of the Reich, often pose the greatest threat of cultural disruption, and so are useless and dangerous for "practical cultural achievement". There will be no going back.'[103] There were some clear thinkers present at the conference; they must have asked how consistent this was with the fact that in the Berlin Philharmonic 'half-Jewish' musicians still contributed as much as ever to that 'practical cultural achievement'. As it happened the questions did not go away, and ideological uncertainty persisted. Furtwängler's general plan, although perforce not fully realised, had left its mark.

No sooner had tolerably friendly relations – not least as a result of successes abroad and at Bayreuth – been established with those 'on high', than the conductor made it clear that he wanted this to be of benefit to musical activity rather than just an end in itself. As part of his efforts both to achieve organisational order and to create an all-embracing camaraderie between egotistical and anti-social artists, Goebbels had just eliminated the 'damaging consequences' of art criticism. In his speech to the Reichskulturkammer he had announced that he felt obliged

> to prohibit any form of criticism whatsoever, and to replace this with the observation and description of art. This should not be taken to

mean the suppression of freedom of speech, but that only those who have an original opinion should be allowed publicly to state it, and furthermore only those with the relevant knowledge and experience, as well as accomplishments and skills, should have the right to sit in judgement on those who appeal to the public with the products of their imagination.[104]

Today it is obvious that this was a sacrifice the minister made to 'his artists' in order to appease them, and that it was only a half-hearted one, because it turned out, after a period of uncertainty, that the 'prohibition' had been no more than a beautiful gesture. However, some musicians – especially the second-rate ones – once again had reason to be grateful. Surviving files show that artists, and especially musicians, had been seeking to muzzle the press for years with letters, complaints and legal actions. It was not a case of Goebbels giving in to their pressure; it was far more that the perpetual commotion and guerilla warfare between podium and editor's office, as well as the demands for official intervention, all got on his nerves. To establish peace in this area would be to progress towards popular unity. That is the explanation for the decree on criticism. The fact that its originator set up no apparatus to ensure that it would be enacted and that he strongly rejected advance censorship is evidence of the intention behind it. Right up until the end of the regime the press continued to print criticism as it had done since time immemorial. It was only initially that the decisive tone adopted in the minister's speech deceived people into thinking it meant something other than it actually did. Furtwängler had received a hint from the ministry some days earlier that in future criticism would no longer be allowed.[105] Even as the minister wrote his speech for the Kulturkammer, the conductor was pondering a memo on the same theme. He saw music criticism as a corrective which was as indispensable as the applause or disapproval coming from the public; criticism in the press also provided the public with necessary guidance and something by which to measure their own judgements, especially given that any particular programme of music was generally only played once. He summarised:

It is only by adherence to the principle of competition that great heights of achievement are possible, and it is only these, i.e. truly great artists and works of art rather than mediocre ones, which are significant and representative of a nation. Only mediocrity would benefit in the long run from an absence of criticism. No – there should be more, much sharper, and above all more truthful criticism today, not less, if the intolerable claims of mediocrity, which are becoming

205

ever more noticeable in German musical life, are to be kept within limits.[106]

This was jotted down spontaneously, without any consideration of the details which Goebbels was to announce the following day; it was burningly defiant, and the musician had visibly forgotten to work into it his own general dislike of music criticism. To make sure his petition would not be ignored he roped in ministerial adviser Hanke, and asked him to hand this statement of professional objections to the minister, who at the time was not in Berlin, as soon as he returned, and to do so in person. The advice to proceed in this way came from the manager of the Reichsmusikkammer, Heinz Ihlert, who knew the ropes. Hanke must have acted immediately, because Goebbels immediately responded to the memorandum, and calmed him with evasive statements; he was 'firmly convinced that the worries you express will be shown as groundless by later developments. Furthermore, these developments will of course be carefully observed by myself, and should any harmful consequences arise I will intervene in good time.'[107]

That the conductor did not let himself be deceived or persuaded to let this – and other matters – rest was thanks to Berta Geissmar, working from a distance. Through no fault of her own, while contact with her former boss had not died away completely, it was considerably diminished, but the fact remained that she still – unrequested and occasionally to his embarrassment – sorted things out for him, whether by sending him information about the details and plans of the music business in London, Paris, Vienna or Switzerland, or smoothing the way for guest contracts. She felt herself secure and so sought to allay his fears:

Given that, as I am told, even the Propaganda Ministry had issued orders concerning me, it would be simply laughable if you of all people were to start to moderate your tone. On the other hand I only did what was absolutely necessary, I have also heard how the negotiations in Berlin are progressing, and it appears that things are ready to go, and that the most important thing, namely fixing the prices, has been done, unlike last year when it all went wrong despite my advice to you.

With a sigh she then got round to discussing the most recent developments in the Reich:

Our country is renouncing all normal laws. Having suffocated the

206

natural play of supply and demand, it is now the turn of public opinion, in so far as it still exists at all, to be ignored. Someone like you has an audience, but otherwise . . . there is much discussion of these matters here, and nobody can understand why public figures do not take a stand on them. (Naturally this is easier said than done.)

This observation was clearly meant for Furtwängler, whom she was thus asking to protest; in her own handwriting – even more urgently – she added:

There is something else I should tell you; it seems you were expected to approach the Führer, as agreed, to talk about the question of criticism. There is no report that you have done so. The gentleman concerned has just been to see me. He claims you would have had considerable support from within the government. The gentleman said you had firmly agreed to intervene. According to the latest authentic report you are in a position to do what you like at this juncture.[108]

If this letter had been intercepted by the Gestapo it would have provided grounds for a further charge against the musician, namely of conspiratorial links with the 'Jewish enemy' abroad; the text carelessly illustrated that he entertained imprudently close and influential relations with Geissmar and arranged actions with her via a third person. To keep up his courage, his former assistant, who had just been promoted to organising manager of the London Philharmonic, reassured him that she considered him

basically independent of all political situations, as long as you do not let yourself be used by those back home for a certain sort of publicity. I urge you most strongly to insist on freedom in this respect. In the interests of both yourself and their mission they have to treat you with special consideration. I learned yesterday that there is a great deal of understanding at the highest level for your individuality in this regard.[109]

Furtwängler heeded the exhortation and applied himself more intensively to a number of questions. On 10 December, knowing how useful friendly gestures could be, he visited the minister. Goebbels did not recognise it as a tactical move, noting: 'He is now fully on our side. He appreciates our great achievements. He still has some small requests,

207

primarily to do with criticism and Hindemith. Otherwise he is in line.'[110]

Thus – now practically the helpmate of emigrants – he prepared for his return to musical activity. This began with a charity concert in aid of the needy in winter given on 10 February together with the Berlin Philharmonic; once again Hitler, Göring and Goebbels sat in the box of honour while the stalls thronged with leading figures from Berlin's social, political, business and artistic circles. The press took delight in registering individually the ambassadors from Argentina, Brazil, Chile, England, France, Italy and Poland, as well as the envoys from Bolivia, Colombia, Denmark, Estonia, Finland, Greece, Guatemala, Haiti, Iraq, Yugoslavia, Latvia, Austria, Spain, South Africa, Czechoslovakia and Hungary, a veritable parade of prominent diplomatic figures. Tickets cost as much as 30 RM, and in the interval von Benda, the manager, handed the minister of propaganda a cheque for the net proceeds of the evening – 21,065.40 RM. The public gave the conductor several ovations, which were mirrored in the newspaper reports:

> But why do we love and honour the artist in him to such a degree? Because his manner of working, and his brilliant interpretations allow us to feel and recognise the German in him, and because he allows us to feel and recognise in our master composers our own truly German being. We grow with him and are thankful to him for his cheering and deeply stirring sensitivity to our great musical composers, who broaden our spirit and our souls.[111]

He had deliberately chosen a popular programme; the *Freischütz* overture, Brahms' Fourth Symphony, and Beethoven's Seventh to end with. The interest which his return aroused abroad made the functionaries tolerate him as a necessary evil. Goebbels received this difficult man on 2 March at 12.30 p.m. Although the agenda[112] has not survived, the ban on criticism was high on a list of pressing matters, and it seems likely that this was discussed, as well as a guarantee for his existence as an 'apolitical' artist. The minister also had something else in mind; to get such a man into the party, even if only on the fringes, was a task fit for this master of propaganda. As he was an honorary member and patron of the Fellowship of German Artists it was quite natural for Furtwängler to be invited to join by the president of the association, Benno von Arent.

Included with his letter of 2 April was a sheet of paper describing the aims and purposes of the Fellowship of German Artists; among other things it was supposed to

Der Präsident

DER

Kameradschaft der deutschen Künstler e. V.

GRÜNDER: BENNO v. ARENT

 v.Ar./Hy.

BERLIN W 35 den 2.4.37
VICTORIASTRASSE 3—4
FERNRUF: KURFÜRST 81 47/94 95

Sehr geehrter Herr Reichskultursenator!

Die Kameradschaft der deutschen Künstler als Stätte kameradschaftlicher Zusammenkunft aller künstlerisch-schöpferisch tätigen Künstler von Rang ist Ihnen seit langem bekannt, und Sie wissen, dass ihr Schirmherr der Präsident der Reichskulturkammer, Herr Reichsminister Dr. Goebbels ist.

Es ist in seinem Sinn, wenn wir Sie als Mitglied des Reichskultursenats hierdurch kameradschaftlich auffordern, der KddK beizutreten und damit ihre ideellen Bestrebungen zu unterstützen. Wir würden uns sehr freuen, wenn Sie unserer Bitte nachkämen und teilen Ihnen gleichzeitig mit, dass seit einem Jahr die Aufnahme in die KddK gesperrt ist und Aufnahmen nur in besonderen Fällen genehmigt werden. Doch legen wir den grössten Wert darauf, dass gerade die Mitglieder des Reichskultursenats, auch wenn sie ausserhalb Berlins wohnen, sämtlich Mitglieder der KddK sind.

Wir legen Ihnen Aufnahmeformular, "Sinn und Zweck" und die Mitgliederliste zu Ihrer Orientierung bei. Selbstverständlich ist für Sie als Mitglied des Reichskultursenats die Nennung von Paten nicht notwendig.

In der Hoffnung, Sie bald als Mitglied bei uns begrüßen zu können, bin ich im Namen der Kameradschaft der deutschen Künstler in Kameradschaft

Heil Hitler!
Ihr

THE PRESIDENT OF THE FELLOWSHIP OF GERMAN ARTISTS

Founder: Benno v. Arent

Honourable Reichskultursenator!

209

You have known for a long time about the Fellowship of German Artists as a friendly meeting point for all well-respected creative and performing artists, and you are aware that its patron is Dr Goebbels, president of the Reichskulturkammer and minister of the Reich.

It is at his request that we are asking you, as a member of the Reichskultursenat, to join the Fellowship of German Artists, and thereby support its strivings to achieve its ideals. We should be delighted if you choose to accede to our request, and would also point out that since last year the Fellowship has barred any new members and now only grants membership in special cases. Yet we feel it most important that all the members of the Reichskultursenat, even if they live outside Berlin, should be members of the Fellowship.

For your information we include an application form, a description of our 'aims and purposes', and a list of current members. Naturally as a member of the Reichskultursenat you would not be required to name sponsors.

Hoping to be able to welcome you soon as a member here I remain, in the name of the Fellowship of German Artists, yours in comradeship.

Heil Hitler!

Yours, Benno v. Arent

---

bring together artistically creative individuals of recognised achievement in a comradely association which takes National Socialism's philosophy as its defining principle. Its members make it their duty to cultivate comradeship amongst themselves and to renounce the egocentric stance encouraged by fame, to the benefit of the community spirit within the Fellowship, and more broadly to the benefit of the German people. Its endeavours are purely artistic, in harmony with our Führer's programme for cultural growth.[113]

In other words an artists' club to be used for politics as and when required; in practice it was a meeting-point where prominent individuals, being among their own, could eat well and drink – even to excess if they so desired.

Furtwängler, the non-conformist, did join, was given membership no. 868, and paid a year's subscription of 120 RM. On the surface it was a matter of form, but as the club was also supposed to allow informal meetings with politicians he may have hoped that in this relaxed atmosphere he would find somebody who would listen to his politico-cultural problems. It was only later that he noticed that even the patron of the association only made very rare appearances.

On 10 April he began at the Staatsoper with *Der Ring des Nibelungen*: one day after *Die Walküre*, the guest contract, which had been postponed by orders from the very top and contained new changes, was signed. Two days before Hitler's birthday he conducted a special performance of Beethoven's Ninth with the Kittel choir and Erna Berger, Gertrude Pitzinger, Walther Ludwig and Rudolf Watzke as soloists. The party press observed that it was a fine opportunity to demonstrate the choir by 'having them in the solemn performance preceding a national day of celebration. Beethoven's Ninth yesterday, with its moments of fighting and struggling, supremacy and final joyous victory, formed a deeply symbolic prelude to the Führer's birthday.'[114]

'Artistic observation' which was little more than description of political events was quite the norm at that time; its task was to 'testify' and assist with the political appropriation of art and artists. The fact that Schiller's text advocates the brotherhood of man – which would mean the abandonment of racial division – in other words, ran directly counter to the brown-shirts' ideology, could not of course be mentioned; if it had been, some reader or another would have got the idea that Bruno Kittel, a party member, and Furtwängler, not a party member, had formed an alliance to use the double meaning of this work in order to put the Führer in the wrong. There is even one American source which, if there were no doubts about its accuracy and veracity, might persuade one that the conductor acquitted himself obediently on the occasion of this important birthday; according to this source a US soldier was given the task, after the war was over, of putting documents from the German ministries in safe keeping, including Hitler's 'fan mail'. While doing so he came across a telegram dated 20 April, 1937:

Adolf Hitler, Berlin
On this day most sincere best wishes to you and your work. Wilhelm Furtwängler, General Director of Music and Prussian Staatsrat.[115]

To have convinced anyone of the reality of this telegram, the fortunate finder and reporter, who was in fact a fervent opponent of the conductor even when he had been exonerated by the commission, would have had to demonstrate either perfect recall of the exact wording or to have produced a copy. Yet despite an intense search in the Bundesarchiv and elsewhere, the original cannot be found, even though, had GI Sonnenfeld cared to do so, it would have been easy to make a facsimile at the time.

Thus it seems all too transparently obvious that the quotation is a fake. From surviving documents it can be shown that the conductor never used the title of general director of music, which was only given him by the City of Berlin and prior to 1933 anyway:[116] it would have been ludicrous to try and use either that title or that of Staatsrat to impress the dictator, who knew perfectly well who Furtwängler was. In a list of things to be done noted in Furtwängler's diary on 19 April, there was a reminder to write firstly to Ribbentrop, secondly to Göring about Pfitzner, and thirdly to Frau Hindemith, but no other names were mentioned, either then or on 20 April. Just assuming that the telegram really did exist and was reported even semi-accurately, it could be that he was making the 'diplomatic' gesture of returning the greetings which Hitler had sent the musician on his fiftieth birthday, in other words repaying his debts. This would have been more like him. There is no evidence that they were on particularly good terms at this time, which might otherwise explain it; on the contrary there is evidence of a renewed distancing. On 21 April the Berlin Philharmonic set off on its spring tour, including Halle, Bielefeld, Dortmund, Düsseldorf and Cologne on their way to Paris and London. The following day, the journalists who gathered together in the Propaganda Ministry for a press conference on politico-cultural matters were told: 'Furtwängler has asked that it be noted that his journeys abroad and his guest performances abroad are undertaken as an independent artist, not within the framework of official exchange concerts. Only at the Paris exhibition will he conduct in an exchange concert.'[117]

This demonstration of independence cannot have been to the liking of the Propaganda Minister, who had initiated the press conferences as a means of ensuring that the official line would be propagated, rather than the truth. This truth conflicted with his interest in politicising art. How had this happened? Had this slipped through because the bureaucratic mind could not conceive of anybody turning such a tool against its inventor? At all events the officials at the Propaganda Ministry believed that despite this declaration things were not too serious, that here was just an artist who was detached from reality and did not know what he wanted. They took no retributive action, merely passing on a commission from Goebbels:

The cultural symposium at the National Party Congress has been declared by the Führer and Chancellor of the Reich to be the occasion at which the German National Prize (anti-Nobel prize), created by the Führer and Chancellor of the Reich, will in future be awarded. As a result the character of the cultural symposium will undergo far-reaching changes. The cultural symposium of this year's party congress will take place on Tuesday 7 September in the opera house in Nuremberg. Would you and the Philharmonic Orchestra please undertake to provide the music before and after the Führer's speech and at the celebration described above. I would further ask you to submit your proposals for the programme to me as soon as possible. I would be grateful if, apart from an overture to be chosen by you for the beginning of the event, it were possible to end with a performance of one of the Beethoven symphonies, again to be chosen by you.[118]

Furtwängler, whom they had not even bothered to address at the beginning of the request, informed them coldly, also without any form of address, 'that I cannot conduct in Nuremberg, as I have already accepted other engagements for the time in question'.[119]

They should have known this at the ministry, having after all been involved in the preparation of that other engagement, namely the German Week of Culture at the World Exhibition in Paris; as one can see, even a dictatorship cannot guarantee that minimum of information necessary for its own functioning. In the end Peter Raabe and Siegmund von Hausegger, together with the Munich Philharmonic, provided the music for the presentation of the Nazi regime's anti-Nobel prize at Nuremberg – performing the 'Entry of the Gods into Valhalla' from Das Rheingold and the Finale of Bruckner's Fifth Symphony.

Furtwängler by contrast was preoccupied with worries which were only indirectly connected to matters musical; he hoped that he would be able to endure the atmosphere at Bayreuth despite its being so uncongenial for his work, but other evils were at the door. In the middle of July – by order of the Führer's deputy – a new series of actions against non-Aryans began, starting with the ninety-one officials of mixed blood or 'related to Jews' employed by the Reich's Education Ministry; with a few exceptions they were all to be retired – a clear breach of the law concerning the rehabilitation of the civil service. As it was obvious that this would have repercussions elsewhere, the conductor wrote to Hitler and pressed for an audience at a place where it would be difficult for him to refuse: 'The things which I wished to discuss with you are partly of a factual nature and partly – and these are the most important – personal, and I would be grateful if you would grant this much-delayed audience during your stay in Bayreuth.'[120] Once again he did not sign off with 'Heil Hitler', offering his 'profound respects' instead; the 'respectful' Furtwängler wanted to use the Führer as an effective crisis manager, and for this he had to treat him in a direct rather than a byzantine manner. It was high time. The Chancellery stirred itself at the beginning of July with the offer of a meeting. The tone remained reserved.

A few days later the Propaganda Ministry did in fact begin to carry out the deputy's orders; the minister for the interior had responded quickly to a hint from the chief of staff at the Führer's Chancellery, and was now trying to remove all those with a suggestion of 'non-Aryan' blood, by applying the same criteria as had been applied to the civil service. As the Reich had long since ceased to be run by rule of law, this ploy stood a good chance of success. The Propaganda Ministry actually also had lists of those employees with long-term contracts and those whose contracts could be terminated at less than one year's notice: at the German Opera House these included the director Hans Batteux, and the singers Elise von Catopol, Margarete Slezak and Günther Treptow; among the members of the Philharmonic Ernst Fischer, Otto Hess and Hugo Kolberg, who all three had Jewish wives, and the 'semi-Aryans' Hans Bottermund and Bruno Stenzel. The official assessor responsible, Baumann, was so unacquainted with his subject matter that he gave Kolberg the wrong forename, Paul, and mistakenly promoted him to chief conductor! It was now up to Goebbels to decide whether or not these artists were to be removed; to Furtwängler's astonishment Goebbels took the risk of jeopardising his cultural policies which having these 'unsound' second-class musicians around allegedly entailed. Funk scrawled a memo all over the proposal which had been submitted, using a thick crayon and many underlinings: 'The minister decided after hearing my report that no further action should be taken on this matter, as the minister had already decided that in all the cases justifiable exceptions for the purposes of further employment could be made for the musicians in question.'[121]

This threat was accordingly set aside for the time being; Hindemith's case however was still in the balance. There was a lot going for the composer; against him – now as ever – stood Rosenberg, but even he was no longer opposed to him on principle, but merely on the question of how long the humiliated composer's 'probation period' should be. He had after all obediently done what was demanded of him. Minister Rust had urged him in December 1934 to ask for the suspension of his professorship. Hindemith did so. Then he took up – with the agreement of the relevant ministries – a temporary contract with the Turkish government, which was welcomed in Berlin as good propaganda for the Reich, because Ankara was now learning to use German methods in its creation of a 'Western' musical culture: 'Hindemith won this commission against very strong competition from Russia and France, and was esteemed so highly by his employers that he was given far-reaching powers which put him in a position to assure the predominance of German cultural influences in the sphere of music in Turkey.'[122]

In April 1935 the Propaganda Ministry informed Rust that it had no objections to Hindemith resuming his teaching activities. The education minister declared him no longer suspended, but then, after protests from the powerful Rosenberg, extended the suspension until July after all. After some further indecision the matter was referred to Hitler; he – normally so very willing to take decisions – did not wish to take a stance personally and left it to Rust to make the final decision. Rust wanted to avoid any awkward repercussions, above all the possibility of a spectacular resignation:

> All those foreign countries which are ill disposed to the National Socialist Reich are just waiting with a row of excellent offers for the moment when he [Hindemith] is labelled an emigrant. Such a development would certainly not benefit German cultural propaganda abroad. In particular the possibilities of exerting an influence on Turkish cultural life, which are currently developing so pleasingly and could be expanded, would be lost.[123]

In January Hindemith took an oath of office to Hitler, because Rust sought to avoid causing a sensation; an extension of his work in Ankara allowed the decision to be postponed. Rosenberg still demanded a longer 'probation period', but was simultaneously relaxing the boycott on the works of this prominent German composer; he was never quite prepared to impose a total prohibition. In one of the press-conferences on politico-cultural matters the journalists were then also told: 'The announcement that Hindemith would in future be withdrawn from concert programmes was made here as well, with particular calls for the information to be kept confidential.'[124]

In an effort to prevent this Furtwängler had already remonstrated several times, both verbally and in writing. As he was now due to meet with Hitler he took up the question again, and while still in Bayreuth drafted a memo in which he elaborated on his trusted arguments and pointed out the paradox that to lift the ban on this music would be to signal its ruin, since it was precisely because of the boycott that a large proportion of young people, including not only members of the Hitler Youth but also almost all the younger critics, had gone over to Hindemith's side. And he asked – discussion topic no. 1 – on what basis assessments of intellectual achievement were actually being made:

> Max Reger is currently officially described as the Third Reich's most

215

representative musician. Has the Führer ever heard a typical piece of his? In my opinion Max Reger is the true initiator of the present decadence in music. There is a massive contradiction in banning Hindemith, while Max Reger is characterised as the no. 1 contemporary musician. It would be better if neither of these things happened and it were left to the public to make their own judgements. [. . .] Abroad, Hindemith has until now never played anything like the role he presently has in Germany, and it is only in the last few years that he has been seen as Germany's political martyr. He is particularly suited to the role because morally and theoretically, as well as in his personal conduct, he is quite irreproachable and has never given anyone the least occasion to blame him for anything. This all strengthens his image as a martyr in the eyes of impartial observers.[125]

It was a plausible reflection, which furthermore had some grounding in facts, such as the astonishing sales success of the recently published *Unterweisung im Tonsatz* (The Craft of Musical Composition), part 1, which within a short space of time had sold more than two thousand copies; the publishers Schott's Söhne could hardly satisfy demand. There is a note on the draft version of this memorandum that it was 'not handed in', but one can be certain that at their meeting Furtwängler would have reasoned with Hitler along the same lines as he had laid down in the draft. However, he met with rock-like resistance and succeeded in making the dictator even more mistrustful.

On the other hand some things happened that summer – possibly as a result of his success as a conductor at the coronation celebrations in London – which suggest that his relations with other high-up officials were at least temporarily consolidated. As part of the reorganisation of the Prussian Academy of Arts Goebbels had done away with the old statutes and Funk now appointed Furtwängler an ordinary member for music, along with Armin Knab, Hermann Reutter and Heinrich Kaminski, who was having problems proving the purity of his Aryan origins; those who had left included 'the majority of members of a previous era in the arts, who did not wish to stand in the way of a National Socialist revival of the academy'.[126]

The conductor also gained the 'very highest' recognition at Bayreuth again, even though he no longer liked the atmosphere at the festival and a big row was in the offing. On the 'green hill', he discussed with Goebbels the details of a new music periodical which was to be published by Schott's Söhne, and in connection with this too he noted a success: 'I was above all interested in how freely it would be allowed to express opinions, i.e. to criticise, as that would decide my opinion on the whole

216

thing. The minister was most accommodating and assured me that if I were to take responsibility for the content we would have no difficulties.'127

The high spirits of this work-laden month were somewhat marred by a dispute with Toscanini in Salzburg; it had to do with politics, and probably other things as well, given that, as on previous occasions, two giants of the conducting world were invading one another's preserves, only more flagrantly this time. It is possible that the Italian maestro, who always wore his heart on his sleeve, said more than he could really afford given the course his own development had taken. A contemporary biographer of Furtwängler reported that Toscanini had declared:

Anybody who conducts at a Bayreuth which has been tainted by the evil Nazis will find no welcome in Salzburg. Wilhelm Furtwängler responded to this point of view with intelligent and well-chosen words. But almost the whole non-German press agreed with Toscanini. It was as if the whole world had to agree with what was said at Salzburg, with the exception of the nasty Germans.128

The different versions of what happened conceal the possible motives; it is more than likely that Toscanini was trying to compensate for something. His surprised adversary came out of it offended but unscathed, because he was convinced that it was not emigration which determined the difference between Nazis and anti-fascists. Also in August those 'on high' had yet to decide to whom to award the newly founded German National Prize for Arts and Sciences; this was a political matter, an act by which the Führer hoped to defy the world, because, as he let it be known,

this year the Nobel prize committee awarded the international Nobel Peace Prize to the pacifist Ossietzky, one of the worst misfits and corrupters of the German people, whom the Reich Court of Justice had condemned for treason! This award was an unashamed attack on National Socialist Germany [. . .] Germany's answer to such defamation lies in its deeds – in cultural achievement. And there is no doubt that there has never been a statesman who has done so much to promote cultural activity as Adolf Hitler has. One glance at the cultural achievements of his Reich is enough to confirm that all Jewish assertions are no more than poisonous slander.129

On the list of twenty-six suggestions which the Propaganda Minister's personal adviser sent to SA-Brigadeführer Schaub at Berchtesgaden on

BERLIN W 8. DEN   1.7.37
REICHSKANZLEI

DER FÜHRER UND KANZLER DES DEUTSCHEN REICHES
ADJUTANTUR

Hauptmann a.D. Wiedemann

W/Mi

Herrn

Staatsrat Wilhelm F u r t w ä n g l e r

P o t s d a m

Viktoriastrasse 36

Sehr geehrter Herr Staatsrat !

Ich habe den Inhalt Ihres Schreibens vom 16.6.37
dem Führer vorgetragen. Der Führer ist bereit, Sie
in Bayreuth zu empfangen.

Ich bitte Sie, sich unter Berufung auf dieses
Schreiben beim diensttuenden Adjutanten dort anzu-
melden.

Mit der Versicherung meiner
vorzüglichsten Hochachtung !
Ihr sehr ergebener

Adjutant des Führers

Berlin
1.7.37

To Herr Staatsrat Wilhelm Furtwängler
Potsdam, Victoriastrasse 36

218

Honoured Herr Staatsrat!

I have informed the Führer of the content of your letter dated 16 March 1937. The Führer is prepared to receive you in Bayreuth.

Would you please refer to this letter when you report to the duty adjutant there.

I remain your obedient servant

Adjutant to the Führer

---

31 August, Furtwängler was alphabetically in ninth place, proposed by Goebbels himself. The prize however did not go to him – there was after all a dossier on him – but to the surgeon Prof. Dr August Bier, the geophysicist Wilhelm Filchner, the surgeon Prof. Dr Ferdinand Sauerbruch, Alfred Rosenberg and the Führer's deceased architect and 'master builder', Prof. Ludwig Troost. This was supposed in all earnestness to leave the Nobel prize in the shade. Furtwängler was not bothered, and carried out his duties at the German Week of Culture in Paris from 3 to 12 September, at which the Reich's leading artists were presented; it had been arranged by the Propaganda Ministry, which had also unquestioningly put up the 30,000 RM demanded by the Berlin Philharmonic to cover the cost of the trip. Furtwängler began with Beethoven's Ninth Symphony in the Salle Pleyel on 7 September; following the next day with *Die Walküre* in the Théâtre des Champs-Elysées, which was then repeated on the 11th, all of which used star performers and were priced accordingly. The German press was jubilant, and reported that even at the first concert there were twelve encores, and that it was attended by the French president, numerous ministers and nearly all the heads of the diplomatic delegations, emphasising that 'Furtwängler [. . .] has strengthened his world reputation once again as a result of this evening. Through him and with him the German music which he interpreted celebrated a great – one might even say its greatest – victory.'[130]

The public could learn from this real-life example that artistic achievement did not originally have the slightest connection with any regime which might seek to share in its glory; these musicians, even the party members among them, were not subjects of the Nazi government, even if their passports were decorated with the imperial eagle and the swastika. It was not the government in Berlin which produced art. They created the organisational and technical preconditions for a future

219

expansionary rule of force, the details of which the Parisian papers discovered a little bit more every day; what had been intended as a deception turned out – thanks to the intelligence of the metropolis' concert-going public – to be something quite different:

> It was a German success in the most European or world sense of the word rather than in the National Socialist sense, and the ambassadors of this Germany were called not Ribbentrop, Ley or Funk, but Furtwängler, Schlusnus, Krauss, the members of the Berlin Philharmonic and the men and women who make up the German opera. It was the old Germany which was evident here, despite all the political storms of recent times.[131]

That the public almost to a man not only stood up when the French president entered the theatre and the national anthems were played, but also stretched out their hands in the Hitler greeting, surely did not affect this. The press noticed one thing: the anthems were conducted by the manager, Hans von Benda, not Furtwängler. And something else: at the invitation of the Reich commissioner to the World Exhibition a celebratory reception was held at the Hotel Georges V after the performance of the Ninth; the German artists, State Secretary Funk, French politicians including the foreign minister Delbos, the US President Roosevelt's mother, and many other prominent personalities all gathered there. Furtwängler only showed up after midnight, once the official speeches were long past. Hitler – at the time attending the party congress in Nuremberg – responded to the enthusiastic reports of the success in Paris with a spontaneous invitation to the best known of the participants. On 10 September the embassy in Paris informed the Foreign Office that the ladies Martha Fuchs and Ruth Berglund, and the gentlemen Rudolf Bockelmann, Erich Zimmermann and Josef von Manowarda were pleased to accept and would fly to Nuremberg on the morning of Monday 13 September. Furtwängler had withdrawn once again.

Regardless of this he sought to bring his Bayreuth problem, which in the meantime had come to a head, to the attention of those in power, and once again requested an audience with Hitler for as soon as possible: 'I shall only be in Berlin for a short while, as I shall very soon have to leave for Vienna for several weeks.'[132] He again closed with 'sincere best wishes' but added a post-script publicising his new symphonic concerto for piano and orchestra, which had been fixed for the Philharmonic's second concert, with Edwin Fischer as soloist. Hitler announced that he was under a lot of pressure from official duties, and so no audience took place. However, as the conductor wished to publicise the difficulties

220

which were causing him to leave the team at the Wagner festival, he wrote them out in detail for Winifred Wagner and sent a copy to Hitler; the Führer's adjutant ensured that he was informed. It was a weighty accusation, which he sent to Wagner's heiress. What the conductor had in the past taken for granted,

namely the possibility of using Bayreuth to set the standard, an example which will influence the build-up of a tradition – in the best sense of the word – of cultivating Wagnerian art the world over, this you have made impossible for me. You quite seriously believe that a first-class musician is unnecessary to lead Bayreuth. You are so ignorant of the role which the music, and therefore the conductor, plays in the overall concept of Wagner's works of art; you are so unaware how deeply at risk Bayreuth's position is in the world today, and of how it is here of all places that only the best should be used, if Bayreuth is even to be able to justify its existence in the future [. . .] You put your trust in the powers of the authoritarian state. It is precisely because they are kindly disposed to Bayreuth that you should be acting doubly responsibly.[133]

In order that the accusation would not be wasted Göring and Goebbels also received copies. These reminded them once more just what a difficult person the conductor could be whenever he had to work in collaboration with artists whose ideas about aesthetics, or even just about how to organise things, differed from his own. This problem was the subject of several discussions at the highest level. Hitler eventually reacted sharply. Goebbels noted in his diary on 3 November: 'He wants to drop Furtwängler from Bayreuth after all. I have shown him all the objections. It will be a heavy loss for Bayreuth. Tietjen is a wily intriguer. And now he is conducting the whole *Ring*. Yes, Bayreuth indeed suffers when women are in charge!'[134]

The Führer of the Reich obviously did not like this type of artist, a lone ruler who wanted a monopoly, who was absorbed in art, but so much so that he would accept no compromise in this area. This was his strength but it was also his weakness. The prime minister especially recognised his Achilles' heel. Again and again he would become infuriated because the musician did not behave as he was supposed to, despite all the advance commitments and concessions, and because he did not repay his debt of gratitude with good behaviour, taking it for granted instead that the leaders of the Reich should court him. In December 1937 Göring decided to put an end to the sabotage of his politico-cultural intentions by this man who thought himself indispensable and irreplaceable.

6

ATTACK FROM THE REARGUARD

At the end of 1937 the conductor's situation was more or less satisfactory. Despite politico-cultural crises he had decisively renounced the regime's enticements and thus kept his freedom;[1] he was conducting as he always had done, enjoyed great national and international acclaim, and no informed culture buff could justifiably accuse him of working for the brown barbarians. There is no doubt that as time went on he came to a more realistic assessment of Nazi policies; but neither is there any doubt that he and many other Germans hoped the regime would sooner or later be overthrown by means of foreign intervention or an internal coup. There are also indications that initially, although constantly seeking to distinguish very carefully between National Socialism and his own intellectual system, he still considered it a painful procedure of 'self-purification', until the wholesale and irrational course of official action taught him otherwise; the *Kristallnacht* in 1938 was to mark a decisive turning point in this respect. For the moment there were problems, but he felt in full possession of the necessary powers to deal with them. He had learnt from politico-cultural conflicts to date. Was there really anything worse which could befall him?

The Bayreuth affair certainly angered him, and the growing politicisation of the festival may have disturbed him as well; moreover his work at the Staatsoper – still under the initially deferred and then changed contract — also was more or less under duress. But the support of the public and the regular, glowing praise he received from the press were ample recompense. And did he not also have a possible basis from which positively to influence the politicians? Surely his morality and integrity would in the end carry the day quite irresistibly? Now that Hitler and his gang were here they could not be ignored because the power lay in their hands, and he would have to submit to them if he were to change those things which in his opinion needed changing. To accuse the conductor of not having been sufficiently whole-hearted in his involvement in the Jewish problem, which after all was a symptom of the seriousness of the situation, is to leave circumstances at the time out of account. The ferocious pogrom – which appeared to be a one-off – was one incident; the passing of anti-Jewish laws concerning Jews in the professions, their legal status, wealth and the like, derived considerable plausibility from propaganda. The things which tore other civilised countries apart simply could not happen in the 'land of poets and thinkers'; the British massacres in the Boer War and in India, the extermination of the Armenians by the Turks, the slaughter of the Kulaks by the Soviets, the bloodbath which France, the nation of culture, caused among the Kabyls . . . anything like that was still hard to foresee in 1937. Inflammatory anti-Semitic speeches, Jew-baiting cartoons, 'scientific' studies of racial inferiority: all seemed excrescences which could nevertheless not endanger the underlying cohesive legal order. For Furtwängler, just as for the majority of Germans, there was no reason not to trust the government.

One reason he was not very quick to pick up what was happening in the musical world was that there were things he did not get to hear. He was unaware that Tietjen was wont to rail against him, whereas Göring knew the director's complaints, even the private ones:

> Tannhäuser was going well until that primadonna turned up, just like in 1936 with Lohengrin, ruined everything but still had Berlin at his feet. When he conducts Wagner he's like a woman with perfume – always adding touches. It is the last time in my life I ever try and produce Wagner with him; for ten years now I have been trying to make him stick faithfully to the work, but he's always turned it into an act of public hypnosis and then it appeared that it was Wagner who was the idiot – and so we split![2]

This moan was written before the third performance of the new production of Tannhäuser; the 'charming girl', as the inscrutable director was wont to call Wagner's granddaughter, had his measure as a schemer and was more kindly disposed towards the apparently helpless conductor, especially as the matter assumed ever larger proportions. Furtwängler found the allegation that he was not 'faithful to the work' deeply painful from the very first time it was suggested that he was not being sufficiently exact. He repeatedly tried to explain: what mattered was neither sticking to the music down to the last marking, nor keeping a rigid tempo, but being 'truly faithful to the work i.e. to the original sense of the work'.[3] However, what he was now most concerned with was not to do with aesthetics, but with an organisational arrangement which threatened his prestige: after Krauss's departure, Göring, unable to find a suitable replacement director for the opera – Furtwängler's contract having been deferred at Hitler's orders – had done away with the position in accordance with the finance minister's recommendations, and entrusted Tietjen with the overall charge of the institution. The press was instructed 'to desist henceforth from any criticism of the artistic work of the Berlin Staatsoper under the new artistic director, General Intendant Tietjen'.[4]

Thus the conductor suddenly found himself subordinate to the wily director, who could pull all the strings and made no bones about his dislike of Furtwängler. When the press mistakenly reported that he was to accept an engagement at the Vienna Staatsoper, Furtwängler sent a letter rectifying the error, and used the opportunity to make a complaint: 'I find I cannot bring the necessary enthusiasm to my work in a situation which seems to me to be unworthy of me both as a person and as an artist. Because under these circumstances there can be no future for my work at the Staatsoper anyhow, it is perhaps better than I should give it up now.'[5]

Göring reacted with visible displeasure, and raised a warning finger; he was concerned

> that your calling should not suffer excessively from the incessant difficulties which you seem to encounter all over the place, whether in Berlin or Bayreuth, the opera or the Philharmonic. [. . .] Just as for the rest of us your first and foremost duty is to Germany. But you can by no means expect me to put up with the clockwork regularity of a Furtwängler case every year at the Staatsoper.[6]

The conductor sought to calm him, but would not be moved from his wish to be released from the contract at the Staatsoper, and furthermore held the politician partly to blame for not recognising that he, Furtwängler, had been willing to devote all his energies to the Staatsoper:

> You made no use of this. In your concern for your opera you (just like Frau Wagner in Bayreuth) obviously thought only of getting Furtwängler the popular conductor, rather than Furtwängler the artist who was prepared to take shared responsibility for this leading opera house, which would also have meant responsibility for the whole standard of Germany's musical life.[7]

Göring made a note on this letter instructing his chief secretary to 'inform F. at once that I will receive him if that is what he wishes', because it was vital to him to try and find a compromise solution which would keep the conductor at the opera house. But nothing of the sort happened . . . apart from a few sporadic appearances up until the end of that season. The Staatsoper had lost Furtwängler. Therefore, if the business was not to sink to provincial standards, an equally good and popular conductor had to be found; Berlin was after all supposed to be the last word in opera. The first few months of the new year were marked by an intensive search for a successor who, it was hoped, would be able to put Furtwängler, who had proved just too difficult, in the shade. Tietjen was trying to find a contender through whom he could get back at Furtwängler.

Furtwängler did not suspect that dark clouds were gathering over him, and carried on as he always had done in the German and international music life. For the seventh Philharmonic concert, which fell on 30 January of all days, he abruptly decided to cut Gottfried Müller's Orchestral Concerto from the programme and replaced it with a first performance of Bartók's Music for Strings, Percussion and Celesta, which was originally to have taken place in November. Müller was a twenty-three-year-old and much acclaimed *Wunderkind* whom Hinkel had seriously proposed for the title of professor that autumn, before it was decided that he lacked the necessary age and dignity. Those with inside information knew that he was working on a piece which incorporated some of Hitler's sayings. It was obvious that this young and ambitious musician found favour with the Führer, but to the conductor at that moment Bartók seemed more fitting, and the public showed their appreciation with their applause.

Some days later the Philharmonie was closely packed with members of the Hitler Youth; as their leadership wanted to acquaint the rising generation with German culture, they had acted as concert organisers and arranged a series of master-concerts with well-known artists and ensembles. Furtwängler conducted one of these, and one only. This took place on 3 February, and when he looked at the audience he realised that this was more than just a concert for school kids in uniform; a whole collection of prominent political figures were sitting there as well: the Führer's deputy Rudolf Hess, the leader of the Hitler Youth von Schirach, General Inspector Dr Todt, SS-Obergruppenführers Litzmann and Prince August Wilhelm, Rosenberg's chief of staff Gottfried Urban, state secretaries from many ministries, members of the military, and many other party officials as well of course as almost the entire leadership of the Hitler Youth, including chief of staff Lauterbacher, Obergebiets-

226

führer Axmann, and Obergebietsführer Karl Cerff, the head of the Hitler Youth cultural department and initiator of this series of concerts. This may well have been the last straw for Furtwängler. It was the last time he raised his baton for this particular purpose. Apart from the rapturous applause he received no further thanks. Political calculations were once again working against him.

This time it was to do with the Salzburg festival. High-level official talks about what policy to adopt on this issue took place in early February, as the prestige of the Reich was after all at stake: to retreat or to attack? The Chancellery demanded an expert opinion – from the offices of the Reich's extraordinary and plenipotentiary ambassador to Austria – and received among other things a résumé of events:

> While Furtwängler was staying in Salzburg, Toscanini publicly declared that Furtwängler did not have the right to conduct in Salzburg, because he had brought politics into artistic and musical life. However, the only conductor who could maintain the Festival at the same, if not higher, level, as would be the case with Toscanini conducting, is Furtwängler, who despite the campaign conducted against him by certain international circles, enjoys a very great reputation abroad. This raises the question whether it would not be as well for the Austrian side to approach Furtwängler and ask him to take charge of the musical direction of the Salzburg Festival. Would it be possible for Captain Wiedemann, after checking with the Führer, to drop a hint to this effect to the Austrian department in question?[8]

The interesting thing about this advice is not only that it was to do with Salzburg – after all a foreign festival – but that if Hitler's adjutant could drop hints to settle politico-cultural matters which were really incumbent on Austria to decide, then by this point the government in Vienna was clearly no longer master in its own house. This was not surprising however, given that the National Socialist Seyss-Inquart had already moved into the Austrian Ministry of the Interior, the first step towards *Anschluss*. It turned out that Hitler did not wish to put the disobedient Furtwängler of all people in such an exposed position. The ambassador was informed: 'The Führer is opposed to Furtwängler taking part in the Salzburg Festival.'[9]

Thus the suggestion that he should be musical director was dropped completely, and even his participation was considered inopportune. At this time he was already dealing with the artistic director of the Salzburg Festival and director of the Vienna Staatsoper, Dr Erwin Kerber.

Amtliche Mitteilungen
der
Reichsmusikkammer

5. Jahr Berlin, den 1. Juni 1938 Nummer 11

Zehn Grundsätze
deutschen Musikschaffens

In seiner großen kulturpolitischen Rede anläßlich der Reichsmusiktage in Düsseldorf führte Reichsminister Dr. Goebbels u. a. folgendes aus:

Dieses Musikfest ist zum ersten Male eine Heerschau über die Musikkultur unserer Zeit. Es legt Rechenschaft ab über das, was wir erreicht haben, und fixiert die Zielsetzungen für die nähere und weitere Zukunft. Hier möge sich der Ruhm Deutschlands als des klassischen Landes der Musik aufs neue beweisen und erhärten. Hier mögen vor allem die Grundsätze wieder festgelegt und anerkannt werden, die seit jeher Ursprung und Triebkraft unseres deutschen musikalischen Schaffens gewesen sind. Und diese lauten:

1. Nicht das Programm und nicht die Theorie, nicht Experiment und nicht Konstruktion machen das Wesen der Musik aus. Ihr Wesen ist die Melodie. Die Melodie als solche erhebt die Herzen und erquickt die Gemüter; sie ist nicht deshalb kitschig oder verwerflich, weil sie ihrer Einprägsamkeit wegen vom Volke gesungen wird.

2. Nicht jede Musik paßt für jeden. Es hat deshalb auch jene Art von Unterhaltungsmusik, die in den breiten Massen Eingang findet, ihre Daseinsberechtigung, zumal in einer Epoche, in der es Aufgabe der Staatsführung sein muß, neben den schweren Sorgen, die die Zeit mit sich bringt, dem Volke auch Erholung, Unterhaltung und Erquickung zu vermitteln.

3. Wie jede andere Kunst, so entspringt die Musik geheimnisvollen und tiefen Kräften, die im Volkstum verwurzelt sind. Sie kann deshalb auch nur von den Kindern des Volkstums dem Bedürfnis und dem unbändigen Musiziertrieb eines Volkes entsprechend gestaltet und verwaltet werden. Judentum und deutsche Musik, das sind Gegensätze, die ihrer Natur nach in schroffstem Widerspruch zueinander stehen. Der Kampf gegen das Judentum in der deutschen Musik, den Richard Wagner einmal, einsam und nur auf sich allein gestellt, aufgenommen hat, ist deshalb heute noch unsere große, niemals preiszugebende Zeitaufgabe, die allerdings jetzt nicht mehr von einem Wissenden und genialen Außenseiter allein betrieben, sondern von einem ganzen Volke durchgeführt wird.

4. Die Musik ist die sinnlichste aller Künste. Sie spricht deshalb mehr das Herz und das Gefühl als den Verstand an. Wo aber schlüge das Herz eines Volkes heißer als in seinen breiten Massen, in denen das Herz einer Nation seine eigentliche Heimstätte gefunden hat. Es ist deshalb eine unabweisbare Pflicht unserer Musikführung, das ganze Volk an den Schätzen der deutschen Musik teilnehmen zu lassen.

5. Unmusikalisch sein, das ist für den musikalischen Menschen so viel wie blind oder taub sein. Danken wir Gott, daß er uns die Gnade gab, Musik zu hören, sie zu empfinden und leidenschaftlich zu lieben.

6. Die Musik ist jene Kunst, die das Gemüt der Menschen am tiefsten bewegt; sie besitzt die Kraft, den Schmerz zu lindern und das Glück zu verklären.

7. Wenn die Melodie der Ursprung der Musik ist, so folgt daraus, daß die Musik für das Volk sich nicht im Pastoralen oder Choralen erschöpfen darf. Sie muß immer wieder zur bewegten Melodie als der Wurzel ihres Wesens zurückkehren.

8. Nirgendwo liegen die Schätze der Vergangenheit so reich und unerschöpflich ausgebreitet wie auf dem Gebiete der Musik. Sie zu heben und an das Volk heranzutragen, ist unsere wichtigste und lohnendste Aufgabe.

9. Die Sprache der Töne ist manchmal durchschlagender als die Sprache der Worte. Die großen Meister der Vergangenheit sind deshalb Repräsentanten der wahren Majestät unseres Volkes, denen Ehrfurcht und Achtung geziemt.

10. Als Kinder unseres Volkes sind sie damit auch die eigentlichen Majestäten unseres Volkstums, in Wahrheit von Gottes Gnaden und dazu bestimmt, den Ruhm und die Ehre unserer Nation zu erhalten und zu mehren.

Stiftung eines Nationalen Musikpreises

Zur Förderung des musikalischen Solistennachwuchses verfüge ich mit dem heutigen Tage die Stiftung eines Nationalen Musikpreises.

Dieser Preis wird jährlich in Höhe von 20 000 RM. je zur Hälfte an die besten deutschen Pianisten und den besten deutschen Geiger des Nachwuchses zur Verteilung gelangen.

Berlin, den 28. Mai 1938
Der Reichsminister
für Volksaufklärung und Propaganda
Dr. Goebbels

41

OFFICIAL ANNOUNCEMENT BY THE REICHSMUSIKKAMMER, year 5, number 11, Berlin 1 June 1938

THE TEN PRINCIPLES OF GERMAN MUSIC

In his major speech on cultural policy on the occasion of the Reich's Day of Music in Düsseldorf, Reichsminister Dr Goebbels set forth *inter alia* the following points:

This music festival is the first overview of its kind of musical culture in our times. It renders account of what we have achieved so far and fixes goals for the immediate and more long-term future. It is an opportunity once again to testify to and affirm Germany's fame as the classical land of music. Above all, this is an opportunity to restate and recognise the principles which have always been the source and driving strength of our classical achievements here in Germany. They are as follows:

1. The essence of music lies not in its programming, nor in musical theory, nor in experimentation or particular construction; it lies in melody. Melody as such lifts our hearts and quickens our spirits; the fact the people sing it does not make it corny or reprehensible.

2. Not everybody likes all kinds of music. This is why there is so-called 'light music' which appeals to the masses. And it is this appeal which justifies its existence, especially in this difficult epoch, when the government must make it its task to provide relaxation, entertainment and stimulation for the people.

3. Like every other art form, music arises from deep and secret forces which are rooted in the people of the nation. Therefore only the nation's children can create and perform it in a manner which befits the desire and musical inclinations of that nation. Judaism and German music are opposites which by their very nature stand in sharp contradiction to one another. The fight against Judaism in German music, which Richard Wagner once took upon himself, quite alone, is for that reason still today the great and never-to-be-surrendered fight of our time, in which we can never surrender, and which is no longer being fought by one single brilliant and knowing outsider, but by a whole people.

4. Music is the most sensual of all the arts. It thus addresses our hearts and our feelings more than our minds. Where else though does the heart of a people beat than in its broad masses, amongst whom the heart of a nation finds its real home? It is therefore the clear duty of those who lead our musical activity to allow the whole people to participate in the treasures of German music.

5. To be unmusical is for the musical individual like being blind or deaf. We thank God for his bounty, by which we can hear, feel and passionately love music.

6. Music is the art which moves people most deeply; it has the power to soothe pain and illuminate happiness.

7. If melody is the source of music it follows that music for the people

229

should not limit itself to pastorales and chorales. It should always return to the stirring melodies which are the root of its being.

8. The treasures of the past are nowhere so rich and abundant as in the realm of music. To gather them up and bring them to the people is our most important and rewarding task.

9. The language of music can sometimes say more than the language of words. That is why the great masters of the past represent the true majesty of our people, and are worthy of their respect and esteem.

10. As the children of our people they are thus also the kings of our heritage, truly blessed by God and fit to maintain and further the fame and honour of our nation.

FOUNDATION OF A NATIONAL MUSIC PRIZE
To encourage the rising generation of soloists I today decree the foundation of a national music prize.

This prize will be worth 20,000 RM each year to be divided equally between the best young German pianist and the best young German violinist.

Berlin, 28 May 1938
The Minister of the Reich for Popular Enlightenment and Propaganda Dr Goebbels

---

He had said he was prepared to take on some opera performances and concerts in Salzburg and to conduct four of the Vienna Philharmonic's concerts and a number of Staatsoper performances. When he came back from Vienna on 5 March he noticed that everything had changed, and so by way of the music division he informed the Propaganda Minister:

> I have heard that the Führer has outlined a firm statement as to the task and the programme of the Salzburg Festival which differs from mine on certain key points. As I wish to avoid even the shadow of a 'collision' of my interests with those of the Führer I herewith request that you allow me to withdraw from our agreements concerning taking over the direction of the Salzburg Festival.[10]

It must have dawned on the conductor on this occasion at the latest that a collision course would give rise to permanent difficulties, with regard not only to his own personal and artistic advancement, but also to the

230

ideal of musical activity which he sought to represent. This was the point at which everything seemed to press towards a renewed attempt at bartering. The opportunity came quickly. Hitler wished to hold a plebiscite on 10 April which would ratify his annexation of Austria in the eyes of the world and so persuade them to further appeasement; people abroad should be taught that the whole German people stood behind him 'as one unified whole', which now included the 'annexed' Austrians, who were to be called *Ostmärker*. The press again publicised the election speeches of prominent personalities. The conductor of the Gewandhaus, Hermann Abendroth, began by saying that there had never been any division between music in Germany and Austria, and continued in propagandist fashion: 'The fact that this homogeneity has been re-established on a political level by the Führer's unique deed, is something that German musicians will know to thank the Führer for, and to a man they will all demonstrate their gratitude on 10 April!'[11] The President of the Reichsmusikkammer, Peter Raabe, proclaimed with that certainty of victory which was the mark of a recent party member: 'There is no need to tell any German musician how he should vote on 10 April [. . .]; he knows that the final goal of our Führer's policy is the consolidation of our German being, and that our German being finds its purest expression in German music.'[12] The general director of music Karl Böhm, although not even a party member, made the point even more explicitly, if in the somewhat crude language of a provincial politician: 'Anybody who does not say a big YES to our Führer's action and give it his one-hundred-per-cent support does not deserve to be called a German!'[13] Wilhelm Rode, an old party member and general intendant at the German opera house in Berlin said in positively byzantine fashion: 'Whatever the Führer wishes and demands, him I will follow, ever and always enthusiastic, with an obedient, faithful and grateful "Yes!" '[14]

This, or something along similar lines, was the tenor of all the spontaneous declarations in support of the vote, as well as those 'requested' by the various Reich propaganda offices: they were all calls to people to give their votes in favour of annexation. Even Furtwängler was involved, but he wrote in such a way that the editors had to add a couple of lines to the beginning in order that the reader would even notice that it was to do with the plebiscite; the text itself could have come from a history text-book: 'Ever since St. Germain the point of an independent Austria has been lost. Its return into the great and unified Reich had become a necessity, even self-evident. But to have turned this necessity into reality is the unchangeable historical act of Adolf Hitler.'[15] After the end of the Third Reich the conductor was asked about this statement and he declared that he could 'still subscribe to it today if one takes it very literally. [. . .] I said then to my friends that it would be an unchangeable historical act. What meaning one attributes to that "unchangeable" is another matter. Why don't you compare it with what others who were also forced into doing so wrote?'[16]

The statement of fact he made, double significance and all, outlined a historical situation, nothing else, and, owing to its unenthusiastic tone and lack of a personal statement of support, was of so little use in the pre-plebiscitary propaganda that it did nothing to interrupt or even slightly hinder the campaign against the awkward artist. This was why even a performance of *Die Meistersinger* – which was described in the programme as being in honour of 'the Führer's birthday' – was of no use any longer. Göring's mind was firmly made up. Chance came to his assistance.

It had almost become a tradition with the Berlin Philharmonic Orchestra to present less well-known conductors at those concerts which were not either reserved for Furtwängler or were shared only with other famous master conductors. It was a sort of trial, because the Berlin public was known to be choosy and critical. To work with such an orchestra was the dream of every aspiring conductor. Since it had been incorporated into the Propaganda Ministry however, the Philharmonic was impossible to hire; the management now sent an invitation if they felt it was right to do so, and if Furtwängler agreed. This arrangement survived, even though Furtwängler was now only the most prominent of the guest conductors and no longer the 'boss'. Quality had come to play a more important role in the choice of guests than ever before: in Aachen in recent years the town's young general director of music, Herbert von Karajan, had been gaining an ever higher profile, and so an invitation was now sent to him too.

Seen from the western border of the Reich through the eyes of an ambitious and highly gifted musician, Berlin must have seemed the fulfilment of every dream. Karajan came. He cast a spell on both the public and the press – and it was not the case that he benefited overly from the ban on criticism, because at this point the papers did still voice their reservations. The concert which he gave with the Berlin Philharmonic Orchestra on 8 April 1938 offered Mozart, Ravel and Brahms. More than one reporter registered satisfaction,

> because the man has all the gifts of a born conqueror, regardless of which troops he has to work with. [. . .] His is a very strong conducting talent; that of a man who stands at the very forefront of the rising generation. The moment he steps on to the podium and

picks up the baton one is spell-bound by a rare synthesis of under-standing, will, and ability: comprehension of the nature of music, the will to produce it, and the ability to do so.

The critic testified to the young conductor's great hopes, talked of an unprecedented artistic success, stressed his youth, and expressed the conviction that 'great tasks will also be set him in other areas of German musical life'.[17]

Shrewd as he was, the music reporter – had he heard rumours? – together with some of his colleagues was one step ahead of events; no miracle occurred and Karajan returned to Aachen. But thoughts about the opportunities in the Reich's capital gave him no peace. Furtwängler just noted the success of this gifted conductor from the provinces and concentrated on his own work. While Karajan had been rehearsing with the Berliners, Furtwängler had received visitors from Vienna in Potsdam. A delegate from the Vienna Philharmonic poured out the bad news that twenty-one of his colleagues came under the 'Aryan' clause, and that party officials there were trying to curtail the orchestra's independence. That very day the conductor drew up a plan for rescuing this orchestra, which was so rich in tradition; if the orchestra were to retain its neutral status he would be happy to take on the role of chief conductor. He immediately began putting his connections to use.[18]

The manager returned to Vienna full of hope. While Karajan was in Aachen conducting a celebratory performance of the new production of *Fidelio* on the occasion of Hitler's birthday – the Führer was of course to be identified with Fidelio, the hero who rescues victims from the dungeon, rather than with Pizzaro – Furtwängler brought the Vienna Philharmonic to the capital of the Reich to present the orchestra and draw attention to its plight. For all eventualities Goebbels had issued a protocol forbidding the press to draw any comparison between the Berlin and the Vienna Philharmonic. The concerts on 22 and 23 April were triumphs which achieved their purpose. They demonstrated that this was an independent musical enterprise which merited protection, and should be seen as completing and enriching German musical culture rather than competing with it. Hitler and Goebbels, sitting in the box of honour, seemed to understand this, even though they both had plans for the cultural merging of 'Ostmark's' unloved metropolis. The fact that it was Furtwängler who was reminding them of Vienna's musical tradition and greatness damped the top officials' already severely weakened sympathies still further, but they could see from the public's uninhibited enthusiasm for the guests that it would not be expedient to use overly brutal means to attain their goal.

The Berlin Philharmonic's next journey, too, was a success all the way, faithfully reported by the papers in Berlin. The musical public in Rome, at the May Festival in Florence, then in Zürich and Basel and finally in Paris as well, responded to the German musicians with resounding ovations. This was Furtwängler's chance to convert his success into suitable remuneration; he did not want a repeat of what had happened in 1933 when, owing to the orchestra's dire circumstances, he had received no honorarium for three quarters of a year. So he put in a request to Dr Funk, who at the beginning of the year had risen from state secretary in the Propaganda Ministry to the position of minister of economic affairs, to double his fees from 2,000 RM per concert to 4,000 RM. Goebbels agreed to the new clause in principle, and, while the budget department of his ministry objected that the additional expenditure could not be paid for from the orchestra's budget, a note in the file shows that the officials were very well aware what the political consequences would be if they refused:

> Dr Furtwängler's demand is quite appropriate given that when abroad he receives these honoraria automatically. And so it is clearly necessary to meet it because a lower fee at home would cause him to spend more time conducting abroad, which would leave the orchestra with another season like the 1935–6 one (no F.-concerts = empty halls).[19]

Rather than make demands on the orchestra's budget, the increment was met with a grant given by the ministry.[20] However, there were frequent delays in payment, such that by January 1940 Furtwängler was once again owed 50,000 RM by the management.

All in all though the summer of 1938 was once more – despite the noticeable distancing of top Nazis – almost free of worries for Furtwängler, carried along as he was by his fame, success, and the liking of both his musicians and the public. There was no one in sight who could challenge him, the greatest in German music. There was also no lack of offers, and he could pick and choose. The Hans Pfitzner Association in Berlin, which had only been founded in February and which operated within the framework of the NSKG, chose him as their honorary chairman, from which arose the obligation to take baton in hand at the first concert staged by this club. Now the chairman, the music critic Wilhelm Matthes, was planning a large Pfitzner festival, and he turned to the conductor with his programme suggestions, hoping that he would manage to book him and the Berlin Philharmonic for a date some time in the spring of 1939. Due to the festival preparations in Salzburg Matthes only received an answer three weeks later; Furtwängler regretted that he did not have the time, but recommended a colleague instead: 'For the time being I believe that you will really have to entrust this to someone else, perhaps Herr Karajan.'[21]

If any proof were needed to show how innocent he still was as far as the security of his own position in the music business was concerned, this recommendation provides it, because in effect it meant that Karajan would have to come back to Berlin where the Pfitzner festival was to be held. Aachen by contrast was a place at a safe distance on the periphery of the Reich; but Furtwängler did not consider the young general director of music as a possible competitor, certainly not as a danger to be taken seriously. He knew the man was good, the members of the orchestra had told him so, and they certainly knew what they were talking about; but however talented he might be, the difference in their greatness remained . . . as did Furtwängler's self-confidence, and so he involved himself in the preparations for the party congress. The organisation of the music programme was once again in Rosenberg's hands, and he called on his music expert Gerigk for help. They wanted Furtwängler to conduct;[22] he however informed them by way of party member Ernst Ludwig, adviser for domestic musical events in Division X of the Propaganda Ministry, that he was prepared to do *Die Meistersinger* before the party congress, but nothing else. Hitler was vacillating between Böhm and Weisbach and so, once he had decided on the soloists for the Wagner opera, as was his custom, he gave Rosenberg a free hand. At this point Furtwängler discreetly but firmly began to edge the problem of Vienna's musical life on to the agenda. From Salzburg he sent a personal telegram to Goebbels, of which a carbon copy went to Captain Wiedemann at the Chancellery:

> Believe on artistic grounds essential to have first-class ensemble for *Die Meistersinger* at party congress therefore at Nürnberg ask apart from soloists chosen by the Führer to use orchestra choir and minor soloists from the Vienna Staatsoper whom have very carefully rehearsed in Salzburg stop
>
> Only then can manage artistic performance of this very difficult to pull together opera in short time available in Nuremberg stop
>
> Please obtain Führer's assent to this proposal which would also stress the Austrian part in the performance for this party congress.[23]

The suggestion was based on more than just artistic motives, and even the 'Austrian' part was not the key issue – although he may have meant to stress that the annexation could not simply be papered over by functionaries using the protocol term *ostmärkish*. The main issue was

235

the Vienna Philharmonic, for whom he wanted an exceptional ruling to be passed which would save the orchestra from the Viennese officials who were in the process of destroying it. Only a few days earlier Furtwängler had requested of the director of the Staatsoper, Dr Kerber, that he 'apply to the relevant authorities for special licences for the nine members of our orchestra indicated on the herewith enclosed list, and ensure that they are granted, so that the artistic capabilities, standing and good name of the Vienna Philharmonic can be preserved'.[24]

There were nine 'full-blooded' Jews, as well as two musicians with 'non-Aryan' connections, whom there was never any question of being able to keep because of the regime's racial policy, which by comparison with 1933 had gained assurance and momentum. The cases an exceptional ruling was being sought for were orchestra members with 'non-Aryan' wives, as well as those who were one 'quarter-Jew'. If they left this would cripple the orchestra's ability to play at all, because it would involve the loss of one clarinet, one trombone, one bassoon and the first horn. The forced retirement of the eleven 'racially unworthy' musicians had already caused enough damage, even if the director, a party member and SS man whom the Nazi Party had appointed as a commissioner, tried to pretend the consequences were minimal: 'So when in those historic March days of 1938 slight changes took place in the orchestra – they really were slight – the members were also faced with new tasks.'[25]

The 'slight changes' had consisted among other things in removing the eminent concert master and virtuoso violinist Arnold Rosé, who had already been denounced in Hans Brückner and Christa Maria Rock's notorious lexicon of Jews as 'Josef Rosenbaum, Jew'. Furtwängler's resourceful move saved the remaining musicians; all the cases listed received a special licence from the Propaganda Minister; only Hugo Burghauser the bassoonist had to leave, but as his divorce from his Jewish wife was already under way this was for political rather than racial reasons.

The performance of *Die Meistersinger* by the Viennese, on the evening before the party congress in Nürnberg, took place in front of the leadership corps of the Nazi Party headed by Hitler, the diplomatic corps, the Gauleiters and ministers of the Reich, and a delegation from the Italian Fascist Party. It thus prepared the ground for the preservation of this traditional Viennese orchestra without the conductor having to compromise himself, as the performance – on 5 September – was scheduled before the political event which was only formally opened in the congress hall the following morning. But it affected enough of the 'right-minded' public – those who would be attending the congress – to raise

𝕹𝖆𝖙𝖎𝖔𝖓𝖆𝖑𝖋𝖔𝖟𝖎𝖆𝖑𝖎𝖋𝖙𝖎𝖋𝖈𝖍𝖊   𝕯𝖊𝖚𝖙𝖋𝖈𝖍𝖊 𝕬𝖗𝖇𝖊𝖎𝖙𝖊𝖗𝖕𝖆𝖗𝖙𝖊𝖎

Der Stellvertreter des Führers
Stabsleiter

z.Zt.Obersalzberg, den 5.Aug.38
Bo./Bm.

Durch Eilboten.

Herrn
Reichsleiter Rosenberg

Berlin W 35,
Margaretenstraße 17.

> Kanzlei Rosenberg
> Eing. Nr. 2122 Am.-3/4 38
> E 1c

Betrifft: Musik bei der Kulturtagung.

Den Inhalt Ihres Schreibens vom 28.7.1938 - Dr.Gk/G.-
konnte ich erst heute dem Führer vortragen. Bitte über-
senden Sie mir die Platten des Beethoven-Werkes so rasch
wie möglich nach dem Berghof, wo der Führer sie sich an-
hören will.

Heil Hitler!

(M.Bormann)

By express messenger.
Herrn Rosenberg, Reichsleiter

Berlin W35
Margaretenstrasse 17.

Re: Music for the cultural symposium.

I was only able to inform the Führer of your letter of 28 July 1938 today –
Dr Gk/G. –. Please send me the records of the Beethoven pieces as quickly
as possible at the Berghof, where the Führer wishes to listen to them.

Heil Hitler! (M. Bormann)

---

a great deal of interest. The press was so full of praise it could hardly
contain its approbation:

> After the final act the applause, which the Führer repeatedly contri-
> buted to with particular enthusiasm, attained [. . .] the dimensions
> of an enthusiastic demonstration, which was certainly provoked in
> equal measures by the wonderful work and the matchlessly executed

performance. [. . .] Manifest here is one single spirit, one single working of the German mind and soul. What was once formed there by the highly gifted creator is here elevated and transformed into a total proclamation of all that Germany signifies and always has signified throughout the centuries.[26]

Of course this afternoon of opera also had something to do with music. As in the previous year, only this time even more severely, Hitler restricted his circle to a chosen few by way of a circular which his deputy sent out; the office for guests of honour at the party congress passed on the wish 'that only such visitors as are really interested should attend. By order of the Führer therefore [. . .] guests of honour too will only receive tickets on receipt of payment.'[27] Price list attached, pre-payment using enclosed payment card, ticket transfers not allowed. One had to pay for one's honour with money, but this did give a certain guarantee that even those of the Nuremberg opera house's 1,500 seats reserved for 'political' purposes would be occupied by music lovers rather than by philistine officials.

Furtwängler was in no doubt that the opera was a success, especially as he was not only strengthening his own position but also helping the Viennese. His reputation grew, and because there was such a run on the far too few tickets issued for the Philharmonic concerts the management of the Berlin Philharmonic Orchestra decided to allow a repeat, which meant that the dress-rehearsal was now to be followed by three further performances. This caused the Berlin press to take a renewed interest in the personal and professional development of this extraordinary artist; Edwin von der Null[28] was one of those to state his opinion very clearly, in an article published in a widely read newspaper:

Furtwängler represents German music like no other today. Although he conducts anything which he feels worthwhile, from Bach to Stravinsky, and although he has a knowledge of and the ability to bring forth two hundred years of European music, his artistic focus remains on German music. And in particular that German music which derives life from the conflict of mind and soul, the music which causes us (to adapt a line of Kant's) to see the starry heavens above and feel the moral law inside ourselves. It is the music in which man struggles with himself and the eternal forces, the music which seeks to express elevation, redemption, release, strife, victory or annihilation. [. . .] In him our experience is mirrored with indescribable power. His soul ranges across all the levels between heaven and hell, expresses them to the outside world using his eyes, gestures and movement, and sucks the orchestra and the singers into the maelstrom of his visions as powerfully as the public.[29]

The conductor accepted this as one of the ovations the music reporters on the *BZ am Mittag* customarily wrote, and does not seem to have realised that behind all this the attack from the rearguard, which he had yet even to recognise as such, was gathering strength. Benda, the manager, because of the positive feedback after the spring concert, had invited the Aachen general director of music again, this time to give a master concert for the Nazi association Kraft durch Freude (Strength through Joy), and for the Berlin Concert Association, both either affiliated to political organisations, or political organisations in their own right. Both could mobilise considerable audiences and regularly 'bought up' Berlin Philharmonic concerts at very low cost, because they wanted to offer their members preferential treatment. The first of these concerts that season was the one conducted by Karajan on 27 September. It was a prelude to greater things. Ever since the dispute with Furtwängler, Göring and Tietjen had been searching for a conductor with whom to pay him back in kind; they gathered expert opinions, such as that of Rudolf Bockelmann for example, who had played Wotan in Aachen that February.[30] The claim made by Walter Legge, the music producer, namely that he was the one who advised Tietjen to fetch Karajan, is a dubious one, as he was obviously more concerned with gaining attention for himself than with historical fact.[31] One can safely assume that the general intendant needed information in his own field, but not advice. Anyway, a report given him the previous year by his dramatic adviser, Julius Kapp, had left him with a positive picture of the young general director's achievements, and so he invited him to work as a guest at his venerable institution. Karajan's first appearance at the Staatsoper – on 30 September – resulted in a memorable *Fidelio*: 'It was one of those rare evenings when all the strengths contained in the work were released and came into their own. The performance had a quite remarkable tension. [. . .] Within a few minutes the young conductor had won over the whole apparatus of the Staatsoper.'[32] No hand had been raised to greet him, but from the second act onwards the public celebrated this previously almost unknown conductor with a wild enthusiasm that could not have been prearranged; it was for Karajan – the conqueror. The public's spontaneous reaction even caused von der Nüll to reflect analytically on the change in the audience's behaviour: 'The public decided at once. It decided that this was transcendental achievement and behaved accordingly.'[33] It was not just because of the effect he had on the public that Tietjen at once agreed to a contract for guest appearances with Karajan. This man could be useful for settling accounts with Furt-wängler; he was after all not only an artist, but also an obsessive climber who would ignore no opportunity to further his success. The intendant understood so much of the psychology of this broad and conflict-laden culture industry from his own experience.

While in Ulm the young conductor had been thwarted in his ambition by a provincial lack of success; the leap to one of Germany's great musical stages would have suited him, but there were so few vacancies that a beginner could hope at best for a post as a repetiteur. Then Hitler came to power. In the first few months of 1933 the newly appointed intendants, faithful to the party line, had put their Jewish conductors out on the street; but this appeared to have been done in what might only have been a passing mood. One day however, the Reichstag con-firmed the situation with the notorious law for the rehabilitation of the civil service passed on 7 April 1933, really a post-hoc legalisation of the boycott of Jewish civil servants. Karajan, twenty-five years old and driven by a desire to reach the top, was at the time staying with his parents in Salzburg. On that Friday evening Munich Radio reported the legal reform, and the following morning a paper sympathetic to the National Socialists brought the news in black and white – before the other Salzburg newspapers. Now, there for all to read, 'the precon-ditions enabling the removal of all Jewish officials and others at odds with the party from public service' existed at last.[34]

Anyone who works in theatre knows that conductors of both regional and national opera houses are always, so to speak, 'temporary'. In the house in which Karajan's parents lived, no. 1 Schwarzstrasse, there was a small shop where one could find not only the *Salzburger Volksblatt* but also publicity for the Austrian offshoot of the Nazi Party; thus in order to find out about the latest developments the young musician would not even have had to cross the road; and it would have been easy for him to work out that the 'Aryan' clause would lead to a mass dismissal of Jewish theatre directors which would necessarily result in some twenty to thirty positions, including a few highly desirable ones, falling vacant. Competition would be stiff of course, but there were steps one could take to help oneself . . .

On that Saturday 8 April, Karajan signed an enrolment form for the Nazi Party, paid a five-schilling registration fee and returned the slip to the recruiting officer, party member Herbert Klein, who would later become a historian and head of the regional archives in Salzburg; Klein delivered the certificate to the party recruitment office, which as it happened was in the shop in Karajan's parents' house. There is no proof that the decision to declare his political colour was a calculated move;

240

one could of course assume that it was one of those improbable coincidences which only happen once in a blue moon, though with the most significant consequences: it is just possible that even though he had listened to the radio and scanned the 'people's paper' and realised the political situation, the musician's next move was dictated not by his ambition but by a fanatical admiration for Hitler. At any rate there are no obvious motives apart from these two.[35]

He must at least have had a purpose in mind when he made this early show of allegiance, otherwise, as he already had one party membership no. 1,607,525, he would certainly not have bothered to sign a second enrolment form for the Ulm regional branch, for which he was given the number 3,430,914. One is again struck by the way this was linked to a particular date: 1 May 1933, the day on which he joined for a second time, was the last day for four years on which the party still accepted new members fairly indiscriminately; from then on Hitler decreed a 'closed season'.[36] Just how useful this membership might be for the conductor is demonstrated by a series of cases in which rather untalented artists were – even if only temporarily – given positions on the grounds of their 'political merit' whether they were up to them or not. Karajan was actually too gifted and therefore a nuisance, which was why the intendant for Ulm, after trying him out for a while in the vacant position left by the dismissed Jewish chief conductor, Otto Schulmann, finally sent him on his way in March 1934.

The unemployed musician went to Berlin in search of conducting work of any kind. Now at that time the capital of the Reich was home to the Stage Recruitment Agency, as well as several concert agencies, and also to a concert department which had been founded that February by the 'Musicians of the Reich' as a part of the Reichsmusikkammer. At Havemann's suggestion the non-party member Rudolf Vedder had been appointed as manager of this so-to-speak 'official' employment agency. He was an extremely pushy and successful climber with a less than savoury past, and he now got down to business, distributing engagements and filling vacancies, gaining support for himself from the artistic community to the point where it seemed he was indispensable. For a conductor without a job the obvious thing to do would have been to look up Herr Vedder. Athough there is only evidence of contact between Vedder and Karajan from 1935–6 onwards,[37] their acquaintance may well have begun in April or May of 1934; it was inevitable if the unemployed artist was really doing everything he could to explore new possibilities. In the autumn of 1938 – having in the meantime become a successful general director of music in Aachen – he was certainly on Vedder's register, and although the agent had quit the since-dissolved

241

concert department with much ado, he now worked independently and more effectively, was downright obsequious to the top artists, and did a number of favours for Karajan; whether the idea of bringing him to Berlin was thought up and set in motion by Vedder's concert agency – which had moved from the Neu-Westend on the edge of town to the Potsdamer Platz in the centre – is no idle question; Furtwängler was to the agent what a red rag is to a bull, and the feeling was mutual.

At any rate 21 October marks the beginning of a large-scale attack on the difficult 'old man'. That evening Karajan was conducting *Tristan und Isolde* at the Staatsoper. It was his second appearance in this opera house. There was one paper – of the five or six large ones in Berlin – which blew up what was indubitably a success to the proportions of a world sensation. It was the *BZ am Mittag*, and the highly personal and wholly exaggerated article was written by Edwin von der Null. Its title: 'In the Staatsoper: Karajan the miracle'. This banner headline celebrating his unique genius – as well as Null himself, who had indirectly helped discover this phenomenon – was spread across the whole page. In the article itself Null was modest. He preferred to credit the 'great artist and organiser' Tietjen with the honour of the find, after which he launched, fortissimo, into a hymn of praise: 'What we were shown yesterday borders on the inconceivable. A thirty-year-old man creates a performance for which our great fifty-year-olds can justifiably envy him. [. . .] Karajan is a gift. I believe he knows exactly what he is worth. Shortly the opera capitals of the world will be fighting over him.'[38]

To make it quite clear to everybody just which of the 'great fifty-year-olds' this was addressed to, mention was made of Furtwängler in one of the two introductory paragraphs, alongside his photo. One of the critic's editorial colleagues later described some of the details of what happened on that day and also quoted parts of the review, although abbreviated and somewhat changed from the original.[39] According to this description, Null burst into the editorial office he shared with Bernd Ruland on the morning of 22 October, full of enthusiasm, and read out the report to his colleague. Ruland suggested the attention-grabbing title as a joke, and it was also his idea to set it across the whole width of the page so it would catch the eye. The text in its own right was obviously calculated to hit Furtwängler below the belt, and now it could be seen how little the minister's decree on criticism, which was supposed to prevent such excesses, was really worth. The conductor, although an opponent of the ban on criticism, was definitely keen to teach the newspaper people a degree of editorial discipline, and he now found himself in a somewhat difficult situation. Since 1933 quite a few things had changed. Official departments now offered more hope of success than a telephone call to the chief editor; in other words there was no choice but to go via official channels. But could he – now himself a victim of his own cause – go begging to one of those 'on high'? Especially as Goebbels would be able to turn him away with a gloating reminder about his memo concerning criticism from the previous year?

Prior to 1933 disciplining any critic who became too forward had been no problem. There are several pieces of evidence for this, including this draft of a letter to an unnamed chief editor:

> I have hitherto always refrained from responding to the more than impertinent stance which your contributor A. B. has taken against me for many years. It seemed unnecessary to bother to refute his statements, which are always as correct in theory as they are wrong in practice. But this time, when he claims that in the Andante of Schubert's C-major Symphony I beat vigorous crotchets (he says this twice), when in fact I never beat anything but quavers and actually on average take this movement slower than other conductors, one is justified in asking whether this is a case of deliberate misrepresentation or just unbounded dilettantism. I refuse to submit myself to the judgements of such a critic; could you please give me your assurance that in future he will no longer discuss my concerts. Should this not be forthcoming I shall no longer come to Munich and will make a public statement of my reasons, as I do not see why as an artist one should have to put up with gross misrepresentations of the facts of the case as well as with everything else.[40]

The target of this fulmination was probably Alfred Burgartz on the *Bayerische Staatszeitung*; it is not clear whether or not his departure to Stuttgart is linked to it. The conductor habitually collected critiques and evaluated them. He not only observed the effect he himself had on the public, but also that of colleagues such as Böhm, Sabata, Kabasta, Talich and the like. In this case it was a purely factual matter which was at issue: his already controversial manner of beating time; the force of his reaction really attributed more importance to the accusation than it merited. Another case happened in Hamburg shortly before Hitler's accession to power; the gist of it is sufficiently clear from a letter:

> Lütgert has just rung me after having conferred for an hour with Professor Roth. He says Roth was shocked that there is the threat of such consequences, but had slowly retracted his statement and said he would make clear that he had done so in his next review. But if you

243

dine with Chevalley you are not supposed to know anything about this, because Chevalley wants the honour of having achieved it on his own.[41]

What formerly had always succeeded – although with an effort which would have been better spent elsewhere – namely making the newspaper people realise when they could go no further, and who was important, now ran up against difficulties with which the politically vulnerable Furtwängler had to calculate if he wished to avoid being compromised. To begin with he asked his secretary, Freda von Rechenberg, to approach Dr Drewes; she discovered that the music division of the Propaganda Ministry which he headed had no responsibilities for matters to do with art criticism. Her boss then talked to Drewes, who until recently – as Furtwängler's successor – had been vice-president of the Reichsmusikkammer, in other words a 'colleague' of sorts, who was also a general director of music, but a long-standing National Socialist. Drewes probably advised him to try going higher up, to State Secretary Naumann, head of the ministerial office. This Furtwängler did. Despite all his reservations about the musician, Goebbels saw this as a chance to get even with his rival, Göring, and he intervened on Furtwängler's behalf. The editorial office of the *BZ am Mittag* received a serious complaint from the ministry about the 'bombastic form' the review had taken.[42] The chief editor passed this on and made sure that Nüll stayed away from the belligerent conductor. Whether a request dated 16 March 1939 and renewed on 8 May 1940, which the head of the politico-cultural archive in Rosenberg's department, Dr Gerigk, made to the Berlin Gestapo – for information regarding Nüll's earlier political activities or possible hostility to the Nazis – is connected to this case, remains an open question. At any rate whenever there was a Furtwängler concert to be reported on it was always done by somebody else.[43] This did not go unnoticed by music lovers. The hapless individual was even publicly rebuked by a colleague:

> Even a good review can cause damage if it is obvious that it is getting at someone. It can make people believe that even the best are 'in for it'. [. . .] If the reader no longer finds any distinction being made between a novice composer and a Hans Pfitzner, or between a newcomer to conducting and a Wilhelm Furtwängler, then the discussion of art loses any value at all.[44]

Now it was Karajan's turn to feel bitter, because – quite rightly – he felt that to be labelled a 'newcomer to conducting' was discriminatory and as it was plain for all to see who was behind it all, his anger was directed at Furtwängler rather than at Matthes or the minister. For Furtwängler's second Philharmonic concert, which took place on 5, 6 and 7 November and featured among other pieces the original version of Bruckner's Fifth Symphony, the *BZ* now sent Matthes, who extended measured, unequivocal praise and explained 'how it is that such deep intellectual relationships can surface in a music which flows so broadly. One feels that the furthest possible limits of interpretation have been reached here.'[45]

The minister had not suddenly started checking in every corner to try and stop comparisons of any sort being drawn between the two conductors, and he certainly did not intend to introduce advance censorship; the press however had begun to behave more cautiously. For example some days later the *Berliner Illustrierte* published a page of pictures, with a picture of Furtwängler conducting which was twice the size of the one of Karajan printed beneath, placed at the top of the right-hand column. The caption said: 'The winter's music has begun: Wilhelm Furtwängler, Germany's leading musician, the most spiritual and introspective conductor of symphonic music, celebrating his first triumph of the season.' Under the photo of his competitor one could read: 'Herbert von Karajan, at only thirty years of age already general director of music in Aachen and with an unprecedented talent for operatic drama, is the big discovery of Berlin's musical winter. He was appointed to the Berlin Staatsoper by the Prime Minister, General Field-Marshall Göring.'[46]

The superlatives used for Furtwängler contained a clear message; they were intended to show that he remained Germany's unquestioned number one. On the same day the *BZ* settled another debt; Nüll's 'miracle review' could not be simply ignored; it had to be toned down to a more moderate level. This was a matter of protocol which was dealt with in sophisticated and clever fashion by the third music reporter on the paper's editorial staff, Walter Steinhauer. He reduced everything in the article by half; instead of ninety-seven lines there were now only forty-three; a title covering two columns replaced the full-width one, and there was no mention of a 'miracle', even though the same *Tristan* was being discussed; the critic attested only to 'an uncommonly gripping and intensive production'.[47]

One cannot be surprised that Furtwängler had begun to try and get a picture of what his young rival's achievements were and where the important differences might lie. The whole affair had churned him up considerably and had no doubt affected his self-respect to some extent. He studied this allegedly sensational *Tristan* by the intruder from Aachen and came to a noteworthy analysis:

The intellectual conductor (Karajan, *Tristan*), who does not experience the piece afresh each time, conducts only what he knows and wants, in other words the nuances. Which is why the nuances are all exaggerated. The slow tempi are too slow, the fast ones too fast, there is no total experience of harmonic-polyphonic orchestral sound, just deliberately over-emphasised individual voices. This detracts above all from the overall sound (strings). The only thing which is expressed is the immediate 'here and now', which is hysteria-laden, or at least becomes exaggerated and hysterical in re-interpretations of this kind. [48]

This was an astonishingly unemotional view which at the same time expressed everything which Furtwängler saw as dividing them; there is still no evidence that at this point he might have feared Karajan as a threatening and dangerous rival. The effects of the 'miracle' review seemed to have been damped; his standing had been reaffirmed, and with his peace of mind restored he could address himself to his musical tasks. At this moment in time he was not terribly interested in who or what lay behind it all. But the anger was now deeply rooted. Anyone who wanted to could easily bring it to the surface; they needed only to assert that Furtwängler was jealous of Karajan. This was the sort of thing that von Benda, the manager, did with consummate skill after the 'boss' had turned on him for wanting to misuse the members of the Philharmonic by dividing them into chamber groups which he would then give pretentious names and send off on concert tours; the conflict ended with Benda being released from his duties when it had become obvious that he was serving as Vedder's front-man in the dispute with Furtwängler. The latter rejected all allegations of jealousy, protesting, 'I only complained about the fact that from one day to the next Karajan was presented by a certain paper as if he were the great God Almighty himself.' [49]

There were some matters in which he had certainly put two and two together; after all Nüll must have undergone a sudden change of heart at some point between 4 and 22 October, because prior to that he had already attended Karajan's first appearance at the Staatsoper without reacting with such wild enthusiasm, and the difference cannot have been due to the impression which the guest conductor made on him, because Karajan's first appearance had been no less extraordinary than his second. Is one to assume that Nüll was affected only the second time? Or that his hymn of praise in *Der Stern* at the beginning of the month was insincere? Perhaps calculated to lull Furtwängler into a false sense of security? On the other hand he had no apparent reason for wanting to take any such revenge. During the de-nazification commission proceedings concerning Furtwängler, the witnesses were agreed that the critic

246

Karajan conducts *Tristan und Isolde* at the Staatsoper, October 1938

cultivated close relations with the Reich Air Ministry, which Göring directed, and that he was wont to brag about this to his colleagues. This may have been good for his self-confidence – which he needed because he made a point of sticking up for modern music, causing frequent offence. Even in his – now untraceable – book *Lebendige Musik* (Living Music), published in 1943 in Leipzig by the air force's defence branch and immediately distributed with help from the Nazi leadership of the air force, by order of the Air Ministry – which in fact meant the edition quickly sold out – Null hailed composers such as Egk, Orff and Wagner-Régeny. This was the logical continuation of a development begun ten years earlier with the study *Modern Harmony*. In other words even from an aesthetic point of view he was one of Furtwängler's opponents.

As one of Berlin's twenty music critics, and not a particularly prominent one at that, he could well use support 'from above'. Records show that both Göring and Tietjen knew him;[50] it is possible that other more personal relations were cultivated outside professional ones. This would not have been unusual and could have been in the interests of both sides. As Göring did not have his own publicity organ – unlike Rosenberg, Ley, Goebbels and other top figures in the regime – he was almost certainly interested in being able to influence the press. Such a direct link saved him from having to ask the propaganda minister for favours.

Another personality who knew Nüll well, had many dealings with him and also enjoyed excellent relations with the Air Ministry was the concert agent, Rudolf Vedder.

Vedder was a sort of *éminence grise* in the conspiracy against Furtwängler; a talented player in behind-the-scenes intrigue, this steely businessman knew more about business and the music world than any of his competitors, and moreover was barbarically ruthless. He had been in charge of the concert department of Steinway & Sons where he pocketed for himself several fees which were owing to artists. That was in 1927. As Steinway had to compensate those who had been cheated for the not inconsiderable sum of 10,200 RM, Vedder was given a neutral testimonial and dismissed; however this embezzler was spared legal proceedings because the firm acted on the principle that someone sitting in prison would not be able to repay the damages. Vedder quickly realised how he could profit from this situation; he let his former employers support him with recommendations and the like. Because of the general economic situation this was only partly successful, and consequently he tended to be dilatory in his debt repayments to the firm's Hamburg office.

Naturally the now-independent concert agent went for the best musicians. He even made approaches to Furtwängler, but the latter had a secretary who was excellent at dealing with the arrangements for guest performances, and already worked with the Wolff & Sachs agency whenever the Berlin Philharmonic was involved, and so he roundly rebuffed the over-eager Vedder. That was in 1929. Now Vedder was using all the means at his disposal to put Furtwängler down; obvious method: build up and deploy a counter-force. He tried to do this with Eugen Jochum, boasting: 'Jochum is an ace. He is the rising star and will soon put Furtwängler in the shade!'[51]

This attempt was unsuccessful; Jochum did not make it because the Berliners remained loyal to their trusted idol. Another incident sheds light on the agent's work and organisational ethics: Furtwängler was due to conduct the *St. Matthew Passion*, and needed the soprano Mia Peltenburg, whom Vedder was supposed to 'deliver'. However, she did not turn up to the rehearsal. The agent paced up and down the hall, nervously to begin with, then with gestures of profound frustration and repeated apologies about the singer. He found it unbelievable, he had never known her do this before; could something have happened to her perhaps? Mia Peltenburg took part at the next rehearsal as though nothing had happened, and revealed that the evening before, Herr Vedder had found her an engagement at the last minute and told her

248

she need not go to the rehearsal. Furtwängler saw it all very clearly, got rid of the dishonest agent and never worked with him again.

It was by such methods and lack of scruple that Vedder had reached his influential position in the music business. He had begun the climb as an artist's secretary working for Edwin Fischer and Georg Kulenkampff. He benefited his already prominent clients by demanding ever higher honoraria, but he suppressed hopefuls from the rising generation who might threaten the great ones; he did this not least through his good relations with the press. He did deals of all kinds, though he was still bound by his links to Steinway. He was a virtuoso in the latest trend in agency ploys, not only loudly plugging his own artists, but trying to do down and cast suspicion on those of his competitors. Thus he succeeded in making himself appear indispensable; loved by some, feared by others. With Hitler's accession to power on 30 January 1933 he really was in a position to gain the upper hand.

In November 1933 he set to work on the Wolff & Sachs agency, which had broken its ties with Erich Sachs some months previously and had reverted to calling itself Hermann Wolff Concert Management. He began by surveying the situation in almost military fashion – more evidence for how dangerous a person he was. He gathered all the useful information together in a memo, including the economic situation of the firm, which naturally was suffering under the anti–Semitic boycott and had announced a deficit of 4,000 RM on 1 July; he was also interested in details about the personnel, as with the departure of her Jewish business partners Erich Sachs and Erich Simon, Frau Wolff was the sole boss:

Louise Wolff is ostensibly a Christian, her daughter half-Jewish. Objections to her daughter's employment have been voiced on all sides, above all by the manager of the Philharmonic Orchestra (Herr Höber). [. . .] The contract with the Philharmonic (ten Furtwängler concerts) has been abrogated this year. It is not clear whether it will be extended. Höber, the manager, does not wish the contract to be extended if there is no change regarding the owners and the daughter.[52]

The confidential information that the firm had not paid its taxes correctly seemed particularly useful, given that what he was after was the partnership. Because of the pressure of circumstances at the time, Frau Wolff did actually negotiate with him and even offered him a contract – obviously without yielding to the upstart's demands and with the following telling clause: 'The current clerks, Frau Stargardt and Frau

249

Brandenburg, can only be dismissed with the permission of the assembled company.'[53] The 'half-Jewish' daughters were the very people Vedder wanted nothing to do with, and he turned the offer down point-blank. Even with a second draft they failed to reach agreement. On 5 January his lawyer informed Frau Sachs that he was not interested in the appointment as manager and that material matters were only of secondary importance in his decision. The director of Steinway, Theodor Ehrlich, observed this development and worked behind the scenes in aid of his dilatory debtor. Other people also intervened, such as the wealthy singer Carl Clewing, a party member and SS-Führer who had served as a fighter pilot in the First World War and there got to know a flight officer by the name of Hermann Göring, and this led his old comrade – who himself had only just climbed to Reichsjägermeister – to make him his commissioner for music.

With so much help Vedder was able to take the decisive step. He became head of the Reichsmusikkammer's concert department when it began work in February 1934. His contract was dated from 16 March. The first thing he undertook – in grateful association with his sponsor, Havemann – was to remove all Jews from musical positions in the provinces, simply by not sending any Jews there. Although he knew that by doing this he was acting against Furtwängler he tried once more to approach the conductor. On 22 March he knocked on Frau Geissmar's door, and she found him pleasant and their conversation useful: 'He put things in a quite new light for me. I now see many things much more clearly, and there is not one of your advisers or assistants who can tell you so much so concisely in the space of quarter of an hour. I believe it would be a very good idea if you were to receive him sometime, and I will tell you why when I see you.'[54]

She had told the now-official agent about her boss's meeting at the Propaganda Ministry a week earlier, and after hearing her guest's comments she became convinced that Furtwängler had been dealt with very strangely there, and that his interlocutors had had quite unjustifiable preconceptions. Vedder was well informed, and he was using this as an attempt to re-establish contact. He tried several more times, the last occasion being after Berta Geissmar had left; that time he wanted to use Lucas, who was chief producer at Telefunken and whom Furtwängler trusted, as an intermediary. But Lucas refused to cooperate in trying to set up a one-to-one meeting. Quite apart from all this Vedder was becoming hectically busy under the mantel of the Reichsmusikkammer. He had a hand in all aspects of the music business; with none of the reservations he showed at home, he liaised with the Jewish concert agency, Organisation Artistique Internationale, which the emigrants

Erich Simon, Horwitz and Dr Schiff had opened in Paris, obtaining famous artists such as Dusolina Giannini, Poldi Mildner, the Don-Cossacks Choir and Jack Hylton's Jazz Orchestra. He was only too happy to allow others to take care of his work for him. Thus for example the pianist Erwin Gräwe, regional head of the Reichsmusikkammer in Westphalia, sent a circular to important conductors and music associations in his area and informed them that the Reichsmusikkammer would like more use to be made of the concert department.

When Gaspar Cassadó, the Spanish cello virtuoso, no longer wanted Vedder to organise his tour for him, his secretary was brusquely informed by Vedder that he did not want to stop him going elsewhere, but that he would regret it, if only because of the licences which the artist needed; he would try and see what he could do, but it was possible that there would be problems with the licences and that limits would be fixed. This sort of blackmail was normally successful. It is not surprising that the private concert agencies complained about this official competition, which according to the statutes of the Reichsmusikkammer was inadmissible. They appealed several times to the Reichsmusikkammer and finally pointed out the way Vedder was mismanaging his business: he had taken a loan of over 19,600 RM from the musicians in the Kammer but ended the business year 1934–5 with a further loss of about 13,500 RM; takings did not even cover the concert department's salaries and day-to-day costs. When this was also followed by a verbose but well-documented denunciation from the pen of his arch enemy Max R. Müller, sent initially to the Chancellery of the Reich before being passed to von Keudell, ministerial adviser in the Propaganda Ministry, the management of the Reichskulturkammer finally took action. A note by Moraller showed he was ready to do battle: 'Action! Please discuss this with me!'[55]

Action there was, and in a letter dated 5 July 1935 the Reichskulturkammer informed Vedder that he had been dismissed 'with immediate effect'. However, when the Berlin police chief tried to start enquiries into accusations of unfair competition, the Reichsmusikkammer dragged the whole procedure out and came up with no evidence. Somebody was protecting the man, and something quite astonishing happened next. When the Reichsmusikkammer dissolved the leaderless concert department on 1 October, dozens of artists who had until then dealt through it declared that they wanted to stay with Vedder, who had immediately founded a new firm – with the help of a false testimonial from the president of the Reichsmusikkammer, Raabe: 'Herr Vedder always led the concert department with great skill and untiring diligence. Under his leadership the department had a record of great successes. Both his equals and subordinates always found him very companionable and easy to work with.'[56]

Those who continued to put their trust in the versatile agent were almost without exception top musicians from at home and abroad, soloists of all kinds, and chamber ensembles. A number of them dropped away in the course of the murderously competitive war with which he soon began to take his revenge on the 'hostile' concert agencies. But this man was good for still more mischief: in 1937 he complained of hard times to his creditors, Steinway & Sons, and managed to reduce his debt repayments to 50 RM per month. When the Reichsmusikkammer failed to give him the agreed severance pay immediately, he asked them – wily as he was – to transfer payment of it to Steinway, which meant the firm then chased up the Reichsmusikkammer on his behalf. Legal proceedings ensued. The Reichsmusikkammer gave in. Steinway received money and saw themselves rewarded for the exceptionally accommodating stance they had adopted towards Vedder, because whenever he could, Vedder promoted the firm's products; in 1937 for example, true to the motto 'You scratch my back and I'll scratch yours', he negotiated the sale of a Steinway to the singer Karl Schmitt-Walter, as well as offering second-hand Steinway grand pianos to a lawyer and to the composer Dransman.

He did not need to civilise his approach, because from the position of power he was in he could afford to do anything. Anyone who was his enemy suffered. When he was commissioned by the management of the 1941 Berlin Arts Festival to organise the festival, he insisted on being given precedence, and booked up the Beethovensaal for his own festival concerts on three evenings which the Geo Albert Backhaus concert agency had already firmly booked in advance, whereupon the artists engaged by Backhaus all backed out, leaving their agent with a loss of 600 RM. Once again Vedder had won. Those he took care of were impressed by such acts because they benefited from them, and so as hangers-on they clustered around him. By the beginning of the 1941–2 season he had become the sole agent for the conductors Benda, Eugen Jochum, Karajan, Paul van Kempen, Gustav König, Clemens Krauss, Willem Mengelberg and Hans Swarowsky, as well as the pianists Eduardo del Pueyo, Claudio Arrau, Arturo Benedetti-Michelangeli, Ornella Puliti Santoliquido, Edwin Fischer, Conrad Hansen, Rosl Schmid and Hugo Steurer, and the violinists Georg Kulenkampff, Gioconda de Vito, Jan Dahmen and Antonio Abussi, the cellists Hoelscher and Mainardi, the sopranos Irma Beilke, Tilla Briem, Helene Fahrni and Marta Schilling, the alto Marta Rohs, the tenors Peter Anders and Walther Ludwig, the baritone Karl Schmitt-Walter, the basses Wilhelm Schirp, Fred

252

Drissen and Hans-Friedrich Meyer; he also represented the duos Fischer/
Kulenkampff, Elly Ney/Ludwig Hoelscher and Kulenkampff/Siegfried
Schultze, the trios Fischer/Kulenkampff/Mainardi, Kulenkampff/Mai-
nardi/Schultze and Santoliquido/Pelliccia/Amfiteatrov, the Breronel
Quartett and the Strub Quartett, a further three duos specialising in
romantic waltzes and gipsy songs, Edwin Fischer's chamber orchestra,
the Berlin Chamber Orchestra which Hans von Benda conducted, and
finally the accompanist Ferdinand Leitner.

At one time Vedder's supremacy was so absolute that even former
competitors began to work with him – on his terms; good relations
with Dr Otto Benecke, the head of the Concert Office, a joint venture of
the Reichsmusikkammer and the Association of German Municipalities,
assured the agent of influence over the middling and small towns which
were accustomed to organising concerts independently. This meant that
he could extend his power far into the provinces. Soon after the beginning of the war he also seized some of the contracts for entertaining the
troops. In this instance he was helped by the conductor Erich Seidler,
who came from the NSKG and was an important member of the SS.
Until 1936 he was head of music for the Reich's Königsberg radio
station, after which he had a short spell directing the NSKG. He returned
to radio in Hamburg, but finally lost his useful connections, which
meant that from 1938 onwards he had to make do with conducting the
Munich Hitler Youth radio ensemble. Göring then had Seidler appointed
as head of his office organising concerts for the welfare of the air force;
through him Vedder was able to place his clients in this expanding and
profitable business as well; as he had learnt that it pays to demonstrate
gratitude, he put a lot of pressure on Paul van Kempen who, quite apart
from their business connection had been known as 'Uncle Paul' in the
family for a long time, and did actually succeed in getting Seidler the
second conductorship of the Dresden Philharmonic. That was in 1941.

His gambler's nature, which takes and makes risk, was displayed in
his personal life as well. It was confused, littered with legal proceedings
including a divorce; this was largely because his wife was opposed to
the Hitler Youth and sent her daughter to the Heliand Catholic Youth
Group, but had her unruly sixteen-year-old son against her, roundly
denouncing her as an enemy of the state. Vedder fled from this tragic
state of affairs into a new relationship, a new marriage to a twenty-
nine-year-old adviser in the cultural department of the Hitler Youth
head offices. That this man led a hectic existence is testified to on many
hundreds of sheets of file paper. Although he had beaten down many
of his enemies, some, the strongest, remained, and one of these was
Furtwängler, who in the meantime had discovered the source of the

conspiracy. By the autumn of 1941 the Vedder–Nüll–Karajan connection could no longer be kept hidden.

The music critic had been called to arms, but did not have to go to war.[57] He merely had to apply what he had already learned, taking over Seidler's job of arranging the concerts for the air force, for which Vedder now provided the artists. Karajan's agent now took a further step to consolidate his empire politically. On 1 March 1940 he applied to join the Nazi Party. The regional group granted him membership on 1 August 1941. To the newly fledged party member (no. 8,742,192) this did not seem sufficient, and so – once again – he roped in influential friends to help; in this instance a brigade leader in the SS, who offered him a higher position as music agent for the SS as well as taking on the rank of an SS-Untersturmführer. He wrote a special recommendation: 'Vedder is serving the air force in an honorary capacity and has had great success organising entertainment for the troops. His knowledge of cultural circles and consequently his connections at the highest levels can be of use to the Schutzstaffel [SS] in the same way.'[58] The intercession of this patron, whom Vedder had known since 1938, amounted to an order, because Alvensleben served Reichsführer-SS Heinrich Himmler as chief adjutant. It was carried out immediately. The music agent was given the SS-number 413,729, and by 27 November the SS's head personnel office had already made him a special SS leader attached to SS and Polizeiführer, SS-Brigadeführer von Alvensleben. Alvensleben was not his only 'god-father'; someone else was acting on his behalf, one level up:

Vedder has been commissioned by the various ministries to initiate a large-scale effort to aid the recovery of wounded soldiers in the Crimea. His advancement to Untersturmführer in the general SS is also desirable because Vedder could be used to great advantage within the framework of the education office as one of those responsible for organising concerts and education in Europe.[59]

Thus towards the end of 1941 the concert agent enjoyed a politico-cultural monopoly – extending beyond the borders of the Reich – of such strength that he believed himself unassailable. It is a classic situation which leads people to make mistakes. This was why Vedder, who had effortlessly subordinated weaker opponents such as Müller, or the bass-baritone and college teacher Josef Maria Hauschild, now pitched into Furtwängler. He did so quite deliberately, as a decisive test trial of strength, so to speak.

The conductor, always on the lookout for outstanding instrumentalists,

254

had discovered the highly talented eighteen-year-old violinist, Gerhard Taschner, and immediately taken him on as leader of the Berlin Philharmonic Orchestra. At the beginning of 1942 Vedder approached the youth, who was somewhat disoriented by his early fame, and entrapped him in a conversation. He asked him his salary, which he found quite ludicrous.[60] In the Staatsoper he said, one would get far more, and of course, he was wasted in the orchestra and must choose to make a solo career . . . he would be crazy to enter into a longer contract with Furtwängler. He ought really to play under Karajan, because he was the best conductor and was already raking in four to five thousand marks per concert, and because the future belonged to Karajan, who would shortly have all the others up against the wall . . . It is obvious what Vedder was hoping to achieve. First-rate violinists were rare. If this one could be enticed away the Philharmonic Orchestra would immediately be ranked second to the State Orchestra. Taschner told Furtwängler who recognised that a decision had to be taken once and for all. He alerted the ministry. At the same time he followed this with a memo on the Vedder case, adding some thoroughgoing criticism:

It should also be mentioned that in the present state of affairs one is faced with the ascendancy of an unhealthy form of power, such as that exercised by Vedder. For one thing there is far-reaching centralisation; good 'connections' to the Concert Office, the Municipal Association and thereby to the towns, the Kraft durch Freude movement and the armed forces, can work wonders. If to this is added the suspension of both the press and the public as deciding factors, agencies and concert-promoters are put in a position where they are less controlled and more able to act autocratically than earlier. [. . .] Vedder's presence cannot be tolerated much longer in our musical life, especially in Germany as it is today. It should make no difference that Vedder is a virtuoso when it comes to playing on his 'connections', even to the point of taking refuge in the SS, as he managed to do at the last moment.[61]

The conductor – did he not realise that he was making enemies of high-ranking SS officials? – presented this memo at an investigation which the ministry and the Reichsmusikkammer had at last initiated. The agent, summoned before a number of witnesses, including Taschner, tried every means he could to talk his way out of it. Karajan's name was mentioned frequently. Unquestionably Karajan had not unleashed the campaign against his older rival, but he did take part in it. He was now quite deliberately challenging his competitor on the concert

255

IM NAMEN DES FÜHRERS

VERLEIHE ICH

DEM

ᛋᛋ-Untersturmführer (F)

Rudolf   V e d d e r

"Höherer ᛋᛋ- und Polizeiführer
Schwarzes Meer"

DAS

KRIEGSVERDIENSTKREUZ 2. KLASSE
MIT SCHWERTERN

Feld-Kommandostelle, DEN 20. April   1944

H. Himmler.

REICHSFÜHRER-ᛋᛋ

The concert agent receives a (second-class) war decoration

podium. At Vedder's instigation the Staatsoper concerts had begun again at the beginning of the 1940–1 season; Karajan was at the podium, and now the press really did have the opportunity to compare the two conductors. The very first concert produced a partisan response; the renowned *Frankfurter Zeitung* gave Karajan forty-four lines coverage and Furtwängler only twenty-six and this despite the fact that the former had given them only the usual standard programme to review while the latter had conducted the first performance of Pfitzner's new symphony.[62]

The parade of prominent figures which Goebbels called on for the armed forces' fiftieth request concert included not only Zarah Leander and Wilhelm Strienz, but also Karajan. He was compensating for the fact that since mid-April 1939 Furtwängler had not let him near the Berlin Philharmonic, and he also enjoyed the press attention. The older man was not happy at the press's openly partisan stance, and he complained to Goebbels, who saw that some redress was called for: 'I will stop all that. Otherwise Furtwängler is behaving very well. And he is after all our greatest conductor.'[63] The minister could not really understand why this notoriously awkward customer had for some time now been a model of good conduct and seemed to be hoping for protection in the highest places; but as he too had certain reservations about Karajan he used his ministerial adviser, Wilfried Bade, to reprimand the journalists: 'It is clearly an undesirable habit to set a scale by which to evaluate conductors. In order to play off Karajan against Furtwängler, for example. We should view diversity of artistic achievements as a matter of pride, not as an excuse for making comparisons.'[64] This protocol was not immediately effective, and fearful as he was, Furtwängler once again asked the minister for protection. Goebbels noted almost compassionately: 'Furtwängler angry about Karajan. The press are excessively gushing about Karajan. Furtwängler is right about that. He is after all world-renowned. I will put a stop to it.'[65]

There is no doubt that in his new state of uncertainty Furtwängler needed reassurance, and it came from various sources, including to some extent from the Chancellery of the Reich. At Christmas he received a small gift accompanied by a greetings card with the Führer's gold stamp: 'I hope you will accept the accompanying packet of coffee as a small present. It is part of a larger consignment which was sent to me from abroad. With very best wishes for Christmas and the New Year. Yours, Adolf Hitler.'[66]

Lest anybody believe that he kept a hoard of goodies down in the vaults of the Chancellery of the Reich for all his bosom friends, the virtuous Führer explained how he had come by the scarce colonial goods. He had already received similar donations before the war, for example from the overseas Germans who farmed beneath Kilimanjaro; this time it was the Imam of Yemen who had outwitted the Allies' export controls and sent a shipment of his country's domestic products. The conductor – who did not like coffee – was not the only one to receive some of it. Others included Gauleiter Bohle and Heinrich Schlusnus, the latter no Gauleiter nor even a party member, but a singer who did not even have the mandatory proof of Aryan descent. The fact that Furtwängler was seeking protection from the very officials whom he had previously both fought and used to achieve his aims in the music business, shows nothing other than that he was aware how serious his own situation was, especially as the constellation of power was not in his favour. In the first instance it did not change. The minister's protocol did mean that for journalists there was greater risk attached to speculations about 'who is the greatest in all the land', because they might always be reprimanded, but as a prohibition it whetted the appetite, such that the music reporters positively specialised in making the comparison. For example:

> 'Furtwängler's art is like life, surging forth unhesitatingly, inexhaustible, spontaneous, touching all with compelling inspiration, its sense of total fulfilment so convincing one feels there is nothing left to ask. [. . .] While words such as 'life' and 'art' served to describe what was essential in the artistic work of others, in the case of Karajan's achievements one can stick with the ambiguous concept of *Geist*. We do not mean the thinking mind which serves the intellect, but the subconscious 'organic' spirit of art (because art too has its own spirit), which drives to choice and decision, which knows the strength to be found in control and single-mindedness, which unlike life does not aim for all-encompassing wisdom, seeking rather to prove itself in the passionate struggle to uncover that truth which is peculiar to its own epoch.[67]

This was printed in the new weekly review for intellectual and 'liberal' readers – one of Goebbels' bright ideas – skilfully tailored to allow a comparative evaluation, and culminating in the malicious insinuation that Furtwängler's style of interpretation was the unspiritual one. The conspiracy included many one would not have suspected, and was moreover furthered by events in the war. During the night of 9–10 April the Staatsoper was reduced to rubble and dust in an air raid. Despite resistance from the 'master of the house', Karajan was given permission – even though only temporary – to give his series of concerts with the State Orchestra in the Philharmonie, and there is no doubt that he preferred to be there rather than anywhere else. The struggle to oust his rival was yet to bring its biggest reward for the antagonist. The question of concerts in competition which those of the Berlin Philharmonic had always been a very real one, which was why the management of the orchestra had gone to some lengths to protect itself: since 1937 there had been a contract with the association which ran the Philharmonie and the Beethovensaal according to which the association was forbidden to stage any symphony concerts other than those given by the Berlin Philharmonic. This was in return for a rent guarantee of 67,500 RM, which between 1938 and 1940 was increased by a third. But contracts are of no avail against enemy bombs, which had now helped Karajan to Furtwängler's very own podium, one of those unexpected 'spoils of war' which were so much to the taste of Furtwängler's challenger.

The conflict was becoming more acute. Comparisons were pursued pitilessly in the press, as if the observers of art preferred to be critics. The sensitive and uncertain elder man repeatedly felt under attack; being compared with the younger man – especially in a period when a barbaric cult of youth prevailed – it must have seemed to him that his importance and abilities were being questioned:

Furtwängler is primarily a sculptor of sound, inspired by strong impulses and spiritual powers. Karajan is more of a painter and designer, even though he too has a strong sense for creating an organic whole and for three-dimensionality. Furtwängler's is a passionate temperament, Karajan's a gentler one. The former is a very expressive musician, the latter – and one not only hears this, one can also see it from the way he beats time – more reticent and introspective, although also capable of ecstasy. With Furtwängler one is immediately aware of the formative individual at work, while with Karajan one is aware more of the finely strung and sensitive individual who feels himself above all to be a medium, but at the same time retains visible distance from the work. There we are seized by the driving force of the work and the interpreter on the podium, here we are drawn in more gently. Furtwängler shows us the drama in music, Karajan more its epic and lyric qualities. [68]

Naturally the musical public eagerly seized on the musical expert's neatly formulated antithesis. During the winter of 1941 Berlin was divided, with supporters of Furtwängler on one side and of Karajan on the other. Each party fought the other, and many bets were placed on who would eventually make the running. Furtwängler defended himself, firmly decided that he would not abandon the field, and was happy to get any allies he could. He even condescended to play in front of Hitler at the Christmas reception given by the Chancellery of the Reich; he was after all a good pianist, and the situation was such that he wanted to take defensive action at the highest level; he could count on being listened to as the Führer did not like Karajan, whom he considered an arrogant fop. But at about this time the conductor of the Staatsoper made a mistake which Goebbels noted in his diary on 5 June 1942; he presented Tietjen with megalomanic demands – to become the number one in the Reich capital's musical life – which the general intendant at once, apparently hoping for help, passed on to Goebbels, who was not strictly speaking responsible for such matters. To ensure, though, that Furtwängler would also be punished, Tietjen added a note on how unscrupulously Thomas, the Viennese general cultural adviser, was working against Berlin in politico-cultural matters; in fact in many musical matters Thomas really was an echo of Furtwängler, who by choice would have been Viennese himself.

In the course of the proceedings against the agent Vedder, it turned out that there was no need to go higher than the ministerial level. By Goebbels' personal instructions the concert agent was finally banned from the Reichskulturkammer on 30 July. Hinkel informed the head of the SS personnel office confidentially: 'Vedder thereby put himself in a position sharply opposed to that of the government of the Reich, although he must have known that the perpetuation and improvement of the Philharmonic Orchestra as Germany's most representative orchestra is dear to their hearts.'[69] Vedder took this banishment and the loss of his agent's licence very calmly and – for all eventualities – maintained contact with most of his clients with the help of a reliable and faithful secretary. Karajan however was shocked. He could imagine what it would mean to lose his agent in the middle of preparing for the 1942–3 season, without the regular guest engagements which until now Vedder had always arranged for him. He would be reduced to his work at the Staatsoper, which he could not rely on either. This is what happened because the other concert agents now paid the stricken agent's clients back in his own coin, pretending all sorts of difficulties when it came to providing work for an 'orphan'. As in addition to all this his plan to become chief musical director at the Dresden Staatsoper had been blocked by Goebbels, he now fell on hard times. He even suffered the humiliating experience of being – temporarily – driven out of the Staatsoper house, which had been restored at great expense, while on 7 December 1942 Furtwängler conducted *Die Meistersinger* in celebration both of the institution's two-hundredth anniversary and of the reopening of the opera house.

On the other hand Karajan managed that same month – though by order of the Propaganda Ministry this was again only temporary – to break into the older man's domain once more, as the Berlin Philharmonic's guest conductor for three concerts in aid of winter charity. One was a public concert in the Philharmonie, the second was for armaments workers in Borsigwalde, the third was back in the Philharmonie playing to war-wounded. The calculation behind all this was that because it was supporting the national cause nobody would dare to attempt sabotage, as to do so would be to invite public opprobrium and Goebbels' enmity. In those days and weeks Hitler's soldiers were fighting desperately from their encircled position in the ruins of Stalingrad, initially still with some supplies reaching them by air, but soon with no new provisions at all. Karajan perceived how he could benefit from this military and political situation. The Berlin Propaganda Office was of the same opinion and sent a secret circular asking the press to 'pay good attention' to these concerts.[70]

Despite this success in the struggle to displace Furtwängler, Karajan felt sorry for himself; at any rate when he met Luis Trenker during his winter holidays on the ski-slopes of Cervinia he poured out his heart to him. He complained that he had no 'suitable' orchestra – as if the State Orchestra were not good enough – and added pusillanimously: 'In Berlin Furtwängler will not allow access to the Philharmonic, in Berlin I have nothing, hardly even a measly three-room apartment.'[71]

He must have been perturbed by the thought that while the Berlin Philharmonic Orchestra was still bound to its long-time master his victory would get him nowhere: in addition he was struggling with political adversities. Some months earlier he had married for the second time. The woman of his choice, Anna Marie Sauest, whose maiden name was Gütermann, and who called herself Anita, was by law Aryan despite being a quarter Jewish, and there had been no problem obtaining the special permission required for their marriage: Karajan was however no ordinary citizen, belonging as he did to the political élite of the party, as a result of which he had to obey stricter laws. He was certainly serious about the Nazi Party. For years he had only had a provisional membership card, but in the summer of 1938 had finally put in an application to his area group which was passed to the Cologne-Aachen regional office.[72] His motive is plain to see. This document in one's pocket, which always had to be produced if requested, could be something of a silent ally, not only for the purposes of conquering the Staatsoper, but also during the detailed vetting procedure which was intended to ensure that no unworthy individual would be distinguished by a favour from Hitler – and with regard to which the 'conductor to the state' was at the time under discussion. Of those who had been appointed conductors to the state since the Führer and Reich chancellor's second decree concerning the granting of titles had been issued on 22 October 1937 (Karl Elmendorff, Hans Gahlenbeck, Robert Laugs, Walter Lutze, Wilhelm Franz Reuss, Hans Schmidt-Isserstedt, Johannes Schüler, Kurt Striegler and Ernst Zulauf), nearly all belonged to the Nazi Party, and every single one had had to prove his political reliability.

Even if there was no doubt about Karajan's membership, the document arrived too late because the present conductor's letter of appointment was dated 20 April, Hitler's birthday. Karajan's membership book was only issued on 13 July because the application had revealed his double membership and in the interests of bureaucratic tidiness the membership no. 1,607,525 which he had received in Salzburg had had to be annulled first, especially as Karajan had only paid the joining fee and within the month had moved to an unknown address and then failed to meet the requirement that he register within a month at the local group in his new area, Ulm. Thus his Ulm membership of 1 May 1933 was the one which finally counted.

A party member who married a 'quarter Jew' was acting in a 'shameful' manner and was breaking his oath of allegiance: 'I vow loyalty to my Führer Adolf Hitler. I promise always to respect and obey him and the leaders he appoints above me.'[73] Such cases were punished with expulsion by an ordinary party trial which had to take place even if the disloyal member in question tried to preempt expulsion by declaring his resignation from the party. At the later de-nazification commission in Austria Karajan claimed that because of his marriage he had been brought in front of such a party tribunal in 1942 and had at that point declared his withdrawal from the party. This was a half-truth which he hoped would help exonerate him. It is contradicted by the fact that on neither of the two cards for Karajan in the Nazi Party's central index is there any note of his withdrawal – or of his expulsion – which meant that despite having infringed the rules he was still considered a party member up to 8 May 1945. The full truth is revealed in the way the party's jurisdictional proceedings functioned: they could recommend a member's expulsion but not actually carry it through. Its execution was in the first instance the responsibility of the leader of the area group, but it was permissible to appeal against the party tribunal's decision – and thereby delay its implementation. There is no doubt that loss of membership brought disadvantages which could be quite considerable:

Self-evident as it is that besides their membership ex-members automatically lose whatever leadership positions or employment they may have within the party and all its organisations as well as all honorary state and municipal positions taken up by invitation of the party when they withdraw from the party, it is generally quite undesirable that individuals who have left the movement should also be thrown out of their private employment.[74]

If it was necessary to mention this specifically then it must have occurred

262

more frequently than was desirable and been a real possibility. Karajan – might he be removed from the Staatsoper as well? Someone who knew how to fight so fiercely for promotion also knew how to maximise his chances here, however nebulous. The last resort for party members wishing to obtain exemptions from the Nazi Party's Aryan requirements? Hitler himself. Unfortunately it was not the best moment at which to seek favours from on high; the Führer had already begun to sniff at the young genius' excessively Austrian airs and graces, and no longer really believed quite so firmly in his exceptional musical talent. Two years earlier, at a performance of *Die Meistersinger* of all pieces, which took place at the Staatsoper in honour of the prince regent of Yugoslavia and his consort, Karajan had failed him, as his adjutant noted: 'Hitler was disappointed by the performance. I heard him mention inaccurate entries and that he found it pretentious of a young conductor to conduct a great piece without the score. Even Wilhelm Furtwängler would not have done so.'[75]

Despite this Karajan's future career was smoothed by a word from Hitler. There is still no documentary evidence that this favour was granted, merely the clue given by a confidential order from the Reich's minister of interior to the governors of the Reich on 28 June, 1937.[76] However, at the time there could have been no other way: there is no doubt that in November 1942 the main office for dispensations, in other words the penultimate place of resort in the hierarchy and immediately beneath the Führer's Chancellery, was busy with Karajan's case, file no. IIIr–201 055, and that under such circumstances only a personal decision from Hitler could have rescued Karajan's membership of the Nazi Party; proof that it had been rescued came in June 1943, when Goebbels called some zealots to task for being too thorough in their investigation of the genealogy of Karajan's wife.[77]

And so the crisis passed. Karajan once again knew what he was worth, but as the possibilities of work and status did not correspond to this worth he once again began to advance on Furtwängler. As usual Tietjen had fixed six concerts for the State Orchestra in the 1943–4 season and entrusted them to his state conductor; as events staged by the Staatsoper they should have taken place in the opera house. But Karajan had a better idea. He wanted to conduct in the Philharmonie – as he already had done following the destruction of the Staatsoper house, but this time for no better reason than to hem in Furtwängler. Furtwängler appealed to Goebbels, giving his expert opinion on the question of where the performances should take place and adding why he thought it unsuitable for Karajan to be in the Philharmonie:

However, if he were to decline the generous offer he has received from the Staatsoper I would not – out of loyalty to the Staatsoper's sister institution – feel in a position to ask him to do concerts with the Berlin Philharmonic Orchestra, especially as in such a case his stance would be an unashamed snub to the Staatsoper – in fact to the whole of Berlin's musical life, which certainly could not be in the interests of your bold policy of reconstruction.[78]

The minister took steps to ensure that these hostile brothers were kept apart, in order to prevent an open conflict developing. He was, though, not in the least averse to allowing a degree of conflict, because it could be used to check Furtwängler's extravagances; Karajan was the whip with which to lay into Furtwängler when necessary. Goebbels did not doubt for a moment who was the greater of the two:

I have had a detailed talk with Furtwängler. He has been very ill and even now appears quite poorly.[79] For all that, he cannot desist from attacking everything about the young conductor Karajan. I will try to help the two of them to reach some sort of agreement. I would like under all circumstances to keep Karajan in Berlin, either alongside Furtwängler or behind him. Of course as an artistic figure Karajan does not bear the least comparison with Furtwängler.[80]

This more or less sealed the aggressor's defeat; his ruthless attempt to edge Furtwängler out of his position of power in Berlin, and even possibly out of the capital altogether, had been a failure. However, while the aggressed had defended himself as best he could, the balance had really been tipped by a couple of coincidences, and even then only in the short term. Karajan had all the strategic advantages.

It was on these that Vedder built after being thrown out of the Reichsmusikkammer. This explains his composure. The SS were informed almost instantaneously of what had happened in the Kulturkammer. The leader of the SS Upper Elbe Division had met with Vedder to discuss inquiries concerning the leader of an orchestra and was left with an uneasy feeling; as a result he asked the SS head personnel office to 'keep an eye on this SS-Untersturmführer because I feel he should be treated with some caution'.[81]

The personnel office had however already been informed; following a suggestion from the head office of the SS tribunal they began disciplinary proceedings against Vedder, but regardless of this decided that with effect from October he should be appointed to the SS upper division's Ukraine headquarters. The investigation of the evidence was quickly

264

completed. At the beginning of January 1943 the head office of the SS tribunal was informed that 'the disciplinary proceedings against Vedder are about to be concluded and look set to end with Vedder's rehabilitation.'[82]

Naturally the Propaganda Ministry was also interested to hear how the case was progressing; Goebbels mobilised his state secretary Gutterer, an SS brigade leader with connections to the Reichsführer-SS. In June Vedder heard that the proceedings had been closed 'because the investigations undertaken have shown the allegations of professional misconduct brought against you to be unfounded'.[83]

This was a thorn in Goebbels' flesh; Himmler was once again showing who was really in charge, and the minister was so perplexed and unpleasantly surprised that he initially did nothing at all. Eventually he instructed Hinkel to look into Vedder's SS particulars, and received the information he had requested in mid-December. How he felt about the whole affair is indicated by the fact that he either refused to answer or only answered evasively the repeated reminders sent by the SS regarding Vedder's rehabilitation. It was April 1944 before the president of the Reichskulturkammer summoned the music agent in order to clarify the details of his reinstatement into the music business, but by that time the situation on the eastern front, where Vedder was serving in the army as a liaison officer for SS-Obergruppenführer and Police General Hildebrandt who was head of the SS and police in the Black Sea area, was such that the meeting could no longer be avoided. So Vedder asked friends to find out how the situation looked for him. From SS-Hauptsturmführer Walraven Genth, for example, he found out that the Reichskulturkammer wanted to incorporate him into the newly created Arts Services; SS-Sturmmann Diefenbach, who although low ranking was a lawyer and on his way to becoming a senior SS judge, informed his friend more about the background and tactical changes:

There are a number of things which are obviously different now. Most importantly Naumann has been appointed a state secretary and so no longer has to be so careful. And of course the RF SS has more say in such matters now that he is minister of the interior. If the Propaganda Ministry were now to refuse one would have to start the PK again [. . .] So if it cannot be settled directly between the RF SS and Dr N., it will be necessary to get involved in doing that.[84]

Diefenbach himself contacted the Chancellery of the Reich – by way of an acquaintance – but nothing happened; it was 20 July before an official from the Reichskulturkammer received someone sent by Vedder to present his demands; these amounted to little less than full compensation: '1. Unconditional readmission to the Reichsmusikkammer. 2. Restoration of his concert agency with the rights which are due to the agent by law.'[85]

This would have led to his complete rehabilitation and it did actually only seem a question of time before this would happen; amidst the confusion of the retreat from the Red Army, Vedder was already planning his professional future as if nothing had happened. There were old connections to be revived. What else were his SS connections for? He took advantage of them by way of the Black Sea SS and of the police leader's telegraph post, asking the SS regional command in Vienna to send a certain box to the general director of music, Paul van Kempen, and he used an SS courier to give Kammersänger Karl Schmitt-Walter something he had wanted from him. He also asked one of his SS-Hauptsturmführer friends to 'ring up Baron von Holzing at the Dresden Bank in Bucharest to ask whether he still has those two pairs of shoes for Frau Karajan, and if so please to send them. I will forward them to Karajan's wife.'[86]

Although the concert agencies had long been closed as part of wartime measures, Vedder was preparing for his own personal 'final victory'. In the meantime he was moved to the SS head offices for race and colonisation. While he was there he was at last informed that after repeated examinations of his case by the Reichskulturkammer the decree ordering his expulsion had been lifted on 5 January 1945. In an attempt to play a last trump the official responsible observed two months later:

> In my opinion there is no need for the state secretary to send Herr Staatsrat Furtwängler a letter as proposed. At the present juncture Furtwängler has neither good reason nor opportunity to attack Vedder in any way. If he should later try to do so when, with our permission, Vedder resumes his activities, then there will still be the opportunity of taking steps against this.[87]

The planned warning to the conductor that it would be in his interests to take no further steps in the matter was never posted. It would not have arrived anyway. Furtwängler was already in safety. From Clarens, Lake Geneva, he sent a letter to Goebbels via the consulate in Bern to ask for permission to take leave on grounds of ill-health. But in the chaos of the collapse it too went missing.

266

7

. . . SAY NOTHING IN FUTURE

Among the many newspaper cuttings which Furtwängler collected and evaluated, there is a short report which appeared in the review *National-sozialistisches Bildungswesen* in November 1938:

> In the light of the conductor Toscanini's political behaviour while abroad, the Italian authorities feel it would be inappropriate to renew Toscanini's passport. In Italy there are however no restrictions on Toscanini's artistic activity. Toscanini's conduct on his last journey to Palestine, where he was celebrated by the Jews as an anti-fascist, his public pronouncements against Germany and the ridiculously exalted demeanour which he affects in political matters as well, have all been subject to much public criticism.[1]

This came just at the beginning of what he saw as another campaign against him which, involving state authorities and even ministers, may have triggered a warning signal to the German conductor. The public horror of the persecution of the Jews during *Kristallnacht* may have been an additional indication of the merciless nature of the regime.[2] In future he would have to be more careful, perhaps even be ready to show a little more willingness to compromise than had hitherto been the case. A valid passport was a prerequisite for his continued artistic activity in itself, but his standing abroad also allowed him to get away with his many undertakings on behalf of threatened individuals and art. He could not risk his passport being withdrawn a second time – as after the Hindemith affair in 1934; any sort of constraint on his work would be an attack on his existential foundations. This was why he had to do everything he could to avoid any row over ideology. He appreciated that his programme for the fourth Philharmonic concert from 11 to 13 December 1938 was proof that he had succeeded in considerably extending the limits of the aesthetically acceptable: between Haydn and Beethoven on the one hand and Wagner on the other were Stravinsky's ballet music 'The Fairy's Kiss' and Ravel's Piano Concerto for the Left Hand, both German premières. However, worse conflicts outside the realms of music could be a provocation from one day to the next. What would he do then? He knew from experience that Berlin, where nearly all his enemies lived, presented ever-present dangers. Perhaps he could settle matters by withdrawing from the town. He could not abandon his Berlin public or the members of the orchestra, but there was a means by which both goals could be met, and in such a way that his work would be augmented. It would also allow him, at least for a part of the year and in addition to his tours abroad, to put a safety zone between himself and the centre which threatened such danger. Ultimately it came down to a conflict of loyalties – though making the long journey to Vienna was not the same as a journey to a foreign country, being more like a return to a second, though non-Prussian, spiritual home, which anyway suited him better now than the capital of the Reich. A conflict of loyalties arose because of the rivalry between the Berlin party and state authorities and the cultural metropolis of 'Ostmark', for Vienna was the perennial meeting point for cultural exchanges between countries which had earlier been part of the Hapsburg Empire. Hitler did not love this city which had witnessed the defeats of his sorry youth, and Goebbels at once extended the Kulturkammer's law (concerning among others Jewish artists) to the 'annexed' artists and set about making Vienna into a colony of Berlin, not only by appointing commissioners from the Reich with corresponding special powers, but also by less direct means. For example he wound up the International Bruckner Society which had hitherto been based in Vienna, and amalgamated it to form a national association to demonstrate that the composer – whom Hitler esteemed very highly – was a German possession. Even before the new association was inaugurated he appointed Furtwängler as president and on the same day informed the Viennese lawyer Dr Friedrich Werner: 'I hereby appoint you as manager and commission you to found the German Bruckner Association in Vienna forthwith, on the basis of the statutes authorised by me, and subsequently to ensure that it is entered into the register of associations immediately.'[3]

Thus the conductor suddenly found that he was the minister's right-hand man when it came to dealing with the 'German' master, Bruckner, who was no longer allowed to be an Austrian; this rather dubious honour would be a source of many matters for dispute in the years to come. For while Goebbels at times meddled in the association's affairs, at others he had to be called on to mediate internal quarrels. On the other hand as president Furtwängler was able to bring many of his own politico-cultural policies to bear in the association and even, with the help of Schirach, who would later become a Gauleiter, to help it achieve and defend considerable independence from Berlin.[4] At the turn of the year 1938–9 and against the background of the conspiracy to edge Furtwängler out, the minister was rejoicing in the certainty that he had 'broken Furtwängler'.[5] But he had not reckoned with the musician's powers of resistance; Furtwängler put up a fight to the best of his ability, always aware of the advantage offered him by the regime's inability to take the severest measures against him, the Reich's artistic ambassador abroad. He travelled as freely as before, and when at Christmas he conducted Wagner's *Siegfried* at the Paris Opéra, he met up with Friedelind Wagner who responded to his repeated expressions of admiration for her decision not to return to the Reich by saying dryly: 'Well, you are out now. Throw away your return ticket.'[6]

But this was not the right moment to go into free-fall.[7] There were several reasons for this, of which the most important must have been the memory of the boycott of his planned guest trip to America in 1936, for he felt certain that he would have to reckon with similar or even worse things in the future. Thus thoughts of emigration, and a mixture of fear and 'frightful hope' for some contingency, all conspired to induce a traumatic state of mind. He was also driven by a sort of 'Nibelungen' loyalty to his people; he would try to hold out despite everything, even if only as an almost powerless witness. His people were the fellow individuals and fellow victims whom he felt obliged to through his art; the Führer and his officials were certainly not counted among them. He repeatedly took action in non-musical matters whenever he felt the necessity to do so was self-evident. For a number of weeks in February 1939 he hid the actor and cabaret artist Werner Finck from the clutches of the Gestapo. Finck had not taken the closure of the cabaret *The Catacombs* in the spring of 1935 very seriously, despite being warned about his anti-state and anti-party jokes, and had continued to work 'without the slightest sign of a positive attitude to National Socialism'; now Goebbels had ordered his expulsion from the Reichskulturkammer, effectively banning him from working. As the musician's then partner, the doctor Maria Daelen, owned a country house in Pieskow near Bad Saarow, he was able to take refuge there until the trouble had passed and everything was calm again.

In the meantime – not without certain diplomatic complications – the French Republic had paid tribute to Furtwängler's cultural achievements at the 1937 World Exhibition in Paris by awarding him a distinction which indicated that the French government had not considered those concerts 'fascist' propaganda. As it was obligatory to obtain permission before accepting marks of distinction from abroad it was some time before Furtwängler was informed: 'The Führer and Chancellor of the Reich, by an order issued on 11 March 1939, has given permission to accept the Commander's Cross of the French Légion d'honneur which has been conferred on you.'[8] This order certainly did nothing to change the cautious assessment which the Nazi officials had built up – on the basis of the files and frequent reports on the musician's latest achievements. Goebbels, still enjoying the mood of victory, once let slip what role in the cultural activities of the Reich he still conceded to this genius, living in a higher world of his own, and to ensure that it reached the ears of the right people he decided on a meeting after the closing ceremony of the Reich's music congress in Düsseldorf on 21 May with the holders of the national music prize, because one of the two he had chosen to distinguish was Siegfried Borries, leader of the Berlin Philharmonic: 'What does this Furtwängler want with his miserable two thousand listeners in the Philharmonie. What we need are the millions, and we have them with the wireless!'[9]

The following day the conductor wrote a letter to the Propaganda Ministry and complained once again about the unfair treatment bestowed on him by the papers. Had he wished, Goebbels could have read this to mean that he had been understood, and that the press were not the only ones to be guilty of injustice.

In June Furtwängler took over the direction of the Vienna Philharmonic. They had asked him to because of their threatened situation, and Furtwängler had thought that showing allegiance to Vienna could well serve as a lesson to the minister. From this position – in a speech given at the closing ceremony of the Bruckner festival – he immediately took the politicians to task again for the aesthetic and politico-cultural problems (including banal, strident music) which resulted from brash mass consumption of the arts being organised in a quasi-official manner:

An inevitable consequence of one-sided intellectual efforts is that the vital sphere does not receive sufficient of what the artist wishes to share, and so the source of art is suppressed and [. . .] must yield to banality. From this results what has only now become real fact, namely the unbridgeable divide between serious and light music, the former the expression of an all too problematic life, the latter that of far too easily achieved enjoyment.[10]

270

His incidental mention that an artist should 'never lose his beloved mother earth from under his feet' may sound today like the use of ideological clichés; this late Romantic used them ingenuously and without being able to draw a sharp distinction even at a theoretical level between his world and that of the barbarians, because he lacked the necessary analytical and critical tools with which to do so, the tools which angered him so much when his opponent Goebbels used them. These tools were something he hated quite fundamentally, and so he did not regret his own lack. It was for this reason that his ability to recognise political connections and to understand the causes and effects behind them was so extremely limited and flawed by misunderstandings. Whatever else he may have been he was above all a product of an era overwhelmed with myths from tradition and propaganda, and from our present-day point of view his attitudes appear deeply distorted.

Just where Hitler's policies would inevitably lead – the Munich conference had only just helped avoid war – was something he failed to see long after it had become obvious. His respect for authority and government, which was essential to his self-respect, would not allow him doubts, doubts of the kind which had led him astray concerning the Weimar Republic. Power and the law must come from God, whatever harm they might cause, and even at their worst they could still be seen as a test from God. He wanted to be trusted by the regime, some of whose principles he thought he could not do without. So he tried once again to speak with Hitler. He drafted a letter requesting an audience. So that the Führer would not be put off at once he intended to stress

> that I do not wish to touch on things of a personal nature which are merely to do with the past, and that it is nothing to do with matters which have in the past demanded on-the-spot decisions or opinions of you, my Führer. These are matters of very general importance. Furthermore, both as an artist and as a person I would finally like the opportunity to speak to you with trust. As you will understand, it is of decisive importance for my work as an artist in Germany that I should have your trust, and therefore this meeting is essential for you to demonstrate it.[11]

What he wanted to talk about then was the question of trust, and he had every reason to wish to do so. At that moment the conductor seems to have felt that nearly everything he had hoped and striven for and tried to see implemented was at the mercy of hostile forces, and he was also prey to a horrible suspicion that his existence as an artist and as an authority in the artistic world was not properly valued by those in power. The above letter however was not posted, although a different one was – to Minister of State Meissner, the head of the Führer's presidential chancery, because he had urged Furtwängler to apply once more for an audience. The idea that he had to talk with Hitler was becoming an obsession. It was not that Furtwängler wanted to prevent the war. He did not even realise that that particular time bomb was already ticking away. He was still deeply concerned about artistic activity and its organisation and – not least – with having his very existence justified by favours from on high. Was he really such a broken man?

Notes in his diary suggest roughly what he hoped to say to Hitler. He was still troubled by the situation in Bayreuth; he did not want to go to Bayreuth while Frau Winifred was still under Tietjen's influence. He wanted 'Herr Tietjen to accept responsibility for it, rather than shamelessly blaming and blackening my character and even my art behind my back in such a way that I cannot defend myself.'[12] Then there was the problem with Göring. The field-marshal, still fretful about Furtwängler's withdrawal from the Staatsoper, had had it in mind to create a position which would put him alongside rather than beneath Tietjen. Furtwängler returned to the matter again and again: 'Tietjen. Some people seem to be of the opinion that in the realm of art the organiser is worth more than the artist – an opinion which will always remain incomprehensible to the public's sound instinct.'[13]

Could he not understand that, and why, such a regime required 'Apparatchiks'? Or did he feel threatened by these powerful positions? He complained that 'today the organiser is replacing the artist. The organiser in the world of art should have no other functions than those of an exalted policeman. People whose main talent is for organisation and whose artistic gifts can only be described as of a rather modest secondary nature, are coming to the fore. Benda, Drewes, Tietjen. They are the ones who control the artistic world today.'[14]

This was not just the usual problem which arises in every artistic organisation which the artists are personally involved in running. It was also a question of quality. The head of music at the ministry was one of those Furtwängler saw in a negative light, accusing him of wanting to nationalise everything, of using leading musicians such as Elmendorff, Hugo Balzer and Herbert Albert to exert influence in appointments, of using his own position to get conducting jobs, and even of threatening to forbid the international music festival in Baden-Baden because he feared competition with the Reich music congresses in Düsseldorf. This was all summed up in the form of a diary entry: 'Doubts about the

272

suitability of authoritarian leadership of the music world by a personality who is not qualified in any way, whether musically or as a person.'[15]

One is surely not mistaken if one assumes that in judging such an appointment as ill-chosen – heedless of the many positive qualities and actions of the official in question – he always measured everything against what he himself would have done; he was still thinking of all the benefits he could have brought to the music world had he not been removed from the vice-presidency of the Reichskulturkammer back in 1934. There is no doubt that this still pained him. On the other hand the musician seems at times to have recognised that the Reich system did give rise to such events and so could be held responsible for them; then he would get to grips with the fundamental characteristics of such a system:

Central planning is in order where there is a definite need to be met. The same principle when applied to an area in which different values are in constant competition and in which old ones adapt and new ones are created, such as in art, has a downright destructive effect. It is however a principle with appeal for mediocrities.[16]

He wanted to tell Hitler all this and much more besides, he considered it to be of the utmost importance. The Führer had more pressing matters on his mind. Only Goebbels was available for a talk, but it was very short, and he made it clear how precious his every minute was. Furtwängler was not put off by this, and because he still persisted in his wish to talk to the Führer himself he soon wrote to the Minister again:

You tell me of the great workload on the Führer's shoulders and then say that even you yourself had to wait a very long time for a meeting; these arguments are of course a great blow to me, quite devastating in fact, especially as I would be the last person to fail to realise what mammoth tasks the Führer has to accomplish every day. Despite all this I must stress again that – as things are at the moment – the possibility of my continued productive work in Germany is firmly dependent on whether or not the Führer gives me the opportunity to speak to him.[17]

It is very doubtful whether the minister understood as such the threat of emigration which can be read between the lines here, especially as his experience was that the musician could never get enough of suffering . . . Goebbels would surely have formulated it more ironically. Hitler really did not have any time to spare for musical and personal problems. He was hard at work preparing a repeat of the tactics which had won him both the Sudetenland and Prague, but this time they were

273

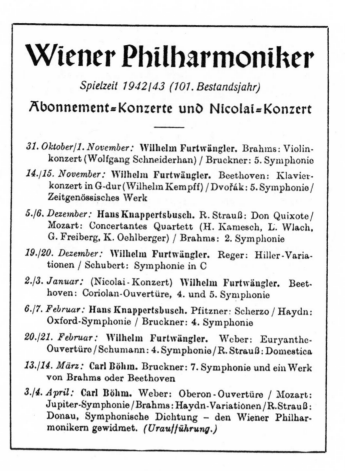

to be employed against his Polish neighbours: namely the use of force. He had already succeeded in provoking acts of terror against the German minority in Poland's western border region, a classic situation which called for military redress. He had also given it a propagandist slant, maintaining that there was 'accurate evidence' that tiny and weak Poland had launched a cowardly attack on her neighbours, who were armed to the hilt and ready for anything, thus leaving him no option other than resistance. But Furtwängler was not in the least aware of what Hitler was planning and the consequences this would have; he was just terribly concerned that he could not talk to him . . .

At least the propaganda minister was not playing hard to get, as it was now necessary to negotiate concessions from him for members of the Vienna Philharmonic, whose independence as an orchestra was under threat; it was important to try and prevent it from being turned into just a provincial Reich orchestra when it was nationalised, because all the signs suggested that plans had already been made to do just this. The conductor wrote to Vienna that he would lay the case before Goebbels; he added reassuringly: 'Moreover may I assure you that, were your independence really to be curtailed in such a way that you lost the free choice of conductor, I personally would resign immediately from conducting any concerts with you.'[18] There is no doubt that Furtwängler was serious; he even planted a permanent observer in Vienna in the person of Agathe von Tiedemann, who in Berlin had headed an association of young musicians, organised concerts of contemporary music, and was now keeping an eye on 'Ostmark's' music business, sending regular reports and sounding the alarm when necessary. The ministry's serious attempt to nationalise the Vienna Philharmonic by way of an offer to subsidise them had miscarried and now they were attempting to carry out their plan by means of political organisation. The conductor met with Goebbels on 11 August; the subject of their intensive discussion was the future of this orchestra, whose current status as a private association of musicians could no longer be tolerated. The next day Furtwängler dejectedly reported that the minister had told him 'that the free choice of conductor by the orchestra would be contrary to a basic National Socialist principle. Therefore, this demand must be dropped. I regret this; however, I will always try to use my position to support you, in so far as this is possible.'[19]

But was he now capable of offering any support at all? The empty formula 'basic National Socialist principle' could mean anything at all, could be given any content one chose and therefore always fulfilled its purpose, which was to nip opposition in the bud. The most stupid functionary could make use of it. It was this that now caused Furtwängler to check his attitude to ideology; he did so in an improvised dialogue with his diary rather than in public. It is not surprising that he had most difficulty with the 'new order' when some of its extraordinary regulations from other disciplines infringed on his own. But he separated theory from practice as if the one were not determined by the other, and so he could not accept 'that National Socialism and mediocrity are supposed to be synonymous where art is concerned'.[20]

Was it then the case that the unremitting propaganda about 'German' quality had blinded the musician to how much this philosophy – especially as personified in Hitler – represented everything he loathed, was that of a regiment of unashamed *arrivistes* who thought that they could measure everything against their own achievements, but who nevertheless only ever attained mediocrity at best? It is quite clear that Furtwängler saw at least the 'intellectual' principles of the regime as absolutely necessary, as an antithesis so to speak to the 'lawless, libertine Republic': 'In so far as fascism is revolution its ideas are transitory. In so far as those ideas include the law it is not; despite its mass character it is significant and alive. With the joining of law and National Socialism something truly new and previously unrecognised has come into the world.'[21]

Even now – apart from his dislike of anything revolutionary – he refused to pass any judgement; his rather clumsy objectification completely blocked all possibility of criticism, which was why he did not even begin to analyse the Nazi ideology and mythology. He only went halfway with his review of his own political stance; it was inevitable that he would reach totally wrong conclusions as to the historic importance of the regime and the extent to which it had established itself, because he never really weighed up the meaning of concepts such as 'law', and because he was always trying to make comparisons with art which were completely off the mark:

Why will Germany win in this war? Why will the authoritarian system necessarily win through with time? Because it is a feature of human nature that individuals cannot cope with limitless or even with just too much freedom. This is equally clear in art. Reger and Strauss, to say nothing of the atonal composers, are representative of that condition. They are already out of date and finished with. What is needed is a new compliance with the law.[22]

Here spoke a conservative who viewed the temptations of freedom with mistrust and saw the law and conformity to the law as offering the cohesion with which to fight off chaos. It is quite likely that his adhesion to such a line of argument was a result of his upbringing; how often had teachers and tutors warned the rebellious child to be good? Certainly it was of great importance to the impulsive, desire-driven adult to have a higher order – self-chosen or imposed from above – which sanctioned his not doing the things he was afraid of. It was beyond his comprehension that a government could be capable of decreeing laws which made a mockery of all morality. His attempt to work out his relationship to National Socialism in the summer of 1939 failed because he got stuck just before reaching the crucial question.

At this time Hitler was preparing not only to overrun Poland, but also – only in a minor way – the next party congress, which was announced as the 'Party Peace Congress'. And so on 25 July Furtwängler received a call from Hitler's deputy at the Chancellery, telling him he was to participate in the party congress and that the programme would contain such and such. At the same time Rosenberg, who was involved in the preparations for the cultural symposium, was informed:

> The Führer has decided that Herr Staatsrat Dr Furtwängler will conduct at the cultural symposium rather than any of the conductors suggested by you, and in fact it will open with the overture from *Iphigenia in Tauris* as you suggested, with Beethoven's Fifth Symphony to be played before the Führer's speech.[23]

This meant that unlike in 1935 and the year before, Furtwängler was supposed to conduct not only the pre-congress performance of *Die Meistersinger*, but the musical ritual surrounding Hitler's culture speech as well; the Nuremberg Opera very appropriately announced the 'Party Peace Congress' with a 'Day of Peace' on 1 September, celebrating with a dance suite as the German tanks were rolling into Poland. However on 3 September the opera performed Lehár's *Tsarevitch* instead of *Die Meistersinger*. When Hitler understood that the British and French meant their ultimatum to withdraw his forces from the occupied country seriously and that his 'campaign' in Poland was going to bring about a great war, he cancelled the party congress. The conductor was not required to give service to the party; yet that was by no means the end of his political problems. On 22 September the post office in the Propaganda Ministry recorded the arrival of a hand-written letter, which caused astonishment in every one of the three departments it went to. It was a denunciation with no named sender and an illegible signature – although ostensibly it came from the wife of a musician in the Berlin Philharmonic Orchestra:

> As is well known there are even now many members of the orchestra who are married to Jewesses. It is very painful to watch how these women, in their hatred for National Socialism, have a negative influence on their husbands; they gnaw and dig away at them with real Yiddish cunning, and sow dissatisfaction wherever possible. [. . .] There must be some way of getting out of this. After all every other organisation has made a clean sweep; can it really be that it is not possible to do the same in our most famous orchestra, whose head is our honoured minister of the Reich, Goebbels?[24]

Kohler, as senior government adviser to the personnel department, remembered that there had been earlier proceedings to do with 'Jewish

277

marriages' in the orchestra, and he sent for the details; the director of the ministry, Dr Greiner wrote furiously under the scribble of the anonymous sender, 'A coward into the bargain!' Nevertheless the ministry took up the matter. The orchestra's management stressed that there were only three musicians left with Jewish wives, adding soothingly: 'Given that the informant did not sign with her real name we are inclined to assume that this is an act of vengeance or something similar.'[25]

There is no doubt that Furtwängler was the target of these new attacks from the rear, because he had been the one to insist on retaining the 'suspect' musicians, and had always put himself out for them when danger threatened; but these were incidents in the musicians' daily lives which even the most influential of helpers could do nothing about: the spiteful glances from neighbours, the whispers, the cold mistrust, and other similar private signals against these 'subversive elements'. It was a form of psychological terror which the concert master of the orchestra, Hugo Kolberg, had not been able to put up with any longer. On 1 January 1939 he played Beethoven's Violin Concerto under Leopold Reichwein, an old party member and anti-Semite who had been favoured by the party, and for the fifth Philharmonic concert from 7 to 9 January Furtwängler used him for the première of Pfitzner's Duo for Violin and Cello with Orchestra; but lest Kolberg's success awaken any suspicions it had to be damped; this was achieved through a short protocol announcement to the press: 'When discussing the concert given by the leader of the Berlin Philharmonic, Hugo Kolberg, restraint had been requested (the reasons are well-known).'[26] Fortunately the violinist had prepared the ground in the USA just in time, during a guest tour in 1938 which had been approved by Goebbels himself, despite a futile warning from his Department IB:

> One does have to reckon with the possibility that during the trip he will use the opportunity to establish connections so that he can later go to America for good. Kolberg is currently indispensable in the Philharmonic; however, Herr von Benda does think that next year or the year after he could be replaced and so he is not worried about permitting the trip.[27]

The minister heeded the manager of the orchestra, Benda, rather than his adviser and so Kolberg was allowed to travel, make firm arrangements in the USA, return to Germany, finally leaving the inhospitable Reich soon after his January concerts with Reichwein and Furtwängler, even though his contract officially ran until 1940. Once again Furtwängler felt alone. How little he understood of the situation is shown by an

278

incident in Winterthur, where he was due to conduct the orchestra of the music college. This small Swiss town was also the place where Hermann Scherchen had settled as conductor of a series of subscription concerts. The two met and despite the fact that the emigrant had been labelled a 'communist' both in the Reich and in Switzerland, Furtwängler invited him to share the Philharmonic concerts in Berlin . . . as though time had stood still and 1939 lay somewhere in the future. And in fact, Scherchen, demonstrating unbelievable naïvety, did want very much to return to Germany, even though it was not as if after France's capitulation Switzerland had remained 'untouched' by the Germans; Scherchen's musicians were turning against him because German authorities were not prepared to exempt the German members of the Winterthur Orchestra from doing military service for the Reich while an emigrant continued as conductor. That under such circumstances he could think about a 'homecoming' suggests a touch of madness. He blindly sought to use Furtwängler's mediation, but in the summer of 1940 received news from him that in official circles he was still considered an enemy of the state, and that therefore it would be advisable to seek new work in America immediately. At least Furtwängler had realised why he must refuse to help in this case: unfortunately time had not stood still after all.

The first year of the war did mark a certain artistic turning point for him. Despite all his reservations about its poor quality of sound, he discovered radio as a musical medium. It is possible that he was impressed by the minister's callous reference to millions of listeners, or maybe it was the fact that Karajan showed a lively interest in this new technology. Previously the Reichsradio had occasionally transmitted concerts – as part of a contract intended to ease the finances of the Berlin Philharmonic Orchestra – even ones conducted by Furtwängler, but had hardly made any of its own wax recordings with the orchestra. The radio's war-time role however demanded more than just broadcasts of pre-recorded music, which was why the Berlin Philharmonic was invited, together with its prominent conductor, to make intensively advertised national broadcasts from the main recording auditorium in the Reich broadcasting house. One of these broadcast concerts took place on 22 September; the press revealed what it was all about:

Noble music has always been the balm of noble souls, and if at crucial times a nation needs uplifting, then its music too must be 'uplifting', causing all lesser and lower concerns to fall away. And yet great music, especially that of Beethoven, expresses far more than just comfort or escape: all the passions are raised to a magnificent pitch of

279

heroic pathos and the sound of the hammers of fate reinforces our resolve to be strong.[28]

This primitive association of ideas was in keeping with the spirit of the times; greatness and loftiness, and their associated fictions, were essential in the process of removing the national inferiority complex; Plato attracted the Nazi cultural policy-makers, believing as they did that music was a drug which could banish certain facts and evils from the world, or at least from people's minds and hearts. The public was keener than ever on the balm of music. The orchestra's management noted with relief 'that the initial fears that necessary war measures (black-outs, restricted transport etc.) would have a negative effect on concert attendance have proved groundless; in fact the opposite has been the case: the experience of war has evoked an even more lively concern for and greater interest in the performance of serious music'.[29]

The concerts broadcast in this season – there were eleven in September alone, of which two were conducted by Furtwängler – were eagerly listened to. Goebbels ordered the ten Philharmonic concerts to be trans-mitted as well, at least the first half of each, recording the second half on wax to be broadcast later. Even in 'Ostmark' there was evidence – like in the old Reich – of an increased appetite for music; the Vienna Philharmonic, although presented in many places by 'their' Furtwängler, still needed someone to intercede for them when it came to asserting their status in political quarrels. When the Gauleiter congratulated them on their centenary they took it as a sign of fate and answered:

> The Vienna Philharmonic was very pleased to receive the good wishes of the Gauleiter and of the Commissioner of the Reich. In the name of the Philharmonic Orchestra would you please tell the Gauleiter that he is invited to the opening concert of the eightieth subscription series which will take place in the Musikverein's great hall. The box of honour will be at the Commissioner of the Reich's disposal.[30]

Gauleiter Bürckel was an unmusical person and quite helpless when it came to dealing with the inter-factional struggles and groupings with which he was confronted in Vienna. This was why, as of 9 December, he named Furtwängler his plenipotentiary responsible for all musical matters in the city of Vienna; more specifically this was to include

> above all, the promotion and nurturing of music in so far as this falls within the responsibilities of the state and parish administration of this department of the Reich. This will primarily involve exerting

280

influence on Vienna's concert life, music halls and music teaching institutions [. . .] Because all musical matters have been entrusted to my plenipotentiary all other departments in the Vienna region should act to promote and nurture music in Vienna only with his knowledge and permission, after first reaching agreement with you.[31]

What the conductor had in vain been seeking to achieve all these years now fell into place because one Nazi official was honest enough to admit, as Goebbels would never have been able to bring himself to, that he needed professional support. Now there would be no obstacle to implementing a broadminded musical policy informed by detailed knowledge of the town's historic role in music. However, while Furt-wängler, with these hopeful prospects in mind, was in Munich present-ing the Vienna Philharmonic for a second time on 11 and 12 December, opposition gathered in Vienna, so blatant that the political police got wind of it; they observed that there was an ugly public reaction: 'Although it is widely recognised that Furtwängler has been appointed because of his artistic ability, fears are already being voiced about the opinions he is known to hold. People in Vienna have not yet forgotten his intimate friendships and they fear that those circles will now once more gain influence.'[32]

The Security Service's report also named names; these included the – Jewish – musicologist Dr Elsa Bienenfeld; a ministerial adviser, Dr Alfred Eckmann; the head of the state theatre management, Hofrat Dr Karl Wisoko-Maytsky; a sectional adviser, Dr Friedrich Dlabać who before the *Anschluss* had headed the Friends of Music Society, and, despite being a party member, Professor Franz Schütz, director of the Reich Musikhochschule. In their next report the Security Service said regretfully: 'The general public heard nothing about a withdrawal or restriction of the contract and so there is still widespread dismay in circles affected by these measures. For example Weisbach is said to have reported sick immediately and apparently it was only with some difficulty that Knappertsbusch could be persuaded to stay in Vienna.'[33] This may have been somewhat exaggerated, because Weisbach quickly recovered and resumed his work at the radio and in the Friends of Music Society, and Knappertsbusch remained first conductor at the Staatsoper and did not run away. Both came to understand that their common interests could be better met by intervention from above than by behind-the-scenes intrigues. Nevertheless the head of the music department, Drewes, was sent by his minister to try and turn Bürckel against Furt-wängler; Goebbels was pressing towards Vienna. For example, because he wanted a bridgehead he had appointed the general intendant from

Hamburg, Heinrich K. Strohm, to be senior director of the Vienna Staatsoper. Strohm cracked under the strain of being in such an exposed position and suffered attacks of paranoia, until after a hard fight Furtwängler – supported by Vienna's new Gauleiter, Schirach – managed to convince Berlin that a change was necessary. In this instance his threat of not wanting to conduct any longer was effective in bringing pressure to bear. However the incident had shown that on the basis of political calculation Goebbels would use a clinically sick man, even if it meant coming within a hair's breadth of scandal, so keen was he to bring Vienna under his rule.

All this work on matters of music policy took time, and the title 'plenipotentiary', which was only ever a title, never a paid position, acted like a magnet, causing a considerable increase in the conductor's mail. This burden was in addition to the grinding routine of concerts in Vienna and Berlin and to the exertions of concert tours. It may seem unbelievable that there was still a European capital left in which he was a novelty, yet he was able to celebrate another début – in Oslo. This occurred at the beginning of April 1940. Times were uncertain. At his headquarters Hitler had long ago perfected the plans for project 'Weserübung' and was only waiting for the right moment; the purpose was to secure the supply of ore from Sweden, using the Norwegian port of Narvik. On 28 March at about nine o'clock in the morning Furtwängler flew from Berlin, right over the marshalling area for the planned attack, without noticing the reason for the delay in his flight. When he landed in Oslo nine hours later everything seemed normal, but at that time the Norwegians too were still living in 'the good old days', welcoming their guest as 'Wilhelm Furtwängler, the famous German conductor and Beethoven expert, successor to Richard Strauss and Nikisch in Germany's most distinguished music post, the equal of Toscanini in New York, vice-president of the Reichskulturkammer, general director of music, head of the Berlin Philharmonic and the Staatsoper etc. etc.'.[34]

Those of the particulars which were correct at all mostly related to out-of-date facts which had long since been superseded. However, in the space of four rehearsals the Oslo Philharmonic adapted to the conductor and they put their all into the concert. The great hall of the university, the largest concert hall in the city, was sold out despite the high ticket prices. Norwegian music enthusiasts regarded the concert on 1 April as having been a rare artistic experience, which was why the German Embassy could report jubilantly that the concert 'has left a strong and lastingly positive impression in Oslo, and was very suited to waken and animate sympathy for German art and for Germany'.[35]

It is questionable whether the Norwegians saw Haydn's Symphony no. 88, Strauss's *Tod und Verklärung*, Beethoven's Seventh and the *Tannhäuser* overture (which was added at the last moment) as being peculiarly German, given that this music formed part of the repertoire of both the Oslo orchestras, with no mention of its national origins, in other words formed an integral part of Norway's cultural heritage. In any case their sympathy would only have been very short-lasting as only a week after the concert Hitler's warships entered the Oslo fjord and bombarded the city; the Reich flag of war was raised over the Hotel Continental. Only a short while later a music corps from the invader's infantry was marching on the square in front of the university, playing to the Norwegians music which was *really* German: military marches and even a rendition of 'Erika'.[36]

The idea of using Karajan the young competitor to bring down Furt-wängler had many eager advocates in Rosenberg's department; they were also keen to entangle Furtwängler in the regime's rituals in a way which would destroy any self-respect he had, because they knew exactly what the man's political position was, and how to undermine him. In mid-July 1940 Reichsleiter Bormann was informed by Rosenberg that the Berlin Philharmonic were prepared to provide the music for the cultural symposium of the party congress in the autumn, at short notice if necessary. Rosenberg's music expert, Gerigk, already knew that Furt-wängler would also be available, although he had said he 'would want to conduct the cultural symposium [. . .] only if the Führer also entrusts him with the traditional performance of *Die Meistersinger*'.[37]

He was thus offering to do what five years earlier – with the excuse of already having too much on – he had decisively refused to do, and this must have struck his interlocutors; had the musician really 'converted' so quickly and recognised that it was his duty to serve the party? No, Furtwängler was actually creating a trap the party could not avoid falling into. Beethoven's Fifth Symphony – Gerigk had kept to his programme suggestions from the previous year – was really not so suitable after all, as he explained to the official, however the finale of the Ninth would create a far more magnificent effect; he elaborated enthusiastically:

The final choral movement lasts for almost thirty minutes and offers a grandly conceived cantata which would guarantee a very special effect even if performed just for its own sake. Nuremberg has the technical preconditions for putting together a choir of several hundred singers. If one wished to one could place the choir out of sight behind flower arrangements or light curtains.[38]

Really a very persuasive suggestion, and furthermore made with no thought for himself; to Gerigk's confusion he added that for aesthetic reasons he, naturally, would not conduct just one movement of a complete symphony, and so suggested Professor Karl Böhm instead. Four days later Hitler decided to cancel the planned party congress. Things did not always work out so smoothly.

As the Berlin Philharmonic's employer the Propaganda Ministry was in a position to give commissions; for example the previous year Furtwängler had been asked to conduct the *St. Matthew Passion* at the May Festival in Florence. It did not seem corrupt to him to do so because at worst it was an attempt to gain sympathy for Germany, and certainly did nothing to further Nazi Party interests. Furthermore he was not the only person to be similarly commissioned. The Propaganda Ministry engaged foreign guest conductors, all good but not the best – the 1940–1 season included the Spaniard José Cubiles, the Japanese Hidemaro Konoye, the Italian Franco Ferrara and the Croatian Lovro von Matačić – to conduct the Philharmonic Orchestra, in the hope that they would be impressed by the superior culture of the Reich.

A guest performance commissioned by the ministry was also intended as sympathy propaganda – and perhaps a little more than that. The capital of what had formerly been Czechoslovakia and was now a protectorate of the Reich, Böhemia and Moravia, was legally speaking not counted as occupied territory; Hitler had instead decreed that the protectorate was an integral part of the German Reich, and so anyone not in a position to question the morals behind this 'right' had to make do with the belief that the Czechoslovak president had 'put the fate of the Czechoslovak people in Adolf Hitler's hands'[39] on 15 March 1939, which meant that any remaining moral objections to giving a guest performance in Prague fell away. The ministry's intention was obviously to prove that the capital of Böhemia had always been in the past, and was now once more a centre of German culture, rather than a fascinating melting–pot of Czech, German and Austrian influences. For the inauguration of the German Opera House – which was given the task of putting the Czech one in the shade – Furtwängler appeared with the Berlin Philharmonic. Naturally the local party and state dignitaries – this was the administrative centre for the Reich's protector – used the opportunity offered by this festive occasion to seize the limelight. The guests of honour in the front two rows, wounded soldiers from Prague's military hospital, were almost forgotten about. The reporter for the capital's

Nazi newspaper avoided passing political comment, concentrating on the conductor instead:

> There are occasions which stand so far above the day-to-day 'business' of musical activity that their very existence calls for special scales by which to measure them. And yet these are the real, in principle the only carriers of artistic culture, for only the exceptional, the highest achievements should decide and be counted in spiritual matters. It is one of the mysteries of all artistic activity that the most rarified spirituality can have such a deep and magical relationship to the soul of the people, however much it might appear to be distanced from it. It is only thus that the broad appeal of a man like Wilhelm Furtwängler can be explained.[40]

That was on 7 November. The first item on the programme: Smetana's 'Moldau'. This might cause a few shrugged shoulders today. At the time it was intended as a clear signal rather than an apologetic gesture to Czechoslovakia. This piece is part of a cycle in which the Czech master celebrated 'Ma Vlast' (My Country), and at the time it was composed, in the second half of the nineteenth century, was intended to support his compatriots' fight for independence from Austrian domination. In 1940 the situation was being repeated, only now the oppressor was Hitler. Just how much ideological weight Smetana's cycle carried here is proved by the fact that towards the end of the war – although performances of the piece had not actually been forbidden – a patriotic review of *Ma Vlast* resulted in the murder of its author at the hands of Gestapo killers.[14] When Furtwängler began with the 'Moldau' it was not a deliberate risk, but a statement of his stance towards the oppressed Czechs. This homage to the local genius was just about acceptable in Berlin, as long as people closed their eyes to the fact that the genius was in fact a 'foreigner'.

The group of Nazi ideologists around Rosenberg were also united in their opinion on the politico-cultural innovations which the new Gauleiter in Vienna, Schirach, had introduced and defended against local party representatives. His concern was to prevent Vienna being degraded to a museum piece, and just what the functionary, himself a cultured man, meant by this was demonstrated among other things by a week of contemporary opera and drama which degenerated into a political storm when Wagner-Régeny's opera *Johanna Balk* was performed for the first time. Schirach used the opportunity to make a speech about the plans he had for the future of cultural policy in Vienna:

We do not want to live in a graveyard. Let today's younger generation have their own cultural experience, even if others have the right to reject it. So many sticks have already been broken over the heads of these 'cultural criminals' that one would even feel justified in attempting some form of reparation. We are not acting in the spirit of the great individuals who have lived in this town if we see our task merely as that of maintaining tradition.[42]

This could have come straight from Furtwängler's own heart, and was somewhat similar to his own opinion that contemporary works should be carefully integrated into concert programmes so that they could be well performed and their effect on the public tried out, rather than left to bigots and party hacks. That he was too reserved about the ephemeral efforts of self-important composers was an accusation frequently levelled at him by advocates of 'progress'. And it is true that he chose carefully. Scores came to him from all over the world with requests for his expert opinion, which gave him a good overview of trends in composing. For example the Munich composer Alfred von Beckerath, whose job as a music teacher in a country boarding-school in Ambach, Upper Bavaria, left him with a lot of time for composing, sent Furtwängler a selection of his works; obviously not his March and Fantasia on Hans Baumann's war song 'Brittle Bones are Atremble', nor the music he had written for radio series such as 'The Führer's Path' or 'The People's Observer – the Story of a Wartime Newspaper', but some harmless concert items instead. Having leafed through the odd piece the conductor observed incredulously: 'Nowadays composition seems to have become a society game – except of course that only the composer derives any pleasure from it, not society.'[43]

By contrast Furtwängler was happy to give Heinz Schubert, the director of music in Rostock, a recommendation, despite his being a party member, testifying that he was 'a genuine musician, a composer of great musical talent (I myself have performed a work of his, Prelude and Toccata, at a Berlin Philharmonic concert, with great success), who would surely achieve great things as a conductor. I at any rate can only recommend that this genuine, unpretentious and sound musician be given every support.'[44]

A recommendation like that and with that signature was the dream of every musician, which explains the large number of requests for his expert opinion. Sometimes he obviously acted according to motives other than just musical ones. There lived in Bergen auf Rügen a musical entertainer, a pianist and violinist who had worked for a long time at the town theatre in Guben and – as he was a very capable musician –

Herr Heinz S c h u b e r t

ist ein echter Musiker, ein Komponist von grossen
musikalischen Qualitäten (ich selber habe ein Werk von
ihm(Praeludium und Toccata) mit ausgezeichnetem Erfolg
in einem Berliner Philharmonischen Konzert zur Aufführung
gebracht) und dürfte sicherlich auch als Kapellmeister
hervorragendes leisten. Jedenfalls kann ich eine Beförde-
rung dieses echten, schlichten und wahrhaftigen Musikers
nur befürworten.

Wilhelm Furtwängler

had helped out in the Berlin Philharmonic, as a result of which
Furtwängler knew him personally; but Paul Henckel had failed to meet
the requirements for proving his Aryan descent and was suspected on
other grounds as well. After receiving a report from the local schools
inspector Rügen, his local Nazi Party group had come to the following
conclusion: 'H. is politically unreliable and refuses downright to offer
the "Heil Hitler" greeting. His contribution to collections is poor, and
he never attends party gatherings.'[45]

Furtwängler put himself out for this man of all people, and in the
spring of 1940 – in other words in good time for planning the next
season's programmes – asked him by way of his secretary to send in his
scores. As Henckel's compositional achievements were not sufficient for
such a distinction no performance took place. This shows that despite
everything Furtwängler always made his selections on the basis of everything that was offered, leaving little doubt that the work of composers
such as Karl Höller and Theodor Berger really did deserve to be prem-
ièred. In the first Philharmonic concert in October 1941 Höller was
allowed to present his Cello Concerto Op.26, played by Hoelscher, to
a public accustomed to classical and romantic music, followed in the
very next concert by Berger's Ballade op.10. Berger, a 'young genius'
who many hoped would make an '*ostmärkisch*' contribution to contemporary music, had been given a 5,000 RM commission by Goebbels for

287

the 1939 Reich music festival in Düsseldorf, and although this may have been partly motivated by political purposes, it is certain that the dynamic minister – unlike the Rosenberg clique – perceived in Berger's work, which took stylistic inspiration from Stravinsky, not only nothing 'degenerate' but even a symbol for the political *élan*, the arousing and motivating aspects of National Socialism, a reflection of the 'Erleben unserer Tage' (Experience of Our Times). However, when Berger used this significant phrase in the programme notes to describe his work, the Rosenberg faction was not pleased. The music observer Hermann Killer, now no longer burdened by his work on the recently published *Lexikon der Juden in der Musik* (Lexicon of Jews in Music), had become head manager of the politico-cultural archives in the arts promotion department and so was empowered to make allegations of all sorts; he criticised the text of the programme because it went on to say that the ballad reflected an 'apocalyptic atmosphere' . . .

> which is no doubt supposed to convey something like the atmosphere at the end of the world. With this in mind, the listener, who could hardly consider the great freedom fight of the German people anything like a biblical apocalypse, was then astonished when waves of sound broke forth in quick tempo, [. . .] a host of dissonances peppered with bursts of percussion which was more reminiscent of a nightmare than of visions of great and uplifting events.[46]

It was not only critics and public who were divided over novelty; conflict also broke out between old and young, with one side welcoming the 'aesthetics of progress' while the other damned it. The conductor found himself accused by various factions of having been commissioned by 'world Jewry' to smuggle in by the back door all the musical depravity which everyone had believed had been fortunately and easily got rid of along with Hindemith. Furtwängler did have an argumentative tactic up his sleeve which could silence such harmful allegations. He had developed it in response to the situation in the twenties, when factions in musical circles were having a very similar effect to party dictatorship and state directives a decade later; at that time he repeatedly had to put up with the accusation coming from 'left-wing' advocates that the format of his programmes with their well-known masterpieces was actually suffocating them. In fact statistics proved the opposite, but they could be spirited away by the objection that what Furtwängler did do was far too little and always benefited the wrong people rather than the 'real geniuses', namely the favourites of the advocates of change. The tactic which Furtwängler would repeatedly use in his fight for Hindemith was already decided on when he made a diary entry in 1927:

> Consideration for the general public has gone so far that it is sometimes necessary to perform a work just so it can be discussed and to prove that it is not all that it is made out to be. It goes without saying that this occurs *ad absurdum* and that such performances demand the same high standard of performances as the greatest works of art. It is therefore a mistake to believe that I am equally keen on all the works which I conduct.[47]

Of course he knew very well that stylistic modernity need in no way be a bar to success. Discussion of a piece was often the first step towards its having a broader influence, and this was clearly what happened with the Berger pieces which the conductor adopted; but he could prevent lovers of classical music from deserting by giving them proof that he had done nothing special to help Berger, that it just was a good and successful piece, as had been proved . . .

There was certainly no need to excuse the minority status of contemporary composers. Not even the Philharmonic concerts had a wide influence, even though each was now given three performances and was always sold out. Through the radio the new music, and more importantly the great masterpieces could reach unbelievably large audiences, which meant that

> the broad masses of the German people have the opportunity to participate in and enjoy an artistic experience which without the radio the majority would never have had. [. . .] A new procedure is being used for the recordings, the magnetophone. This procedure reproduces every slight gradation in sound, and therefore a fully accurate sound picture of the concert.[48]

Although there was a Radio Symphony Orchestra, the Berlin Philharmonic – especially under Furtwängler – was a firm favourite in the Sunday broadcasts. However, even with the magnetophone there were quality defects; there was an attempt at an FM transmitter, which achieved better reception than medium- or long-wave, but this system too was still not technically proven and was liable to have problems. It is not in the least surprising that the conductor, who was so insistent on the highest quality, should often have complained of defects. The minister acknowledged the orchestra's importance when he excused its members from all military service 'because they have important tasks

289

to fulfil at home, and also it is so priceless a body that one cannot now dismantle it'.[49]

Goebbels now intended to demonstrate how 'priceless' it was in connection with a political event. The Soviet winter offensive had disappointed the Germans' certainty of marching into Moscow as victors, and pushed them back from large areas, especially around Leningrad and in the central sector. Hitler had called a halt to the retreat and ordered 'fanatical resistance', at the same time removing the commander-in-chief of the army and appropriating command of the 'Russian campaign' to himself, a jack-of-all-trades who could turn his hand to anything and who was now going to show his incompetent generals how to do their job. It was necessary to project his new image as a general accordingly. Goebbels took responsibility for this, using the opportunity to prove just how great his propagandist capabilities were. For Hitler's next birthday he unleashed a sympathy campaign in all the media, extending it over the border into friendly countries. He also planned a ceremony with speeches written by himself; he requisitioned the Philharmonie, part of which he filled with the usual representatives from the state, the party and the armed forces, and the remainder with soldiers, wounded servicemen and armaments workers. He also engaged the Berlin Philharmonic Orchestra for the whole ritual – but then found he had problems with Furtwängler. Understandably enough the minister wanted to enhance the Nazi Party's celebrations by the presence of the German master conductor, and the ground had seemed well prepared, because in talks at the end of February Goebbels had found Furtwängler apparently completely changed, even converted. He had been astonished to note that the conductor

is practically bursting with nationalist enthusiasm. This man had undergone a profound transformation, which it gives me great pleasure to witness. I fought for years to win him over and can now see success. He approves wholeheartedly of my radio and film policies and is very willing to put himself at my disposal for any work I may require him for. His judgement of Karajan has become far maturer; he no longer takes part in the public dispute and now views these attention-seeking squabbles from a position of deep and absolute confidence. He made an extraordinarily likeable impression at our talk. I am looking forward to getting to know that side of him some time.[50]

With the advantage of hindsight it seems unbelievable that this intelligent minister could have let himself be duped by the musician's new stance, especially as he had been informed that the moment of decision in the conflict with Karajan and his patron was in the offing. Had he really failed to grasp why there was only ever mention of Germany, never of the Nazi Party and Hitler? Or that the musician, who knew nothing about radio and film policy, was simply agreeing with everything the expert said in order not to annoy him? An angry Goebbels at this point in time could cost Furtwängler victory over his ruthless rival. This also explains what the minister took to be his willingness to cooperate. However, that is what Goebbels wrote in his diary, and just how wrong his assessment had been soon became apparent. When he wanted Furtwängler to come to Berlin and perform at the ceremony for the Führer's birthday the conductor did everything he could to get out of it. Furtwängler had actually arranged his concerts and rehearsals in Vienna in such a way that he could not leave the city, and he turned to the Viennese Gauleiter Schirach for help when Goebbels insisted that he come immediately. Schirach attempted to mediate but was also loth to stretch matters too far, which put him at a disadvantage, such that he had the concert postponed. Now there was no pretext for not going; had he continued to refuse, the conductor would have been open to accusations of sabotage, especially as Goebbels had linked his personal prestige to the success of the whole event. Although pressured into it this time the conductor began to think of unobtrusive ways to avoid such obligations in the future; happily an idea came to him, and in the following years during the springtime he would be 'taken ill' with something which completely prevented any public appearance: not just flu or a stomach disorder, but spondylitis – an inflammation of the back and neck vertebrae which of course made conducting impossible. In 1943 the necessary testimonial was written by Dr Johannes Ludwig Schmitt, a renowned doctor consulted by all the prominent members of Berlin's artistic circles, especially actors. At this time, Schmitt was no longer practising from home, having been put in prison as a suspected accomplice in Rudolf Hess's (one of his patients from the political camp) crazy flight to Scotland Whenever a famous personality required treatment the doctor, indispensable as he was, was allowed out. So Furtwängler would avail himself of Schmitt for weeks on end, partly as a gesture of revenge. It was obvious that his affliction, so typical in conductors, lasted much longer than just a day, and, as it would have been a bit suspicious to fall ill of spondylitis exactly on 20 April for one day only, the illness had to be made to stretch over several weeks. Dr Schmitt certified the whole thing. In 1944 this spring malady was diagnosed by Dr Egon Fenz in Vienna, and – two is better than one – Geheimrat Prof. Dr Sauerbruch in Berlin, thanks to whose testimonies Furtwängler was freed from his responsibilities. Thus in 1943 and 1944 the music on the eve of the Führer's birthday was conducted by Knapper-tsbusch, but without this ever giving rise to accusations from emigrants and post-war authors; double standards allow an easy life.

In 1942 however, as Schirach had been unable to protect him, the conductor yielded to pressure and appeared on the podium of the Phil-harmonie late in the afternoon of 19 April, reluctance written all over his face; the evening performance had been moved to the afternoon as a result of the Anglo-American air attacks – as had cinema and theatre performances – but this did not detract from the ceremony, especially as transmitters from Norway to Greece and from the Atlantic coast to Dnepropetrowsk were tuned in and the cameras of the UFA Newsreel set up. To set the mood the ceremony began with the Air from Bach's D-Major suite. This was followed by a pithy speech from the minister, which – in the light of the recent release of the film *Der Grosse König* (The Great King) – began with a reminder of the historical importance and achievements of Frederick II, after which he stressed the parallels between that historic period and the present, equated the Prussian king with the Führer and made a renewed avowal of loyalty and faith to the latter in the name of the German people before returning to the Philharmonic:

> This time the sounds of the most heroic music of Titans ever to have flowed from a Faustian and German heart will elevate this declaration of loyalty to a serious and ceremonious event. When at the end of our celebration the voices of people and instruments join in the great final chord of the Ninth Symphony, when the rushing chorus of joy sounds forth, carrying a sense of the greatness and scope of these times into every last German dwelling, when its hymns ring out over the great distances and far countries where German regiments are standing guard, then every one of us, whether man, woman, child, soldier, farmer, worker or official, will simultaneously sense the grav-ity of this hour, in which lies also the happiness of being privileged witnesses and participants in this, the greatest historical epoch of our people.[51]

The propaganda minister knew his trade, and there is no doubt that this skilfully packaged performance – right down to the coda, a prayer to the Almighty 'to keep our Führer, give him strength and blessings to continue and extend his works' – did create a convincing atmosphere . . . until the next wail of the sirens. Newspaper reports from that time do not reveal any details, nor are witnesses as reliable as the film on which the minister is captured suffering a set-back: Goebbels is sitting in the front row, his face puckered, his discomfort the result not only of his eczema, which was always worsened by stress, but also of the certainty that Furtwängler had only travelled up from Vienna under threat of force, and not out of great enthusiasm to honour Hitler. Their greeting was correspondingly icy. The musician bent down to take the hand the undersized Minister stretched up to him, and then, the cameras capturing his hardening expression, he turned brusquely away. It is still possible today to follow the whole sequence in stills as can be seen in the selection of photographs herein.

At this time Furtwängler also had another quite different political task. The viola player, Erich Bader, who was already considered less than sound politically, had attracted renewed attention. While making a street collection for Winter Aid to the Needy on 28 February and 1 March, the two party members, Kleber and Woywoth, the former a shop-steward and the latter an SA man, began to collect inside the Philharmonie and to draw up a list of who gave what. This was not strictly speaking allowed, as it was only supposed to be a collection in the open air. This was why Bader did not contribute. Kleber called Schuldes, another party member, to be a witness, and took his colleague to task for pettiness. One thing led to another; Bader accused them of dishonest practice and ended by assuring them: 'I will give nothing to a collection just so that others can earn themselves a badge.' It was one of many similar disputes between ordinary citizens and Nazi Party members, though not without its dangers. Kleber made a report to the managing director, Dr von Westerman, and to Furtwängler. Bader threatened to lodge a complaint with the NSV[52] if the matter were not cleared up within a week. The deadline passed; the NSV drew up an official statement and yet the viola player refused to apologise to the two collectors. On 9 April Westerman suspended the obstinate Bader and also ensured that negotiations with his lawyer came to nothing; the lawyer had taken the case to the Labour court where it threatened to have repercussions. The Propaganda Ministry sought to mediate and drew in Furtwängler, who managed to initiate an amicable solution allowing the musician to remain in the orchestra.

The whole process took months. The war was making itself felt in the form of further restrictions, which affected the music business as well: 'As a result of the request that everybody make as little use as possible of the Reich railway, we undertook no concert tours at all in the Reich during the fourth winter of the war. We even had to drop the traditional subscription concerts in Hamburg and Dresden.'[53]

Tours abroad were also reduced. In September 1942 Knappertsbusch took the orchestra to Romania and Bulgaria by way of Krakow and

BERNISCHE MUSIKGESELLSCHAFT

GEGRÜNDET 23. NOVEMBER 1815

Dienstag, den 26. Januar 1943, **20** Uhr

Konzertmässige Hauptprobe: Montag, den 25. Januar 1943, 20 Uhr

Extra-Abonnements-Konzert

im

CASINO BERN

Leitung: **Dr. Wilhelm Furtwängler**

PROGRAMM

Ludwig van Beethoven Symphonie Nr. 1 in C-Dur, op. 21
Bonn 17. Dezember 1770
Wien 26. März 1827

          Adagio molto — Allegro con brio
          Andante cantabile con moto
          Allegro molto e vivace (Menuetto)
          Adagio — Allegro molto e vivace

Ludwig van Beethoven Ouvertüre zum Schauspiel „Coriolan"

Pause

Anton Bruckner Symphonie Nr. 4 in Es-Dur
Ansfelden 4. September 1824
Wien   11. Oktober 1896

          Ruhig bewegt
          Andante
          Scherzo
          Finale, mässig bewegt

Ende 22.00 Uhr

Billett-Vorverkauf im Musikhaus Krompholz & Co., Spitalgasse 28, Telephon 2 42 42

Die Tombolalose H 5 und A 5 sind gültig für das VI. Abonnementskonzert vom 8./9. Februar

Abendkasse im Casino am Konzerttag von 19 Uhr an geöffnet

Preise der Plätze: Fr. 12. —, 10. —, 8. —, 6. 60, 4. 50

Konzertmässige Hauptprobe: Fr. 6. 60, 4. 50

GARDEROBEGEBÜHR und BILLETTSTEUER sind in allen Preisen inbegriffen

---

Beethovens sämtliche Streichquartette, Kammermusikkonzerte des Berner Streichquartettes, im grossen Saal des Konservatoriums, 1. Abend: Dienstag, den 2. Februar

VI. Abonnementskonzert: 8./9. Februar. Leitung: Luc Balmer, Solist: Wilhelm Kempff, Klavier. Werke von Bach, Mozart, Beethoven, Schumann

---

Slovakia, returning via Yugoslavia and Hungary; in May he and Robert Heger travelled through France, Spain and Portugal with the Philharmonic. Furtwängler made a guest appearance – without his own orchestra – in Sweden, and strengthened his involvement in Vienna, as is suggested by the fact that he entered the telephone numbers of the Reich governor of the town and Reichsleiter Schirach's home number into his

294

How Australians saw the 'spies' in the Berlin Philharmonic

diary. There were more concerts – a *Tristan* here, a *Fidelio* there –
an excursion to Budapest, preparing the programmes for the coming
season . . . all the routine work of a conductor. However, there was a
war on, with all the associated propaganda and counter-propaganda. A
German orchestra which toured not only occupied territories but also
neutral states was highly suspicious, at least as seen from London or
Paris. As early as 1940 there had been one quite successful propaganda
coup by the French. The French news agency Havas spread the news
that the Berlin Philharmonic, at that moment in the middle of a tour of
the Balkans with Karl Böhm, was underway with 500 accompanying
personnel and suitcases laden with bombs and weapons. In Belgrade
and Zagreb, the next stops on their tour, the press seized eagerly on
this report and added its own anti-fascist commentaries. For fear that
the musicians might come under attack, the German ambassador, after
conferring with Berlin, cancelled the concerts in Yugoslavia.

Now in the autumn of 1942 a new offensive was launched, this time
by the London rag the *Daily Sketch*. It was a story which went around

the world and was even given a whole page of coverage in the Australian *Radio Times*. In vivid detail, as if the reporter had been present himself, the story told how the Danish anti-fascists had discovered that at the last concert given by the Berlin Philharmonic in Copenhagen there had been musicians sitting on stage who were only pretending, not actually playing, and who must therefore – obviously! – be spies sent along with Furtwängler by the Gestapo; one fake flautist and two fake violinists, and to make the story more credible the paper even gave their names: Adolf Mann, Franz Leuchtenberg and Hans Boekel – the sort of nice German names one could look up in the Berlin telephone book. It obviously did not occur to the inventor of this sensational news item that by giving the names he made it possible to check up on the story . . . although of course at that time none of the English readers would have done so and the fact that the German press immediately treated the story as a huge joke could just have been seen as Nazi propaganda. Nowadays the archives provide sufficient information to prove otherwise.

The fact that the above names do not appear in the music lists for those years does nothing to support the story; they would have been missing if they had been made up, and anyway they were at best amateurs, not professional musicians. Yet, had they existed, the alleged spies Boekel, Leuchtenberg and Mann would certainly have been listed as heads of households in Berlin, unless one is prepared to assume that they were all subtenants, and probably – as Gestapo personnel as a general rule belonged to the Nazi Party – in the main index of party members. Both sources contain all three names several times over. However, all have work histories suggesting 'harmless' activities rather than membership of the Gestapo – one was even a cobbler – or else they were advanced in age and therefore could be discounted. Thus the following can only have been a straightforward propaganda lie: 'Now artists and politicians in foreign countries know that the Berlin Philharmonic Orchestra does not come in a purely friendly spirit. Their art serves the Nazis as a pretext for sowing dissension, for spying and fostering fifth-column activities.'[54]

To have done all these things would have required more time than a musician who was constantly on the move would have had at his disposal; such activities were the responsibility of the embassies and their agents and of the Nazi Party's foreign organisation or department of foreign affairs, all of which provided the Gestapo with sufficient informers and accomplices to carry out such tasks in their own time and under good cover. If it had just been a matter of observing the members of the orchestra there was an easy solution available when needed, namely hiring one of the – few – musicians who were also involved in the party, although such matters generally fell to the orchestra's shop steward. And yet there was a kernel of truth in the lie. Furtwängler kept a list of the names of musicians and other people who did not belong to the orchestra but who required protection for racial or political reasons. In an emergency he would pretend they were members of the Philharmonic; thus, for example, he managed on several occasions to save Hendrik, the son of the 'half-Jewish' violinist Max Leuschner, from difficulties. This meant that not only extra musicians went along, including one solo-cellist who was a party member acting also as a 'diplomat', but also the odd individual who pretended to be a musician without ever playing an instrument. But such people obviously did not – as the British report had imaginatively suggested they did – sit in the orchestra during rehearsals in Berlin where the conductor would have been forced to acknowledge their incompetence.

Late that spring however, there was an example of how action taken to help could fail tragically. In May the Gestapo had, following a denunciation, arrested the young and highly talented pianist, Karlrobert Kreiten. It was the usual sort of thing: a thoughtless word against Hitler, in the wake of Stalingrad – a truly hopeless battle; it was thus no great act of resistance, just a silly moment of carelessness. 'Enemies are listening' was a warning posted on all public transport and on every hoarding, but although the artist travelled frequently he did not take it seriously. Such chat, as long as it was not a gesture of resistance and was not inspired by some group, was not considered a capital crime by the judiciary; most people got off with a couple of months in prison, at worst a year or two. But as artists were a grouping which had failed to show solidarity in the 'fateful fight against the Jewish–Bolshevist world conspiracy', it was felt necessary to make an example of Kreiten, although initially this was kept a secret. Furtwängler had very quickly intervened with the relevant authorities on behalf of the young musician while he was being held for questioning, and had been given certain reassurances which led him to believe that the matter would be resolved without any serious consequences. However, on 3 September 1943 the First Senate of the People's Court, chaired by its president, Dr Freisler, passed the death sentence: 'Such a man can never regain his honour. In our current struggle he is – despite his professional achievements as an artist – a danger to our victory. He must be sentenced to death. For our people must march strong, unified, and untroubled to victory.'[55]

Normally there would still have been hope even after the sentence had been passed because there were reprieve procedures which could delay execution of the sentence. However, the Plötzensee Penal Institute

297

had suffered in an Anglo-American bombing raid on Berlin and as Hitler feared that those on death row – in mid-August there were about 900 – might be able to escape because the walls were now shaky, he allowed Bormann to empower the Minister of Justice to order execution without reprieve in those cases where there was no doubt. This is what happened to Kreiten. He died under the guillotine on 7 September, giving Werner Höfer material for a leading article on the problem of artists' solidarity – or lack of it – which appeared in the *12-Uhr-Blatt* on 20 September 1943, and in which he lauded the act. This was the first Furtwängler heard of it. The young artist's fate was a personal blow to Furtwängler, which also opened his eyes to how limited his room for manoeuvre was. And yet he did not give up.

In May 1943 he and the Vienna Philharmonic toured to Copenhagen, Malmö, Stockholm and Uppsala, passing through Berlin on their return journey without experiencing any political difficulties, although the route taken showed how impossible it was to avoid performing in occupied countries. Denmark's capital city was on the way to Sweden; there was no other conductor available for Copenhagen, and, because the trip had to be financed, this concert could not be cancelled. This meant that he had no option but to appear again in Copenhagen, which since his previous visit had been occupied. It was however for the last time. In connection with this tour of Scandinavia Furtwängler had noted in a pocket diary – ironically under 9 April, the third anniversary of the occupation of Denmark and Norway by Hitler's forces – a plan to help someone, namely the rough draft of a letter of recommendation to 'Luschek, Security Police, Victoria Terrace, Oslo'; it concerned the conductor Issay Dobrowen; Dobrowen had worked at the Great Theatre in Moscow before coming to Germany in 1923 to work in Dresden and the Berlin Staatsoper and later moving to Sofia, New York, San Francisco, Rochester NY, Philadelphia, Los Angeles, and even Palestine, although he always kept one foot in the Oslo Philharmonic, where he was overtaken by the arrival of the Germans. As a Jew, Dobrowen's life was always in danger, especially after the launching of the 'Final Solution'. Furtwängler's recommendation sought to get permission for the artist to emigrate to Sweden as he already had a contract at the Royal Opera in Stockholm. In this instance Furtwängler was successful, and during his tour in May he was able to spend a considerable amount of time with the rescued conductor in Stockholm.[56]

That May it became known that Furtwängler wished to start a new household and family, not just for the sake of external appearances, which had suffered under his very disrupted life-style, but also so to speak as a sheet-anchor in the mad tide of events. In Elisabeth, a war widow with four children, he found both the ideal wife and companion. At a meeting on 29 May he informed the propaganda minister that he wished to remarry, and Goebbels discovered: 'He has a number of family worries. I will try and be of assistance in overcoming them.'[57]

At least some of these worries did require help 'from on high'; as part of the divorce settlement with his first wife, Zitla, he had assumed maintenance responsibilities. She however, Danish by birth, although holding a German passport after her marriage, did not wish to live in the Reich, and so had withdrawn to Switzerland and lived there in a house in St. Moritz belonging to Furtwängler. By the time of Furtwängler's meeting with Goebbels it had become almost impossible to transfer the maintenance sums, because the valuable Swiss francs which the Finance Ministry had at its disposal – some were only on credit from 'neutral' capitalists – were of course not available for private transactions. Goebbels was able however to arrange a solution by which part of the considerable sums which the conductor had earned for the state coffers by his guest appearances in Switzerland in fact flowed back again.

It was at this point that Hitler expressed the wish that Furtwängler should be engaged for a number of concerts in Munich the coming concert season to conduct some of the Bruckner and Beethoven symphonies he loved so much. One concert had already been arranged for 30 September with the Munich Philharmonic for their fiftieth jubilee, but the conductor turned the others down: 'I sincerely regret that it will not be possible for me to take on more of the Munich Philharmonic's concerts this winter as I am already fully booked for the whole winter and it is now too late to change any of these bookings.'[58]

As all this was going on the wedding drew near; the marriage ceremony took place on 26 June, the day after a Beethoven concert with the Berlin Philharmonic in Potsdam. It was a short ceremony, lacking in ritual, just like other such occasions in that war-time summer. Goebbels did however take it upon himself to find a fitting home for the new – already six-strong – family. This proved too difficult even for a powerful minister. The bombing was forcing the population to live in increasing proximity, as more houses were reduced to ruins every day. Furthermore Goebbels wanted something 'befitting' Furtwängler's status. Hitler was having similar problems 'house-hunting'. Frau Bechstein, heiress to the piano builder's empire, had placed her property in Berchtesgaden at the disposal of guests at the Obersalzberg and demanded another house as compensation, either in the environs of Berlin, or by the Starnberger See or the Tegernsee. Bormann enquired of the finance minister on Hitler's behalf whether it would not be possible to use one of the properties expropriated from the Jews, whereupon the minister charged one of his advisers to come up with suggestions. The hunt dragged out however, because enquiries had to be made with local authorities. And now here was Goebbels asking for a house for Furtwängler as well. This request too landed first on Bormann's desk and then on that of the finance minister. When Dr Helmut von Hummel of the Chancellery asked at the Finance Ministry how the situation stood, the conductor had already learnt to his astonishment that the propaganda minister was thinking of him, and had gratefully but firmly declined, just as he had the earlier offers of honorary positions and of an honorary pension. Thus he managed to avoid living in a house whose Jewish owners had been evicted and perhaps 'resettled' in Auschwitz.

He did find his own solution, and a more satisfactory one at that, though it took some months. While visiting Schloss Achleiten near Krems at Christmas his hostess, Bernarda von Aichinger, invited both him and his family to take up residence in the castle. The question of the Munich concerts however, had yet to be settled. Hitler's wish was his command. As there was no way of changing the arrangements Furtwängler had already made, the Munich Gauleiter, Paul Giesler, who had taken the matter in hand, sought to placate Bormann: 'Please note that I will ensure that Furtwängler gives more concerts in Munich next year.'[59]

Meanwhile Furtwängler – alongside Abendroth – was conducting *Die Meistersinger* for the 'war-time festival' in Bayreuth. The Reich organisation chief, Dr Ley, reassured everybody at a press conference held at the Gauleiter training school in Bayreuth that

> this unique war-time festival is a visible manifestation for all to see, of our people's holy faith in our Fatherland and their unbending will to determine their own lives, which a criminal and barbaric enemy seeks to oppose with unprecedented cultural annihilation, with the destruction in many German towns of both our most noble cultural memorials and of peaceful residential areas.[60]

As the functionary had lost all sense of the sequence of cause and effect it seemed logical to him that the festival chorus should be strengthened with members of the Hitler Youth, maids from the BDM and men from the SS Viking Division. The population however had lost all patience with an undertaking which resulted in the already overloaded railways being packed with 30,000 extra people, the majority of whom dropped out of vital war production efforts for the space of five days. Furthermore, while soldiers on the front could not even get a glass of wine or cognac, the artists treated themselves almost as if it were still peace time. Even worse, the Security Services noted

> that Kammersänger Lorenz was in Bayreuth with his Jewish wife, and she stayed in rooms allocated to the festival and enjoyed special privileges in the restaurant along with all the others. This provoked genuine outrage not only among the people of Bayreuth, especially party members, but among all participants in the festival who were aware of the fact.

However, at least this year there were no cases of guests invited by the KdF falling asleep during performances or selling their tickets or exchanging them for liquor. The Security Services' report ended on a positive note: 'It is evident from the many spontaneous declarations of participants at the festival that they really consider their experience in Bayreuth a gift from the Führer and that this great experience has made them feel personally indebted and grateful to the Führer.'[61] There can be no doubt that – by this stage – such propagandist utterances were made by party members. Furtwängler could once again, as in 1940, consider his appearance at Bayreuth a victory over Tietjen, as the general intendant had once again been loth to put him on the podium in the festival hall.

In the autumn of 1943, coinciding punctually with the announcement of the Berlin Philharmonic's tour dates for the winter season, the *Daily Sketch* in London reheated the old story about secret agents; it was too late to disrupt the Spanish concerts under Knappertsbusch in August and September, but perhaps something could be done about the spring tour to Spain and Portugal . . . this must have been more or less the thinking behind it. Even the most provincial of German newspapers heaped ridicule on the story:

> At any rate it is once again very indicative of the English artistic imagination that they think that merely by putting a fiddle in a secret agent's hands it is possible to turn him into a perfect first fiddle. Perhaps the Secret Service has tried this method on occasion? That at least would explain why there has never yet been a world-ranking British orchestra![62]

Furtwängler opened the Philharmonic season with a first performance of Ernst Pepping's Second Symphony, had a meeting with Goebbels on 2 November at 12.45, travelled to Vienna the day after the third performance of the programme, conducted a concert there and then continued

301

to Budapest where he rehearsed and gave a concert on 10 November before getting the train back to Berlin, arriving back on the podium in the Philharmonie in time to take two rehearsals, one a public one, and then conduct the second Philharmonic concert on 14 November . . . two weeks of a conductor's routine. At the beginning of the month he had received an invitation from the Stockholm Concert Association to conduct a number of performances of Beethoven's Ninth in the Swedish capital. On 18 November he travelled to Vienna, rehearsed *Die Meistersinger* and left for Scandinavia on 23 November.

Rehearsals went well, and the work was performed in Stockholm on 5, 6 and 8 December. But it now became clear that even here Furtwängler was more of a political than an artistic symbol, perhaps because British propaganda had gained a foothold, or maybe the arrest by German occupiers in Oslo of Norwegian students and professors had given rise to Scandinavian solidarity. The students at the University of Stockholm drafted a letter of protest, asked well-known personalities to sign it, and gathered further sympathisers. The leader of this action was Marianne Hillbom. On Friday 3 December a protest demonstration against the Oslo mass arrests took place, led by one of the student leaders, Folke Lyberg, a postgraduate. The letter to Furtwängler went as follows:

Many subscription holders and other visitors to the concert association feel they will have to forego the pleasure of attending one of your concerts. We consider you one of the finest representatives of German musical life, but you are at the same time the representative of a nation whose policies present a great threat to Nordic culture. If we now appeal to Stockholm's musical public not to attend the concerts conducted by you, this is meant as a protest against the excesses perpetrated very recently by the German occupiers. To maintain Swedish–German cultural relations under present circumstances would be to show a lack of solidarity with our brother nation.[63]

This was certainly the most sophisticated and unusual protest ever aimed at the conductor, but it never reached him and he only heard roughly what was going on. For reasons of foreign policy the Stockholm students were silenced – with no public explanation given. The Swedish government had sent a *démarche* to Berlin concerning the events in Oslo, but was told diplomatically but firmly by Foreign Minister Ribbentrop to mind its own business. Someone therefore must have thought it expedient to call off the student protest, although the authorities responsible, the Foreign Ministry and the Information Services, denied having anything to do with it, and the college secretary, Allan Hellstrand, refused to say who had asked him to pass on the request that the protest should be cancelled. In order to be forearmed Furtwängler sketched out in his diary under 1 and 2 December two texts of an argument which was supposed to protect him from such undifferentiated accusations; the second, a more complete elaboration of the first, ended on a note of certainty: 'It seems to me that the message which Beethoven put across to mankind in his works, and in particular in the Ninth Symphony, the message of goodness, trust, and unity before God, has never been more necessary than today.'[64]

He was once again presenting himself as the apolitical artist who had ceased to sign contracts and now only took guest or honorary positions – as he had in Vienna. Matters were not such though that formal legal arguments would have encountered much understanding, especially among the excited young people of Stockholm, and when the conductor returned to Germany he brought with him not only a diary for 1944 and a blue jumper which he had bought for his housekeeper in Potsdam, but also the knowledge that such subtle distinctions were no use when trying to overcome global resentment.

While he was spending Christmas in Castle Achleiten – after the fourth Philharmonic concert in Berlin and the concerts in Vienna – the head of the security police and Security Services set to work in the capital. He did this in a professional capacity, looking at the question of the performance of German music abroad, which of course also involved Furtwängler:

Both German and French reports are agreed that the guest performance given by the Berlin Staatsoper under Karajan in Paris in May 1941 surpassed by far all pre-war German artistic successes, and even months later still dominates the thinking of many influential French circles. [. . .] It is considered regrettable that Furtwängler has in the last few years conducted only in neutral or friendly foreign countries, never in the occupied territories, even though it is precisely there that he would have had a lasting impact.[65]

The Security Services complained that the planned trip to Turkey was also encountering awkward problems, because Furtwängler was showing no interest in conducting in the Balkans and had only given a provisional agreement to conduct in Istanbul or Ankara in March or April 1944, providing this did not affect other commitments or his health. The police authorities cannot have guessed that he was already dropping hints as to his future tactics for avoiding the coming 20 April. As far as the last tour of the Balkans was concerned the Security Services noted several deficiencies:

> The main complaint is that Furtwängler did not take part in the tour. The Furtwängler-Berlin Philharmonic combination is said to have a reputation all of its own, with the result that many people bought tickets they would not have bought if they had known he would be absent. It is feared that the knowledge that in many other capital cities the orchestra had played under Furtwängler, but on this tour had been led by less famous conductors, might easily cause the sensitive Balkan peoples to be affronted and feel they were being treated as a second-class country.[66]

Anyone listening to the Security Service report was definitely receiving the echo of official opinion on the matter, in other words not the voice of the people but that of the functionaries who were interested in arranging such concert tours not for their artistic value but for politico-cultural purposes, and from their point of view the following explosive suggestion was the high point of the Security Services report:

> Thus every performance is related to the interests of the Reich. [. . .] Many people therefore consider it astonishing that personal dealings with the conductor regarding concerts which are crucial for the Reich continue in the same way as before the war, and they think it imperative that those directing the intellectual war should see the great conductor's activities as part of the war-effort.[67]

But this final step of conscripting orchestras' conductors to make concert tours in politically important countries had so many negative aspects to it, including from a propaganda point of view – Goebbels trembled to think of headlines appearing in the 'enemy press' such as 'Nazis in command of Beethoven' – that it was never taken. It is no longer possible to tell whether it was even on the agenda of Furtwängler's talk with Goebbels on 12 January 1944 – another of their beloved midday meetings at 12.15 p.m. – although it may have been one of the complex of issues under the heading 'political' noted by the musician in his diary. On that occasion however they did talk about appointing a price commissioner to restore a degree of economic order to the music business, if at all possible Giovanni di Bella, whom Furtwängler had already recommended to Dr Drewes. They also talked about Prague . . . The commission to go to Prague was one which the minister was merely

304

handing on. Celebrations for the fifth anniversary of Hitler's politically skilful move, which had wiped Czechoslovakia off the map, were to take place in March in the present capital of the Reich's protectorate of Böhemia and Moravia. Such an occasion demanded pomp and propaganda, and Hitler, although he was aware of the conductor's dislike of appearing in connection with political events, had chosen none other than Furtwängler. The discussion with Goebbels degenerated into dogged negotiations. The musician, who did not yet know whether a medical certificate would suffice to free him from the coming celebrations for the Führer's birthday, presented the politician with carefully worded doubts, saying that really his state of health was less than ideal, but if one were to consider Prague, well at least it was less politically exposed than a concert on 20 April, which two years ago had provoked such unpleasant attention in neutral countries and been so damaging to cultural relations . . . this must have been the line of his argument for this instance of political jobbery to have succeeded: Prague yes, Hitler's birthday celebrations no. It was a risky business, because Goebbels behaved almost slavishly when it came to matters affecting the Führer.

Two weeks later – poetic justice on the eleventh anniversary of the takeover of power on 30 January 1933 – the Philharmonie was a smoking pile of rubble; the orchestra had to move to the Staatsoper whenever it performed a Philharmonic concert, while Knappertsbusch gave concerts in the cathedral and smaller concerts took place in the main hall of the Lichtenberg vocational school. Because the Staatsoper contained 600 seats fewer than the Philharmonie it was necessary to repay subscriptions for 1,800 seats until the end of the season. Despite such difficulties Goebbels often engaged 'his' orchestra for special occasions, for example an event staged by the Propaganda Ministry in the cathedral; this was to be a big thing, a public demonstration against the barbarism of the western 'plutocracies', because the roof of the cathedral had been destroyed in an air-raid and snow now lay on the steps and between the seats. Furtwängler conducted a Concerto Grosso by Handel and Beethoven's Fifth – a repeat of the seventh Philharmonic concert he had given some days earlier, although with the omission of Mozart's G-minor symphony. Did Goebbels wish to make a speech to the invited guests between the two pieces? Something must have deterred him. He forbade the camera team from the weekly news programme to film in the ruins of the cathedral, and only gave permission shortly before the event began for the filming to go ahead in front of the cathedral, but at such short notice that there was not enough time to do it at all. The press also kept silent, even though they were aware of the political situation and on the same day stressed that Furtwängler's performance of *Die Meistersinger* at the Staatsoper – with some new singers – was another high point: 'In their faith in Germany's immortal genius our people repeatedly show, particularly in difficult times, how deep are their links with their great masters, the masters whose unique art widens the people's hearts and fills them with new courage to live.'[68]

Then there was the festival concert on 16 March in the Spanish Hall of Prague Castle. Reichsminister and Protector Dr Frick was host; the papers reported a large audience. Henlein and Eigruber, Gauleiters of Sudetenland and the Upper Danube region respectively, were there as was Schaal, the army's plenipotentiary to the protector, commander of the army in Böhemia and Moravia and general of the tank command. The entire government of the protectorate, both German and Czech, also attended, and wounded soldiers from Prague military hospitals were the guests of honour. Furtwängler – very demonstratively – began with the Czech Dvořák's E-minor Symphony, followed by Beethoven's Fifth:

In the deeply symbolic framework of this concert Beethoven's Fifth, a secular document of the powerful spiritual and ethical power of European culture and the heroic feeling for life which this culture honours so deeply and defends so invincibly against every attack by soulless forces, provided an overwhelming, fulfilling, eternally valid symphonic response to this profound call of yearning, in which all the intense and beautiful aspects of Dvořák's native folk music are expressed in more refined artistic form.[69]

The fact that Dvořák's symphony owed its existence to the composer's eighteen-month stay in the USA and is a creative commentary on 'folk music' there, including the negro spiritual, all heightened its political significance as the choice for this occasion. The politicians' defective instruction in music history of course ensured that no suspicions were aroused, and so they were less hesitant in their judgement of the conductor than ever before. Goebbels was almost swooning:

An artist like Furtwängler [. . .] compels my deepest admiration. What a highly accomplished person! He has never been a National Socialist. Nor has he ever made any bones about it. Which Jews and emigrants thought was sufficient reason to consider him one of them, a key representative of so-called 'inner emigration'. Furtwängler, whose stance towards us has not changed in the least, showed by his conduct during the bombing of Berlin just how far he stands above this rabble. Not only did he not quit in the way many other so-called

306

M 2157/44

(1) Berlin, den
Pariser Platz 3
Ruf: 11-00-52

ZA/Ch/Kr.

An
Herrn Reichsminister Dr. Goebbels
Reichsministerium für Volksaufklärung
und Propaganda

(1) B e r l i n W 8
Mauerstr. Nr. 45

*zur Absendung
an Büro*

Lieber Parteigenosse Dr. Goebbels,

      Generalmusikdirektor Dr. Wilhelm Furtwängler hat
- wie mir Reichsleiter Bormann mitteilte - den in Abschrift
beiliegenden Brief an den Führer gerichtet. Der Führer hat
inzwischen angeordnet, dass der Keller des z.Zt. von Dr.
Furtwängler bewohnten Hauses soweit wie irgend möglich ge-
sichert und verstärkt werden soll, ich habe entsprechende
Weisungen gegeben.

      Ich würde nur wünschen, dass der von Dr. Furtwäng-
ler hinsichtlich des Bunkerbaues eingenommene Standpunkt von
recht vielen Prominenten geteilt wird. Leider ist dies z.Zt.
nicht der Fall! Ich würde es für sehr zweckmässig halten,
wenn in ähnlichen Fällen auf den von Dr. Furtwängler eingenommenen Standpunkt als Vorbild hingewiesen würde. Vielleicht
haben Sie, lieber Parteigenosse Dr. Goebbels, hierzu auch
Gelegenheit. Ich habe Herrn Dr. Furtwängler gegenüber über
den von ihm eingenommenen Standpunkt vor allem als General-
bevollmächtigter für die deutsche Bauwirtschaft meine Freude
zum Ausdruck gebracht.

      Ich begrüsse Sie herzlich mit

            H e i l H i t l e r !
              gez. *Speer*

3453

Anlage!

24 June 1944
(1) Berlin, Pariser Platz 3
Tel: 11–00–52
ZA/Ch/Kr.

M 2157/44

307

To Minister of the Reich, Dr Goebbels
Ministry for Popular Enlightenment and Propaganda
(1) Berlin W8
Mauerstr. Nr. 45

Dear Party Comrade Dr Goebbels,

General Director of Music Dr Wilhelm Furtwängler has – I am informed
by Reichsleiter Bormann – sent the letter of which a copy is herewith
enclosed to the Führer. The Führer has ordered that the cellar of the house
Dr Furtwängler is currently living in should be strengthened and made secure
in so far as this is possible, and I have given instructions accordingly.

I only wish that the stance adopted by Dr Furtwängler with regard to the
building of a bunker were shared by many other prominent figures.
Unfortunately this is not the case at the present time! I believe it would be
very to the point if in similar cases Dr Furtwängler's stance were used as an
example. Perhaps you, dear comrade Dr Goebbels, will have opportunity
to do this. I have expressed my pleasure to Dr Furtwängler at receiving his
letter, especially in my capacity as plenipotentiary for the German
construction industry.

With sincere greetings, Heil Hitler!
signed: Speer
Copy enclosed!

---

artists did, he also in these difficult weeks and months used all his
artistic skills in the service of Berlin's bomb victims and armaments
workers.[70]

Naturally he put the conductor together with Strauss and Pfitzner on
the list of 'irreplaceable artists'; these 'divine talents' were to be protected
from destruction at all costs. It was to this end that Hitler ordered in
the course of the spring that a private bunker be built for Furtwängler
and his family, not however in Berlin, which was being bombed almost
daily, but in Achleiten, far removed from any possible bomb target,
next to the castle which housed the conductor and his family, with its
deep medieval cellars and foundations of up to three metres thick. It
was a case where the recipient's argument against so much pointless
disturbance was to the point:

Naturally I am very grateful if during an enemy air attack on an
endangered city – such as Berlin – I can make use of a bomb-proof

308

matter of assuring this work with a contract. The radio service's hyper-efficient management presented the Berlin Philharmonic with a new version of the old agreement, according to which for one single payment the Philharmonic concerts could be broadcast on all stations as often as the management wished. The orchestra management and Furtwängler both objected to this, Furtwängler stressing his protest by refusing to conduct in front of the radio's microphones before the matter was settled. The trustee was called in; the radio services yielded because unrestricted utilisation of the musicians' artistic achievements would have ruined the orchestra's financial situation. To begin with the radio services recorded without a contract; in the end such recordings were legalised by a revised new version of the orchestra's contract and a special contract for Furtwängler. The problem of quality remained and on more than one occasion the conductor forbade transmission of a piece.

That August – for the last time in the Nazi regime – the Bayreuth war-time festival concerts were staged again and Furtwängler shared the conducting with Abendroth, naturally nothing but *Die Meistersinger* which was played repeatedly to hoards of spectators, a sort of mass-administrating of a musical tonic, though it was really only a placebo. The papers wrote what they were supposed to write, placing the festival

in the great tradition of a German race whose people find their national essence expressed in works of art and over many generations have entrusted these documents of German culture to the younger gener-ation, which then has the historic task of protecting the ideas and heritage of centuries from the threat of destruction.[80]

This was someone performing his duty and – as usual – confusing cause and effect by adhering strictly to official guidelines, which allowed the exploitation of the heroic myth of rescuing the West from the rampaging 'Bolshevist subhumans'. Occasionally other voices made themselves heard, more distanced and even sceptical:

It is clearly a 'peace-loving' Germany which appeals to us so guilelessly and distractedly in this work. But this glimpse of a peaceful world, and the relaxed sense of well-being which it wakens in us, need not necessarily lull us. At a time like this the sharp contrast to reality offered by our glimpse of it is likely to call forth different feelings and emotions when, the immediate moment of enjoyment passed, we take pause to reflect on what we have heard.[81]

313

The growing recording industry: Karajan competed here too

314

Scepticism was now being voiced more distinctly than ever in Switzerland too, though it took a considerable time before the Federal Council could get its act together sufficiently both to announce – on 1 October – a total ban on the export of war materials, and also to proscribe the presence of the Nazi Party in the country . . . which happened just in time on 7 May 1945, the day before the unconditional surrender of Hitler's successors. The press on the other hand saved itself even the slightest risk and launched – as never before when he had conducted guest concerts in Switzerland – an attack on Furtwängler, who had been invited to the music festival in Lucerne, as had Arthur Honegger and Paul Paray from occupied France; the fact that they did not come was blamed by alert newspaper reporters on the German occupying authorities in particular, and on the Third Reich's cultural policies in general, of which the prominent guest was an unwelcome representative. Furtwängler of course knew better, but how could he make himself understood? The organisers of the festival had discussed the whole programme with him; as the matter stood in January 1944 the Swiss Volkmar Andreae, the French Paray, and the Jewish Paul Kletzki were to conduct as well as Furtwängler, and among others Carl Flesch was to perform as soloist, according to a note made by the German legation in Bern:

> Furtwängler too says the participation of the French conductor would be desirable and he has declared himself prepared, if necessary, to sort out travel difficulties with the relevant German authorities. Staatsrat Furtwängler, as this is a Swiss undertaking, has no objections to Professor Kletzki (Polish) or Professor Flesch, and he will make this clear in Berlin.[82]

This however meant no more and no less than that the Propaganda Ministry was allowing the conductor to appear abroad together with Jews, in other words to do something which ten years earlier had been one of the main points of accusation against Hindemith, and this permission rested on the artist's own recommendation in his own domain. It would have been a gripping task for Swiss journalists to research this further, but they all spared themselves the effort, as people do when they believe they are adequately informed. They might even have discovered how mistrustfully Furtwängler's moves were being followed by the Reich. When he asked for his manuscripts and his special cook to be sent after him, it was assumed in the Propaganda Ministry that he wanted to prolong his stay in Switzerland, perhaps even to flee; they sent a coded telegram to Bern: 'Please stick to return

Get out of Basel. Baby certainly doesn't like music controlled by Himmler

date of 1 October, especially as Furtwängler is expected for recording sessions in Berlin at beginning of October. Also ensure that he does not accept any commitments there past 1 October.'[83]

One of the key champions of the Swiss 'enlightenment' was Otto Maag, editor of the *National-Zeitung* in Basel; formerly a Protestant vicar, who had officiated in Heidelberg before losing his parish for undisclosed reasons – which might explain a twelve-year-long 'gap' in his life – he had surfaced again as a journalist in Basel in 1927, progressing to editor in 1932 and receiving Swiss citizenship two years after that. He was a valiant anti-fascist who was quite happy writing snide commentaries on the Nazis at the same time as drawing royalties from the Nazi state, as for example for the first staging of a version of Millöcker's *The Beggar Student* which he co-scripted with the emigrant Eugen Gürster under the pseudonym 'Eugen Otto'. Maag polemicised against the German conductor as follows:

> How is it that we, champions of genuine internationalism in the realm of art, are repeatedly prepared to take into account the political 'concerns' of a nationality which would never allow a Furtwängler to play Mendelssohn, let alone give a concert with a non-Aryan soloist? These artists from the Third Reich have known for a long time, even if they did not want to know, that the state whose honorific title they bear is bringing mothers and children to the gas chambers, from life

316

to death, in the most horrific manner imaginable, simply because they belong to another people than that of the 'master race', and we should at last refuse to accept art from these people in whose 'totalitarian' state everything, but everything is connected to politics, a people who do not believe or allow artistic expression to be without political meaning, a country where one has to begin a concert of chamber music with the Horst-Wessel Song.[84]

Unintentionally Maag's skilful formulations betrayed how much he needed to compensate for leaving his country; even the untruths which he stated were calculated to appeal to the feelings of bourgeois readers who were now proud to feel that they were 'champions of genuine internationalism', and so, their self-respect strengthened and from a position of moral righteousness, they were supposed to chase Furtwängler the scapegoat out into the wilds. The journalist was stirring up emotions, and this was his intention; he could of course have taken the opportunity to ignore the Furtwängler concerts and thereby teach the organisers of the festival a lesson, but that would have meant an unreasonable sacrifice, and so he added to his propaganda text, as if he had not meant it seriously, a rather distanced but factual critique of the musical event. Other Swiss papers – including *Die Tat* – and some members of the Lucerne town council were provoked into taking a stand against Maag. A controversy gathered pace involving various party factions well beyond the confines of Lucerne; Furtwängler had to serve as ammunition. However, there was another rumour going around that Maag had only been using the political situation as a front; the real reason for his attack was allegedly that his twenty-five-year-old son, Peter Maag, at that time conductor at the Biel-Solothurn Theatre, had not been given the chance to make his mark in Lucerne in front of the festival audiences.[85]

The conductor left Switzerland again for the time being . . . alone. His wife Elisabeth had to stay behind with her three-year-old son Thomas Ackermann. She was now expecting their child and he wanted her to remain in the security of Switzerland, which was not involved in the war. However alert, he cannot have known at the end of August what lay in store for him; perhaps he felt he risked a parting which could last an unforeseeable length of time. He may have been thinking of possible consequences of his refusal to subscribe to the homage to Hitler, or maybe of the more immediate danger of the bombing which was reaching ever further and more brutally into German territory, and – as we know today – was for strategic reasons aimed at the civilian population. Whatever the danger, whether of an air attack or of being arrested, he

317

wanted to make sure that his wife Elisabeth, Thomas and the unborn Furtwängler child would not be affected by it.

Perhaps it was the failure of prominent intellectual figures to make a declaration of loyalty which aroused Hitler's anger. He made Bormann responsible for undertaking a monstrous plan. This is touched on in a circular which also reached the politico-cultural archives in Rosenberg's department, where it aroused lively interest – in the head of the department, Gerigk. The head of the party chancel, now also a Reichsminister, announced:

> Furthermore I would ask you to make known as quickly as possible the names of any other people whose behaviour in the past or currently has raised doubts as to their commitment to National Socialism or the soundness of their opinions. It goes without saying that the personal details must be accompanied by proof which can be verified or even used as the basis for taking immediate action.[86]

The Gestapo and the security police already had a stock of files available for such tasks; but to have used it would have demanded an impossible amount of work, as the 'intellectuals' only represented a tiny minority of cases, which would have been very tedious to sift out. By contrast the department's politico-cultural archives had been accumulating incriminating material on this group in particular for a period of over ten years, and sorting it into more than 60,000 named files; not all those working in cultural activities were there, but the group Bormann wanted was. Thus it sufficed to go through the records from A to Z. Gerigk informed the party chancel that he welcomed this initiative and would place his archives at its disposal: 'The material was collected expressly regarding the politico-cultural reliability of those concerned. Generally those cases were dealt with where the exposed position of the individual men in question gave reason to do so, or where checks were required following complaints.'[87]

Bormann's grateful answer went direct to Rosenberg. Its aim: to root out all traitors and defeatists. He alerted Himmler's RSHA (security headquarters), and sought to use the documents in Rosenberg's department. Rosenberg however wished to keep control of this treasure, and wanted to allow only the RSHA to inspect them; on 4 December Bormann responded by toning down his request: 'The inspection of your archives and possibly further details from your office will be a valuable aid to the RHSA in their screening of personalities from cultural and academic circles.'[88] The surviving files end with that letter; nevertheless there is sufficient evidence to reconstruct what was supposed to happen

318

next. Among the files in the politico-cultural archives there was one which owed its girth to a particularly assiduous drive to collect material. It was labelled 'Furtwängler'. The file itself did not survive the end of the war, but large parts of it can be reconstituted from the copies which were sent to other offices or received a response from them. This file contained every denunciation, every official report on pro-Jewish statements or interventions, notes on any telephone conversation in which he criticised Nazis, every detail of the musician's conduct abroad – for example the fact that on 2 February 1939, shortly before the return journey from a guest tour of Holland and Belgium, he went to the station post-office and sent all the money he had left to Jewish friends, as a result of which the train could not leave on time and Hans von Benda came running to him and impressed on him that if he persisted despite all warnings he would be risking the death sentence.[89] One piece of information after another must have built up a picture in this file of a person whose nationalist feelings had not led him to National Socialism, with much evidence instead of how little he thought of the regime's theory and practice, a degree of dissent which extended far beyond the Jewish question into the realms of religion, morality and culture. The fact that such a man, distanced as he was, was allowed to maintain personal contact – even if not uninterrupted – with Hitler, Goebbels, Göring, Schirach and many others, made him even more dangerous, at least in the opinion of the Rosenberg clique and Himmler, who had already warned him in 1942 that anything he did for a Jew, or anyone related to Jews, would henceforth be considered subversive behaviour.

Furtwängler, however, showed no sign of being worried about his security. He discussed broadcasting plans with advisers from the Propaganda Ministry as he wanted his own radio series of six Berlin and five Vienna concerts; he travelled to St. Florian in October to appraise the new Reich Bruckner Orchestra which was already earmarked for Karajan, though Goebbels had originally promised it to him. Some conflicts were unavoidable, because Hans Fritzsche, head of the Ministry's broadcasting department and with no knowledge at all of matters musical, was constantly blocking Furtwängler's wishes and suggestions, and represented quite different concerns. Very soon Ministerial Director Fritzsche complained:

Herr Furtwängler seems set on causing the broadcasting organisation difficulties. For example he recently failed to complete recordings in Vienna under the most trivial of pretexts. Furthermore he broke off the recording of Brahms's Third Symphony in Berlin's Beethovensaal on the grounds [. . .] that the Beethovensaal was too small – while

319

only a short while before he had conducted Bruckner's far more demanding Ninth Symphony in the same hall, although it has to be said he did not complete the last fifteen minutes of that either. Herr Furtwängler treats all the assistants at the radio, including the chief, as good-for-nothings. [. . .] Although we initially got on well he now tries to avoid me. He tries to play on the minister's love of art.[90]

The musician's complaints were primarily of an artistic nature; Fritzsche even had to promise him that the concerts would be recorded in such a way that they sounded the same on radio as in the hall. In a further discussion on 5 December he was full of worries that the recording technique using the magnetophone would conserve music for eternity which would leave musicians without any income, and that the rooms still available – after the loss of the Philharmonie – could not guarantee sufficiently good acoustic quality. At the programme planning session the next day Dr von Westerman, artistic manager of the Berlin Philharmonic and also head of the Reichsradio's programme group dealing with 'lesser known and therefore difficult music', suggested making a special feature of Furtwängler on various occasions, such as the fiftieth broadcast of 'Eternal Music . . .' (mid-January), Remembrance Day in March, and the Führer's birthday.[91] Fritzsche however, did not wish to impose any such dates, which meant that the conductor did not have to rethink his avoidance tactics all over again. All these broadcasting issues were waiting to be discussed at Furtwängler's next meeting with Goebbels, which took place on 11 December – again at 12.15 p.m.

Only a week earlier the Minister had once again suddenly been reminded of the fact that Furtwängler had spoilt another propaganda hit of his. On 4 December the very first showing of the film *Philharmoniker*, which had been praised by the most senior film director as 'of great artistic merit, and also valuable from a cultural and political point of view', was screened in the Tauentzien-Palast. This film, based on an idea of Friedrich Herzfeld and directed by Paul Verhoeven, showed many of the conductors connected with the Berlin Philharmonic Orchestra, including Richard Strauss, but not Furtwängler, who had been the head of this world-famous orchestra for so many years; he – although the key protagonist – had declined the offer to take part in a project which was so obviously intended to fulfill cultural propaganda purposes not only for Germany, but also for the Nazi regime. This incidentally was also something which Goebbels criticised. In December 1943 the film was already finished; when the minister watched it he complained about its roughshod approach, its lack of nuance, and he ordered a second attempt. But its greatest fault could not be corrected. There

320

can be no doubt that Furtwängler's non-participation set film-goers wondering, especially those who were music enthusiasts.

At the programme meeting on 13 December Fritzsche reported the outcome of the conductor's visit to the minister, and that both control of the recordings and artistic control were at issue. In fact the radio service had recorded the première of Kurt Hessenberg's second symphony. In general though the musician was not happy with the quality. This was because he did not listen to the recordings in the recording studio, but only when they were broadcast over the loudspeaker of his wireless set. Reception was especially poor in Achleiten, just as in other mountainous areas. Fading and crackle meant that listening to the music was extremely painful to Furtwängler; the ministerial director even sent a technician to Achleiten to check the receiver and instruct the musician in how to use the set correctly. Karajan complained of similar quality defects, especially regarding his recording of Bruckner's Eighth. Of course he was not satisfied with the advice of the radio technician, and suggested instead that the swings in frequency could be resolved by building in a resistor; once this was done, he said, he would allow the symphony to be broadcast. Those present at the programme meeting responded to this absurd suggestion with roars of laughter.

At the beginning of the 1944–5 season the minister for armaments and war production, Albert Speer, had booked a series of eighteen Philharmonic concerts, which were outside the main programme, and which were intended for all those working in the Berlin armaments industry; they were not however 'work-break concerts', but were to take place like any ordinary concerts in the Staatsoper, in the Beethovensaal and in the Admiralspalast. As conductors he engaged Eugen Jochum, Karl Elmendorff, Clemens Krauss, Fritz Zaun, Abendroth, Rother, Böhm, Heger, Schmidt-Isserstedt and the Flemish Hendrik Diels. Two of the concerts – on 22 October and 12 December – were entrusted to Furtwängler. Speer had several motives for this unusual undertaking. For one thing he wanted to show these workers, who were so vital to the war effort, that they were a kind of élite, and for another he wanted to use the fact that the orchestra was now occupied uninterruptedly with the no less 'vital' task of serving this public to protect it. He later explained:

As the war was now rapidly coming to an end one could detect a sort of nihilism in Goebbels, and he was downright pleased whenever any valuable *objet d'art* in Berlin was reduced by an air raid to rubble and ashes; after the wonderful building by Schinkel which housed his own ministry had burnt down for example, he was moved to say:

'The Russians shall not have any of this. They are not allowed to have it.' And then he also made remarks to the effect that he had really been the one who built up the Philharmonic Orchestra [. . .], and that he found the thought of their playing to the Russians quite intolerable.[92]

Speer was in fact exaggerating in order to emphasise his own role as a rescuer; it is however a fact that the culture department of the Propaganda Ministry decided on 23 February 1945 to send the entire orchestra to join the people's army, but only to the fourth reserve, which meant that the musicians – until further notice – were freed from military service for the duration of their important orchestral war duties in order to perform. On the other hand, Goebbels, faced inescapably with the *Götterdämmerung* of the Nazi regime, was behaving very unpredictably; at any moment his claim to have the power to take this or that person, friend or enemy, with him in the final 'heroic' moment of destruction, could become a terrible reality.

Furtwängler learned in November and December 1944 what a catastrophe the collapse of the Reich would be, and that there was nothing which could avert the end. One report came from an authority in matters of war economics, namely from Speer, who was requested by the conductor to come to his room during the interval of the Philharmonic concert on 11 and 12 December. Speer remembered this conversation:

He said to me: What is the war situation? Now at that time this was definitely a risky question, I have to admit, because the general line was that you had to believe in the victory and be convinced that it would happen, and so the very question made it quite clear that he had more than just doubts about the victory. By asking that question Furtwängler put himself in my hands, which made me surer of my answer, and I told him very clearly and openly that there was no longer any hope, that the end was drawing near. After this we had a conversation the details of which I do not remember, but I do know that in the course of the conversation I advised Furtwängler to go to Switzerland and not come back.[93]

To convince an artist so far removed from everyday life, who was ignorant of facts which would inevitably change his isolationist existence, was difficult indeed, especially as he did not even notice how Himmler was having him watched. He needed to have it pointed out to him by well-wishers, and even so he was inclined to turn a deaf ear to any warning. Already in November Frau Dr Richter, assistant to Dr Schmitt, the fashionable doctor for Berlin high society, had told him that the destruction of Germany in the final phase of the war had been prepared down to the last detail. This information was absolutely reliable, because as Frau Himmler's doctor, Frau Dr Richter was consulted several times a week in Reichsführer-SS Himmler's house, where she kept her eyes and ears open and discovered the most hideous details of the planned *Götterdämmerung*. Furtwängler's name was also mentioned: 'She emphasised that care had been taken to ensure that people like myself, who had always been considered "traitors", could not escape.'[94]

A second conversation covering the same information, but more urgently this time, occurred in mid-December; the doctor made an effort to find out what concrete plans had been made for the musician, and she succeeded in doing so. In the days of the Mozart and Brahms Philharmonic concerts in the Admiralspalast – on 22 and 23 January – Frau Dr Richter startled Furtwängler by appearing suddenly and surreptitiously in Potsdam, where she gave him another report:

> She told me that this time she had come in secret, and that nobody must learn of her coming, because I had been declared *persona non grata*. No National Socialist or SS man was allowed to speak another word to me. My telephone, my every step was being watched, and I had to reckon with the possibility of arrest every day. I was under suspicion of being party to the assassination attempt in July 1944.[95]

In the meantime the Gestapo had begun to take an interest in Dr Maria Daelen, believing that she must be able to provide some clues from the early days of the conspiracy in 1942–3. The officials took diaries, letters and photos belonging to the conductor's long-time friend from the surgery and from her country house in Saarow, and they forced her housekeeper Erna Geske and the surgery's locum, Frau Dr Ulla Momsen, to make statements. In January Maria Daelen had to appear several times before a Gestapo hearing. On each occasion they were particularly interested in how much Furtwängler had known of the preparations for the assassination attempt. They knew about his friendships or acquaintance with the insurance director Otto Hübener, Major-General Hans Oster, the one time ambassador to Rome Ulrich von Hassell, Erwin Blank and Hans Bernd Gisevius, all of whom were more or less part of the circle of conspirators, and some of whom had already been executed. The Gestapo used its usual tactic: lull the victims into a feeling of security, collect peripheral evidence and then finally lay into them. In mid-January the situation was more or less as follows: the Reich's security headquarters had begun the evaluation of documents from Rosenberg's politico-cultural archive, which included the file on Furtwängler; however, it was a slow process because the demands of war frequently necessitated the release of personnel to go to the front. Goebbels, Himmler, Hitler and their high-ranking entourage were irremediably caught up in one of those insoluble conflicts of ancient tragedy. To extend their lives for a mere few days, they had to sacrifice every available man in the final battle, especially the political police's young, well-educated experts, who were supposed to be preparing Hitler's final act of vengeance on suspect artists and intellectuals. For the Red Army had just passed Posen and the Upper Silesian border. This meant that although the Nazi chiefs were primarily concerned with taking revenge at home, they would have to pay for it with the loss of a few days or weeks of their own lives if they used young men to execute it who could otherwise be sent to the front. They decided to delay, for however brief a space of time: this allowed the suspects a reprieve. It was certainly to be expected that the apparently legal procedure of detection, judgement and execution would be replaced by the use of a less personnel-intensive death squad the moment the desire to maintain legal appearances disappeared. Whether the conductor had such misgivings as he hung around in Berlin waiting to conduct a concert with the Philharmonic Orchestra is anybody's guess. He was probably troubled by vague fears, which are always worse than those of something concrete. He certainly understood that there was great danger lurking in Berlin:

When he was positive that designs were harboured against him, he began to think of how best to avoid another trip to Berlin, and as he used to love going for walks on his own – always at a great pace – he was walking one day considering what excuse he could make when he slipped a bit on the ice, and it came to him in a flash that that was the solution; he could pretend he had concussion, because his eternal flu really convinced nobody any longer.[96]

No sooner said than done. On 30 January at 18.40 he sent a telegram from Vienna to the Berlin Philharmonic Orchestra which arrived the next day: 'Concussion due to fall on back of head under strict doctor's orders to rest in bed regret cannot do Berlin concerts suggest make up beginning April.'[97] This was indeed *force majeure*, and so the concerts on 4 and 5 February, which were to have included Pfitzner's overture 'Christelflein' and his cello concerto, ending with Bruckner's Seventh

Symphony, were cancelled without anybody to stand in. The dangers of Berlin were happily avoided, just as events were occurring there which affected Furtwängler more or less directly. 800 four-engined bombers attacked the capital of the Reich on 3 February; the state opera house Unter den Linden was reduced to rubble for the second time, and Roland Freisler, president of the people's court, died at the scene of his crimes, amidst the wreckage. Undoubtedly the news of the destruction of the artistic institution, with all its traditions, would have reached Vienna, where they had only four more weeks in which to enjoy their own Staatsoper before it too burned down. The conductor must have seen this as a sign of fate, and yet he still behaved as if things were relatively normal, because if they were he should in any case leave for Switzerland where he was due to conduct, especially as Bormann's office – responsible for even the most trivial of details – had procured him an exit visa.

This was the first point at which he began to exercise a degree of caution, leaving for the West sooner than necessary. His friend Julia Janssen, an actress at the Burg Theatre, telephoned people she knew in Vorarlberg and asked them to play host to the artist for a few days, and Arthur Haemmerle's family in Dornbirn, cultivated people who were prominent in the small town and still believed that Hitler would win, were pleased and proud to welcome this famous person as their guest of honour.[98] From here to the border post at Buchs was only another twenty kilometres. Almost as if he had nothing to fear, he dealt with correspondence while staying with the Haemmerles, putting at least five letters in the post. They were addressed to Karl Straube in Leipzig, the actress Irme Schwab in Weil, his housekeeper Helene Matschenz in Potsdam, his sister Märit Scheler in Heidelberg and the composer Kurt Rasch in Berlin; he need not have worried about any of them being checked, because the post was only forwarded irregularly and slowly and it would have been two or three days before he could have been arrested. Furthermore the Gestapo knew the dates of his concerts, so an official request for help at the border control post would have sufficed to prevent him from leaving the country. Perhaps by way of precaution he announced in four of the five letters that he would be going to Switzerland but returning in ten days' time, on 28 February – with his wife and her young son. He did express some doubts about whether he would encounter difficulties crossing the border, and he was also worried about the boycott against him in Switzerland, of which he already had some experience. He made a date with Rasch for the 'next concert', in other words for the beginning of March, in Berlin. Despite the reservation – 'of course, who knows what the world will look like by then?'[99] – anyone from the Gestapo reading this could assume this to mean that the suspect did not intend to emigrate, would soon be within easy reach again, and was considered a 'Nazi' in Switzerland.

He crossed the border on 7 February with no problems. The boycott was tightening up, but at the same time gaps were appearing. The Zürich council forbade the two concerts announced for Zürich's Tonhalle, but Winterthur kept to its contract – as did Lausanne and Geneva. The Swiss press, however, was hounding him: 'And when the Prussian Staatsrat travels abroad to conduct concerts he is of course not only dedicating his talent to art, but is also following the wishes of the National Socialist powers by appearing as a propaganda merchant for a German culture, which, as is well known, is no longer allowed to include Mendelssohn.'[100]

In the meantime he had noticed that the key people at the German Embassy in Bern were on his side. Diplomats from the Reich elsewhere also sought to delay his return to Berlin for as long as possible. On 16 February the German embassy in Milan – the base for the Reich's plenipotentiary in Italy – consulted with the embassy in Bern and suggested that Furtwängler might like to conduct two special concerts and a performance of *Die Meistersinger* in La Scala. There was an added inducement: 'I believe it will be possible to persuade Dr Furtwängler to make this trip if its importance is stressed, and if it is possible to tell him *entre nous* that he should bring some of his francs with him.'[101]

Thus Berlin seemed ever more distant as a guest tour to Milan was arranged from Bern, but the increasingly hostile atmosphere in Switzerland was cause for anxiety. By way of precaution the head of the Zürich Atlantis publishing house, Dr Martin Hürlimann applied on 21 February to the foreign department of the Swiss police for an extension of a residence permit for Furtwängler and his family, in the confident expectation that his profession and his fame would be a good recommendation. The authorities refused brusquely however: 'There is no supporting evidence, nor is it even credible, to suggest that on his return to Germany Herr Dr Furtwängler would be liable to any particular persecution. When Dr Furtwängler returns he will merely be sharing the fate of all his fellow countrymen in Germany.'[102]

Shortly before the concert in Winterthur the left-wing press published formal complaints against the German musician, written in tones of unbounded moral outrage, obviously intending to use his case as one of the arguments in party political agitation against the bourgeousie, which was why the complaints were so short on facts. The campaign was dangerously intense:

Just by his participation in dozens of concerts and other events, Furt-wängler has allowed the immortal works of the great German masters to be used for National Socialist propaganda purposes. For years he has allowed himself to be misused, witness that the cries of victims in the concentration camps were masked by solemn music; his activity was supposed to ensure that the horrific crimes against countless individuals would not be heard and not be considered possible.[103]

The press managed to create such an atmosphere of tension that it gave rise, so to speak, to a Swiss 'civil war' in the papers. Sometimes the musician seemed to be considered an enemy of civilised humanity. However, lest the old Swiss understanding for democracy and peace be lost, the most famous musicians in the country decided to defend the attacked conductor, and on 6 March began to collect signatures for this warning message:

We are deeply afflicted by the shameful fact that in our own country intellectual freedom is being ignored and art is being misused in the power struggles of political parties. It is impossible to foresee what the effects of the Furtwängler case will be, and this fills us with serious concern. [. . .] We therefore demand of our authorities that artistic activity and the right to intellectual self-determination, which are inalienable for us Swiss, should in future be protected.[104]

This appeal was supported by the signatures of Volkmar Andreae, Ernest Ansermet, Edmond Appia, Wilhelm Arbenz, Luc Balmer, Samuel Baud-Bovy, Ernest Bauer, Jean Binet, Robert Blum, Joseph Bovet, Alphonse Brun, Fritz Brun, Adolf Brunner, Willy Burckhard, Leopoldo Casella, Robert Denzler, Oskar Disler, Henri Gagnebin, Walther Geiser, Emil Jacques-Dalcroze, Walter Kägi, Ernst Kunz, Walter Lang, Joseph Lauber, André-François Marescotti, Frank Martin, Karl Matthaei, Albert Moeschinger, Hans Münch, Othmar Nussio, Robert Oboussier, Alfred Pochon, Werner Reinhart, Kurt Rothenmüller, Paul Sacher, Erich Schmid, Othmar Schoeck, Walter Schulthess, Max Sturzenegger, Carl Vogler, and Roger Vuataz. Some others were not obtainable, and Heinrich Sutermeister was plain forgotten, as a result of which he wrote to the German embassy in Bern to apologise in writing. Of course Furtwängler's opponents insinuated more or less explicitly that these personalities were no better than 'Nazi friends', such that the troubled waters were not stilled at all. There was further excitement when the socialist paper *Volksrecht* announced in tones of outrage that the conductor had handed in an application for asylum to the relevant authorities.

Naturally this news travelled quickly to Berlin. Furtwängler denied it: 'Of course I never made any such request; it is a lie by the press in connection with the left-wing parties' campaign against me.'[105]

Even without being granted formal asylum the concert dates were up in the air. Milan had not been settled; those for 4, 5, 18 and 19 March in Berlin remained open, as did those for 11, 12, 24 and 25 March in Vienna; in the second concert the Berlin Philharmonic were supposed to play a programme of Beethoven only, with the Eighth Symphony, the 'Coriolan' overture and the 'Eroica' symphony. On 5 March the Red Army was pushing a broad front along the lower Oder and fighting in Forst and Lauban, 120 kilometres from Berlin, and in the west the Allies had reached the centre of Cologne. The conductor had to make a decision. On 11 March he wrote a letter to Goebbels applying for an extension of his visa for another six weeks – for health reasons; he sent this through the legation in Bern so that it could be forwarded from there to Berlin by courier. This suggests that he was not thinking of emigrating, preferring to wait and see whether there was any question of returning to Germany. In the meantime the Americans had won the bridge at Remagen with no losses and created a bridgehead on the east bank of the Rhine. The press in Switzerland was spreading a – false – report from the USA, that with the loss of Remagen Hitler was prepared to enter into a peace treaty. Such developments might mean the chance of a safe return. The controversy in Switzerland had still not settled, and this strengthened his resolve, excessively sensitive as he was to the slightest attack, to distance himself from such hostility at the earliest possible opportunity. In an outburst of sentimentality a few days later the conductor Carmen Weingartner-Studer, widow of the famous Swiss conductor, publicly demanded that 'Beethoven's music, our symbol of the fight for freedom of the spirit, should not be played until the atrocities stop and we are able to walk before him with a clear conscience.'[106]

Her protest against Furtwängler and those of her colleagues who supported him provoked an unpleasant response in turn:

In what year did the worthy Herr Felix von Weingartner divorce his fourth wife,[107] who was a full-blooded Jewess? I do not wish to insinuate anything by pointing out that in that year Hitler was already 'in power'. A second question seems to me to be more important: When was the last time that Herr Felix von Weingartner performed in Greater Germany? And – additionally – when was the last time Frau Carmen Weingartner-Studer performed in Greater Germany?[108]

328

On 23 March – the Soviet army command was busy on the Oder-Neisse front preparing large forces for the final attack on Berlin – an urgent coded telegram from Berlin arrived at the German legation in Bern: 'Propaganda Ministry requests immediate return of Furtwängler to Berlin, to conduct here. Postpone Milan trip.'[109] The officials at the embassy agreed, however, that they would spare the conductor this message, and hold things up by making enquiries with Berlin. This seemed feasible because in the meantime it had been possible to postpone the earlier deadline on Furtwängler's stay in Switzerland by lodging a complaint with the Chef du Département Fédéral de Justice et Police in Bern, to Councillor Eduard von Steiger. Steiger in his time had proposed to the most senior executive authorities that they exchange records to confirm their agreement of 10 October 1938 with the Third Reich regarding the marking of Jewish passports, and had later declared the horrific news of the destruction of the Jews unbelievable and insisted on a restrictive refugee policy – which included handing over refugees to the border police of the Nazi state. He was not the sort of man to recognise a certificate of *spondylosis deformans*, even if it was signed by a well-known medical authority such as Dr Paul Niehans; this man was harder and more inhuman even than Goebbels.

However, the staff at the legation helped wherever they could; on 13 April the artist's passport was extended to May. A week later – the Soviets were beginning to surround the capital of the Reich, and their tanks were rolling through Strausberg and Bernau in the north and Jüterbog in the south – he managed to come to a decision: 'I do understand that the political factors which make it desirable for the ministry and the embassy that I should return to Germany are of great consequence. The minister and Dr Köcher will not hold it against me if for me the most important thing is to restore my health.'[110] The diplomats in Bern were in agreement with this, especially as Goebbels – in a surrounded Berlin – no longer seemed in a position to take any action, and they now adopted a quite different tone: 'Recent developments have solved a problem which had put us in the difficult position of doing justice to all sides. [. . .] The matter [. . .] has now resolved itself thanks to the tide of events.'[111]

There was no longer any need to pay heed to Berlin, and the musician and his wife readily obtained an extension of their passports to last for six months after their visas had expired. In the beleaguered capital of the Reich the Propaganda Minister had burned his personal papers, once again celebrated Hitler's birthday, describing him over the radio as the 'man of the century', and decided that he would hold out with his family 'by the Führer's side'; he was still left a few days in the bunker of the bombed-out, bullet-ridden chancellery, his last chance for reflection. Did Goebbels reflect on the highs and lows of his – political, personal and ideological – trial of strength with Furtwängler? Did he delude himself that his failure to draw the musician back within reach was really an 'eternal victory', or did he perhaps ponder without bitterness what it would be like for Furtwängler to live in a post-war world which was no longer his own?[112]

On 1 May, at the same time as in the Chancellery garden Goebbels abdicated responsibility with one shot from his pistol, the musician in Clarens was noting his political thoughts in his diary. Shocked by ever-bolder intimations that the Reich would be militarily defeated, and by global accusations of collective guilt, he was now trying to work up history, find explanations. As ever this was a form of defence against attacks which he felt were directed at him personally. Hitler had initially been welcomed as unifying Germany, and then, with the use of deceit and terror, lies and propaganda, he had reduced the people to silence, and by the proclamation of racial hatred and his subsequent policy of extermination had undermined the very foundations of the former Germany. The following was the result of further reflection:

The Treaty of Versailles [. . . .], whose main aim was to dishonour Germany, was the ladder up which Hitler climbed to power. What is happening today is the same only far more acute. Anyone who blames a whole people for the concentration camp atrocities is thinking in the same way as the Nazis, who, by raising the Jewish question, were the first to declare and practice mass responsibility. Those who blame us are doing something worse still; to deny the honour of a very great people – a people whose inner nobility can compete with that of any other people, having produced Goethe and Beethoven and innumerable other great benefactors to mankind – is not only dangerous, it is terrible. The German people will never accept it. In which case it would be better if one were to be honest and logical, and destroy it completely.[113]

Furtwängler was so much the artist, and so distrustful of a historical approach, that he could not even begin to achieve a reliable analysis. His personal distress made it impossible for him to obtain the necessary objectivity, and personal identification gave rise to helpless compassion for 'his people'. It did not occur to him that political 'honour' is itself an expression of ideology – as are 'shame' and 'inner nobility' – not an objective value on the basis of which to build a stable political order. It did not even occur to him to ask what it was that really linked the

330

German people – as they were in May 1945 – with Goethe and Beethoven; it had after all been a quite different and far earlier German people which had produced them, and if that were the case then what, other than providing a very shaky alibi, did these 'great beneficiaries', if that is what they really were, have to do with the German people of 1945?

Art, and especially music, cannot in itself be held up as a moral absolute; it is now taken for granted that every state will use art for its own ends, regardless of who happens to be in power. The large-scale technology to meet the consumer's needs for energy, information, water, freedom of movement and living space – and of course music by way of orchestras, opera houses, radio and television – is now spread worldwide and is an accepted feature of advanced civilisation, independent of day-to-day politics or culture. Such facilities can be organised, they are goods, and just like goods an artist can be purchased, however expensively he prices himself. In just the same way Beethoven and Goethe are consumable commodities. To attribute anything else to music is ideology and illusion. This was why Furtwängler had to create a protective mythology between himself and the threat of such 'devaluation' if he was to spare himself from facing bitter reality.

His naïve, clumsy semantic interpretation of history was – like all his notes – never thought through. He could not be more exact and factual because this would have undermined his own existential foundations, demolished his world view in which the certainty of his own greatness shone forth like a great central sun. The trial of strength he underwent between 1933 and 1945 can be explained as a frustrated attempt to safeguard this view of the world and of himself as a spiritual and moral high priest, whatever catastrophe might befall him, and with as much room to manoeuvre as was possible under the circumstances. Thus he attempted to rescue a mythological 'other Germany' – of which he was proud to be a symbol – as proof that there existed a 'German' essence.

This means no more and no less than that he sacrificed himself to his own fiction.

NOTES

Abbreviations

AMZ	*Allgemeine Musik-Zeitung*
AStA	Austrian State Archives, Vienna
AUT	Author's archives
BA	Bundesarchiv, Koblenz
BBZ	*Berliner Börsen-Zeitung* (Berlin Financial Times)
BDC	Berlin Document Centre
BDM	Bund Deutscher Mädel (League of German Maids)
BPhO	Berlin Philharmonic Orchestra
CDJC	Centre de Documentation Juive Contemporaine, Paris
CStA	Central State Archives, Potsdam
DAF	Deutsche Arbeitsfront (German Workers' Movement)
DAZ	*Deutsche Allgemeine Zeitung*
DNVP	Deutschnationale Volkspartei (German National People's Party)
DTZ	*Deutsche Theater-Zeitung*
Gestapo	Geheime Staatspolizei (Secret Police)
GDM	General Director of Music
GStA	Geheimes Staatsarchiv Berlin (Secret State Archives, Berlin)
HY	Hitler Youth
KDDK	Kameradschaft der deutschen Künstler (Association of German Artists)
KdF	Kraft durch Freude (Strength through Joy)
KfdK	Kampfbund für deutsche Kultur (League for the Defence of German Culture)
DCM	Director of Church Music
MNN	*Münchner Neueste Nachrichten*

NSBO	Nationalsozialistische Betriebsorganisation (National Socialist Business Organisation)
NSDAP	Nationalsozialistische Deutsche Arbeiterpartei (National Socialist Workers' Party, i.e. The Nazi Party)
NSKG	NS-Kulturgemeinde (NS Cultural Association)
NSV	NS-Volkswohlfahrt (National Socialist People's Welfare)
NYT	*New York Times*
PAA	Politisches Archiv des Auswärtigen Amtes, Bonn (Foreign Office Political Archives, Bonn)
Pg, Pgn.	Parteigenosse, Parteigenossin (Male and female party members)
PMWKuV	Preussisches Ministerium für Wissenschaft, Kunst und Volksbildung (Prussian Ministry for Sciences, Arts and Popular Education)
ProMi	Reichsministerium für Volksaufklärung und Propaganda (Reich Ministry for Popular Enlightenment and Propaganda)
RKK	Reichskulturkammer
RMK	Reichsmusikkammer
RMVP	Reichsministerium für Volksaufklärung und Propaganda (see ProMi)
RPA	Reichspropagandaamt (Reich Propaganda Department)
RSHA	Reichssicherheitshauptamt (Security headquarters)
SA	Sturmabteilung (Storm-troopers)
SD	Sicherheitsdienst (Security Service)
SS	Schutzstaffel (Army Police Squadron)
STAGMA	Staatlich genehmigte Gesellschaft zur Verwertung musikalischer Urheberrechte (State-approved association for determining musical copyright)
VB	*Völkischer Beobachter* (People's Observer)
VPhHA	Vienna Philharmonic, historical archives
WFA	Wilhelm-Furtwängler Archives, Zürich

Sources

All quotations are as accurate a rendition as possible; corrections have been made only where necessary to make the sense clear. Use of the available material has been limited for reasons of space. All sources given are in the author's archives in the form of microfilm, microfiche, photocopies or other copies. The author was responsible for all the translations into German from French, Russian and Swedish originals.

Notes	Wilhelm Furtwängler: *Aufzeichnungen 1924–1954* (Wiesbaden, 1980); page numbers refer to this edition; manuscript (MS) page numbers are given for unpublished diary extracts. English edition: WF: *Notebooks 1924–1954*, trans. Shaun Whiteside, Quartet Books, London 1989.
Bachmann	Robert C. Bachmann: *Karajan. Anmerkungen zu einer Karriere* (Düsseldorf/Wien, 1983). English edition: *Karajan: Notes on a Career*, trans. Shaun Whiteside, Quartet Books, London 1990.
Letters	*Wilhelm Furtwängler: Briefe* (4th edition; Wiesbaden, 1980).
Geissmar	Berta Geissmar: *Musik im Schatten der Politik* (Zürich/Freiburg im Breisgau, 1945). See also new shortened critical edition (Zürich, 1985). English edition: *The Baton and the Jackboot*, trans. Berta Geissmar, Columbus Books, London 1988.
Gillis 1	Daniel Gillis: *Furtwängler Recalled* (2nd edition; Zürich/New York, 1971).
Gillis II	Daniel Gillis: *Furtwängler and America* (New York, 1970).
Muck	Peter Muck: *Einhundert Jahre Berliner Philharmonisches Orchester*, vol 2: 1922–1982 (Tutzing, 1982).

Riess	Curt Riess: *Furtwängler. Musik und Politik* (Bern, 1953).
Legacy	*Wilhelm Furtwängler: Vermächtnis. Nachgelassene Schriften* (5th edition; Wiesbaden, 1975).
Wessling	Bernd W. Wessling: *Furtwängler. Eine kritische Biographie* (Stuttgart, 1985).

Wessling's book cannot be considered as a product of historical research; the Wilhelm Furtwängler Association was right to warn of its dangers. Wessling has been shown up for inventing sources and asserting as fact things which are false. On the basis of the findings of several legal hearings it is permissible to describe him as a forger, and to state that all his assertions collapse as soon as proof is required. See also Harvey Sachs: *Toscanini* (Munich 1980), p. 285.

1 (pp. 1–26)
THE SCAPEGOAT

1. The mutual antagonism of anti-Semites and those who hate anti-Semites has been part of history ever since the emancipation of the Jews. At the highpoint of anti-Semitic feeling in the Reich even a personality of Thomas Mann's standing participated, unfortunately on the wrong side. By contrast, the Jewish philosopher and cultural critic Theodor Lessing (1872–1933), after decades of fighting racial chauvinism, was slain in exile in Marienbad at the hands of a Nazi murderer. At the time a Zionist response came from the Hamburg author, Cheskel Zwi Klötzel, with an aggressive essay entitled 'The Great Hatred' (see *Janus* 11/2, November 1912, pp. 57–60). Expressions of Jewish counter-hatred in the light of the internal pogrom carried out in the Nazi state, such as Theodore H. Kaufman's book, *Germany Must Perish* (Newark, N.J., 1941), also served German propaganda as welcome material with which to incite anti-Jewish hatred.
2. The comparison refers to the French '*camps de hébergement*', more commonly referred to by the press and in every-day speech as concentration camps. The comparison is not the author's own, but one made by emigrants from the Reich, who knew what they were talking about, e.g. Friedrich Wolf (see Alfred Kantorowicz: *Exil in Frankreich*, Bremen 1971, pp. 74, 96), Arthur Koestler (see Arthur Koestler: *The Scum of the Earth*, London 1968), Walter Mehring (see Walter Mehring: *Wir müssen weiter: Fragmente aus dem Exil*, Düsseldorf 1979, p. 83), Lotte Eisner (see Lotte Eisner: *Ich hatte einst ein schönes Vaterland: Memoiren*, Heidelberg 1984, p. 199). An absurd comparison between the British transit camps for illegal Palestinian immigrants after 1945 with Dachau, Belsen and Maidanek (!) can be found in Ira Hirschmann (see Ira Hirschmann: *The Embers Still Burn*, New York 1949, p. 34).
3. See *Hessische Nachrichten*, no. 45, 16 May 1946.
4. Erika Mann: 'The Furtwaengler Ovation' (*New York Herald Tribune*, Paris, 6 June 1947). For German text see Elisabeth Furtwängler: *Über Wilhelm Furtwängler*, Wiesbaden 1979, pp. 135–7. This is a reader's letter printed

on the page 'From the Mailbag', not – as E. F. said, and Wessling adopted – a telegram. Frau Mann's sense of events was somewhat deficient. As early as 1937 Hitler passed the following judgement on Furtwängler: 'That man is one of the most unpleasant people I know' (see Victor de Kowa: *Als ich noch Prinz war von Arcadien*, Nürnberg 1955, p. 358). Frau Mann was also a pitiless opponent; when WF was being considered for a guest engagement in Chicago in 1948, she tried to provoke the well-known journalist Walter Winchell into conducting a smear campaign by sending him letters containing slanderous allegations about the conductor's 'Nazi past'. See Erika Mann: *Briefe und Antworten vol. 1: 1922–1950*, Munich 1984, pp. 250–2.

5. Bruno Walter to WF, Beverly Hills, 13 January 1949, see Bruno Walter: *Briefe 1894–1962*, Frankfurt am Main 1969, pp. 308–9.

6. Fritz von Unruh: *Der nie verlor*, Bern 1948, p. 263.

7. Lies (*Basler Arbeiter-Zeitung*, 3 March 1948). WF did not congratulate Hitler 'warmly' on the invasion of Austria, nor did he conduct the Horst-Wessel Song, nor did he receive 'huge sums of money'; the quotation does not originate from the Horst-Wessel Song.

8. 'Zum Fall Furtwängler: Es bleibt dabei', *Tageblatt der Stadt Zürich*, 5 June 1948. The censors were silent – no doubt intentionally – about some easily available evidence, even though it came from a solid, well-known 'left-wing' author, namely Heinrich Mann: 'The regime's cultural propaganda, which is aimed at throttling our people's shared heritage, is complemented by the use of force and by spying. The innumerable political agents with which one country is infiltrating all others, and the assassinations, conspiracies, and corruption which are their doing, are all to remain secret; and people are stupid enough to say nothing. Up front in the limelight there is a marvellous orchestra performing the old German music in the capitals of the world, on the regime's incomprehensible assumption that their audiences might think it was the regime's own music, and hold the regime responsible not for assassinations, but for music' (Heinrich Mann: 'Ziele der Volksfront', *Neue Weltbühne*, 30/XII/ 37. See also Heinrich Mann: *Verteidigung der Kultur: Antifaschistische Streitschriften und Essays*, Hamburg 1960, pp. 295–6). Before Mann wrote this the BPhO had performed in the following capitals: with Eugen Jochum in Riga, Reval, Helsinki, Stockholm, Oslo, Copenhagen; with WF in Paris and London.

9. See 'Einfach untragbar. Zum Verbot der Zürcher Furtwängler-Konzerte', *Volksrecht* no. 46, 23 February 1945.

10. *National-Zeitung*, Basel, to WF, 26 April 1952, signed by A. Moser. Source WFA. This source anticipates others. Some of the documents are in private hands.

11. Unsigned typescript, December 1948. Source WFA. Edward L. Ryerson was president of the Chicago Orchestral Association, George Kuyper the manager, and Aaron a member of the committee.

12. 'Das war Furtwängler', *Israelitisches Wochenblatt*, Zürich, 10 December 1954.

13. Ira Hirschmann: 'Setting the Record Straight on Furtwängler', NYT, 30 September 1983.

14. *New York Herald Tribune*, 11 December 1945, and quotation in an unpublished letter to the NYT by Gillis, 25 October 1983.
15. ARD TV transmission 'Dresden: Theaterplatz 1' by Klaus Lang, produced by SFB 1985, script in author's possession.
16. Ludolf Herbst: 'Deutschland im Krieg 1939–1945' in Ploetz: *Das Dritte Reich. Ursprünge, Ereignisse, Wirkungen*, eds. Martin Broszat and Norbert Frei, Freiburg/Würzburg, 1983, p. 69. Wolfgang Porth in *Konkret*, March 1984, p. 66 describes a concert in the armaments factory in Borsig in 1944 by the BPhO under WF as even more shameful, an 'intellectualisation of barbarity'; he failed to discover that WF did not conduct such a concert in Borsig in 1944 or at any other time. Karajan conducted the BPhO at Borsig in front of armaments workers in 1942.
17. Tamara Lewaja/Oksana Leont'ewa: *Paul Hindemith. Shisn' i twortschestwo*, Moscow 1974, p. 89.
18. Anna Geissmar to WF, London, 26 October 1945. Source WFA.
19. Notes 1929, p. 113 of MS, unpublished. Source WFA. The published edition (Wiesbaden 1980) contains only some of the surviving papers, because the editors Elisabeth Furtwängler and Dr Günter Birkner were unable to add explanatory comments.
20. Notes 1924, p. 69 of MS, unpublished. Source WFA.
21. Notes, p. 128.
22. Notes 1937, p. 159 of MS, unpublished. Source: WFA. He was thinking of the *Buch vom persönlichen Leben* which was banned by the RSHA.
23. See Harry Graf Kessler: *Tagebücher 1918–1937*, Frankfurt am Main 1961, p. 733.
24. Notes, p. 198.
25. Ibid.
26. Notes 1939-IV, p. 30 of MS, unpublished. Source WFA.
27. Christoph Steding: *Das Reich und die Krankheit der europäischen Kultur*, Hamburg 1938, p. 481.
28. Ibid., pp. 251–2.
29. Notes, p. 163.
30. Johanna Thoms-Paetow: 'Wilhelm Furtwängler und die Musik', AMZ LXI/41, 12 October 1934, see p. 555.
31. Oswald Schrenk: *Wilhelm Furtwängler*, Berlin 1940, p. 14.
32. Notes 1930, p. 10 of MS, unpublished. Source WFA.

2 (pp. 27–56)
THE DYNAMIC STRENGTH OF THE NATIONAL MOVEMENT

1. A. Berndt to B. Geissmar, Berlin, 27 July 1927. Source WFA.
2. WF to Chancellor of the Reich Brüning, St. Moritz, 30 August 1930. Source BA R 43 I/828, pp. 174ff.
3. BA R 43 I/828 p. 175.
4. Adolf Hitler: Introduction to the programme notes for the 1934 Bayreuth Festival, see Paul Bülow: 'Der Führer und der Bayreuther Kulturkreis', *Die Bühne* V/8, 20 April 1939, p. 183.
5. Ottmar Weber to Albert Osthoff, Bayreuth, 7 January 1933. Source WFA.
6. Notes 1933-X, pp. 17–18, 20–20' of MS, unpublished. Source WFA.
7. H. H. Stuckenschmidt: 'Furtwängler äussert sich', *Melos* XI/5–6, May–June 1932, pp. 196–201.

8. *Goebbels-Reden*: Volume 1 1932–1939, Düsseldorf 1971, p. 225. Speech on 17 June 1935.

9. Ibid., p. 219.

10. K.U.: 'Furtwängler und die Philharmoniker', *Westfälische Zeitung*, 23 February 1933.

11. Hans Otto Redecker: 'Grosser Abend mit Furtwängler', *Westfälische Neueste Nachrichten*, 23 February 1933.

12. A. Posse to Göring, 17 March 1933. Source BDC.

13. 'Decision', 12 March 1933. Source BDC. Peter Heyworth in *Otto Klemperer: His Life and Times, Vol. 1 1885–1933* (Cambridge 1983, p. 413 footnote) plays down and draws a veil over what was going on when he claims that five days after that *Rigoletto* rehearsal, 'Busch asked for unlimited leave from the Dresden Staatsoper'.

14. See Fritz Busch: *Aus dem Leben eines Musikers*, Fischer-TB, Frankfurt am Main 1982, p. 204. Busch cites only the outline of the text of the decision, sometimes incorrectly, because he did not have access to the documents which had been left in the Reich. The editor of his book, who could have had access to them, seems to have been incapable of naming even the four singers who stood their ground.

15. WF to Gilbert Back, Clarens, 24 March 1949. Source WFA.

16. Fritz Busch: *Aus dem Leben eines Musikers*, p. 206. Furtwängler is not mentioned once in this work, which was first published in 1949.

17. Grete Busch: *Fritz Busch, Dirigent*, Frankfurt am Main 1970, pp. 64–5.

18. 'Ovationen in der Staatsoper. Festaufführung der *Meistersinger*', BBZ, no. 137, 22 March 1933.

19. J. Goebbels: *Vom Kaiserhof zur Reichskanzlei*, Munich 1934.

20. Thomas Mann: *Tagebücher 1933–4*, Frankfurt am Main 1977, p. 15.

21. See the relevant documents in Joseph Wulf: *Musik im Dritten Reich. Eine Dokumentation*, Gütersloh 1963, pp. 102–3.

22. The Berlin branch of the Conti News Agency, 3 April 1933, author's copy. The procedure was as follows; first of all the politically responsible discussed the matter; their decision was then conveyed to the professionals – who were made to take public responsibility! It was taken for granted that nobody would dare to object.

23. Max Hamm to Reich Commissioner Rust, Bielefeld, 5 April 1933. Source WFA.

24. 'Der Rundfunk gegen hetzende Musiker', VB, no. 96, 6 April 1933.

25. *Hakenkreuzbanner*, 20 March 1933.

26. Fritz Kreisler to Toscanini, BBZ, no. 163, 6 April 1933. The violinist's biographer – Louis P. Lochner: *Fritz Kreisler* (Vienna 1957) – 'forgot' to mention this appeal, even though as an American journalist in Berlin he was well informed. Kreisler's position was the same as that of the national right-wingers, who bewailed the 'tragic fate' of Germany's defeat in the world war they themselves had helped to engineer, and the reforms in government which took place in the republic.

27. At first he made sure to obtain sufficient cover from Hitler. WF, who clearly wanted to denounce the new rulers' anti-Semitism, became impatient, and reminded the minister by sending him a 'revised' version of his letter, in which he asked Goebbels either to ring him or speak to him 'personally after the concert tonight' – in other words on 10 April.

'In view of my many years' activity in the eye of the German public, and my inner oneness with German music, I am allowing myself to draw your attention to certain happenings in Germany's music business which in my opinion are not perhaps absolutely necessary for the process of rejuvenating our national self-esteem, a process we all welcome gratefully and joyfully.

'I feel that I am first and foremost an artist, and that I am therefore apolitical in the sense of party politics. Art and artists exist to create love, not hate; to unite, not to divide. Ultimately there is only one dividing line I recognise: that between good and bad art. However, while the dividing line between Jews and non-Jews is being drawn with a downright merciless theoretical precision, that other dividing line, the one which in the long run is so important for our music life, yes, the decisive dividing line between good and bad, seems to have far too little significance attributed to it.

'Musical activity today, already weakened by the world crisis, the radio, etc., cannot tolerate any more experiments. Music cannot be made contingent in the same way as other essentials such as potatoes and bread. If concerts offer nothing, then people will not attend; that is why the question of QUALITY is not just a nice idea: it is of vital importance. If the fight against Judaism concentrates on those artists who are themselves rootless and destructive and who seek to succeed through kitsch, sterile virtuosity and the like, then that is quite acceptable; the fight against these people and the attitude they embody (as, unfortunately, do many non-Jews) cannot be pursued thoroughly or systematically enough. If, however, this campaign is also directed at truly great artists, then it ceases to be in the interests of Germany's cultural life. If only because great artists, in whatever country, are far too rare for any country to be able to afford to forego their participation without cultural losses.

'It must therefore be stated clearly that men such as Walter, Klemperer, Reinhardt etc. must be allowed to exercise their talents in Germany in the future as well, in exactly the same way as Kreisler, Huberman, Schnabel and other great instrumentalists of the Jewish race. It is only just that we Germans should bear in mind that in the past we had in Joseph Joachim one of the greatest violinists and teachers in the German classical tradition, and in Mendelssohn even a great German composer – for Mendelssohn is a part of Germany's musical history.

'Therefore I repeat: our fight should be against the rootless, subversive and destructive spirits, but not against the real artist, who in his art is always, whatever one thinks of it personally, a creative figure who "loves" his materials, and as such helps build up our culture. This is what I mean when I make my appeal to you, in the name of German art, in the hope that perhaps irreversible damage which would disadvantage the reputation of German art and culture can be prevented from taking place.' (WF's bequest, loan from Andreas Furtwängler; typescript. The editorial markings were made by Berta Geissmar!)

28. Commentary in the DAZ, 12 April 1933.
29. Thomas Mann: *Tagebücher 1933–4*, Frankfurt am Main 1977, pp. 47–8. Entry for 13 April 1933.

30. Nikolaus Pevsner: 'Zum Briefwechsel Furtwängler-Goebbels', *Zeitwende* IX/7, April 1933, p. 70.
31. The correspondence has been published several times, and quoted extensively, e.g. Geissmar pp. 96–9, Riess pp. 142–4, Wessling pp. 260–3.
32. 'Es gibt nur gute und schlechte Kunst!' *Neue Freie Presse*, morning edition, Vienna, 12 April 1933.
33. 'Zu einigen Thesen des Herrn Goebbels', *23*, no. 11/12, 30 June 1933. The unsigned essay in the Vienna music paper was written by Ernst Křenek.
34. Dr John Worpohn and Hilde Stiastny to WF, Berlin, 11 April 1933. Source WFA.
35. Letter to WF, sender unidentified, 11 April 1933. Source WFA.

3 (pp. 57–102)
TACTICAL MOVES

1. Christoph Steding: *Das Reich und die Krankheit der europäischen Kultur*, Hamburg 1938, p. 411.
2. The Mayor, Kunst 4, Hafemann, to the BPhO, 22 April 1933. Source BA R55/1146, p. 141.
3. 'Eine Stunde bei den Philharmonikern', *Neue Mannheimer Zeitung*, 27 April 1933.
4. There is no documentary evidence of the 'banquet' described by Geissmar (pp. 102–3) and Riess (p. 151). The 'Obersturmbannführer, Brigadeführer, Gauleiter und Kulturwarte' mentioned by Riess were added by him for dramatic effect; he was however surpassed by Wessling (p. 266), who talked of 'senior Nazi officials from the whole area', who he alleged attended the concert.
5. H. Eckert: 'Ausklang der Akademiekonzerte', *Hakenkreuzbanner*, 29 April 1933. The date refers to the victory of the Nazi Party at the last Reichstag elections.
6. WF to the director of the Mannheim National Orchestra, Karlsruhe, 29 April 1933. Source BA R55/1138, pp. 105ff.
7. WF to Goebbels, Baden-Baden, 30 April 1933. Source BA R55/1138, pp. 102–3.
8. Facsimile of original in Muck, p. 104. The number of Jews given in the leaflet was too high; in January 1933 there were 525,000 living in the Reich, see H. A. Strauss: 'Jewish Emigration from Germany', Almanac of the Leo Baeck Institute XXV, NY 1980, p. 317.
9. W. Wagner to Albert Osthoff, Berlin, 12 May 1933. Source WFA.
10. See WF, *Ton und Wort*, Wiesbaden 1982.
11. Rudolf Ploderer in: *23*, no 11/12, 30 June 1933, p. 35.
12. This typical example of cultural barbarity and racial hysteria should have made the headlines of the world press. However, even those emigrants who had a head for publicity failed to take this classic opportunity to make fools of their opponents. Only one emigrant – and even then only years later, took the matter up: see Paul Walter Jacob 'Dr Karl Muck', *Argentinisches Tageblatt*, 5 March 1940, and P. W. J.: *Zeitklänge*, Buenos Aires 1945, pp. 108–9.
13. Heinrich Dankert: 'Johannes Brahms' Vaterhaus', *Hamburger Fremdenblatt*, morning edition, no. 143, 25 May 1933.

14. Walter Steinhauer: 'Der deutsche Meister Johannes Brahms', *Die Sendung* X/39, 22 September 1933.

15. K. Straube to WF, Leipzig, 30 May 1933. Source BDC.

16. See Walter Hofer (ed.): *Der Nationalsozialismus. Dokumente 1933–1945*, Fischer-TB, 3rd edition, Frankfurt am Main 1977, p. 131.

17. R. Hernried to WF, Berlin, 1 June 1933. Source BDC.

18. Erich Kleiber to WF, Barmen, 4 April 1921. Source WFA.

19. Thomas Mann: *Tagebücher 1933–4*, Frankfurt am Main 1977, p. 46. Entry for 10 April 1933.

20. Ibid., p. 473. Entry for 15 July 1934.

21. H. Gagnebin: 'De la situation musicale en Allemagne', *Journal de Genève*, no. 298, 1 November 1933.

22. MS, pencil, no date. Source WFA. Transcribed by author.

23. Although he was an 'Aryan', the Danish singer was for many years not considered 'pure-blooded'. He was on the second edition of the notorious 'Semi-Kürschner' list, which was published as 'Sigilla Veri' in 1931. He was denounced because of his 'suspicious' name, which was however only his stage name, and the denunciation was repeated, this time with no question mark, in all three editions of the notorious lexicon *Das musikalische Juden-ABC* (Brückner/Rock); some of the 1938 third edition was corrected before printing.

After 1933 the question of racial descent was of considerable concern to musicians; it affected them all, including foreigners. Since 1929 Melchior had had a contract every year for guest performances at the Staatsoper and City Opera in Berlin, lasting from September till December. The last of these was in the 1932 season. His contract was not extended. For this reason he was entered as 'no contract' in the 1934 German Stage Year Book; he is also missing from the – corrected – lists of engagements authorised by Prime Minister Göring and Education Minister Rust on 30 June 1933. The music lexicons, which all copy each other, contradict this, and suggest that Melchior had performed uninterruptedly in Berlin from 1925 to 1939 (e.g. *Riemann-Musiklexikon*, section on musicians, Mainz 1961, p. 192, and K. J. Kutsch/Leo Riemens: *Unvergängliche Stimmen. Sängerlexikon*, 2nd edition, Bern 1982. p. 459); by way of contrast, a list which got it right because it asked the musician himself is *Kürschners Deutscher Musiker-Kalender*, Berlin 1954, column 816.

In actual fact Melchior was widely boycotted in the Reich; WF knew this, as an entry into his pocket diary on 3 June 1933 shows: '(!!!) Melchior salary or pension (!!!) up to 800'. After Melchior had been engaged – 'by agreement of the Reich government and with the support of Reichscommissioner Hinkel' – for the politically desirable German season in Buenos Aires, which was to run from June 1933 onwards, conducted by Fritz Busch, the KfdK complained about the 'watered-down internationalism' of the artists sent to Argentina, and demanded they be replaced by individuals whose person and thinking 'carry the stamp of the pure German' (see 'Deutsches Operngastspiel in Südamerika', in *Deutsche Bühnenkorrespondenz* II/31, 24/X/33, p. 4). In this situation Melchior thought a proclamation of his political 'soundness' would be expedient: 'On one occasion Melchior was trying to end a dispute and said, "Remember that you are representing Hitler here", to which Seider, the tenor, responded, "I couldn't care less." Melchior answered, "Well, it is a shame that you, a German, couldn't care less. For myself however, a Dane who has been active in German music for twenty years, it does matter!" ' (unsigned report by an agent of the Nazi Party's foreign affairs office, which was sent to the Prussian Ministry of Culture on 9 October 1933. Source BDC file on Busch).

When the Reichstheaterkammer was formed, Melchior was given a membership card, no. 526/2968. The file on him contains a handwritten note that he had not produced proof of descent (!) and his membership was cancelled on 1 October 1935, because 'according to statement by his wife 11.7.34 he will not perform in Germany any longer'. Such incidents strengthened suspicions of a racial 'defect'. However – perhaps protected by Göring's statement 'I am the one to decide who is a Jew' – he did make sporadic appearances at later dates, for example at the Berlin Staatsoper on 3 and 12 May 1936; 10, 11 and 13 April 1937, and Easter 1939 in the German Opera House, Berlin.

24. WF to Reichsminister Rust, Paris, 4 June 1933. Source BDC.
25. Ibid.
26. G. Busch: *Fritz Busch. Dirigent*, Frankfurt am Main 1970, p. 65.
27. Carl Braun to Hinkel, 10 April 1933. Source BDC.
28. Kaufmann of the German Embassy in Buenos Aires to the Foreign Office, 25 April 1933. Source BDC.
29. Neither Busch nor his widow mentioned the name of a singer in their memoirs, let alone the politico-cultural background. Hinkel was not coy about stating proudly at the general meeting of the Deutschen Kunstgesellschaft on 13 July: 'The guest season in Buenos Aires has been arranged to counter propaganda about German atrocities. It has been misunderstood by many in Germany. The main aim is to have a positive effect and act as a counterbalance, as in the case of Ebert' (see BA R56 I/97).
30. ProMi to PMWKuV, 12 October 1933. Source BDC.
31. Letter from the cellist Fritz Schröder to Hitler, Berlin, 18 January 1934. Source BA R 55/1147, p. 43.
32. The author begs for the reader's understanding; the means required to discover the identity of 'Fr.' would have been contrary to his ethics as a researcher.
33. B. Geissmar to WF, London, 12 June 1933. Source WFA.
34. Ibid., 12 June, evening. Source WFA. Hans Sellschopp, head of Lübeck's KfdK group and later *inter alia* head of the concert department of the RMK; Dr Franz Metzner, personal adviser to the Ministry of the Interior, from 1 July 1933 ministerial adviser, and later an SS-Oberführer.
35. Ibid.
36. B. Geissmar to WF, London, 13 June 1933. Source WFA. Dr Erwin Pulay, a medical doctor in Vienna, was one of her many acquaintances.
37. Walter Abendroth: 'Führerloses Bayreuth', AMZ LX/24–25, 16 June 1933, p. 328.
38. 'Erlass über das Konzertwesen in Preussen', BBZ 28 June 1933. Goebbels took responsibility for the decree and extended it to the whole Reich, sending telegrams to all the provincial councils and cultural authorities asking them to acknowledge the decree. However for various reasons the commission deciding on programme content, commonly known as the

Furtwängler Commission, hardly ever met, lasted only a short time, and after Furtwängler's withdrawal was ruled for a time by Strauss.

39. *re* Dr Furtwängler's suggestion, undated typescript. Source BDC.
40. *re* request from Prof. Bernhard Sekles. Source BDC.
41. See Gillis I, p. 108.
42. *re* Prof. Carl Flesch remaining at the Music College. Source BDC.
43. Theophil Stengel/Herbert Gerigk: *Lexikon der Juden in der Musik*, published by NSDAP Institute, *re* Jewish question, volume 21; Berlin 1940, p. 76.
44. RPA Berlin, press section. Rundspruch no. 44, 5 May 1943. Source BA ZSg. 115/17 p. 20.
45. There is documentary evidence to prove that Furtwängler helped at least eighty people who were at risk; he assisted many more by talking to them in person or on the telephone. There is reliable evidence of his help when the following were in racial or political difficulties: Hermann Abendroth, Viktor Adler, Georg Armin, Gilbert Back, Erich Bader, Anna Bahr-Mildenburg, Albert Bassermann, Oskar Bie, Elsa Bienenfeld, Heinrich Boell, Sergei Bortkiewicz, Walter Braunfels, Hugo Burghauser, Fritz Busch, Fritz Alexander Cohen, Jan Dahmen, Issay Dobrowen, George Dohrn, Arnold Ebel, Bill Fiedler, Werner Finck, Ernst Fischer, Carl Flesch, Hans Flesch, Gottfried Freiberg, Norbert Furreg, Berta Geissmar, Richard Geyer, Simon Goldberg, Nikolai Graudan, Josef Hadraba, Rudolf Hartmann, Siegmund von Hausegger, Johannes Heidenreich, Waldemar Henke, Robert Hernried, Friedrich Herzfeld, Theodor Hess, Walla Hess and a pupil of hers whose name is not known, Paul Hindemith, Franz von Hoesslin, (Dr Wilhelm ?) Jarosch, Rudolf Jettel, Johannes Joachim, Fritz Jöde, Kurt Jooss, Robert Kahn, Hermann Graf Keyserling, Arnold Klatte, Otto Klemperer, Raymond Klibansky, Hans Knappertsbusch, (Karl) Köhler, Hugo Kolberg, (?) Krebs, Karlrobert Kreiten, Josef Krips, Richard Krotschak, Felix Lederer, Frida Leider, Erich Leist, Mark Hendrik Leuschner, Hermann Lüddecke, Hermann Wilhelm Ludwig, Herbert Maisch, Karl Maurer, Ludwig Misch, Ernst Morawec, Hans Joachim Moser, Eugen Papst, Hans Pfitzner, Emil Praetorius, Günter Raphael, Max Reinhardt, Alfred Reucker, Otto Rieger, Walther Riezler, Curt Sachs, Hermann Samuel, Hans Schmidt-Isserstedt, Dr. med. Johann Ludwig Schmitt, Friedrich Schnapp, Arnold Schönberg, Friedrich Schorr, Carl Schuricht, Leo Schwarz, Hans Schwieger, Dr. Hermann Seelig, Willi Seibert, Bernhard Sekles, (?) Speydel, Karl Straube, Hugo Strelitzer, Heinrich Strobel, Hans Heinz Stuckenschmidt, Jani Szántó, Gerhard Taschner, Emil Telmanyi, Heinz Tietjen, Max Trapp, Georg Vollerthun, Bruno Walter, Felix Wolfes, Richard Wolff, Heinrich Wollheim, Ludwig Wüllner, Victor Zuckerkandl, a nephew of Fritz Zweig. See note 32 *re* cases where no forename is given. The detailed material concerning such attempts to help, which was available just after the war, has disappeared. After his first visit to B. Geissmar, Martin Hürlimann, the manager of the Atlantis publishing house in Zürich, wrote to WF on 2 August 1945: 'Furthermore she says she had one or two cases full of interesting files, [. . .] and also a large grey suitcase containing correspondence with Bayreuth, Pfitzner etc. and everything taken away from G. at the time. She says the material is also interesting because it contains all the letters requesting help written to you from 1933 onwards.'

This evidence still existed shortly before or just after the end of the war;

Boleslav Barlog claimed in a letter to the *Kurier* to have seen one or more files. In connection with the de-nazification process which was about to take place, WF apparently gave this, along with other 'decriminalising' evidence, to the US journalist Curt Riess, who passed it on to General McClure; once it reached the upper levels of the US occupying forces command, all traces are lost. The evidence was not available at the commission in December 1946. Riess claims that it is no longer accessible if it is in Washington.

46. Norman Lebrecht; *Discord, Conflict and the Making of Music* (NY 1983, p. 151) makes the fantastic claim that 'the Nazis [. . .] drove him to make a quixotic attempt to entice foreign soloists to play in Berlin'.

47. WF to B. Huberman, Berlin, 30 June 1933. Transcription. Source WFA.

48. Clara Klatte, born Senff von Pilsach, to WF, Berlin, 1 July 1933. Source BDC.

49. See Louis P. Lochner: *Fritz Kreisler*, Vienna 1957, p. 228.

50. WF to B. Geissmar, undated. Source WFA. the word [same] has been added which makes sense; the original is illegible.

51. The letter to him which is mentioned here has been published; see Letters p. 76, unfortunately no information about Leist. See also the letter to Schönberg, p. 75.

52. B. Geissmar to WF, Berlin 10 July 1933. Source WFA. Rudolf Hartmann was director at the opera in Nürnberg, Herbert Maisch was the dismissed intendant from Mannheim, Felix Wolfes was a Jewish conductor, formerly in Essen, Julius Kapp was artistic director at the Staatsoper, Berlin; Hi = Hinkel, Ha = Havemann, T = Tietjen.

53. Biographers and music historians have either ignored this letter or quoted it with the wrong date and deviations from the original text. On 7 March 1936 Huberman published an 'Open letter to German intellectuals' in the *Manchester Guardian*, in which he also attacked Furtwängler; in the letter he talked of his outrage at the attacks on German girls who were having affairs with Jews, and especially of a case in Nürnberg in which a girl who was considered 'a disgrace to her race' was driven insane by this inhuman pursuit. There is no evidence to show that the artist had similar difficulties coming to terms with the fact that, after the liberation of occupied countries, e.g. France, Belgium, Holland, Norway, witch-hunts were carried out by courageous heroes of the resistance against women who had had affairs with German soldiers; in some cases these led to murder.

54. B. Geissmar to WF, Berlin, 13 July 1933. Source WFA. Henry Goldmann was a Jewish art collector who had given Menuhin a Stradivarius as a gift.

55. Memorandum from Prof. Dr E. Hoffmann, Heidelberg, 4 July 1933. Source BDC.

56. WF: Note without sender or date. Source BDC.

57. Prof. Dr R. Klibansky to the author, Montreal, 9 November 1984.

58. Boleslav Barlog: 'Für Furtwängler', *Der Kurier*, Berlin 25 January 1947.

59. Gerullis to Hinkel, undated (around 18 July 1933). Source BDC.

60. B. Geissmar to WF, 18 July 1933. Source WFA.

61. 'Freie Künstlertätigkeit ausländischer und nichtarischer musiker', *Die Musikpflege* IV/6, September 1933. p. 185.

62. As note 60; omission in the original.

63. WF: draft on the subject of art and politics, typescript, 16 October 1933. Source WFA. WF appears to have overlooked the fact that state and party had an overwhelming majority in the Prussian Staatsrat; members included not only Himmler and Freisler, a large part of the SS leadership, including SA-Oberführer Prince August Wilhelm of Prussia, but also figureheads such as General Litzmann. The 'professional' element was represented by WF and also some bank directors, university professors, the Catholic bishop of Osnabrück, Dr Berning, and the protestant 'Reichsbishop', Ludwig Müller.

64. WF to Huberman, Berlin, 27 July 1933. Handwritten. Source Huberman Archive, Tel Aviv, Ref. 481/k 1.

65. Open letter from Hanno Konopath to Tietjen, *Nationalsozialistische Partei-korrespondenz*, Folge 69, 11 April 1932, p. 6.

66. P. Schwers: 'Eine neue Tannhäuser-Parodie', AMZ LX/7, 17 February 1933. pp. 87–8.

67. P. Schwers: 'Unwälzungen im Opernleben', AMZ LX/11, 17 March 1933, p. 142.

68. 'Umbau der Berliner Bühnen,' *National-Zeitung*, Essen, no. 144, 27 May 1933.

69. WF to Rust, Paris, 4 June 1933. Source BDC. This letter was an addendum to the main letter written on the same day.

70. WF to Hitler, 4 July 1933. Source WFA.

71. The Reich Federation of German Musicians, Havemann to State Secretary Hinkel, PMWKuV, 12 July 1933. Source BDC.

72. Report from Rosenberg's department, undated, unsigned, no addressee. Source BA NS 8/124, p. 43.

73. As note 70.

74. WF to the member of the BPhO, Berlin, 1 August 1933. Source BA R 55/1147, p. 25.

4 (pp. 103–146)
IN TIME, OUT OF STEP

1. Notes 1933, p. 116 of MS, unpublished. Source WFA. Furtwängler's opposition to Jews controlling the press was the same as that of Thomas Mann; both generalised from isolated incidents.

2. WF: Memorandum addressed in own handwriting to the 'Führer', undated, p. 1. Source WFA.

3. Ibid., pp. 2, 3.

4. WF: further memorandum 'Conversation with the Führer', August 1933. pp. 3–4. Source WFA.

5. Ibid., pp. 7–8.

6. Geissmar, p. 125.

7. WF: draft, MS, undated, not addressed. Source WFA. Transcription by author.

8. WF: draft, typescript, handwritten comment 'F Hitler 8.8.33'. Source WFA.

9. W. Rath-Rex: report to the central office, 17 August 1933. Source BDC. Rath-Rex often made himself of use in this way; for example in April 1933 he mediated between the director of the Deutsche Grammophon

AG, Hugo Wünsch (who wanted to make everyone making records join the KfdK) and Hinkel.

Further denunciations against WF are documented, attempts by party members to draw attention to themselves. One is very obvious; the Stuttgart music critic Karly Grunsky, who worked on the *NS-Kurier*, had been anti-Semitic for many years. He was the regional spokesman for the NSDAP at the end of the twenties, and he attacked the conductor in his book *Der Kampf um deutsche Musik* (Stuttgart 1933) – it was only a passing comment, but all the more effective because of that: 'Furtwängler stood up for Jews, and seems to feel comfortable defending the moderns with words and deeds and vouching for Frank Wedekind, who really is not any of his concern' (p. 71).

The combination of racism and defamation of the modern, including the 'degenerate' writer who had died in 1918, was a well-tried weapon. Any detail could serve as the pretext for a denunciation. At a congress of German musicians held on 17 February 1934 WF – and Strauss – failed to make the 'German greeting' by raising their right arms, which provoked some fanatical followers to call for them to be sent to the concentration camps; in a letter to the national leadership of the NSDAP dated 24 February, Havemann deepened the accusation: 'If worthy officials are to be dismissed from their positions for similar conduct, then at least it should be made clear to the Prussian Staatsrat that he [Strauss] should fit in with the spirit of the Third Reich. One should be able to demand the same German attitude from the greatest artists as from the most enthusiastic and simple Hitler Youth member. I enclose some copies of my letter, and would ask that the national leadership inform the Prussian prime minister, Göring, of it. Given that the majority of German musicians have never been Marxists, the situation might easily turn ugly if similar incidents should be repeated' (see G. Splitt: *Richard Strauss 1933–5* . . . Doctoral thesis, Freiburg 1985, p. 164). Hans Bullerian, a party member, composer and functionary in the KfdK, and Otto Hempel used the same occasion as the basis of a letter to Hess, Hitler's deputy, on 20 July 1934.

10. BPhO to the ProMi, 18 August 1933. Source BA R55/1147, pp. 54–5. Max Donisch, Pg. no. 410,603 since September 1930, head of the music department of the German radio.

11. Notes 1933, p. 93.

12. Hugo Fetting: *Die Geschichte der deutschen Staatsoper* (Berlin/DDR, 1955) 'forgot' to mention the fiftieth anniversary celebrations, in order to be able to claim: 'Richard Wagner's work, which had been excessively nurtured in the years prior to 1933 by Heinz Tietjen, was now misused as a tool in fascist propaganda'; pp. 249–250.

13. Enclosed with letter from Fritz Schröder to Hitler, 18 January 1934. Source BA R55/1147, p. 44.

14. P. Schwers: 'Frisches Blühen im Berliner Musikleben', AMZ LX/38, 22 September 1933, p. 454.

15. Ibid., p. 455.

16. Filed record by Mutzenbecher, 23 August 1933. Source BA R 56I/97.

17. Record for files by State Secretary Funk, 27 October 1933, in response to letter from OB on 26 October. Source BA R55/1141, p. 65.

18. Fritz Schröder to Hitler, 18 January 1934. Source BA R 55/1147, p. 35.
19. Hinkel to Rust, Minister of Culture, 26 October 1933. Source BDC.
20. German consulate to the ProMi, St. Louis, 17 November 1933. Source BA R 55/1175, p. 144.
21. Fritz Busch to the German Arts Association, 12 December 1933. Source BA R 55/1175, p. 138.
22. Sir Thomas Beecham: 'The Berlin Orchestra', *Daily Telegraph*, 20 January 1934.
23. Ibid. The BPhO office prepared a partly erroneous rough translation for their notice-board, which Muck (p. 109) has printed. Beecham was only thinking about anti-Semitic changes; he did not notice that fifteen musicians who were members of the party had also left.
24. e.g. BBZ no. 473, 9 October 1934.
25. See Th. E. = Theodor Eberhard: 'Furtwängler in der Philharmonie', *Der Angriff*, 14 February 1934. This was the pseudonym written under by Friedrich Mahling, Pg. no. 2,588,722 since May 1933, and at that time still in full favour with Goebbels.
26. See E.R. = Erich Roeder: 'Vater und Sohn am Pult', *Der Angriff*, no. 60, 12 March 1935.
27. Otto Steinhagen: 'Neuntes Philharmonisches Konzert unter Max Fiedler', BBZ, 12 March 1935.
28. BPhO to the ProMi, 22 February 1934. Source BA R 55/1148, p. 130.
29. WF: Memorandum, 6 March 1934, p. 1. Source WFA.
30. Ibid., pp. 4–5.
31. Friedrich Welter: 'Hindemith – eine kulturpolitische Betrachtung', *Die Musik* XXVI/6, March 1934, p. 421.
32. Viktor Reimann in *Dr Joseph Goebbels* (Vienna 1971, p. 193) incorrectly states that the performance took place in October 1934, because like Riess (p. 178) he incorrectly copied Geissmar (p. 161); his book is riddled with mistakes and is absolutely useless as a source of information on the Goebbels-WF relationship.
33. *BZ am Mittag*, no. 62, 13 March 1934.
34. See Welda: 'Mit kritischem Ohr', *Deutsche Wochenschau*, Berlin, no. 11, 17 March 1934.
35. Heinz Joachim: 'Hindemith-Uraufführung in Berlin', *Frankfurter Zeitung und Handelsblatt*, 15 March 1934.
36. See Th. E. = Theodor Eberhard: 'Noch immer Paul Hindemith?', *Der Angriff*, no. 63, 15 March 1934.
37. Hugo Rasch: 'Das vorletzte Furtwängler-Konzert', VB, Berlin edition, no. 73, 14 March 1934.
38. Paul Zschorlich: 'Furtwängler und Hindemith', *Deutsche Zeitung*, evening edition, no. 61, 13 March 1934.
39. ProMi to P. Wehe, 29 May 1934. Source BA R 55/197, pp. 166ff.
40. B. Geissmar to Ambassador von Hassell, Paris, 17 April 1934. Source PAA.
41. German embassy to Ulrich von Hassell, Paris, 20 April 1934. Source PAA.
42. German embassy to Foreign Office, Rome, 5 May 1934. Source PAA.
43. L. = Richard Litterscheid: 'Furtwängler wieder in Westdeutschland',

National-Zeitung, Essen, no. 104, 17 April 1934. A diary entry for 20
April reveals that WF was complaining to the editors.

44. Dr Engelmann to WF, New York, 8 July 1954. Source WFA. Frau de
Strozzi was engaged for 16,000 RM as a young dramatic singer; even the
'top' Kammersängerinnen Käte Heidersbach and Margarete Klose only
received 20,000 and 20,502 RM respectively; Göring was tied to a firm
budget controlled by the finance minister.

45. See GstA rep. 151/217, pp. 18–20. The singer was also engaged for the
title role in the première of Rezniček's *Donna Diana* on 29 December
1933, which had initially been given to Margarethe Slezak, and yet the
critics were restrained in their reaction.

46. NSDAP, Austrian section to ProMi, Munich 7 May 1933. Source
BDC.

47. ProMi to WF, 25 May 1934. Source BA R 55/1184, p. 6.

48. See Hanns Eisler; *Musik und Politik, 1924–48*, Munich 1973, p. 231. The
claim that WF 'allowed' the Jews to be hunted out of the country implies
quite wrongly that he could have stopped it happening had he wished to
do so. Eisler knew of course that it was an 'act of the state'; this is an
exemplary instance of scapegoating.

49. Official statement by police inspector Lahl, Essen, 27 April 1934. Source
BA R 55/1147, p. 125. Fritz Alexander Cohen, conductor of a dance
orchestra and a senior producer, was working as ever for Jooss.

50. Note by ministerial adviser Rüdiger, 7 August 1934. Source BA R 55/
1147, p. 128.

51. Draft contract, 3 July 1934. Source BDC.

52. Altered draft contract by ProMi, 20 July 1934. Source BDC.

53. Planned content of the contract with Kolberg, orchestral leader. Source
BA R 55/197, p. 189.

54. Notes, 1934-B, p. 96 of MS, unpublished. Entry of 23 June 1934. Source
WFA.

55. WF: memorandum, undated, not addressed (roughly mid–December
1934). Source WFA.

56. 'Aufruf der Kulturschaffenden' VB, 18 August 1934.

57. WF to Göring, 7 July 1934. Typescript. Source: WF bequest, loaned by
Andreas Furtwängler.

58. NSKG filed record, Music dept. 28 August 1934. Source CDJC document
CXLV–533.

59. WF to Ludwig Curtius, 10 September 1934; Letters p. 77. The addressee,
head of the Rome branch of the Reich Archaeological Institute, seemed
to Rosenberg a typical 'liberal' (letter to Bormann, Party Chancellery, 30
January 1936).

60. Hans Jenkner: 'Wo steht das deutsche Lied?' *Die Musik* XXVII/1, October
1934, p. 138.

61. 'Paul Hindemith Kulturpolitisch untragbar,' *Die Musik* XXVII/2,
November 1934, p. 138. The author of the unsigned article was F. W.
Herzog.

62. At this audience WF had wanted to ask Hitler to read the libretto of
Mathis der Maler, which Hitler did not know at all. The allegation first
made in Riess (p. 177) and then taken over by Joseph Wulf in *Musik im
Dritten Reich* (Gütersloh 1963) and several others too, that the scene of

book-burning in the opera motivated the 'ban', is therefore false. There was no cogent case for the veto against Hindemith; the sole reason behind it was Hitler's prudish response on seeing the 'naked' Laura in the bathtub scene of Hindemith's opera *Neues vom Tage*. The accusation that it was 'atonal music' was only a rationalisation. Hitler's uncertain handling of the composer is well documented, and has deep psychological causes.

63. WF: memorandum, undated, not addressed (roughly mid-December 1934). Source WFA.

64. Karl Silex: *Lebensbericht eines Journalisten*, Frankfurt am Main, 1968, p. 140.

65. WF: 'Der Fall Hindemith', DAZ, no. 549/550, 25 November 1934. This has been reprinted in its entirety several times, e.g. Geissmar pp. 162–5. Riess pp. 142–4, Wessling pp. 285–8. The expression 'without further consideration' led not only the de-nazification commission, but also people whose knowledge of the German language should have been trustworthy – see Alexander Mitscherlich: 'Analyse des Stars' (*Die Neue Zeitung*, 8 July 1946) *inter alia* – to assume that he meant the opposite, and not 'without consequences' for artistic life.

66. E. R. = Erich Roeder: 'Warum Vorschusslorbeeren für Konjunktur-Musiker Hindemith?' *Der Angriff*, no. 279, 28 November 1934.

67. h.g. = Heinrich Guthmann: 'Bannerträger der Zukunft?' *Deutsche Bühnen-korrespondenz* III/94, 28 November 1934, p. 2.

68. e.g. 'Für und wider Hindemith', *Kreuz-Zeitung* no. 280, 30 November 1934.

69. Thomas Mann: *Tagebücher 1933–4*, Frankfurt am Main, 1977, p. 577. The Munich authorities had seized the writer's house and library in order to exert pressure on him.

70. See 'Erklärung', *Die Musik* XXVII/3, December 1934, pp. 215–6. Riess (p. 183) quotes a corrupted text, alleging it is the declaration from Rust's cultural office, but there was no such office in the NS state. At the time Rust was Minister of Education for Prussia and the Reich, and had nothing to do with the case. WF said that Hindemith's early work was 'music of its time', and the NSKG promptly converted this into the allegation that he was an '*Anpasser*', changing his style whenever it was expedient to do so.

71. Hans Lyck = Fred Hamel: 'Die Entscheidungsstunde der deutschen Musik', *Deutsche Zukunft*, 2 December 1934.

72. Geissmar (p. 166) and Riess (p. 182) claim this performance of *Tristan* took place on 25 November 1934.

73. Staatsrat was a title which could only be forfeited, not discarded; it brought with it a yearly endowment of 6,000 RM for members in Berlin, and 12,000 RM for those living outside Berlin; in practice large parts of it went to the winter aid charities and birthday presents for Göring, etc.

74. See Signe Scanzoni: *Wiener Oper. Wege und Irrwege*, Stuttgart 1956, pp. 50–51.

75. Prussian prime minister to WF, 10 December 1934. Source WFA.

A GUEST IN HIS OWN COUNTRY

1. See Notes, p. 57.
2. Ibid., p. 64.
3. See also Legacy, p. 10.
4. Legacy, p. 41.
5. 'Die Frage nach dem Deutschen in der Kunst', Legacy, pp. 88–96.
6. The attaché at the German legation to the ProMi, The Hague, 12 December 1934. Source BA R 55/1174, p. 22. The ProMi only answered on 1 November 1935 with an untrue statement: WF, they said, had withdrawn *after* Goebbels had stated 'the Reich government's stance in the formulation of the nation's cultural will' in his Kulturkammer speech on 6 December.
7. The sum of 180,000 RM which Geissmar mentions (p. 168) and is taken up by, *inter alia*, Muck (p. 116), as having had to be paid back 'on the day after Furtwängler left his post', is incorrect. The foreign press gave the right figures, see e.g. 'Der unentschiedene Fall Furtwängler', *Basler Nachrichten*, 8 April 1935.
8. A. Rosenberg: 'Ästhetik oder Volkskampf?', VB, Berlin edition, 6 December 1934. Note the language of the small-minded official hiding behind National Socialism which he thinks greater than the individual. It becomes clear what sort of person caused so much harm, a sort moreover which has yet to die out today.
9. Teletype, communication to Herr Reifenberg, 6 December 1934. Source BA 25g. 102/1/42. This was a notification to the *Frankfurter Zeitung* by way of its Berlin editorial offices.
10. Printed *inter alia* in *23*, no. 17–19, 15 December 1934, p. 48. The composer flattered the minister like this on 10 December to demonstrate his loyalty; even if it is true that it was his son Franz Strauss who telegraphed the message without his father's knowledge, this does not change the fact that it had the desired effect. See also Gerhard Splitt: 'Richard Strauss 1933–5. Ästhetik und Musikpolitik zu Beginn der nationalsozialistischen Herrschaft' (Phil. Diss., Freiburg im Bresgau, 1985), p. 236.
11. Reference to collection of signatures for Furtwängler who had left his post as GDM, Stapo, Base 9, Berlin-Charlottenburg, 10 December 1934. Source BA NS 15/69, mistake in original.
12. WF: 'Deutsche Musik-Probleme', 17 December 1934, unpublished. pp. 3–4. Source WFA.
13. Ibid., pp. 4–5. WF was alluding to the plebiscite in the Saarland, for which propaganda preparations were being made at that time.
14. 'K istorii s Gindemitom', *Sowetskaja Musyka*, no. 1, January 1935. p. 88. Editorial comment.
15. BPhO to the ProMi, 2 January 1935. Source BA R 55/1148, pp. 26–7.
16. *Anbruch* XVII/4, April-May 1935, p. 109.
17. Friedrich W. Herzog: 'Der Fall Hindemith-Furtwängler', *Die Musik* XXVII/4, January 1935, p. 243.
18. H. Gerigk: 'Auslandspresse und deutsche Musikpolitik', ibid., p. 250.
19. Suggestion from WF to Göring after his withdrawal, December 1934. Typescript. Source WFA. This draft shows that WF was totally wrong

in his estimation of his own situation, and therefore was sulking for no good reason.

20. WF to State Secretary Funk, Munich, 3 January 1935. Source BDC. WF ignored the slight which Goebbels made by naming this GDM his successor as vice-president and presidential adviser of the RMK. Stange had been lobbying the Nazi authorities for a 'suitable' position ever since they had come to power. However, the minister found that he already had to dismiss him again from the position of vice-president on 14 November 1935, as a result of internal conflicts, complaints and denunciations.

21. Ibid.

22. Grete Busch in *Fritz Busch. Dirigent*, Frankfurt am Main, 1970, p. 282, asserts that WF dismissed his secretary, 'because she was a Jewess'. This is not true.

23. See Geissmar, pp. 173–9. There is evidence to show that she was suspected of wanting to force WF to emigrate by compromising him politically. This would explain why the regime, which wanted to keep him, would not let itself be provoked into taking serious measures.

24. 'An die Abbonnenten der 10 Philharmonischen Konzerte!' Berlin, 3 January 1935. Source BA 55/1148, pp. 125ff.

25. Filed note from Walter Funk, 18 March 1935. Source BA R 55/1148, p. 173. The last word is not clear.

26. -tz- = Hermann Matzke: 'Berliner Philharmonisches Orchester', *Breslauer Neueste Nachrichten*, 17 January 1935. Matzke, a member of the KfdK, was originator of a demonstration of gratitude addressed to Goebbels after the 1933 exchange of letters, a demonstration joined by several musical organisations in Silesia; see *Zeitschrift für Musik*, IC/6, June 1933, p. 625.

27. Herman Roth: 'Konzert der Berlin Philharmoniker', *Hamburger Nachrichten*, no. 32, 19 January 1935.

28. Source BA R 55/1148, p. 23.

29. See Gillis II, pp. 46–8.

30. Leopold Stokowski, conductor of the Philadelphia Orchestra; Serge Koussevitzky, conductor of the Boston Symphony Orchestra; Arthur Bodanzky, conductor at the Metropolitan Opera New York and opera director in Mannheim before the First World War, and therefore known to both correspondents; Anthony van Hoboken, musicologist and bibliographer, who was until 1938 responsible for the collection of copies of original scores at the Vienna National Library.

31. Notes 1935, p. 131 of MS, shortened version published in Notes, p. 120. Source WFA.

32. Notes 1935, pp. 131'–2 of MS, unpublished. Source WFA.

33. Notes 1935, pp. 132', 134 of MS, unpublished. Source WFA. Entry on 10 September 1935.

34. WF: draft, four page typscript, date hand-written: 'January-March 35', p. 3. Source WFA.

35. WF: memorandum, undated, not addressed, *c*. January-March 1935, p. 2. Source WFA.

36. WF: 'Hans Sachs wies den Weg. Gedanken über Kunst und Volk', MNN, no. 291, 24 October 1944; see also WF: *Ton und Wort* (10th edition), Wiesbaden 1982, pp. 192–7.

37. As note 35, pp. 5–6.
38. WF: exposé, typescript, undated, not addressed. February 1935, pp. 2–3. Source WFA.
39. Ingeborg Mörschner to Brückner, Berlin, 24 January 1935. Source BDC.
40. Stegmann to Goebbels, Berlin, 2 February 1935. Source BA R55/1148, p. 171.
41. Minutes of the hearing held by the Sub-Commission for the Denazification of Cultural Workers at Magistrat Level in the case of Dr Wilhelm Furtwängler, 11 December 1946, p. 14. Source BA OMGUS AG 1949/88/3; see also Riess, pp. 200–201.
42. Goebbels-Furtwängler agreement, DNB-report, 28 February 1935, BBZ, 1 March 1935.
43. Goebbels-Furtwängler agreement, DAZ, 1 March 1935.
44. See Muck, p. 118.
45. Rosenberg to Hess, 5 March 1935. Source BA NS 8/117, p. 88. The mistakes in the original show how upset Rosenberg was.
46. WF to Hitler, Potsdam, 4 April 1935. Source WFA.
47. See *Der Führer* IX/168, morning edition, 10 April 1935.
48. Erich Ebermayer: *Denn heute gehört uns Deutschland . . . Persönliches und politisches Tagebuch*, Hamburg/Vienna 1959, p. 505.
49. See Muck, p. 119.
50. BPhO, Stegmann to Funk, 17 April 1935. Source: BA R 55/1148, p. 184. Geissmar (p. 185) incorrectly says that Hitler attended this concert.
51. 'Furtwängler får rosor av Hitler', *Dagens Nyheter*, Stockholm, 4 May 1935.
52. Riess (p. 207) talks of the 'Intendant of the Philharmonic'; however, at that time the position and title of Intendant did not yet exist. There were two managers, one commercial, the other artistic.
53. The question of conductors making the greeting to the public was first dealt with in an instruction from the ProMi to the RMK on 28 December 1936, which was in no way restrictive: the German greeting was desirable, but no pressure should be brought to bear on what form of greeting the conductor made.
54. BBZ, morning edition, 10 May 1935.
55. 'Unsere Meinung', DAZ, Reichsausgabe, no. 216–317, 11 May 1935.
56. Ingeborg Mörschner to Hauptmann Wiedemann, no date. Source BA NS 10/161, p. 190.
57. Lorenz Höber: memorandum to the ProMi, 14 June 1935. Source BA R 55/245, pp. 38, 39, 40.
58. The Reich Finance Ministry to Göring, 8 July 1935. Source GstA rep. 151 no. 208 sheet 2. Henry Blair: 'Die Lenkung der Berliner Opernhäuser', in *Musik und Musikpolitik im faschistischen Deutschland* (Hanns-Werner Heister and Hans-Günter Klein, Fischer-TB, Frankfurt am Main 1984, p. 87) mentions this letter, giving the wrong source, as proof of a drop in attendances as a result of the repertoire, without paying attention to the personal connections.
59. WF: draft contract, no date, p. 3. Source WFA.
60. Frauenfeld to State Secretary Funk, RKK, 23 July 1935, p. 3. Source BDC.
61. Ibid., p. 6.

62. 'Furtwängler and Dr Herbert Graf', *Der Morgen*, Vienna, 24 June 1935.
63. Letter from unknown person to Ingeborg Mörschner, 10 August 1935. Source BDC.
64. ProMi, Dept. VI, to RKK, State Commissioner Hinkel, 3 August 1935. Source BDC.
65. Hauptmann Wiedemann to the personal office of the Führer's deputy, 8 August 1935. Source BA NS 10/161, p. 67.
66. Wiedemann to Schaub, 22 August 1935. Source BA NS 10/161, p. 188.
67. 'Erhebende Feierstunden', *Fränkische Tageszeitung*, Nürnberg, 11 September 1935.
68. Oskar Jölli to Hinkel, 17 September 1935. Source BDC.
69. Frauenfeld to Wiedemann, 29 November 1935. Source BA NS 10/161, p. 67.
70. Gerigk to Dr Gotthardt, Gestapo office in Berlin, 18 December 1935. Source BA NS 15/69.
71. Notes 1936, p. 41 of MS, unpublished. Source WFA.
72. Karl Holl: 'Wilhelm Furtwängler 1936', *Frankfurter Zeitung*, Reich edition, 21 January 1936.
73. WF's birthday was noted in Hitler's appointments diary; see BA NS 10/124, p. 267. Politicians have always used newsworthy birthday congratulations as a way of exploiting artists' fame for their own purposes.
74. 'Der Führer ehrt Furtwängler', DAZ, 26 January 1936.
75. BPhO, von Benda to Wiedemann, 30 January 1936. Source BA NS 10/110, p. 82.
76. Stuckenschmidt to State Commissioner Hinkel, PMWKuV, 3 May 1933. The author is grateful to his fellow music critic, Prof. Dr Hans Heinz Stuckenschmidt, for providing the document.
77. WF to Hinkel, ProMi, Vienna, 12 February 1936. Source BDC. As late as 1944 WF gave the boycotted critic a recommendation to the Reich's protector, Frick, in Prague.
78. RKK to Stuckenschmidt, 21 January 1937. Source BDC.
79. WF to Irme Schwab, 26 February 1936, Letters, p. 84.
80. Gillis II, pp. 51–4, a very readable account of events in New York. There was clearly a severe campaign of what might be called anti-product advertising.
81. 'Furtwängler wieder an der Berliner Staatsoper', BBZ, 29 February 1936.
82. This description should not be taken as derogatory. In those of his writings that were published, Hirschmann repeatedly stressed that he was first and foremost a Jew and only then an American citizen. In addition he was a professed Zionist. This was why he dedicated his resources, in a manner both ostentatious and successful, to rescuing east European Jews in the period 1944–6, and later to the state of Israel.
83. On 29 July 1933, Harry W. Garing, the 'Grand Dragon' of the 'Knights and Women of the Ku-Klux-Klan, Inc.' in the state of New York, sent a letter in German to Hitler, cited his own anti-Semitic speeches to the 'association', congratulated Hitler on liberating Germany from its enemies – the Jews – and vowed the support of the Ku-Klux-Klan. Source PAA.
84. 'Philharmonic's Choice', *Time*, 9 March 1936, p. 55.
85. 'Nazi Stays Home', *Time*, 23 March 1936, p. 51. Leo Blech, the only Jewish conductor whom the Nazis tolerated for a few years, cancelled a

US guest tour in 1937 for the same reason, even though by that time he had already emigrated to Riga.

86. 'Telegramm Furtwänglers', *Berliner Lokalanzeiger*, no. 72, 24 March 1936.

87. WF to John Knittel, Zürich, 3 April 1936. (Letters, p. 90). The publisher Frank Thiess observed in connection with the pre-election propaganda – not knowing the circumstances: 'The declaration mentioned in letter 70 that F. "will be working as a German even when abroad" was taken by the press as Furtwängler's way of paying the NS regime for the right to continue working in Germany. F. would never have let himself be used for pre-election propaganda purposes' (Letters, pp. 300–301). Letter 70 refers to the meeting with Goebbels on 28 February 1935; Thiess failed to ask himself why the foreign press should have chosen to wait more than a year before taking up the matter. Paris actually cancelled on political grounds.

88. WF to Hitler, Potsdam, 15 April 1936. Source WFA.

89. Notes 1936, p. 66' of MS unpublished. Source WFA. Entry for 4 May 1936.

90. Ibid., p. 64. Entry for 29 April 1936.

91. See Werner Egk: *Die Zeit wartet nicht*, Goldmann-TB, Munich 1981, pp. 250ff.

92. R. = Erich Roeder: 'Solist Wilhelm Furtwängler', *Der Angriff*, no. 94, 22 April 1936.

93. WF to Hitler, Potsdam, 24 April 1936. Source BA NS 10/110, pp. 77–8.

94. Ibid., p. 78.

95. Thomas Mann: *Tagebücher 1935–6*, Frankfurt am Main, 1978, p. 305. Entry for 21 May 1936.

96. Thomas Mann: *Tagebücher 1933–4*, p. 400. Entry for 27 April 1934.

97. Ministerial adviser Berndt to Reichskulturwalter Moraller, 25 May 1936. Source BDC.

98. Ibid., Hinkel's handwritten record on file. Albrechtstraße refers to the Gestapo Headquarters in the Prinz Albrecht Straße in Berlin; Mo was an abbreviation of Moraller.

99. Pgn. Maria Zinkler: confidential report, pp. 1–2, handwritten, not addressed, Berlin, 24 May 1936. Source BDC.

100. Ibid., pp. 4–5.

101. O. S. = Otto Steinhagen: 'Die Welt hört Bayreuth', DAZ, 20 July 1936.

102. Thomas Mann: *Tagebücher 1935–6*, p. 334.

103. From the politico-cultural press conference on 13 August 1936. Source BA ZSg. 102/62, vol. 1. (Sammlung Sänger).

104. 'Kunstbetrachtung statt Kunstkritik', *Kölnische Zeitung*, evening edition, no. 605, 27 November 1936.

105. In the literature the effectiveness of the ban on criticism as a form of censorship has been immeasurably overestimated, because it was easier to take its stated purpose and the commentaries written by a few ardent party members as if they were the whole story, instead of analysing the spectrum of opinion which was really still present in the press after the key day – 30 June 1937.

106. WF: memorandum without title or addressee, 26 November 1936. Source WFA.

107. Goebbels to WF, Berlin, 26 November 1936. Source Legacy, loaned by Andreas Furtwängler.
108. Geissmar to WF, London, 2 December 1936. Source WFA.
109. Geissmar to WF, London, 3 December 1936. Source WFA.
110. Goebbels: *Tagebuch*, Vol II, Munich 1987, p. 753. Despite his intelligence the minister did not realise that WF was trying to win back sufficient influence on the regime to carry out his own musical and humanitarian goals. He therefore mistook mere lipservice for a political conversion, even though Furtwängler raised his objections and demands quite clearly.
111. Otto Steinhagen: 'Furtwängler dirigiert für die Winterhilfe', DAZ, evening edition, 12 February 1937.
112. The only thing Goebbels noted in his diary, vol. III, p. 64. was: 'He has taken a couple of Jews under his wing again and is standing up for Hindemith. I flare up. Get really furious. That has its effect. He gives way a little. I remain hard and unforgiving. He will gradually learn to see my point.'
113. Memorandum from the Kameradschaft für deutsche Künstler, June 1934. Source AUT. The association was not a part of, or affiliated to, the NSDAP in any way.
114. Erich Roeder: 'Berliner Konzertrunde', *Der Angriff*, no. 93, 22 April 1937.
115. Herbert S. Sonnenfeld: 'Der Fall Furtwängler', *Aufbau*, New York, 2 May 1947.
116. Despite this other people and authorities used both titles in correspondence and conversation with WF.
117. Information from the politico-cultural press conference, 22 April 1937, teletyping. Source BA ZSg. 102/62 (Collection: Singers).
118. State Secretary Gutterer, ProMi, to WF, 11 June 1937. Source WFA.
119. WF to ProMi, 14 June 1937. Source WFA.
120. WF to Hitler, 16 June 1937. Source WFA.
121. Record on file, by Funk, 28 June 1937. Source BA R 55/902, pp. 14–15.
122. The Reich and Prussian minister for sciences, education and popular enlightenment to the secretary of state and head of the Reich Chancellery, 13 December 1935. Source BA R 43 II/1245, p. 111.
123. Ibid., p. 112.
124. From the politico-cultural press conference, 8 October 1936. Source BA ZSg. 102 (Collection: singers).
125. WF: memorandum without addressee, Bayreuth, July 1937. Source WFA.
126. 'Umbildung der Preussischen Akademie der Künste', VB, 16 July 1937. The report ignores the fact that there had been a 'purge' in 1933.
127. WF to Dr Strecker, Bayreuth, 3 August 1937. Source BDC. The plan was never realised. Goebbels remembered other themes: 'He wants more serious music on the radio. He is quite right. Will be done. Should plan for the rising generation more carefully. Violinists should not use shovels while doing service, and singers should not ruin their voices in the Hitler Youth. He also has a couple of half-Jews, but then he always has them' (Goebbels: *Tagebuch*, vol. III, p. 217). Just how much this was a political trial of strength was noted by the minister on 3 August 1937: 'The Philharmonic Orchestra still contains half-Jews. I will try and get rid of them. Will not be easy. Furtwängler is using all his power to try and

keep them' (ibid., p. 223). In 1945 it became clear that WF had won the day.

128. Friedrich Herzfeld: *Wilhelm Furtwängler. Weg und Wesen*, Leipzig 1941, p. 105. For details see Gillis II, pp. 54–7, who also mentions that Toscanini had been a candidate for the fascist party in 1919, last conducted in Italy in 1931, but returned to his country many times before the summer of 1939, and seems to have had no worries about conducting Verdi's *Requiem* at the requiem for the clerico-fascist Chancellor Engelbert Dollfuss. In a still-unpublished interview recorded by Eugeen Liven d'Abelardo for his series on Dutch radio VPRO, celebrating the 100th anniversary of WF's birthday, the conductor Sergiu Celibidache said in Munich on 25 May 1985 that Toscanini was one of the founders of the Italian fascist party, with membership no. 58, and that he came eleventh in their lists of delegates, but only ten were chosen – which was why Toscanini became an anti-fascist.

129. Gerd Rühle: *Das Dritte Reich. Dokumentarische Darstellung des Aufbaus der Nation. Das fünfte Jahr, 1937*, Berlin 1938, pp. 76–7.

130. 'Grosser Erfolg Furtwänglers in Paris', *Der Mittag*, no. 209, 8 September 1937.

131. Paul Schmidt: *Statist auf diplomatischer Bühne 1923–45*, Bonn, 1949, pp. 360–1.

132. WF to Hitler, Munich, 26 October 1937. Source WFA.

133. WF to Winifred Wagner, Potsdam, 15 November 1937. Source WFA.

134. Goebbels: *Tagebuch*, vol. III, p. 323. The last sentence shows clearly that the politician was very envious of Winifred Wagner's influence over Hitler.

6 (pp. 223–266)
ATTACK FROM THE REARGUARD

1. Goebbels noted under 5 December: 'Furtwängler pestered Funk for hours. He is playing the fool in Vienna and Bayreuth, but mostly as a result of his political naïvety' (Goebbels: *Tagebuch*, vol. III, p. 357). He was so sure of victory that it did not occur to him that the conductor was working in a calculatedly political way, or why this might be so.

2. Tietjen to Friedelind Wagner, handwritten, 16 November (1937). Source WFA.

3. Notes, p. 125.

4. From the politico-cultural press conference, 10 September 1936. Source BA ZSg 102/62 (Collection: singers).

5. WF to Göring, Vienna, 11 December 1937, *Aus Görings Schreibtisch. Ein Dokumentenfund*, ed. Theodor Richard Emessen, Berlin 1947. p. 38.

6. Göring to WF, 16 December 1937, ibid., p. 39.

7. WF to Göring, 23 December 1937, ibid., pp. 41–2.

8. Note from the German Reich's ambassador extraordinary and plenipotentiary to Hauptmann Wiedemann, 28 February 1938. Source BA NS 10/110, pp 75–6.

9. Hauptmann Wiedemann to Herr von Wussow, 1 March 1938. Source BA NS 10/110, p. 73.

10. Draft of the letter in Notes 1938, p. 177 of MS, unpublished. Source WFA.

11. *Die Musik-Woche* VI/15, 9 April 1938, p. 243.

12. Ibid., p. 242.
13. 'Musiker bekennen sich zur Heimkehr ins Reich.' Source: Dokumentations-archiv des österreichischen Widerstandes, Vienna, ZL. 1203/46, p. 8.
14. Wilhelm Rode: 'Warum ich "Ja" sage!', DTZ, no. 42, 8 April 1938. p. 3.
15. WF: 'Unauslöschbare geschichtliche Tat', Berliner Lokalanzeiger, morning edition, no. 83, 6 April 1938. By the treaty of St. Germain in 1919, Austria was stripped of its empire and reduced to a nation of one people only. However, the National Assembly in Vienna voted in 1918 to unite with the Reich; plebiscites held in later years in individual regions of the Bund produced the same result, but the Allies brought pressure to bear against the idea. The Austrian Social Democrats kept reunification as part of their party's programme until 1933. The desire for unification was cooled by the Austrian right-wingers and of course by Hitler himself. However, there can be no doubt that a large majority welcomed the Anschluss when it came in 1938. In terms of international law Hitler's action constituted the illegal annexation of an independent state.
16. WF to Riess, 6 January 1953, Letters, p. 238.
17. Hans Lyck = Fred Hamel: 'Aachen erobert Berlin', Deutsche Zukunft VI/16, 17 April 1938, p. 15.
18. See Otto Strasser: Und dafür wird man noch bezahlt. Mein Leben mit den Wiener Philharmonikern, Vienna/Berlin 1974, pp. 148ff.
19. On files of Dept. X of ProMi, 20 June 1938, initialled Lg = Ernst Ludwig. Source BA R 55/247, pp. 322ff.
20. However, despite working very intensively, WF's income remained at the same level as that of other top musicians, and was far less than film stars were making. WF declared the following pre-tax income to the Finance Offices:

67,327 RM (1935)	204,282 RM (1940)
75,945 RM (1936)	129,375 RM (1941)
101,852 RM (1937)	209,049 RM (1942)
155,960 RM (1938)	201,131 RM (1943)
132,467 RM (1939)	c.130,000 RM (1944)

At a tax rate of around 58% this gross income was considerably reduced and amounted to:

45,449 RM (1935)	108,113 RM (1940) 47%
55,749 RM (1936) tax rate	24,987 RM (1941) 81%
67,326 RM (1937) 27–34%	110,143 RM (1942) 47%
106,647 RM (1938)	17,897 RM (1943) 92%
22,068 RM (1939) 83%	25,389 RM (1944) 20%

The assets of 344,501 RM shown in his statement of finances on 31 December 1945 prove the accusation that he profited financially from the Nazi regime to be a deliberate lie.
21. WF to Matthes, 29 July 1938. Source BDC.
22. Goebbels observed: 'Furtwängler does not wish to conduct in Nürnberg. Because of his scruples. What nonsense! He should not be so cautious. I will apply pressure' (Goebbels: Tagebuch, vol. III, p. 470).
23. WF to Goebbels, 24 August 1938. Source BA NS 10/333, p. 239.
24. WF to Erwin Kerber, 20 August 1938. Source, VPhHA.
25. Wilhelm Jerger, Die Wiener Philharmoniker, Vienna 1942, p. 74. This was the way an accomplice who was caught red-handed described it, in an

attempt to salve his conscience. To admit that the 'slight changes' really amounted to a 'purge of Jews' would have been too close to the shameful truth.

26. Otto Burg: '*Die Meistersinger von Nürnberg*. Glanzvolle Festaufführung in Anwesenheit des Führers im Nürnberger Opernhaus', *Fränkische Tageszeitung*, 6 December 1938.

27. Concerns '*Die Meistersinger von Nürnberg*, no date. Source PAA.

28. The misspelling 'van' which first occurred at the de-nazification commission was perpetuated in the literature until Bachmann and Wessling. The Berlin Telephone Directory gives the correct spelling for the widow who survived him. When Nüll signed his articles with his full name he always wrote 'von'.

29. E. von der Nüll: 'Wilhelm Furtwängler. Aufstieg und Leben eines großen Mannes', *Der Stern*, no. 3, Berlin, 4 October 1938, p. 71.

30. See Wessling, p. 337.

31. See Bachmann, pp. 358–9, and Walter Legge/Elisabeth Schwarzkopf: *Gehörtes – Ungehörtes. Memoiren*, Munich 1982, p. 256.

32. Heinrich Strobel: 'Erfolg Herbert v. Karajans in der Berliner Staatsoper', DTZ, no. 102, 5 October 1938, p. 3.

33. E. von der Nüll: 'Zweimal Berliner Theaterpublikum', DTZ, no. 107, 16 October 1938, p. 1.

34. *Salzburger Volksblatt*, 8–9 April 1933, p. 1.

35. For details and inferences see Bachmann, pp. 88ff.

36. Karajan's early biographers, including Karl Löbl (*Das Wunder Karajan*, Bayreuth 1965, and Heyne-TB 1978) and Ernst Haeussermann (*Herbert von Karajan*, Vienna 1978, and Goldmann-TB 1979) claimed ignorance – deliberately? – of the BDC documents quoting Karajan's assertion that he 'had' to join the NSDAP in 1935 in order to become GDM in Aachen. It was an untruth which had already been refuted in 1957 (see Paul Moor: 'The Operator' in *High Fidelity* VII/10, October 1957, pp. 52–5, 190, 192–4), but which Karajan stubbornly perpetuated, even repeating it in an interview on his seventy-fifth birthday. On 31 May 1983 therefore, I, Fred K. Prieberg, approached Karajan's lawyer in Munich, Dr Detlev Wunderlich, and drew his attention to the 'closed season' from 1933–7:
'The 'closed season' affected only new entrants to the party, by Hitler's orders. As before, it was still possible to transfer from one of the organisations affiliated to the NSDAP, if one's political record was good enough. In other words, Herr von Karajan's "subjectively true" story that he joined the NSDAP in order to gain the appointment to GDM in Aachen, gives *carte blanche* to those who one day will wish to discuss the question of whether he was already a member of the SA or the SS who transferred to the party. In this case I would have pleaded "attack in the interests of self-defence". It then becomes clear that the "objective truth" would do less damage to your client's well-established international reputation than insisting on the "subjective truth". Far be it from me to recommend a particular course of action to the maestro, but I can imagine that a person versed in the law, and who enjoys his trust, would wish and would be able to help him to make up his mind.'
I received no reply. Karajan continued to lie. When his American biographer, Roger Vaughan, asked him about it, he denounced the truth as a

'fabrication', adding with no regard for reality: 'Prieberg just said those things in order to get a lot of money for it' (see Roger Vaughan: *Herbert von Karajan – A Biographical Portrait*, London 1986, p. 109). Even when Vaughan showed him copies of the documents, Karajan stuck to his pointless lie, and continued to do so right up to his death.

37. Notes of a statement made by the witness Eduard Lucas to the de-nazification commission, 12 December 1946. Source WFA.

38. E. von der Null: 'In der Staatsoper: Das Wunder Karajan', *BZ am Mittag*, 22 October 1938. The paper was kept by the Uppsala University Library, but that edition just happens to be missing; the author must thank his fellow historian in Vienna, Dr Oliver Rathkolb, for having had the good fortune to come across another original copy.

39. Karajan's biographer, Löbl, p. 65, quotes this second-hand from Bernd Ruland (see Bernd Ruland: *Das war Berlin. Erinnerungsbuch an die Reichshauptstadt*, Bayreuth 1972, p. 279), without giving his source, copying a whole sentence from him which did not exist in the original!

40. Notes 1928. pp. 10–11 of MS, unpublished. Source WFA.

41. B. Geissmar to WF, 18 January 1933. Source WFA. Herman Roth, who later accepted a professorship at the Berlin Academy for Church and School Music, was at that time a critic for the *Hamburger Nachrichten* and the *Hamburger Fremdenblatt*, where Heinrich Chevalley senior was departmental head. Siegfried Lütgert was head of the concert department of J. A. Böhme, i.e. an artists' agent.

42. See Ruland: *Das war Berlin*, Bayreuth 1972, p. 280.

43. The result of many attempts to find the information: it would have required a disproportionate effort to obtain the relevant documentation, and so the author had to make do.

44. 'Loben mit Geschmack . . .', *Signale*, 2 November 1938. Written by Wilhelm Matthes.

45. Wilhelm Matthes: 'Furtwängler greift zu Bruckners Urschrift', *BZ am Mittag*, 7 November 1938.

46. See *Berliner Illustrierte Zeitung* XLVII/45, 10 November 1938, p. 1786.

47. W. Steinhauer: 'Am Pult: Herbert von Karajan. Nochmals *Tristan* in der Staatsoper', *BZ am Mittag*, 10 November 1938. Steinhauer was considered by the Rosenberg faction – according to a letter by H. Killer, politico-cultural archives, written 12 October 1942 – as having a 'hostile worldview'.

48. Notes, 1939-I. p. 23 of MS, unpublished. Source WFA. Entry for 2 February 1939.

49. Official statement on a discussion between Furtwängler and the musicians Dieburtz, Buchholz, Peppermüller, Machula, Kleber and Troester, on 27 October 1939. Source WFA.

50. The contact was made back in the twenties. Null's father owned a house in Paulsborner Strasse, Berlin; the tenants included a famous opera singer and a man called Paul Körner. Naturally the two sons, Edwin and Kurt, knew these people. After Körner suddenly became state secretary in the Prussian Ministry of State, in other words Göring's right-hand man, Edwin used to go to him whenever his press work came under attack from Goebbels' ministry. Körner would inform his employer, who enjoyed the occasional intrigue against his rival, Goebbels. It is not surprising therefore

that the critic boasted of 'his' Göring, or that the latter used him when he wanted to avenge himself against WF.

51. Notes of a statement made by the witness Eduard Lucas to the denazification commission, 12 December 1946. Source WFA.
52. R. Vedder: Notes taken 28 November 1933. Source BDC. One of Wolff's daughters, Edith Stargardt-Wolff, wrote a book of memoirs on the famous concert agent – *Wegbereiter grosser Musiker* (Berlin/Wiesbaden 1954) – without mentioning this massive attempt to aryanise the Wolff & Sachs agency.
53. Employment contract, draft, undated. Source BDC. The text shows that it really was a case of a takeover.
54. B. Geissmar to WF, 22 March 1934. Source WFA.
55. Handwritten note on Max R. Müller's letter to Hitler dated 28 April 1935. Source BDC.
   Vedder could trust his patrons absolutely – above all the RMK's manager Heinz Ihlert, press chief Dr Friedrich Mahling, and Prof. Havemann, head of the musicians' association within the RMK; they also ensured that the new vice-president of the RMK, Hermann Stange, who had uncovered the Vedder affair, was removed from office again in November.
56. Commendation, 5 October 1935. Source BDC.
57. Although not a member of the NSDAP he fell as a volunteer in the final battle for Berlin near Potsdam.
58. SS-Brigadeführer Ludolf von Alvensleben to the Head of SS-Headquarters, Berlin, 14 November 1941. Source BDC.
59. SS-Gruppenführer and Generalleutnant of the Waffen-SS Gottlob Berger, Head of SS-Headquarters, to the head of the SS-Personnel department, 24 November 1941. Source BDC.
60. As second concert master – Erich Röhn was first – Taschner received 1,060 RM gross.
61. WF: five page exposé, undated, not addressed. Source WFA.
62. See Heinz Joachim: 'Dirigenten-Profile', *Frankfurter Zeitung*, Reichsausgabe no. 582–583, 14 November 1940.
63. Goebbels: *Tagebuch*, entry for 14 December 1940. The author wishes to thank his Swiss musicologist colleague Robert C. Bachmann for access to this text; see his *Karajan*, p. 136.
64. Politico-cultural press conference, 20 December 1940. Source: BA R 55/741 (Lothar Band Legacy). The minister – as in this instance – was keen on persuading the press, and often showed great patience in doing so.
65. See Bachmann, p. 136. Bachmann – not knowing the behind-the-scenes intrigues – suggests that 'Furtwängler's conduct lacked dignity' in this incident.
66. Source WFA.
67. Werner Oehlmann: 'Das Berliner Konzert. Wesen und Gestalten', *Das Reich*, 5 January 1941. p. 20.
68. Karl Holl: 'Berliner Konzertleben', *Frankfurter Zeitung*, 16 December 1941.
69. Ministerial Director Hinkel, ProMi, to SS-Obengruppenführer and General of the Waffen-SS Schmitt, 5 August 1942. Source BDC.
70. RPA Berlin, Rundspruch no. 135/42, 18 December 1942. Source BA ZSg. 115/16, p. 66.
71. See Luis Trenker: *Alles gut gegangen. Geschichten aus meinem Leben*, 2nd edition; Heyne-TB, Munich 1965/1972, p. 440.

72. Bachmann's question – p. 124: 'Or is the request connected to the marriage?' – is illogical, because the officials did not demand any proof of political reliability. Furthermore the official procedure by way of the NSDAP's area and national headquarters would have taken longer than the twenty days between Karajan's application and his wedding.
73. See *Die Organisation der NSDAP*, 7th edition; Munich 1943, p. 6d.
74. Ibid., p. 6e.
75. Nicolaus von Below: *Als Hitlers Adjutant 1937–45*, Mainz 1980, p. 166. Biographers have incorrectly dated this famous evening at which the drunken Bockelmann 'cocked up' all his entrances; Löbl (p. 73) is vague, Haeussermann (p. 67) and Bachmann (p. 133) put it roughly in 1940. Wessling (p. 353) uses Bockelmann's repertoire notes to refute his colleagues, but still gets the date wrong; it was 2 June 1939. WF only very occasionally conducted from memory.
76. See *Dokumente über die Verfolgung der jüdischen Bürger in Baden-Württemberg durch das Nationalsozialistische Regime 1933–1945*, Vol 1, published by the Stuttgart Archives, 1966 p. 38–9.
77. In a letter dated 23 June 1943. Paul Moor, who found it in the BDC, mentions it in his essay 'The Operator' (*High Fidelity* VII/10, October 1957, p. 190); the letter has since disappeared from the Karajan file in the BDC.
78. See Muck, pp. 172–3. This letter – WF to Goebbels, Potsdam, 19 May 1943 – was described by Muck as 'to a member of the government', and he went on to simply drop the final relative clause, a scandalous omission. The author is grateful for the copy of the original which he obtained from his fellow documentarist Peter Muck.
79. With a medical certificate, Furtwängler avoided conducting again at the concert given in celebration of Hitler's birthday.
80. Goebbels: *Tagebuch*, entry for 29 May 1943. Source BA NL 118/55, p. 24.
81. The Leader of the SS' Upper Elbe Division to SS-Obengruppenführer Schmitt, Dresden, 3 August 1942. Source BDC.
82. SS-Personnel head office to the Head of the SS Court Head Office, 7 January 1943. Source BDC.
83. SS-Gruppenführer and Generalleutnant of the Waffen-SS Breithaupt to SS-Untersturmführer Vedder, 11 June 1943. Source BDC.
84. SS-Sturmmann Diefenbach to SS-Untersturmführer Vedder, Trebbin, 2 May 1944. Source BDC. RF-SS = Reichsführer-SS Himmler; PK = Parteikanzlei (Party Chancellery); Dr N. = State Secretary Dr Naumann.
85. RKK, Dr Schrade to State Secretary Naumann, 20 July 1944. Source BDC.
86. SS-Obersturmführer Vedder to SS-Hauptsturmführer Emde, 10 August 1944. Source BDC.
87. RKK, Dr Schrade to State Secretary Naumann, 16 March 1945. Source BDC.

7 (pp. 267–332)
. . . SAY NOTHING IN FUTURE

1. 'Toscanini gemassregelt' DAZ, 26 November 1938.
2. Andrew Schulhof remembered later – letter to WF from New York, 1 November 1946: 'On 10 November 1938 you suddenly came to Budapest from Vienna. You had sent me a telegram before leaving, and arrived in

such a state that I could hardly find you in the train. You did not have a penny in your pocket and I had to pay the conductor for your ticket. The reason was that when the first pogrom and burning of the synagogues had begun the previous day, you had shared out everything you had among your Jewish friends' (Source WFA).

The pogrom across the whole Reich began on the evening of 9 November 1938. Schulhof was wrong about the date; WF only travelled to Budapest on 13 November, taking rehearsals on the 14th and holding a press reception in the afternoon. He rehearsed again on the 15th, spent the evening with Ernö von Dohnányi, and conducted the concert on the 16th.

3. ProMi, Dept. X, to Dr Werner, Berlin, 18 November 1938. Source AStA, General administration Archive RSt. III/202/38.
4. See correspondence between German Bruckner Society and Schirach at the ProMi, *c.* 60 pages, March 1938 to October 1941. Source ZStA Potsdam (DDR), ProMi Dept. X/583.
5. See Ulrich von Hassell: *Vom andern Deutschland. Aus den nachgelassenen Tagebüchern 1938–1944*, Zürich 1946, p. 44.
6. F. Wagner: *Nacht über Bayreuth*, Bern 1946, p. 321.
7. Emigration would at least have meant financial profit; at a meeting in the Hague in 1939, Andrew Schulhof, who was manager for Ansermet and Beecham, offered good conditions, i.e. 30,000 US dollars per year without commission, with any further profits being divided 60 per cent to WF, 40 per cent to the agent, covered by a guarantee from a Swiss bank.
8. ProMi, Dept. IB, to WF, 16 March 1939. Source BDC.
9. See W. Egk: *Die Zeit wartet nicht*, Goldmann-TB; Munich 1981, p. 318.
10. WF: *Ton und Wort*, Wiesbaden 1982, p. 119.
11. WF to Hitler, Potsdam, 19 July 1939, according to handwritten comment not sent. Source WFA.
12. Notes, 1939-III. p. 20 of MS, unpublished. Source WFA.
13. Ibid., p. 19 of MS.
14. Ibid.. pp 19–19' of MS. Hans von Benda was the artistic manager of the BPhO; Heinz Drewes the head of Dept. X Music in the ProMi; Tietjen – who had since been given full powers by Göring – general intendant of the Prussian State Theatres: all three were conductors who were hindered to a greater or lesser degree, but were ambitious for all that. Benda certainly did not achieve the standing of the other two, nor did he obtain such a position of power.
15. Notes 1940-I, p. 30' of MS, unpublished. Source WFA. Entry for 19 February 1940. Transcribed from original by the author.
16. As note 12, p. 23.
17. WF to Goebbels, 28 July 1939. Source WFA.
18. WF to Otto Strasser, 2 August 1939. Source VPhHA.
19. WF to Otto Strasser, 12 August 1939. Source: VPhHA. This was typical of the hypocrisy of propaganda experts; although the election of conductors worked on the same principle as the Yes-No vote for Hitler in the Third Reich, the former had problems with a 'basic National Socialist principle', the latter did not.
20. Notes 1939-IV, p. 35' of MS, unpublished. Source WFA.
21. Notes 1939-III, p. 12 of MS, unpublished. Source WFA.

22. Ibid., p. 32' of MS.
23. Bormann to Rosenberg, Berneck, 25 July 1939. Source BA NS 8, micro-fiche from the collection *Akten der Parteikanzlei der NSDAP*, ed. H. Heiber, Munich/Vienna 1984, no. 126.02115.
24. Anonymous denunciation to the RMVP, 21 September 1939. Source BA R 55/197, p. 110.
25. BPhO to RMVP, 13 October 1939. Source ibid., p. 109.
26. Politico-cultural press-conference no. 52, 5 January 1939. Source BA.
27. Record on file, senior government adviser Kohler to State Secretary Hanke, 17 August 1938. Source BA R 55/197, p. 33. As from 8 August 1938 the minister extended Kolberg's special permit, which had hitherto been restricted to the BPhO, to work anywhere.
28. 'Musik in dieser Zeit' *Volksfunk* IX/39, 24 September 1939. p. 4, 11.
29. Report by the artistic director on the 1939–40 season, sent to RMVP, no date. Source BA R 55/247, p. 229.
30. Wilhelm Jerger to Herr Dr Kern, Vienna, 14 October 1939. Source AStA, General administration archives – the Reich's Commissioner for the Reunification of Austria with the Reich 2425/5.
31. The Reich Commissioner for the Reunification of Austria with the Reich to State Commissioner Dr Friedrich Plattner, December 1939. Source AStA, ibid. 2425/0.
32. The inspector of the Security police and the SD in Vienna to Gauleiter Bürckel, 13 December 1939. Source BA R 58/375, p. 91.
33. Ibid., 20 December 1939. Source BA R 58/375, p. 144.
34. See *Aftenposten* no. 156, 29 March 1940. Translation by the German Embassy in Oslo. Source PAA.
35. German Embassy to Foreign Office, Oslo, 3 April 1940. Source PAA.
36. From Oslo WF went to Copenhagen for a few days. His shocked reaction to the German occupation is recounted by Kai Flor; *Store tonkunstere jeg mödte*, Copenhagen 1954, pp. 42–3, and K. Riisager in his article 'En underlig aften', *Berlingske Tidende*, 7 April 1968. The author is grateful to Nils Hemmeth, Copenhagen, for the information, copies and translation. See also Axel Kjerulf: *Hundrede ar mellem noder*, Copenhagen 1957, pp. 136–7. Goebbels' diary entry reveals the tactic WF was pursuing and that – initially – it was successful: 'Furtwängler has reported. Has seen occupation in Copenhagen. Describes the great surprise. Our soldiers apparently behaved in exemplary fashion which was a major factor in the peaceful execution of the occupation [. . .]. I will consult WF more often in future. He may perhaps wish to be Raabes' successor. As president of the RMK. Would be good. Otherwise a little less conducting. He appears to have given himself a little too much to do.' (Goebbels: *Tagebuch* vol. IV, p. 114–15). That this would not work out was immediately obvious in the talk the minister held with Hitler, who put a stop to Furtwängler obtaining any position of power in politico-cultural matters. Thus Furtwängler lost the chance of neutralizing Karajan's rivalry.
37. Gerigk: suggestion for the cultural symposium at the party congress, 20 July 1940. Source BA NS 8, micro-fiche no. 126.02526.
38. Ibid., microfiche no. 126.02527.
39. See *Taschen-Brockhaus zum Weltgeschehen* Leipzig 1940, p. 213.

work required, almost to the point where one might suggest that there existed between them a mystical relationship, along the lines of the Greek Dioscuri, Castor and Pollux, the former a mortal – a lower middle class individual who even managed to be chancellor of the Reich for a few days when there was no Reich left, vain, theatrical even in his suicide – the latter immortal, yet repeatedly dragged down into Hades.

113.   Notes 1945. pp. 56–7 of MS, unpublished. Source WFA. H. = Hitler.

Author's Acknowledgements

For information and references from public and private sources, without which adequate treatment of the subject-matter of this book would have been impossible, the author would like to thank the people and institutions cited below in alphabetical order:

Peter Ackermann, Miltenberg
Akademie der Künste, Pressearchiv und Bibliothek, Prof. Dr Walter Huder, Berlin
Amerika-Gedenkbibliothek, Zeitungsarchiv, Berlin
Archiv der Berliner Philharmoniker, Jutta March, Berlin
Archiv der Bundestheaterverwaltung, Vienna
Aufbau, Publishers, Asst. Editor Robert Breuer, New York
Auswärtiges Amt, Politisches Archiv, Dr Hans G. Pretsch and Dr Maria Keipert, Bonn
Robert C. Bachmann, CH-6354 Vitznau-Luzern
Badische Landesbibliothek, Karlsruhe
Basler Zeitung, Archiv, Basel
Bayerische Staatsbibliothek, Munich
Boleslaw Barlog, Berlin
Berlin Document Center, Berlin
Der Bevollmächtigte der Bundesregierung in Berlin, Geschäftsbereich des Innern
Dr Günter Birkner, D-7891 Küssaberg
Rudolf Boll, Bonn
Bundesarchiv, Dr Wolfram Werner, Koblenz
Centre de Documentation Juive Contemporaine, Paris
Dagens Nyheter, Publishers' Archive, Stockholm

Curt Riess, CH-8127 Scheuren auf der Forch
Gert Ruddies, D-7597 Diersheim
Erna Samuel, Vienna
Helmut Schlövogt, D-8221 Tengling
Adelheid Schmitz-Valckenberg, Munich
Prof. Hans-Hubert Schoenzeler, London
Sam Shirakawa, New York
Sonderstandesamt Arolsen
Dr Gerhard Splitt, Freiburg im Bresgau
Staatsbibliothek, Preussischer Kulturbesitz, Musikabteilung, Berlin
Stadtarchiv, Dr Vogelsang, Bielefeld
Stadtarchiv Mannheim
Stadtarchiv, Dr Helmut Häussler, Nürnberg
Stadtarchiv, Nikolaus Harter, Offenburg
Stadtbibliothek Baden-Baden
Stadtbibliothek Trier
Stadt- und Universitätsbibliothek Köln
Státni Knihovna ČSR, Praha
Prof. Dipl. Ing. Otto Strasser, Vienna
Prof. Dr h.c. Hans Heinz Stuckenschmidt, Berlin
Südwestfunk, Bibliothek, Michael Murer, und Notenarchiv, Siegfried
   Zorn, Baden-Baden
Time Magazine Archive, New York
Dr Uri Toeplitz, Israel
Universitätsbibliothek Bochum
Universitätsbibliothek Bonn
Universitätsbibliothek Düsseldorf
Universitätsbibliothek Erlangen-Nürnberg
Universitätsbibliothek Mannheim
Universitätsbibliothek Saarbrücken
Universitätsbibliothek Tübingen
Universitetsbiblioteket, Kerstin Herelius, Uppsala
Vienna Philharmonic Archive, Dr Clemens Hellsberg
Dr Eva Weissweiler, Königswinter
Bernd W. Wessling, Hamburg
Wilhelm Furtwängler-Gesellschaft, Herr Hildebrandt, Berlin
Johannes Winkelmann, Rottach
Zweites Deutsches Fernsehen, Lothar Seehaus, Mainz
Zentralbibliothek, Musikabteilung, Zürich
Zentrales Staatsarchiv, Potsdam

The author received no reply to his inquiries from:

Dr Henry Bair, Portland, USA
Irmingard Barsoff, Buenos Aires
Bundesarchiv, Abt. Militärarchiv, Freiburg im Bresgau
Ira Hirschmann, New York
Musikverlag Schotts Söhne, Archiv, Frau Dr Marbach, Mainz
Dr Helmut Peitsch, Berlin

Publishers' note: where appropriate, the German language has been retained for the convenience of scholars who wish to pursue their researches.

Illustrative Credits

INDEX

Aachen, 232, 235, 239, 241
Aaron, 337n.
Abelardo, Eugeen Liven d', 357n.
Abendroth, Hermann, 111, 121, 137, 159, 231, 300, 313, 321, 344n.
Abendroth, Walter, 343n.
Aber, Adolf, 58
Abussi, Antonio, 252
Achleiten, Schloss, 300, 303, 308–9, 310, 321
Ackermann, Thomas, 317, 318
Adler, H. G., 368n.
Adler, Viktor, 344n.
Adolph, Dr Paul, 40
AEG, 11
Aichinger, Bernarda von, 300
Air Ministry, 247, 248
Albers, Hans, 165
Albert, Herbert, 272
Altmann, Wilhelm, 58
Alvensleben, SS-Brigadeführer Ludolf von, 254, 361n.
American Federation of Labor (AFL), 196
Amfiteatrov, Massimo, 253
Anbruch, 153
Anday, Rosette, 57
Anders, Peter, 252
Andreae, Volkmar, 315, 327
Der Angriff, 119, 122, 139, 199
Ankara, 303
Anschluss, 159, 227, 358n.

Ansermet, Ernest, 77, 327
Anti-Semitism, 4, 21–2, 28, 36, 46–50, 54–5, 71–2, 336n., 362–3n., chapters 1–5 *et passim*; Aryan Clause, 78, 86, 89, 91, 93; Aryan/ Jewish classification, 43–4, 71, 80, 84, 184, 203–4, 214, 235–6; Jewish/ Bolshevist threat, 46, 166–9, 182; *Kristallnacht*, 223, 267; law excluding Jews from civil service, 51, 62, 68, 74, 95; Horst-Wessel Song (national anthem), 7, 159, 317, 337n.
Apollo Theatre, Nuremberg, 185–6
Appia, Edmond, 327
Arbenz, Wilhelm, 327
Arens, Hans, 312
Arent, Benno von, 208–10
Argentina, 77–9, 208, 342n.
Armhold, Adelheid, 57
Armin, Georg, 344n.
Arndt-Ober, Margarethe, 165
Arrau, Claudio, 252
Associated Press, 173, 195
Association of Berlin Friends of the German Academy, 164
Association of Former Jewish Volunteers, 62–3
Association of German Municipalities, 253, 255
Atlantis publishing house, 326

Kalter, Sabine, 57, 75
Kaminski, Heinrich, 216
Kap, Julius, 58, 90–1, 109, 239, 345n.
Kapel, Gertrud, 44
Karajan, Herbert von, 94, 252, 255,
    303; 'work-break concerts', 11;
    conducts Berlin Philharmonic,
    232–3, 338; WF unaware of threat
    from, 235, 239–40; Pfitzner festival,
    235; rise to fame, 239–42; Nazi
    Party membership, 240–1, 261–3,
    359–60n.; rivalry with WF, 244–6,
    255–7, 258–64, 283; second
    marriage, 261, 262; de-nazification
    commission, 262; Reich Bruckner
    Orchestra, 319; radio concerts, 321
Karlsruhe, 56, 61
Karpath, Ludwig, 58
Kassel, 135
Kaufman, Theodore H., 336n.
Kaun, Hugo, 30
Kellermann, Hellmut, 111
Kempen, Paul van, 252, 253, 266
Kerber, Dr Erwin, 227–30, 236, 358n.
Kergl, Max, 60
Kern, Dr, 364n.
Kerr, Alfred, 71–2
Kessler, Harry Graf, 338n.
Kestenberg, Leo, 33, 59
Keudell, Privy Councillor Otto von,
    108, 125, 131, 132, 162, 251
Keyserling, Hermann Graf, 19–20,
    344n.
KfdK (League for the Defence of
    German Culture), 46, 47, 50, 60,
    65, 97, 108, 111, 121, 128, 135
Killer, Hermann, 288, 360n., 365n.
Killinger, Manfred von, 40
Kipnis, Alexander, 57, 75
Kittel, Bruno, 36, 58, 211
Kittel, John, 195
Kjerulf, Axel, 364n.
Klages, Ludwig, 20
Klatte, Arnold, 88–9, 105, 344n.
Klatte, Clara, 345n.
Klatte, Wilhelm, 58, 88
Klaus, 116
Kleber, Wolfram, 197
Kleber (shop-steward), 293

Kleiber, Erich, 58, 77, 112, 150,
    158–9, 342n.
Klein, Hans-Günter, 353n.
Klein, Herbert, 240
Klemperer, Otto, 49, 58, 66, 77, 85,
    89, 97, 129, 163, 344n.
Kletzki, Paul, 315
Klibansky, Dr Raymond, 93–4,
    344n., 345n.
Klinckerfuss, Margarete, 58
Klingler Quartet, 49
Klose, Margarete, 44, 349n.
Kloska, Hans, 113
Klötzel, Cheskel Zwi, 336n.
Knab, Armin, 216
Knappertsbusch, Hans, 77, 281, 292,
    293–4, 301, 305, 344n.
Kniestädt, Georg, 57
Knittel, John, 58, 147; 200, 355n.
Kober, Alfred, 367n., 368n.
Köcher, Dr Otto, 329, 368n.
Koestler, Arthur, 336n.
Kohler, Herrmann, 277–8, 364n.
Köhler, Karl, 344n.
Kolbe, Georg, 134
Kolbenheyer, Erwin Guido, 19, 134
Kolberg, Hugo, 132, 133, 184, 190,
    214, 278, 344n., 349n., 364n.
Kolessa, Lubka, 38
Konetzny, Anni, 78
König, Gustav, 252
Konopath, Hanno, 97, 346n.
Konopath, Marie Adelheid, 97
Konoye, Hidemaro, 111, 284
Kopsch, Julius, 44
Körner, Paul, 360–1n.
Korngold, Erich Wolfgang, 58
Korngold, Julius, 58
Koussevitzky, Serge, 163, 352n.
Kraft, Assistant Detective, 152
Kraft durch Freude, 239, 255
Krakow, 293–4, 310
Kraus, Lilli, 58
Krauss, Clemens, 143, 156, 163, 170,
    173, 177, 180, 181, 188, 190, 194,
    220, 252, 321
Krebs, 344n.
Kreisler, Fritz, 50–1, 57, 87, 89, 339n.
Kreiten, Karlrobert, 297–8, 344n.
Krems, 300

387

389

Schulthess, Walter, 327
Schultze, Siegfried, 253
Schumann, Georg, 38
Schumann, Robert, 45
Schünemann, Georg, 58
Schuricht, Carl, 111, 124, 159, 344n.
Schuster, Joseph, 111, 130
Schütz, Franz, 281
Schwab, Irme, 325, 354n.
Schwarz, Leo, 344n.
Schwarz, Dr Max Paul, 366n.
Schwarzkopf, Elisabeth, 359n.
Schwers, Paul, 58, 346n., 347n.
Schwieger, Hans, 344n.
Security Services, 301, 303–4
Seehaus, Lothar, 368n.
Seelig, Dr Hermann, 344n.
Seibert, Willi, 344n.
Seider, Paul, 78, 342–3n.
Seidler, Erich, 135, 253, 254
Sekles, Professor Bernhard, 58, 84, 105, 344n.
Seldte, Franz, 45
Sellschopp, Hans, 171, 343n.
Seyss-Inquart, Artur von, 227
Sieben, Wilhelm, 135
Sievers, 59
Silex, Karl, 350
Simon, Erich, 249, 251
Singakademie, 38
Singer, Kurt, 47, 58
Slevogt, Max, 58
Slezak, Margarete, 214, 349n.
Slovakia, 294
Smetana, Bedřich, 285
Smyth, Dame Ethel, 58
Society for Arts and Sciences, 164
Society for Free Philosophy, 164
Society for the Protection of Authors' Copyright, 164
Society for the Support of Retired Artists, 164
Söhnker, Hans, 311–12
Sonnemann, Emmy, 165
Sonnenfeld, Herbert S., 211, 356n.
South Africa, 208
Soviet Union, 25, 121, 290, 329
Spain, 208, 294, 301
Speer, Albert, 308, 309, 321–2, 367n.
Spengler, Oswald, 20

Speydel, 344n.
Splitt, Gerhard, 351
Springer, Hermann, 58
SS, 34, 45, 186, 254, 255, 264–5
SS Viking Division, 300
Staatskapelle, 117
Stage Recruitment Agency, 241
STAGMA, 165
Stalin, Joseph, 5
Stalingrad, 261, 297
Stange, Hermann, 156–7, 159, 184, 352n., 361n.
Stargardt-Wolff, Edith, 249, 361n.
State Academy for Church and School Music, 68
Stauffenberg, Count Claus Schenk von, 311
Steding, Christoph, 22–3, 338n., 341n.
Stegmann, Karl, 131, 171, 175, 184, 191, 353n.
Steiger, Eduard von, 329
Stein, Fritz, 58, 197
Steinhagen, Otto, 348n., 355n., 356n.
Steinhauer, Walter, 65, 245, 342n., 360n.
Steinitz, Dr Wolfgang, 366n.
Steinkopf, Hanns, 47
Steinway & Sons, 248, 249, 250, 252
Stempel, Maxim, 366n.
Stengel, Theophil, 344n.
Stenzel, Bruno, 214
Stern, Richard, 47
Der Stern, 246
Stettin, 114
Steurer, Hugo, 252
Stiatsny, Hilde, 341n.
Stiedry, Fritz, 58, 195
Stock, R. & Co., 11
Stockholm, 298
Stockholm, Concert Association, 302
Stockholm University, 302–3
Stokowski, Leopold, 163, 352n.
Strasser, Otto, 358n., 363n.
Straube, Karl, 58, 66–7, 75, 325, 342n., 344n.
Strausberg, 329
Strauss, Franz, 351n.
Strauss, H. A., 341n.
Strauss, Richard, 46, 55, 58, 77, 84–5

391